THE HOLY ROMAN REPUBLIC

THE HOLY ROMAN REPUBLIC

A HISTORIC PROFILE OF
THE MIDDLE AGES

BY

GIORGIO FALCO

TRANSLATED BY K. V. KENT

London

GEORGE ALLEN & UNWIN LTD

RUSKIN HOUSE MUSEUM STREET

FIRST PUBLISHED IN 1964

TRANSLATED FROM THE ITALIAN
La Santa Romana Repubblica

PRINTED IN GREAT BRITAIN
in 10 point Juliana type
BY EAST MIDLAND PRINTING CO., LTD.
BURY ST. EDMUNDS

A Nelda

caro nome

con l'anima d'allora

TRANSLATOR'S PREFACE

Traduttori traditori—translators are traitors—is a disquieting Damoclean phrase to have hanging over one's head, and in translating this work I have tried to steer an even course between faithfulness to the author and readable English. Italian favours a more Baroque type of eloquence than our austere northern style, and modes of expression which are beautiful in Italian may sound pretentious when turned into English. I have done my best to convey faithfully both the content and the feeling of the author's language, but where necessary I have taken the liberty of simplifying the structure, in order to keep the translation in line with English usage.

In connection with this translation, I should like to thank Professor Weiss, of University College, London, for his suggestion that I should undertake the work in the first place, Professor Dionisotti, of Bedford College, London, for allowing me to work on it while I was an assistant lecturer at the college, and the British Broadcasting Corporation for allowing me to continue the work while serving as a full-time member of its staff.

On a more practical level, my thanks are due to the author, for the patience and dispatch with which he has answered my queries, and in particular to Mr Peter Knop, of the University of Virginia, for his invaluable help with the revision and typing of the manuscript, and his continual support and encouragement throughout.

K.V.K. 1963

AUTHOR'S PREFACE TO THE SECOND EDITION

This book was written more than twenty years ago and published in the troubled days of 1942, through the kind concern and pressure of Benedetto Croce and the truly thaumaturgical powers of Raffaele Mattioli.

It was the result of much study and reflection on the significance and importance of the Middle Ages as a historical period, and was occasioned by an invitation from two kind friends, Maria Rostagni and Cristina Agosti, to give a series of lectures at the society, *Pro Cultura Femminile Yamma* in Turin.

The sub-title printed on the frontispiece, 'A historic profile of the Middle Ages', is really too presumptuous. It is in fact no more than a sketch. As I wrote in the first edition, the pages which follow do not contain a continuous or detailed narrative; they present little more than an evocation of the Middle Ages. The great figures and events which are discussed have been chosen with a view to highlighting the most critical and significant periods in their history. The facts which are treated are in general the inheritance of our common culture; a certain effort has been made to search out the individual character of each period and the coherence of the historical development.

The purpose of this work and the criteria with which it has been written—that is, its questioning attitude, its alternation of summary and individual treatment, its need to follow the main thread of the times and interpret in terms of significant events—should explain why it glosses over so much history and departs from the traditional outline at various points. It should also explain the *raison d'être* of a medieval history which, instead of presenting the feudal age in full flowers, highlights its particularism at the peak of the Catholic hierarchy. Within the limitations already given, it finds Otto III more instructive than Otto I, and Henry VI than Barbarossa. It does not hesitate to sacrifice the greatness of Frederick II, and, while stressing the importance of the great monarchies, which are to be the protagonists of the new Europe, scarcely refers to their formation. It gives prominence to the Benedictine foundation, while refraining from more than a glance at a few of the essential characteristics of the Franciscan movement.

It would be absurd to pretend that these explanations should be as much of a justification to the reader as they are to the author. However, it was necessary to warn the reader that the book had been conceived and written in this way, with a problem and a deliberate plan of its own, with its own light and shadow, and that out of the infinite wealth of history, only those things have been selected which, in the judgement of the author, are best suited to serve as illustrations to explain, albeit very summarily, the significance and importance of the Middle Ages.

Apart from a few amendments and a few corrections, the text has not been changed for this second edition. The bibliographical notes have been brought up to date by the addition of those books which I have been able to lay my hands on, and they make no pretence of completeness. A very full chapter on the *Iconoclastic Struggle* has been added, in connection with which I am not ashamed to confess that I had no sooner finished the book than I realized that, to achieve a completeness of design, it needed a deeper and more incisive treatment of the divorce between East and West and the change in the axis of papal policy in the mid-eighth century. But I allowed myself to be overcome by a certain tiredness and by the difficulties that had been overcome.

As those who have the patience to read on will see, this work belongs to the school of Benedetto Croce. And for me it is indissolubly linked with his memory, with the closeness of devotion and affection, because he read it, took great pains over its publication, and saw in it, in his great generosity, the fulfilment of his 'ideal of a book of history', which was 'to reduce the knowledge of the facts to a story of a drama of the soul'.

GIORGIO FALCO, 1954

CONTENTS

CHAPTER 1

THE MIDDLE AGES

The concept of the Middle Ages, in the sense of an epoch in between the ancient and the modern, was born, naturally enough, when the Middle Ages themselves were waning or even at an end. It is in fact just at this point, in the fifteenth and sixteenth centuries, in the thick of the great crises of the conciliar age, the Renaissance and the Reformation, that we first begin to find writers using expressions such as *media aetas, media tempestas, media antiquitas*, expressions which point to the formation of a new period in the minds of historians. Though empty of meaning for us, these terms were deeply significant for the men who first used them, and remained so for a time, because they expressed their consciousness of a rebirth, especially of religion and culture.

For the humanists and the men of the Renaissance, the Middle Ages were a long period of barbarism, a barrier between themselves and the perfection of the classical art and literature that they emulated. The period was even more strongly modified by the polemics of the protestant historians. The limits were clearly fixed: at one end there was the *inclinatio Imperii*, which covered the decline of culture, the corruption of the primitive Church, the arrival of the Germans, and at the other, the rebirth of letters, the true religion restored by the theses of Luther, a changed Europe, in which the diminished empire still claimed its right to the secular and spiritual government of the world. Between these limits lay the eclipse of learning, monastic superstition, papal tyranny, the immortal glory of Charlemagne and Otto I, the disgrace of Canossa, and the blind and ill-fated heroism of Barbarossa and Frederick II. The passion of their religious faith, of their patriotism and their championship of the German Empire, and of their classicism in both literature and philosophy were all merged to give life to this drama of truth and beauty lost and found again.

So conceived as it was in the antagonism of the Renaissance and the Reformation, this medieval period was indeed a middle age, a kind of tear in the fabric of history, a long muddled time which made no sense on its own, and whose salient traits were the destruction of civilization and culture, and the gradual approach of the antichrist.

The academic writers of the seventeenth century, to whom we are indebted for the first text of medieval history and for the name of the period itself, which was then accepted by historians, did not change either the image of the Middle Ages or the judgements already established; but under the stimulus of the new interests they enriched the period of the transition between medieval and modern by attributing to the Renaissance and the Reformation the great inventions and geographical discoveries of the fifteenth century, and in this they served as a model for the majority of subsequent history books.

The historians of the Enlightenment displaced the salutary crisis from the century of Luther and Leo X to their own, and by this exaggeration confirmed the judgement passed by the Protestants and Humanists against the Middle Ages. To a man who placed his faith in the principles of reason and the rights of nature, his political credo in the balance of power within states and between them, and his pride and pleasure in the new European cosmopolitanism, it must indeed have seemed a primitive and violent age, riddled with anarchy, intolerance and superstition.

Nevertheless, even if we discount the enormous strides made from the sixteenth to the seventeenth century in both sacred and profane scholarship, the work of the eighteenth century historians was anything but sterile. None of them, it is true, even Muratori himself, who although he is not strictly of the Enlightenment circle still fulfils certain of its basic conditions, were capable of experiencing the great organic forces of the medieval world, the papacy and the empire, and of entering into its political and religious consciousness. Even so, it is to them that we are indebted for the wonderful embellishment of the fabric of medieval history: the reconstruction, albeit uncertain and incomplete, of the culture, the institutions and the social and economic system.

The inclinations which prompted them to this research were partly held in common, as for instance the desire to extol the present, and the increasingly complex curiosity in men and things, but they were partly individual. Voltaire and Condorcet, Robertson and Gibbon, Schlözer and Gatterer, were led by the very impossibility of penetrating the world of medieval faith to search out an explanation of its mystery, and impelled by the certainty of the new faith of the enlightenment to track down, if possible in the depths of the Middle Ages, the first hints of reform, and the dawn and evolution of reason: in the resurgence of the people, the liberty of the communes, the economic activities and the advent of the third estate, the formation of the great monarchies, the superior power of the councils, the anticatholic movements whatever their origin, Waldo and the Albigenses, Wycliff and Huss, and in general all those symptoms that pointed to the dissolution of the medieval universalism and the rise of the modern age. Muratori, on the other hand, was moved to his great labour by the passion of a scholar, and by an idea, expressed by others at the same time and applied to great effect by the Abbé Dubos and the Compte de Boulainvilliers to the study of French institutions, namely that we are not the direct heirs of the Greeks and the Romans—the idols of the eighteenth century antiquarians—but sons of the Middle Ages, to which we must turn for the explanation of much of the modern age.

But as early as Gibbon and Robertson, this triumph of reason was tinged with occasional doubt and uneasiness; already the noisy Voltairean polemic was becoming tempered with reflection, equity and a desire to understand. And Muratori, advancing by this newly opened road, reached an exaltation of the Lombards that foreshadowed the idolization of the barbarians and their unspoilt vigour which was to come so soon. Thus the seeds for a new outlook on the Middle Ages were already sown in the historiography of the Enlightenment itself.

The fundamental revision of the earlier interpretations, the complete and substantial revaluation of the 'middle age' were, of course, the accomplishment of romanticism, and perhaps found their most effective expression in Frederick Schlegel's courses held in Vienna in 1829. Schlegel may be accused of simply inverting the propositions of his enlightenment adversaries and thereby falling into an error which was in a way more serious, in sanctifying certain centuries by condemning the following ones; but nevertheless he did recognize the central problem in the politico-religious consciousness of the western world and see the positive value of the Middle Ages, and he overcame the abstract and static qualities of the historiography of the Enlightenment with his idea of individuality and development in history.

This new positive evaluation, even though it is often spoiled by its too immediate ardour, is the greatest progress that has been made in the historiography of the Middle Ages, and we wish to be faithful to it in the course of this work. Our purpose, then, will not be to set up a trial to inflict a severe but useless lesson, but rather to relive, to understand, to gather in the light of the experience of the centuries, the significance of the drama played out in the Middle Ages.

But before we begin, we must clear up an important preliminary question which may well appear ridiculous, in that we have been speaking up to now of nothing but medieval history and historians.

We must find out—and not from any mere journalistic curiosity—whether the period we are accustomed to call medieval is a legitimate one, and if so, what are its limits and its substance, or, in other words, whether we use this name to refer to a definite period and set of historical problems.

Indeed, the question is suggested by the very authors we have mentioned, for in their treatment of the Middle Ages they follow two different methods. One group, under the direct influence of eighteenth century cosmopolitanism, deals with universal history, or rather with the history of the lands and peoples centred on the Mediterranean basin; the other draws its most lively inspiration from romanticism, and its object is the history of Europe. The former is more interested in taking in the vicissitudes of all humanity at a glance, the latter in representing the world of a particular culture, in posing and resolving a definite historical problem.

The pretensions to universality made by medieval history can in effect boast several claims for our consideration. They rest on the universal concept of the Roman Empire and the Christian Church, on the uninterrupted relationship that bound east and west together for a thousand years, and on the length of the historiographic tradition that derives from them. The trouble is that a medieval history of the Mediterranean presents almost insuperable obstacles; or perhaps we should say that even if one does write it, as has been done time and time again, it can never fulfil the fundamental conditions of this or any other history. We may be allowed to speak of a period which we call the Middle Ages, in so far as we imply by the term a true intermediate age between the ancient and the modern world, the heir of the one and the mother of the other, distinguished from them both by its own limits and characteristics, and centred for its own essential significance on a clearly defined political and religious consciousness. But the Mediterranean of this millenium is not the heart of one, but the meeting-place of three civilizations, the Roman, the Arab and the Byzantine, and they can never be made to march in step or be bound into a single 'medieval' history, unless we understand by this term a mere compendium of historical incidents placed side by side or more or less artificially woven together.

It is perhaps this effort to write universal history that has given rise to the at once spectacular and absurd character that the Middle Ages so often assume, bereft as they have been of a spirit of their own, of development and individuality in their various periods, like a landscape of giant peaks and immeasurable whirlpools. The Middle Ages are the foundation of the modern world and the necessary preparation for our civilization, but in themselves they are practically incomprehensible. From the depths of time the succession of the great builders rises as if by enchantment—Charlemagne, Otto I,

Innocent III—all destined to the immense labour of a creation which will not survive their own deaths. And history repeats itself with meticulous uniformity, its creatures engrossed in building, destroying, and rebuilding ever the same things, its empires dying and being born again, its kings, popes and emperors eternally at war, with what result we never quite know.

This explains the crisis of despair at the turn of the century which led a group of worthy scholars—Stieve, Kurth, Halecki, Spangenburg, Haering, Berr, and Vogel—first to point out all the absurdities of a period that begins with the deposition of an insignificant emperor and ends with the discovery of America, and to try without avail to change its limits and cut it into sections so as to give it some organic shape and significance, and finally to decide that the only thing to do was to wipe out the Middle Ages altogether. This, too, can help to explain the scanty sympathy and understanding of those who normally consider the Middle Ages, as their name suggests, as a kind of hiatus, a tear in the fabric of history, a confused tangle of happenings without interest, unity, or individual characteristics of their own, or at any rate with only the negative characteristics of the decline of culture, religious corruption, and political inconsistency.

Using the terminology of that perceptive eighteenth century philosopher August Ludwig Schlözer, we can say that the universal representation discussed above constitutes an 'aggregate', not a system, that is not a history 'systematized from a single viewpoint'. Now medieval history must, like any other history, be 'systematized from a single viewpoint' if it is to be comprehensible, both in its subject matter and its progression, in the vast problem it enfolds and its solution. We must and we can ask the Middle Ages once more for their hidden significance, for they are not, as Lorenz thought, an arbitrary invention of Christopher Cellarius, the poor seventeenth century professor, but historical reality, the mature expression of centuries of experience; and we may hope to draw from our studies a certainty that can take its place in our contemporary consciousness.

Near enough what the secret is, can be read on every page of that millenium, and has, as we have said, been hinted at by the romantics. For our purpose, then, it will be best to leave the scholars of antiquity to deal with the deposition of Romulus Augustulus, as the symbolic limit of their period, and to go back, since we are interested in birth not death, to a great act of life, Christianity, arming ourselves with a solid optimism, which may lead us to see in the fall of the empire and the devastation of the Germanic invasions and occupation, the dawn of a new civilization.

Seen in the light of future development, the first three centuries of the empire, and the persecutions of the Christians, are essentially the conflict of two irreconcilable principles; on the one hand imperial absolutism and political paganism, on the other Christianity, which while respecting the established order, undermines its foundation by its belief in a transcendental Truth and by its dominion over human consciences, and robs its content and action of all value by transferring the meaning of life to beyond the grave. It is not possible, for the citizen or for the believer, to profess the Christian religion and the cult of the emperor at the same time; just as it is not possible for him to reconcile his religious creed with his devotion to the ideals of the state, or of contemporary culture in general. Through a succession of clashes, the gulf is revealed in all its formidable implications, and the difference is seen to be radical and complete. The condemnation moves with equal precision, though with different purposes and means, from both sides. Then little by little the resistance of the empire is coerced into surrender, and Rome herself becomes the instrument of the movement of the future.

When Constantine grants liberty to the Christian cult, when Theodosius recognizes Christianity as the state religion and persecutes the pagans, the empire denies its ancient nature and proclaims the triumph of revolutionary energy over tottering tradition, which has lost its faith and strength. Now this triumph sets a political and religious problem that is unique in all history: beside the universal monarchy of Rome, outside which no other form of civilization has been thinkable for centuries, the Church, which is equally universal, sets itself up, and outside it there can be no salvation. The one and the other, indissolubly, represent and comprehend the whole Roman world, the entire compass of civil life; both of them boast their own right to govern mankind, and mankind in its turn consists of both citizens and believers.

The problem of this twofold yet single universality finds a different solution in the two worlds of east and west, of which the first passed its civilization on to Rome, and the second was civilized by Rome.

The foundation of Constantinople—whatever the actual causes may have been—and the administrative division of the empire after the death of Theodosius, point to a substantial difference in the culture of east and west, to different needs, and to a separation which, slow though it was to start with, was irrevocably deepened by successive events. The faith in the single and ultimate empire did manage to survive, and commercial and political intercourse between east and west continued for centuries. There were renewed pretensions of reconquest and restoration from both sides, but the unity of the Mediterranean world was in fact split.

Byzantium, though faithful in a way to its classical model, creates its own Church and incorporates it in the state; it has its own enemies—Persians, Arabs, Turks and Latins, and it exercises its cultural mission on the Slavs. A lusty offshoot of Romanism and Hellenism, it guards the inheritance of the ancient civilization and carries on its tradition for ten centuries, until, mutilated and exhausted, it finally falls victim to the Ottoman Turks.

The west, in virtue of the stamp of Roman civilization upon it, of the Roman ecclesiastic primacy, and of its appropriation and conversion of the Germans, Normans, Hungarians and Slavs, of their absorbtion into the Roman world, gives rise to a history which, in its liveliness, originality and continuity of development, is profoundly different; and this is the cradle of modern Europe.

The Arabian Empire, which is the third competitor for Mediterranean domination and threatens to submerge the other two rivals, presents us with vague analogies in its politico-religious problems. But we are dealing here with a culture which from the beginning has nothing in common with the Roman and Hellenic world, with a basically Judaeo-Christian religion which yet has no sacramental principles, with an armed conquest of both national and religious significance whose expansion and dissolution cannot, in either its nature or its chronological and territorial limits, be organically united or merged with the history of the Latin and Byzantine Empires.

Once this is clear, it is obvious that if we really want to give shape to a period of general Mediterranean history which can legitimately be called medieval, with a problem and significance of its own, and do this with clarity and conviction, this can be none other than the history of what we should like to call *The Holy Roman Republic*; the history of Europe's Roman and Christian foundations, and of the formation and disintegration of European Catholicism.

The classical world's heritage to the west consists of more than the civil institutions of a legal and military nature; it is one of cities and public monuments, great routes of communication, and processes of production and trade—this last a legacy destined to suffer profound changes, but to survive and come to life again. It is also a heritage of scholarship, techniques of language and style, models of literature and art, the platonic and neo-platonic speculative thought which was to nourish St Augustine and Boethius, and, through them, with the doctrines of Aristotle, the thought of the entire Middle Ages. Finally, it bequeathed a sense of empire and *civilitas*, of political universality that was both refined and humane, and was to permeate the new political and religious consciousness. The Roman tradition is accepted, conserved and nourished essentially by the Church, which affirms its universality on various principles, expresses the need for Christian government of the world, and works its conquest of the spirit with the arts and arms of Rome.

The Christian and Roman, or let us call it the Catholic consciousness, is the substance of the Middle Ages. All the great periods of medieval history must be related to this creed: the expansion and formation of Europe on new foundations, the struggles of the great powers, the wars of conquest and defence against Arabs, Turks and Byzantines, and the final process of the differentiation and disintegration of the Christian republic. All the great aspects of the period lead us back to this religious foundation: the philosophy which is a theology, the physical world considered as a mirror of transcendent Truth, literature and art set to exalt faith, the incessant call to order and purity in the midst of anarchy and corruption, the perennial blossoming of eschatological and apocalyptic prophecies, the fate of men and races on earth conceived as a drama of the human and the divine, lit by the light of Revelation.

The distinct individuality of the Middle Ages lies precisely in its radiation from Rome, in its European setting, and in its unitary and transcendental nature. The *ordinatio ad unum* on earth, which is modelled on the divine government of the world, is no vague ideal or goal to be reached, but an absolute and immediate exigency; the universalism of Church and empire, of Romanism and Christianity, excludes any possibility of civilized life outside itself; the two supreme powers are distinct, but at the same time they are bound together by their faith and their government of mankind; and hence politics and religion become interdependent. This accounts for the prevalence of the religious element throughout the Middle Ages, and the apparently static and uniform nature of the period, which results from the repeated assertions of primacy and supremacy made by the Church with unchanging firmness and varying success. Certainly it is difficult to point to any historical development or to a realizable plan of action in such assertions, but this is precisely because they are neither before their time nor of it, they transcend time, for the principle that informs the Church and the contemporary consciousness is transcendental. This, too, can explain the feeling of many people today that there is a basic inconsistency in the whole of the Middle Ages as a historical period, which arises simply from the fact that the medieval conception of politics is by its very nature unitarian and transcendental, supranational and supernatural, and thus profoundly different from our own conception of the state.

CHAPTER 2

THE CHRISTIAN EMPIRE

CONSTANTINE

In the first decades of the fourth century A.D., between the abdication of Diocletian and his colleague Maximian in 305 and the death of Constantine in 337, comes the decisive point at which the ancient civilization, in the shape of the Roman Empire, admits defeat, albeit without full consciousness of the step, and a new road is clearly opened for the Mediterranean world.

At the close of the third century, the empire was still a powerful reality; comprising at once an organism with centuries of political tradition, a vast web of interdependent economies and a common culture, it could not be shaken without imperilling the Mediterranean-centred civilizations of Europe, Africa and Asia and without inspiring fear of universal destruction. In fact signs of great changes to come had been visible enough to the observant eye. The imperial purple had fallen prey to the unruly power of the legions and the praetorian guard. The vigour of production and trade was failing under the weight of the exorbitant taxes, which resulted from the relentless demands of the army, and perhaps equally the corruption of the bureaucracy. The network of trade routes was torn by invasions and other disorders; and the economic and financial crisis was reflected in uncontrollable inflation. City life sank into a torpor and the population shrank; the middle classes, hardworking and resourceful as they were, declined gradually before the tight aristocracy of the landowners and the vast multitude of the disinherited.

Externally, the restored Persian monarchy was hungry for new triumphs over her age-old enemy; Antoninus Pius' wall had been forced by the Picts and Scots; the boundaries of the Rhine and the Danube were being attacked and penetrated from time to time by various Germanic tribes, Quadi, Marcomanni and Goths; and the armies were given new blood by the very barbarians that Rome had failed to keep from her frontiers.

The last ten years of Diocletian's reign (295-305) mark the point at which the reaction to this decline finally asserted itself; it was the most remarkable effort ever made to arrest the process of disintegration and to restore the immense edifice in all its solid structure. The imperial authority, which had originally been the trustee of the magistracies of the republic, finally became a despotism on the oriental pattern: the Augustus was a creature of heaven, divinity itself of earth; he was the *dominus*, his head was circled by the diadem and before his feet men prostrated themselves, no longer citizens but subjects. Since the government of a single man was not enough for such vast dominions, there were now two Augusti and two Caesars; there were also four capitals—and the mother of the empire was no longer among them—at Nicomedia in Bithynia, Sirmium in Pannonia, Trier and Milan, chosen according to the necessities of government and defence.

The inadequacy and vulnerability of the armies was dealt with by increasing the total number of soldiers and lessening the force of the single legions, and finally by putting chosen detachments at the disposal of the sovereigns in addition to their existing bodyguards. A hierarchic network of civil servants poured forth from the palace to penetrate and administer the dioceses and provinces, which were now smaller and more numerous.

Society with all its civil fabric was steadily disintegrating. Why work, if there was no certainty of the morrow, and the fruit of one's labours—and the more it was the worse—was lost in regular and extraordinary taxes and bribes to buy the tax collectors' favours, to obtain justice or to escape some hateful duty? And so the peasant fled from his ungrateful and undefended holding, from the impositions of man and state, to bury himself in the city and enjoy the easy life of public largess; the miller left his mill, and the armourer his workshop. The aristocracy of the cities, the members of the curial families, sought by every means, even flight, or entry into the priesthood, to escape the once so coveted duties of the duoviri or of the decurions, which obliged them to sacrifice their own wealth to the fiscal demands on their city. And now, little by little, every man was fixed inescapably in his place: the soldier was tied to his standard, the miller to his millstones, the armourer to his armoury, the curial to his class; they and their sons, and their sons' sons too, because the structure of the entire edifice must be preserved intact, for if it were changed it would fall. Bodies of artisans, arts and trades were declared of public utility, and it was made a crime to the state to desert them. Prices rose at an alarming rate, and then came the edict on commodity prices which acted as a general depressant to trade.

Everything was provided for, by innovation or perfection, with so vigilant and thoroughgoing a sense of the necessity of survival, with so systematic an application of reform as to give a distant onlooker the illusory impression of a design conceived and realized at once by the will of an emperor.

But there was an evil much less obvious than the constitutional and military crisis, than the Germanic invasions and the desertion of civil duty, than poverty and underpopulation. It was Christianity, an insidious cancer, profound and substantial, that was all the harder to attack because it was this that was at the root of all the uneasiness, that touched man in his political and religious faith, and was persecuted in his conscience. And the arm of legal persecution was used against it once again.

Scholars have often wondered why Rome, who had welcomed strange and barbarian gods to her Pantheon, the Phrygian Cybele, the Persian Mithra, the Egyptian Osiris, and had tolerated the rigid monotheism of the Giudaic cult, should have been so intolerant solely of the Christians. The apologists of the second and third century, who tried in vain to convince the Caesars of the Christian cult's right to liberty, asked a question which is still raised today: on what legal grounds could a legalitarian people like the Romans persecute the Christians? Whatever the technical reply, the intolerance was born of an essential and irreconcilable conflict between the religious conscience of the Roman subject and that of the Christian believer. And it will be worth our while to investigate this conflict, which does not consist of the opposition of monotheism and polytheism, for the very nature of the Middle Ages will be illumined by it.

What had been happening within the state had happened also in the field of the official religion. Pliny the Elder had called Italy 'nursling and mother of all lands, chosen by the will of the gods to bring to man humanity, and to become the common motherland of all peoples'. More than three centuries later, in the declining empire, Rutilus Naumazianus sang similarly of Rome:

Fecisti patriam diversis gentibus unam,
Urbem fecisti quod prius orbis erat.

And this was no mere oratorical praise.

In effect all free men of the empire were citizens from the time of Caracalla onwards; natives of Spain, Gaul, Illyria, Syria and Arabia all donned the purple. There was a single legal code, a single economic world, in spite of its local peculiarities and its dealings with alien lands, a single predominant culture, Hellenism, pervaded by oriental elements which went back to Alexander's Persian expedition and the foundation of Alexandria. Similarly, all the national cults had been intertwining and mingling with each other, and so long as they did not offend public order or morality they were welcomed into the state religion. And meanwhile out of this multiplicity of rites, a tendency to monotheism was becoming more and more apparent, and was encouraged by philosophical speculation. Its most common form was solar monotheism, which saw the invincible sun as the giver of life, omnipresent and all seeing, and worshipped it in the form of Apollo, Mithra or Osiris, the supreme manifestation of the inaccessible divinity.

As perhaps always happens among men when they undergo the experience of evil, grief and death, when they feel themselves threatened by a superhuman ineluctable force which wipes out life and all its accomplishments, the whole society was caught up in a profound religious ferment, looking for certainty and hope, either in the basest of superstitious rites or the heights of the purest and most austere of moral conceptions. And the empire, whose life-blood was ebbing away, clung ever more desperately to its temples and ceremonies, to the cult of the emperor, and the adoration of the invincible sun.

Let us now read the simple and moving account of a trial held on August 17th, 180, at the time of Commodus, in a city of Numidia called *Scillium*, before the proconsul Publius Vigellius Saturninus; the accused are the Christians Speratus, Natzalus, Cittinus, Donata, Seconda and Vestia. When they are ushered into the hall, 'the proconsul says: "You may merit the indulgence of our lord the emperor, provided that you are prepared to return to your senses!"'

Speratus replies: 'We have never done evil, we have not turned our hands to any act of wickedness, we have never offended anyone; but for the evil we have received we have given thanks, and so we honour our emperor.'

'We too,' retorts the proconsul Saturninus, 'we are religious, and our religion is simple; we swear on the genius of our lord the emperor, and we pray for his salvation, which is what you must do.'

Speratus says: 'If you will let me speak, I will reveal to you a mystery of simple truth.'

And Saturninus: 'As you wish to insult what we hold sacred, I will not hear you; rather you must swear on the genius of our lord the emperor.'

But Speratus replies: 'I do not know the empire of this world; instead I serve the God, whom no man sees or can see with the eyes of the flesh. I have never been deceitful; if I buy something I pay the tax; and this because I know my Lord, King of kings and Emperor of all nations.'

Then Cittinus and Donata and Vestia: 'There is no one we fear, except our Lord God who is in Heaven.' 'We honour Caesar as Caesar; but we fear God.' 'I am a Christian.' And with this cry, repeated by them all, the judgement is complete: the Christians are condemned to death, 'for having obstinately refused to return to the Roman custom'.

The antithesis here is reduced to its clearest and most basic elements. The old religion inherited by Rome is closely bound up with the state; it derives from it, guides it with its mysterious responses, wards off its dangers and consecrates its triumphs. It is not a church, but a citizenship in communion with its gods which prosper and protect it. With the claim of being a national religion, even the rigid monotheism of the Jews had been tolerated by the Romans. But Christianity dissociated the citizen from the believer; it proclaimed its message to a new citizenship, that of the church which knew no difference of nation, sex, state or fortune between men of good will within and without the boundaries of the empire; it transferred the emphasis of religion from the political community and the public lot to the individual's conscience and destiny, and shifted the vital point of interest from earth to Heaven, from cares of this world to hopes and promises of the next.

What crime the Christians were legally accused of may indeed be doubtful; the apologists were right when they raised their voice against the infamy perpetrated against them, when they protested the purity of their lives and even their faithfulness as citizens, who rendered unto Caesar the things that were Caesar's, and prayed God for the health of the emperor. But Marcus Aurelius, the Stoic philosopher emperor, was under no illusion when he refused to give ear to their words, nor were the wickedly brutal mob who stoned them and sent them to the wild beasts in the circus. For these were the destroyers of altars and sacred images, who had made themselves a fatherland in Heaven, avoided civil life as much as they could, shirking spectacles and religious ceremonies, the army and the magistrature, who espied in the calamities of the common weal the fulfillment of the dire words of their prophets. It was no case of misunderstanding; it was a conflict that could not be healed, that had to be settled with blood, the last witness of every faith, a conflict from which one of the adversaries must needs emerge the victor.

On the suggestion of his Caesar, Galerius, the Augustus Diocletian took up the final struggle, and the persecution flared up all over the empire. It was not a momentary or sporadic explosion of popular fanaticism, but rather a more rigorous repetition of the events of fifty years before under Decius, a body of legal provisions throughout the empire which aimed to exterminate the execrable superstition both in the believers and the material adjuncts of their cult. Between 303 and 309 four successive edicts of increasing severity were issued ordering the destruction of the churches and the Holy

Scriptures, the limitation of the civil rights of Christians and their exclusion from office and other honours; the clergy were imprisoned, and all were required to recant their faith by sacrificing on the altars in the presence of the magistrates. There were the *lapsi*, who gave up the Holy Scriptures and threw incense on the altars; there were others who escaped being put to the test by flight; others who got themselves released by bribery or by a *libellus*, a false certificate of their act of sacrifice. There were many, however, who did not yield to exhortations, wheedlings, threats or tortures, many who in the drunkenness of martyrdom strained the indulgence of the governors too far and challenged death.

The intensity, continuity and violence of the persecution varied according to the district and the nature of men and circumstances. In only one part of the empire were people saved, however much this might hurt the sacred structure of the empire; this was in Britain and Gaul, where Christianity was less widespread and where the Caesar of Maximian governed; he was Constantius, known as Chlorus from the pale and sickly look of his face, a valiant soldier and a wise statesman whose court professed the solar monotheism that had become the official religion of emperors and empire under Claudius II Gothicus and Aurelian.

In spite of the extreme gravity and resolution of the provisions, the persecution dragged on indecisively; and unless we take certain facts into account, this surprising fact will seem all the more miraculous and incomprehensible. Between the middle of the third century and the beginning of the fourth, the Christians formed something between a twentieth and a fifteenth part of the total population of the empire; this amounted to several millions and in some cities in the east the Christians were in a majority, or even the sole inhabitants. Though a conspicuous number, this was still a minority, but in this case as in every other, the deciding factor was not the number, but the animating principle, the strength of will, the capacity for sacrifice, the Roman quality of acting and suffering strongly; and this is naturally a distinction of the few, though in time it may become, though more confusedly, the inheritance of the many. Nor was the struggle merely between blind brutality on the one side and divine suffering on the other; it was between a state, religion, and culture of sound and venerable tradition, and, especially from the second century onwards, a new society of believers, energetic, workmanlike, conscious of the truth that must triumph and of a right that must be recognized. Now throughout the two periods—which were only in a very crude sense consecutive—of abstinence, patience and martyrdom at first, and then of defence, declared hostility, and organizing activity, a new body of citizens had been forming both within and without the old, hostile to it; it was alive, fiery, had its headquarters at Rome, called its bishops to council, and announced its faith to the 120 provinces of the empire from 1600-1800 episcopal sees.

The organic fabric that was vital to the new age was already formed when the old organism began to show symptoms of the deep sickness that afflicted it: the failing of the faith in the traditional gods and in the fortune of Rome. Under these conditions, to carry their struggle against Christianity to its appropriate end meant digging even deeper, destroying entire cities, setting off civil war in whole provinces and insisting on extermination on such a scale as to surpass the moral courage of the people supposed to inflict it; and all this could result in no successful resuscitation of the past, and no quenching of the burning thirst that made men seek certainty and hope, away from the storms of the world.

The first to capitulate was the East where the persecution had been enforced more strictly and the failure had been more noticeable. An edict of Galerius, signed also by the other Augusti and published in Nicomedia on April 30, 311, ordered that the churches be restored to the Christians and that they be allowed to meet and hold services. It was a simple edict of tolerance, an act of clemency; justified by the thoroughly pagan consideration, inspired though it was by a religious conception, that the Christians would otherwise be without any cult, and it was at the same time a declaration of the Empire's inability to rekindle a fire that was dead, and to suffocate what was most alive in the hearts of men.

The man who established the Christian empire was the son of Constantius Chlorus, Constantine; not Constantine as a single individual with a prodigious influence on the whole of the Roman world, but as the reflection of the political and religious consciousness at a turning point in history, together with the individuals whose tradition he inherited, with those around him, and with the men who were actually to lead the process that his initiative set in motion to its conclusion. Constantine has suffered the fate of all great initiators in the eyes of posterity. From the first most understandable apologia of Eusebius of Cesarea, to the most recent denigrations and panegyrics, this first Christian emperor has been represented, according to the interests and passions of men and their times, either with all the attributes of piety, inspired and supported by the power of God, or with all the wiles of the politician, professing a religion in total contrast with his conscience and his way of life, solely to further his political ends, or again as a model of military generosity while he was a pagan, but of cruelty and despotism as soon as he embraced Christianity.

Certainly he was a complex figure, full of light and shade. In Constantine we find the continuation of his father's tradition of solar monotheism and tolerance, which appeared to sympathize with the Christians, without denying the traditional religion. He was the valiant general worshipped by his soldiers, always the first in danger, moderate to his enemies and crowned by victory; he was the politician who, with his keen and steady eye, went from fortune to fortune and triumphed over all his rivals, Maximian, Maxentius, Galerius, Licinius, Maximin Daza, Severus: he was the man who silenced the remaining threats of the conquered Maximian and Licinius with death; he was the founder of Constantinople and the true initiator of the Eastern Empire. In him we find the increasingly resolute patron of Christianity; first the devout frequenter of bishops, then the 'bishop for external affairs', as he was to call himself, the catechumen, the Christian. And, yes, there was also, even when his great mission was publicly at its height, the emperor who had his firstborn Crispus killed, who had his wife Fausta suffocated in the bath for some reason that must have been of the weightiest and yet escapes us, and will perhaps be forever a mystery.

Even if it were possible to penetrate into the secrets of his personal life, we would not wish to set ourselves up as judges of Constantine the man. The man interests us, and more than the man the emperor, in as much as he sheds light on the times he lived in and on which he imposed his will. And from this viewpoint the apparent contradictions, the ambiguities of his religious policies and professions, give no grounds for suspicion and scandal. And indeed, the persistence of the old customs such as the practice of public haruspicy, the dedication of temples, and the symbol of the unconquered sun on the coinage, and at the same time the apparent contradictions of the tolerance and favour shown towards the Christians, the even clearer intention to stamp out paganism, the emperor's intervention in internal questions of the church, his formal conversion on the eve of his death, give us a perfect indication of the laborious progress of the Christianization of the empire, centred on the person and the actions of the emperor.

In 312 the political constellation was composed of four Augusti; Constantine in Gaul and Britain, Maxentius in Italy and Licinius and Maximin in the east; the latter two were enemies because of their territorial rivalry, the former because Constantine had defeated his father-in-law, the ex-Augustus Maximian, the father of Maxentius, and had probably forced him to commit suicide and had also blackened his name. This twofold enmity, and in addition, the religious tolerance of Constantine and the corresponding intolerance of Maximin resulted in alliances between Constantine and Licinius on the one hand and Maxentius and Maximin on the other, and finally in the outbreak of two wars, one in the west between Constantine and Maxentius, the other in the east between Licinius and Maximin.

After fortifying the boundary of the Rhine against the Germans, and Hadrian's Wall against the Picts and Scots, Constantine marched on Italy with a small, well-tried army confident in the presence of their Augustus. The Christian bishops that he liked to have around him stood round his standard with the army, and by their devout solicitude offered a pledge of divine favour to his arms. He crossed the Alps by Mont Cenis and set fire to Susa which had opposed him; Turin opened her gates to him, and all Transpadane Gaul as far as Brescia followed her example. Once Verona had fallen, Aquileia and Modena surrendered and in a few weeks the whole of northern Italy was in his hands.

He then crossed the Apennines and advanced by the Via Cassia on Rome where both the people and their leaders began to complain and demonstrate against the cowardly tyrant who left the peninsula to the mercy of the enemy. Maxentius was forced out of Rome, and after crossing the Mulvian Bridge, he lined up his army on the hills that follow the right bank of the Tiber at the junction of the Via Flaminia and the Via Cassia. The auspices and the Sybilline books, consulted before the departure, had replied that 'the enemy of Rome would die'. But which of the two was the enemy of Rome? Lactantius relates that in the night before the battle a mysterious voice told Constantine in a dream to have the monogram of Christ put on his shields and on October 28, 312, under this divine sign and Constantine's prompt, authoritative and wise generalship, his troops gained, at Saxa Rubra and the Mulvian Bridge, the victory that put the whole of the west into Constantine's hands, and which naturally inspired the Christians with burning hopes, although the traditional religious policies remained unchanged. In the east, six months later, on May 1, 313, on the Campi Sereni between Hadrianople and Heraclea, Licinius shattered the army of Maximin, the Augustus of Syria and Egypt, the worshipper of Serapis and now the last persecutor of the Christians. Before the battle the pagan Licinius had made his soldiers raise their arms to the sky and recite the well-known prayer in the sight of the enemy army:

> O God supreme and holy, we pray to you—
> We commend to you every just cause,
> Our salvation, our Empire.
> We live through thee;
> Through thee we gain victory and happiness.
> O God Supreme and Holy,
> Grant, O grant, our prayers.
> We stretch our arms to thee,
> O hear us, God Holy and Supreme.

In the interval between the two actions, the two protagonists had issued the perhaps too famous edict of Milan:

'I, Constantine Augustus and I, Licinius Augustus, being happily met at Milan, and having discussed all that pertained to public security and utility, have decided that of all the things that would please the majority of men, those pertaining to the worship of the Divinity should first be ordained, and therefore that the Christians and all others should be granted the freedom to follow what ever religion they wish, in order that whatever divinity exists in the heavens may show himself pleased and propitious to us and to all those under our authority. We have therefore deemed it necessary to dispose with salutary and most just reason that such freedom be not refused to anyone at all who has embraced either the Christian cult or the religion they feel most suitable for themselves, in order that the highest divinity, whose religion we freely respect, may grant us his accustomed benevolence and favour in everything.'

Who was the 'highest god' to whom Licinius' soldiers raised their hands in prayer? Who the *Divinitas*, through whose *instinctus* Constantine had beaten Maxentius, as we are told by the inscription on the arch raised in Rome in memory of the battle of the Mulvian Bridge and Constantine's triumphant entry into the city? What was the meaning of the 'highest divinity' and the 'whatever divinity exists in the heavens' that we read in the edict of Milan? Whatever the secret faith of the two emperors was, the god of whom they speak is not the God of the Gospels, but rather the personification of the final limit of syncretism, which was the simplest expression of monotheism, and—let us confess it—the least dangerous one for all the subjects of the empire. In short, the edict was not the act of the birth of Christianity or of State Catholicism, but it was an indispensable step towards it: liberty of religious belief.

The trouble was that from 313 onwards, the respective policies of the two emperors drew fatally far away from this precarious equilibrium which had displeased the pagans whom it deprived of their old power, and left the Christians dissatisfied, because they were anxious that truth should triumph over false gods and the hostility of their fellow men. On the one hand, Constantine, with increasingly undisguised scorn for the old gods, gave the Christian clergy first equal and then superior privileges to those of the priests of the old order, recognized manumissions celebrated in church before the priest rather than before a tribunal and judicial arbitration pronounced on civil matters by the clergy even at the request of only one of the contesting parties; he authorized legacies in favour of the 'venerable and holy Catholic Church', promoted and contributed to religious foundations, and entered into ever closer and more binding relations with the Holy See; Licinius, on the other hand, kept the Christians out of the army and out of office, obstructed the practice of the Church and the meetings of the bishops, restored the traditional religious practices and surrounded himself with magicians and astrologers. Finally the victories of Hadrianople and Chrysopolis on July 3rd and September 18th respectively, and with them the death of Licinius, left the whole empire in Constantine's hands, and swung the politico-religious balance decidedly in favour of Christianity.

This, rather than the battle of the Mulvian Bridge, was the moment at which the religious problem, which was also one of internal peace and unity, became a political question of prime importance in the consciousness of Constantine and his contemporaries. Although it was already under way before this date, it was after it that the close interpenetration of Church and state, which had such formidable consequences, was so greatly accelerated. Assemblies of the bishops, convoked or presided over by the emperor, sometimes in person, decided the great questions of discipline and doctrine, such as the Donatist schism which broke out in Carthage between the rigorists and the apologists for the *lapsi* of the latest persecutions, and the Arian schism which denied the divinity of Christ. And according to the personal or political ideas dominant in Constantine's mind, Arius or Athanasius, Donatus or Caecilian and their respective followers, were persecuted or approved. The bishops exercised their contentious jurisdiction under the aegis of the state; in their synods they discussed the question of Christian participation in the army and in public office. The state confiscated the riches of the pagan sanctuaries for the benefit of the churches, and offered to use its authority to see that the bishops' rulings were carried out, and to repress the heretical sects of Novations, Valentinians, Marcionites, Paulianists and Montanists.

In the year 330, only two years after its foundation, Constantine inaugurated his capital on the Bosphorus, the *Nova Roma* which was to keep the tradition of the Christian empire he had founded alive for eleven centuries. And it was near here that his last illness overtook him. He laid down the purple and put on the white robe of the catechumen; and in 337, after asking and receiving baptism from the bishop Eusebius of Nicomedia, he reached the end of his days. It was the seal of a life, and the seal of an age.

The road that Constantine had opened was followed to the end in a few decades. By a decree of Gratianus, all the ancient colleges of the Roman priesthood were deprived of their property and income, and amid the passionate entreaties of the pagan aristocracy, the statue of Victory, witness of the imperial greatness, was removed from the great hall of the Senate. Theodosius, who was the last of the Caesars to hold the reins of both East and West, stamped out paganism and heresy and created the first example of the Catholic Empire, penetrated completely by the new religious consciousness, and ready to serve the Church in all things.

But the premises and substance of the next millenium were already established in the age of Constantine. The conflict between Christianity and Rome had been overcome when the latter had accomplished the mission allotted her by providence, and Eusebius of Cesarea, Constantine's biographer and panegyrist, was able to pronounce the doctrine that was to be believed so widely and for so long: that the authority of the emperor came directly from God, that the empire was the realization of the divine order, destined to govern the world and to make the Church of Christ triumph from pole to pole. The new Catholic society was formed, and fitted into its hierarchies with its requirements, organs and functions. The new Rome on the shores of the Bosphorus went beyond the intentions of its founder, though not against the reality of the situation, by leaving the old Rome as a vast free field of action for the successor of St Peter and thus deepening the gulf between west and east, between wisdom and spontaneity on the one hand and subtlety and servility on the other. The imperial favour granted to Arianism opened the door through which the German races were to enter the orbit of Christianity.

Most important of all, it was from this point on that the fundamental problem of which the history of the Middle Ages consists asserted itself: the problem of the coexistence of two universalities, bound together inseparably, in as much as they had the same object and purpose in spite of their different status. The priesthood was the depositary of a salvation-bearing transcendent Truth, and was forced by historical circumstances to impress its discipline and rule on the temporal world and to become worldly itself and practice politics; the earthly empire, from reasons of power and prestige, and from the deepest exigencies of the faith on which its own legitimacy was founded, was obliged to assume a religious mission and to be Christian in all its actions.

CHAPTER 3

THE GERMANS

STILICHO AND ALARIC

For a long time historians have been accustomed to set the Roman world and the Germanic neatly the one against the other and to represent the invasions as the sudden catastrophic clash of barbarism with the proud structure, civil organization and refined culture of the empire. Now we know that, although there may be some truth in a conception of this kind, this was not quite how it happened; and it is indeed to the credit of modern historiography, especially since the eighteenth century, that it has deepened its research so as to dismiss the notion of the external and accidental causation of the invasions, to reset them in their true historical perspective, and so discover a new significance in them.

The Rhine and the Danube with their garrisons constituted a frontier and a line of defence; they indicated a division, but not the insuperable limit of civilization. Beyond them trade was carried on, money coined, kingships flourished, and even Christianity was propagated in its Arian form. An invincible attraction, the product of countless conflicting desires, was drawing the Germans to Rome, just as the inexorable need for arms in the fading empire was forcing Rome towards the Germans. From Marcus Aurelius onwards, there is an ever increasing infiltration of foreign elements into the army, and gradually up into the highest military posts. At first it is just a few divisions stationed on the frontier, who have been granted land on the condition that they defend it, and conquered tribes who as allies are obliged to furnish military contingents; then finally Theodosius opens the legions themselves to the Germans, and Italy is garrisoned by Batavians, Marcomanni, and Erulians; Egypt by Alemanni, Franks and Vandals; Phoenicia by Franks and Alemanni; Syria by Goths and Mesopotamia by Franks. Then a Vandal, Stilicho, reaches the highest command, marries into the imperial family and is set as guardian over the empire. There is a substantial link binding these two worlds that are so close and yet so different, a fatal circle draws them together, making the state of unbalance more serious every day; and while the one grows weaker, calling for and accepting help which can only aggravate its own prostration and deficiency, the other absorbs its spirit, supports it in its destiny, until the Roman inheritance is transferred to the new world seething at its frontiers.

The barbarian invasions, occupations and rule are only the crisis that sets the seal on this gradual process. If all had consisted of one sudden ruinous clash, the problem would have been considerably simpler and the event more disastrous. But as it was, the development of events was extremely complicated, and the results far-reaching, precisely because this was no case of blind violence, because the Germanic impulse and the decline of the empire were closely interrelated, and each both the cause and effect of the other. Perhaps there has never been a moment of such bitter struggle and such universal suffering—except in times all too near our own. Loves, lives, and fortunes, all could be lost without warning amidst the completely unpredictable and uncontrollable forces that had been let loose. But above all there was the clash and the almost inextricable intertwining of the remaining paganism of imperial Rome and the new Romano-Christian culture, of Arianism and Catholicism, of the Germany that had been more or less assimilated and the foreign Germany, hungry for the lands, offices, and stipends that lay beyond the frontier. And entire peoples and generations, being unable to stand still or return to the past, were pushed inexorably towards a glorious or fearful future, obliged to make their choice, with no way of escape, to work and to suffer to found the new order.

The penetration of the Germans within the territory of the empire became more and more tumultuous and chaotic from 375 onwards. In that year the Ostrogoths and Visigoths, who had settled beyond the Danube on the shores of the Black Sea and were already on the road to civilization, were overtaken by a people with sharp eyes and smooth, flat, yellow faces. They brought with them their flocks, their covered wagons, their women and children, and were preceded by tales of their unutterable cruelty and barbarism. These were the Huns from the steppes of Asia; the Alans fell at their onslaught, the Ostrogothic kingdom of Hermanric disintegrated, and the Visigoths divided. Of these the pagans, under Athanric, took refuge in Transylvania, and the more numerous Christians, under Frithigern, piled up on the Danube, and asked the Emperor Valens to allow them to settle within the frontiers. After lengthy negotiations this request was granted, and in the spring of 376 they crossed the river near Silistria and were received into the diocese of Thrace as confederates.

All possible precautions were taken during their settlement to prevent any disorders: the Visigoths were escorted by Roman detachments, and they were obliged to hand over their arms and their children as hostages. But the most careful precautions could not secure their obedience and tranquillity. The loss of their children, scattered around the Balkan peninsula at the whim of the Romans, necessarily excited the new allies' resentment. Most of them in fact managed to keep their weapons, either through the Roman officers' inability to reduce a warlike people to order under a treaty, or through their corruption, whereby they sold for gold the right to own iron, which was soon to be tried on the battlefields of Greece and Italy. The problem of supplies was a particularly difficult one, and according to the tradition, the military commanders of the diocese of Thrace, Lupicinus and Maximus, took advantage of it to starve the Visigoths and despoil them of their wealth.

But, whatever the crimes of the commanders may have been, no mere human goodwill was or could have been enough to avoid the frictions, remove the obstacles, assure peaceful coexistence, and in short, to absorb rapidly and permanently a large warlike society, with a different language and customs, embittered by exile, organized by its own chieftains, and by now all too convinced by direct experience of its own strength, and of the empire's weakness. The impudence of these invaders increased with their numbers. The Visigoths led by Frithigern reached tens of thousands; then, through the breach they had opened and the Roman garrisons had left unguarded, new bands of Ostrogoths rushed in, headed by Alateus and Saphrax, and took up the cause of their precursors. After threatening Marcianopolis without success—the city's fortifications were strong enough to stand up to the inexperienced aggressors—they set to overrunning Thrace north and south of the Balkans, plundering as they went, while after them there rushed Goths in the imperial service, German slaves, settlers, miners, and finally even swarms of Alans and Huns who had come from over the Danube.

Valens, who was busy with preparations for an expedition against Persia, was unable to reach Constantinople until the end of May, 378. He was received in the circus of the city by the ironic acclamation of a crowd that was worried by the poor performance of the Roman arms and by the presence of the Goths around the city. His colleague of the west, the Emperor Gratian his nephew, who had just successfully checked another invasion of the Alemanni and reestablished the Rhine frontier, set out to come to his rescue, and sent a warning not to go into battle until he arrived and they could join forces. But this prudent piece of advice went unheeded. The jeers of the people were still ringing in Valens' ears; his jealousy was excited by the military success of his nephew, who with another victory to his name would have become the acclaimed and accepted victor of both east and west; his generals, especially Sebastian, the *magister militum*, encouraged him to attack, as did the mistaken belief that he was faced with a force of only 10,000 men. He therefore rejected the proposals of Frithigern, who announced that he was prepared to make peace if the province of Thrace was assigned to the Goths; and thus, on August 9, 378, gave battle on a plain near Hadrianople.

The day of Hadrianople marks the beginning of the final collapse for Rome's world-wide empire. The outcome of the battle was so disastrous as to suggest a second Cannae; except that, while at Cannae soldiers of the Roman-Italian confederation had fought against Hannibal and the Carthaginians, now Germans were fighting Germans, some still rebellious, others reconciled to the discipline of Rome; and while after Cannae the great city had drawn from the defeat the energy to destroy its rival and to put the stamp of its civilization on east and west, now it was making its last effort of self-defence, and could only assert itself by dispensing its inheritance to the invaders. The Roman cavalry was put to flight; the infantry was surrounded and two-thirds of it slain; large numbers of generals and officers were left on the field, among them Sebastian, the *magister militum*. The emperor himself, who had been wounded in the fray, was allegedly carried to a hut, and there met his end in a fire started by the Visigoths, who had arrived shortly afterwards and had been unable to force their way in. In any case his body was never found. Over and against the posthumous recriminations that usually accompany public misfortunes, there were still people to express the greatness of the sacrifice with all the old Roman spirit. 'For my part', said Libanus in his funeral oration composed in honour of Valens and his army, 'I venerate the glorious death that they accepted valiantly, standing firm and fighting in line; I venerate the battlefield stained with their blood and the blood of the barbarians. The soldiers and their leaders were inspired by the virtue of their ancestors, whom they equalled in discipline and in the art of war. Their noble emulation was fed by their love of glory, which incited them to struggle at once against heat and thirst, against fire and the sword, and to embrace an honourable death with rejoicing, rather than give way to flight and infamy.' But when the eloquent orator of Antioch turned from the heroic past to his own times and asked the reason for such ill fortune, he could only give an answer that was of no use for the present or the future, in a phrase devoid of all hope: 'the wrath of the gods', which had led the enemies of Rome to victory.

The enemies of Rome had triumphed; and yet, by an apparent contradiction, which is not surprising when we consider the confused desires and the incompetence of the barbarians on the one hand, and the stability of the empire on the other, almost nothing was changed. The war with the Goths went on for another four years without ever managing to arrive at a definite conclusion. Noricum, Pannonia, Thrace, Macedonia and Thessaly were all ravaged in various raids; Hadrianople and Constantinople were threatened; but for the new Rome to fall, either the Roman consciousness had to evaporate, or the barbarians had to attain military equality with Rome. The war was fought with arms and treachery, and Julius, the *magister militum* for the East, has remained famous for the resoluteness he showed when he assembled all the Gothic soldiers in the towns and camps on a certain day, pretending that their salaries were to be paid, and had them all massacred from first to last, to avoid any further trouble. In the end, either through personal inclination, or by government strategy, or both, Theodosius, the new Augustus whom Gratian had nominated to succeed Valens, adopted a new conciliatory attitude towards the Goths; and on October 3, 382, an agreement was made at Constantinople, whereby Frithigern and his Visigoths were granted land in the diocese of Thrace to the north of the Balkans. The emperor granted them full autonomy, exemption from taxes, high pay, and they in their turn guaranteed to serve in the army under their own leaders. On the part of the empire it was an admission of weakness and necessity, of inability to assimilate these allies settled within its own territory; on the part of the Visigoths it was a proof of strength and resistance to absorption; it was on both sides the sign of a deep difference between two societies, two cultures at once opposed and linked together, hostile and inevitably close.

In this way a political problem arose which, though it passed relatively unnoticed to start with, became more and more pressing as the unbalance between Germans and Romans in the army and the high commands increased; the former became increasingly conscious of their own strength, and the latter, in all ranks and classes, ever more resentful at the growing barbarianization of the empire, the violence and abuse of power, German occupation of high offices and the vast burden of taxation made necessary by the new alliances. An episode recounted by the historians of the time gives a vivid illustration of this conflict of the age and especially of one of the great elements of the drama—the contradiction caused in the minds of the Germans themselves by the contact with Romanism, a contradiction which was linked and even merged with their religious dilemma. Two Gothic chieftains, Eriwulf and Fravitta, were dining one day at the imperial table, the first was an Arian, the second a pagan married to a Roman lady; and in the licence and heat of the banquet they were talking of politics. Now while the Arian, fired by his nationalistic feelings and his hate of Catholicism, which had been so rigidly upheld by Theodosius, declared that in his opinion the final aim of the Goths should be the destruction of the empire, the pagan Fravitta supported the necessity of a close union with Rome. And the best way he could find to support his arguments was to stab Eriulfus as soon as they had left the palace; as a result, he received the highest honours at court, but only to fall victim a few years later to the Roman and Catholic revival.

Even the massacre of Thessalonica, so grievous both in itself and in its consequences for the relations between State and Church, was the result of a demonstration of anti-Germanic reaction. The memory of the Goth's ruinous raids was still fresh in the Thessalonicans' minds, the streets were crowded with barbarian soldiers, and even the governor, Botherich, was a German. It was enough that Botherich should refuse to free a circus charioteer, a boorish delinquent adored by the people, for himself and some of his officers to be killed by an enraged mob. The citizens had won; but while they were all in the circus absorbed in the show before them, they were surprised by the guards, who had received secret orders from Milan, and for three hours the seven thousand of them were systematically massacred.

In 390, the same year as the massacre, the Visigoths broke the peace treaty made with Theodosius eight years before, and for the first time two Germans in their prime found themselves face to face with each other. They were Alaric and Stilicho, who for the next twenty years were to sum up in their careers the dramatic fate of the empire. Alaric was a Visigoth of noble line, who grew up amid the horror of the Hun invasion, amid migrations, wars, peaces, and plunderings; Stilicho was a Vandal of humble origin, who rose by his own ability to the supreme command of the army, and married a niece of the emperor, later his adopted daughter, the Serena whom the poet Claudian praised and adored in his poems and who was destined to so tragic a death. The encounter between the two armies had no decisive outcome. The Visigoths were surrounded and beaten on the Maritza, and obtained a new peace treaty from the prudent Theodosius; then on September 5, 394, twenty thousand of them fought for him under Alaric on the Vipaccus against the rhetor Eugenius, a pretender to the title of emperor.

But on the death of the emperor at Milan on January 17, 395, the Visigoths were sent back to their territory by Stilicho; whereupon, seeing that their leader was disappointed in his desire for a high military appointment in the empire, and that with the disappearance of their threat the payments they had settled for were suspended, they determinedly took up arms again and called on Alaric to lead them into war.

The condition of the empire is now, in a word, considerably changed. Theodosius is the last inheritor of the great Roman imperial and military tradition. Up to his time, the man who wears the imperial purple, be his name Trajan or Marcus Aurelius, Diocletian or Constantine, Gratian or Valens, is above all a military commander, who rushes from one end of the empire to the other, from frontier to frontier, to maintain the unity of the state against rebels and invaders. Now Arcadius, a boy of eighteen, is enthroned within the solid walls of Constantinople, and a child of eleven, Honorius, is cherished at Ravenna, both of them guarded by barbarian troops. They are the Augusti of the east and the west, the sons of Theodosius. On account of his well-earned reputation, his high office, and his close tie with the late emperor, Stilicho would be expected and would like to stand guard over them and the fate of Rome that is bound up with them. But the ministers who follow each other in a succession of blood at Arcadius' side, are doing all they can to deepen the gulf between east and west; they aim to rid the empire of the barbarians, and are hostile to this Vandal who is Honorius' general and the preserver of Theodosius' philo-Germanic policy. Meanwhile, Stilicho—who will ever be able to fathom the depths of his soul?— is cherishing some great ambition, concerned at once with the future of the west and of his own family. He wants to reclaim eastern Illyricum for Honorius and himself from the minister Rufinus who is contesting it in Arcadius' name, and it is said he plans to marry his son Eucherius to Galla Placidia, the emperor's step-sister; certainly he gives his first child Maria in marriage to the emperor in 398 when he is only just fourteen.

But in vain does the court poet celebrate the splendour of the marriage, the happy omens, and the impatience of love, with all the old-time elegance at his command; unspeaking and shadowy, the young empress is to go untouched into her tomb. And similarly untouched and repudiated, after Stilicho's tragic disappearance, his second-born Thermantia is to return to her mother in 408, after she too has been raised for a short while to the honours of the empire.

Between the crafty manoeuvring of Byzantium and the heroic but ambiguous greatness of the general, Alaric plays his desperate game: he is useful to both empires in their hostility to one another, and takes advantage of this for his own advancement and for their ruin. It is hard to say what this clever negotiator, this tireless sacker of town and country really wants. He is pushed on by his own restlessness, the turbid rapacity of his uprooted people. Camping in enemy territory wherever he may be, he is driven on by his need for arms, for land and for provisions and at the same time by the need to destroy or to appropriate the civilization which, in spite of all his efforts, remains foreign to him, by the desire to take the in-

B*

heritance of the impotent into the hands of the strong. Before his eyes there stand the images of Stilicho, Arbogast, and the great German guardians of the empire; and for himself and his Visigoths he longs for a similar but fuller achievement.

With the death of Theodosius the gigantic duel between Stilicho and Alaric began, and it was fought out in Greece and Italy, the very heart of the empire. And then indeed, when the sacred soil of Hellas and of Rome was invaded and violated by barbarians, it may well have seemed that this was no mere formidable preparation, but the very disintegration of the world. Alaric moved first against Constantinople, more to induce fright and to devastate, than from any hope to take possession of the city. He was turned back by a large payment from Rufinus. He then went down through Macedonia and Thessaly and found himself faced with Stilicho, who had rushed to the defence of the empire and to support the western claims on Illyricum at the head of both eastern and western troops. The two armies were drawn up, about to engage in a decisive battle, when an order from Arcadius obliged Stilicho to send back the eastern army and retire. Resistance would have meant falling short of his fidelity to the empire and causing the outbreak of civil war—with what result it was difficult to tell—and he obeyed. After this Alaric's advance was no more than a great race, as it appeared to a contemporary: a game in which chariots and horses rushed from one end of the peninsula to the other, in which places sacred to beauty and knowledge, to civil virtues and sacrifice, that live even today in our memory—the valley of Tempe, Thermopylae, Thebes, Athens, Corinth, Megara, Sparta—now for the first time astonished and satiated the rapacious curiosity for these Germans, who were desperately vowed to the ruin and the triumph of Rome. With the Piraeus blockaded, Athens only escaped being plundered by the payment of a ransom (unless, as the hard-dying pagan tradition would have it, she was saved by the terror instilled by Pallas and Achilles who appeared, huge on the walls, to forbid the sacrilege). Athens was now only a shadow of her former self: but there remained as witness to her greatness, her port, her temples, and her gardens that had heard the words of Plato and Aristotle. And Alaric deigned to visit these ruins, to bathe in the hot baths and to sit at table with the arcons of the prytaneum. At Eleusis the temple of the mysteries was pillaged and destroyed; rapacity joined with religious hatred to plunder and profane. Then the ruinous chase went on, down to the isthmus, and into the very heart of the Peloponnese.

And here a strange thing happened. Stilicho, worried by the fate of the empire and the pleas of the refugees, hurried to the spot with an army, disembarking just south of Corinth (397); but after camping in front of the enemy for some time, he gave up the undertaking and returned to Italy without fighting. There was no lack of suspicions on his account even then. But his departure was in fact inevitable, because one of the habitual court intrigues had caused the Byzantine senate to declare him a public enemy, and a rebellion that had broken out in Africa by agreement with Byzantium threatened famine in Rome and Italy. He therefore tried to turn the unfavourable circumstances to his best advantage by making an ally of his enemy and letting him loose on the east.

Unfortunately the weapon was a dangerous one, and the gamble turned out against him. Indeed Alaric carried out the terms of his agreement with such diligence and devastated Epirus so thoroughly, that Constantinople was obliged to give in and buy the leader of the Visigoths for their own use, detaching him from the western alliance with a large sum of money, the title of *magister militum* for Illyricum, and finally the assignment of Epirus to the invaders, who were thus placed in a position of defence and threat against the west.

In the autumn of 401 Alaric, by agreement with Constantinople, invaded Northern Italy by the Julian Alps and laid seige to Milan. Forced back by Stilicho, he turned west, probably with the intention of attacking Gaul; but he was stopped near Pollentia in the Tanarus Valley, and there in a bloody engagement on April 6, 402, he left his camp and the large part of the women and children, among them his wife and sons, in the enemies' hands. He then pushed down south-east towards Rome; but then the thought of the prisoners prevailed over all his plans and he agreed to leave Italy on the condition that they were restored to him. A year later he was back again under the walls of Verona, where he suffered another defeat; he was pursued up towards the Brenner Pass, and could well have been annihilated, had not Stilicho once more considered it more expedient to make terms, and, as it would appear, to agree with the Visigoths on a common expedition against eastern Illyricum.

With Alaric's first descent into Italy, the death agony of Rome began. In the course of the next ten years the frontiers were broken down on the Rhine, the Danube, and Hadrian's Wall: Picts, Scots, Vandals, Alans, Alemanni and Burgundians took possession of land within the body of the empire, and with disastrous results, and Britain was practically lost. The British troops clamoured for a new emperor, Flavius Claudius Constantine, and the time came when Honorius himself sent him the imperial purple. Stilicho resisted with the force of a soldier and the skill of a diplomat, but in the end he was overcome, not by arms, but by a palace revolution, a tardy and improvident revolt of Catholic and Roman feeling. His enemies hated him for his barbarian origin, his religious tolerance towards the Arians, and his omnipotence; they suspected him of dark designs on the empire on account of his cunning, his military prestige and his family connections; they would have liked, to quote a contemporary, 'to move an army worthy of the name and virtue of Rome against the barbarians, drive them back into their territories or reduce them to the ignominous state of servitude in which the Spartans held their Helots'. It was too late; the time to turn back had passed. Now the problem was a different one: how to fuse the two elements, to create a new world, and, as always, through frightful wreckage. Alaric, spurred on by his restless people, with his impulses and ambitions, was the servant of the great forces of history, which transcended his own person and his consciousness. He seemed to triumph for a moment, and then disappeared.

The treaty made with Stilicho remained a dead letter. Years passed—the terrible years of violated frontiers, Radagaisus beaten and killed under the walls of Fiesole, Constantine acclaimed as emperor—there followed agreements, preparations, orders and counter orders, without the expedition being even begun. Finally Alaric grew impatient, and in 408 moved once more against Italy, resolved to extort a high price for his enforced inertia. He demanded 4,000 pounds of gold as an indemnity. The court was against it; voices rose in the Senate—noble voices, as though from another world—denouncing the shame of Rome being blackmailed by the barbarians. Stilicho, the Vandal, the heir to the Theodosian tradition, intervened, and by his authority the demand was granted.

But the mute hostility of which he was the object, the aversion to the Germans, now broke out in all its violence. He was accused of treason; the general hatred was further enflamed by the zeal of the chancellor Olympius, who believed or pretended to believe that there was a conspiracy afoot to depose Honorius and raise the young Eucherius to the purple by agreement with the Gothic troops. Stilicho got wind of the affair and took refuge in a church in Ravenna, trusting in its sanctuary. He was persuaded to come out by a letter from the emperor promising him his life, but the moment he was over the threshhold, his death sentence for high treason was announced to him from another letter. As far as we can see, he was quite innocent. He could have counted on his soldiers to support him; but he did not want to start a civil war; so he obediently bent his head to the executioner's axe. With his death came the ruin of his family, the slaughter of his friends, the confiscation of many fortunes and the furious hounding of the Goths, their women and children. Thermantia was repudiated and sent to Serena in Rome; Eucherius fled from certain death to Rome, where he was killed soon after, his assassins being rewarded with high offices.

Alaric could now congratulate himself on Rome's loss of her most capable defender, but he had cause for grief as well, the exacerbation of Roman and Catholic feeling rendered agreement impossible and caused him to be rejected as an enemy. He began by negotiating quite moderately, declaring himself ready to leave Noricum and retire to Pannonia against the payment of a smaller sum than the one already considered and granted by the senate. When it was refused, he set out resolutely for Rome. To anyone who pointed out the dangers of such an enterprise, he replied: 'I am compelled to take this step against my will; an irresistible force is sweeping me on and crying, "Move against Rome and destroy it!"' He crossed the Po near Cremona and went down through Bologna, Rimini, and the Via Flaminia to the city. He made no attempt to force the walls, either from lack of adequate resources or from prudence; instead he contented himself with blockading the gates and all lines of communication, so as to stop the delivery of provisions arriving from Africa by the Tiber, the Portuensis and the Ostiensis.

The bewildered citizens hatched the most foul plots against the Germans; and even the tragic widow of Stilicho, the cousin of the emperor, was put to death on the suspicion of having summoned the enemy. They wanted to save Rome, their lives and their fortunes, but they had lost the Roman spirit and lacked both faith and will. The only passions that survived were those of discord: the pagans reproached the Christians for the empty temples, the derision of the ancient ceremonies, and the loss of the statue of Victory from the senate; the Catholics referred everything to the inscrutable judgment of God; the Arians watched, not without hope for the future, and were held responsible for all the ills around them. Instead of going out to fight, they tried to negotiate for the raising of the blockade. Alaric demanded the surrender of all the gold, silver and objects of value in the city and the liberation of the German slaves. When the ambassadors protested at the terms, and spoke menacingly of the readiness of the Roman multitude to take up arms if driven to desperation, the king is said to have replied, 'The thicker the hay, the easier the mowing'. And to those who asked him in dismay what he intended to leave the Romans, he replied, 'Your lives'. Everything in the narrative is so polished and elegant that we cannot but have some doubts as to its credibility; yet, as so often happens in such cases, it shows us something perfectly alive, true and instructive: the German contempt for the effeminate Romans, and the surviving consciousness of past greatness amid the ruins of the present.

Nevertheless, Alaric could not afford to be too rigid in his demands; for, more than an immediate gain, what he wanted from Rome was the means to bend the empire to his will. So he came down to more moderate terms, and imposed the surrender of 4,000 pounds of gold, 3,000 of silver, 4,000 silk robes, 5,000 lengths of purple and 3,000 pounds of pepper, along with a pledge from the senate to intervene at Ravenna to support his requests to Honorius. The sum could not be raised from the contributions of the senators and the minor citizens; so the temples had to be stripped of their treasures, which were melted down. The statue of the goddess Virtus was lost with the rest—a sinister omen to the pagans, who saw in this destruction the end of all nobility and valour.

The ransom paid, the city could at last breathe again. The blockade was relaxed, exit being allowed by some of the gates, and entry of provisions by the river. Finally the army withdrew by way of Tuscia and then Rimini, being reinforced as it went by a large number of barbarian slaves who had fled from Rome, and by several thousand Huns and Goths, brought to Alaric by his brother-in-law, Ataulf. But Alaric was only playing a waiting game; the fate of the city depended ultimately on the results of the negotiations with Ravenna. Here the king asked for an annual subsidy of money and provisions, as well as no less than Venetia, Noricum and Dalmatia in which to station his troops. But in consideration of Honorius' firm refusal, and the improved military position of the empire which had just enlisted 10,000 Huns and was expecting help from Gaul as well, he limited his demands to the possession of Noricum, renouncing all monetary payment. When this attempt too failed, he occupied Ostia and laid seige to the city for a second time.

There then followed an incident, which, though it has appeared laughable to some scholars, is still extremely indicative of Alaric's desire to incorporate himself in the Roman world and to bend the surviving pagan conscience to his own ends, and of the immense intrinsic difficulty of the struggle on either side. In an empire where pretenders to the purple had sprung up more than once and in every land, the leader of the Visigoths never thought for a moment of usurping the empire, any more than did Arbogast and Stilicho before him. He was not a citizen, and his troops were not legions; the gulf dividing the Gothic from the Roman world was still too deep. Alaric as emperor would have betrayed the very nature of his power, his people and his religion; nor would it have been enough for him to put on the purple, for the civil government of Rome to be incorporated in him. The only way to checkmate Honorius was to set another emperor against him. So he bullied the senate into forswearing their allegiance to the son of Theodosius, and appointing as the new Augustus, the prefect of the city, Attalus, a Greek rhetor from Ionia, who had been converted by chance to Arianism, but had remained faithful to the Roman tradition and the circle of pagan-minded senators. The high military offices were equally divided between Goths and Romans, and the supreme command of the army and the title *magister utriusque militiae* granted to Alaric, who thus at last succeeded in legitimizing his ambitions within the orbit of the empire.

But this laborious victory turned out to be completely insubstantial. The creation of a new emperor, or the assumption of a title, was not enough to crush the son of Theodosius and the court of Ravenna. Alaric remained essentially the old leader of the barbarian forces, and Attalus, with his background, his inclinations, and his friendships, was always an unreliable tool, being too weak to command and too inconstant to trust. The possession of Rome was not enough to stop the famine. On the contrary, the *comes* Heraclian, Stilicho's executioner, who had been rewarded with the governorship of the diocese of Africa, remained faithful to Honorius and starved the city by blocking the corn supply. To set the empire on firm foundations, it was therefore necessary to subdue Africa; but Alaric's dream of crossing over with his Goths would of itself have put an end to his audacious enterprise in Italy, and the expedient adopted by Attalus, of sending a new governor out with a handful of soldiers, ended in disaster and an even fiercer famine. And so this hybrid marriage was dissolved: Alaric deposed his Augustus himself, though he kept him with him in a private capacity to protect him from revenge and in case he came in useful against Honorius, and thus he returned to negotiate once more. But all hopes of an agreement were shattered and events precipitated by the successful sally made against Ataulf during the truce by Sarus, the Gothic chieftain in the service of the emperor, and his festive entry into Ravenna.

Alaric now moved for the third and last time against Rome. And on the night of August 24, 410, the Salarian gate was opened by traitors and the Goths broke into the city. Pillage was allowed, but sacred places and, as far as possible, lives were to be respected. The havoc lasted for three days: except for the Sallustian palaces, which went up in smoke, there was little destruction. The horror was in the rape and violence perpetrated against a hated, despised and defenceless people; the only restraining factor was their religious piety. Saint Marcella fell under the blows of the invaders, but her pupils were safely conducted to the church of St Paul, according to her prayers. A 'virgin of Christ' who was asked by a noble Goth to give up all her gold and silver, showed him the precious objects that had been entrusted to her, and laid on his conscience 'the sacred vessels of the Apostle Peter', which 'she did not dare to keep, because she was unable to defend them'. The Goth was seized by reverence and fear, and made his find known to Alaric, who ordered the treasure and its pious guardian to be conducted to St Peter's by a fitting guard. The cortège advanced slowly, the gold and silver objects shining over the heads of the crowd, the Goths walking beside it with their swords unsheathed, and from Goths and Romans alike there rose a Christian hymn that seemed like an invitation. Behind them a throng of warriors and people rushed from all sides to follow the procession to the Basilica of the Apostle.

On the third day Alaric left Rome with his army. He moved down through Campania, devastating as he went, and arrived at Reggio, whence he intended to cross to Sicily and then to Africa. The loss of some of his ships in the straits of Messina, and perhaps the inexperience of his Gothic mariners and the uncertainty of the future, led him to abandon the project and to turn north again. Amid all this confusion and the anxiety of the decision, he was overtaken by death near Cosentia; his people gave him a heroic burial and blood sacrifice, appropriate to his heroic and legendary life. 'They divert the course of the River Barentinus (now Basento) near Cosentia,' writes the historian of the Goths, 'and have a band of prisoners hollow out a burial place in the bed of the river; they let down the body of Alaric, and many precious treasures, then after returning the river to its course, they kill all the prisoners who dug the tomb, so that no one shall ever know the place of burial.'

In actual fact, the capture and sacking of the ancient mistress of the world left little or no mark on her. '*Nihil factum*,' wrote a contemporary, seeing the splendour of the ancient buildings and the throngs of citizens unchanged. Stronger measures, more time, and a fixed purpose to destroy would be necessary to do permanent damage to the architectural and monumental heritage of so many generations. 'Nothing indeed,' we may repeat, when we remember the unbending court of Ravenna and the Goths implacably excluded from Rome.

What an upheaval, though, when we think instead of the stunned amazement of the world, of the recriminations and the burning questions that rise in the hearts of Christians and pagans alike, and become the focal point of religious speculation! The news, first vague, and then ever more precise and terrible, brought by the refugees themselves who have fallen from opulence to beggary, reaches St Jerome as he works in his holy retreat at Bethlehem on his commentary of the Prophets. He is dumbfounded, and can think of nothing else for many days. His friends are dead: the senator Pammachius and Saint Marcella, and the brothers and sisters whose memory had sweetened his exile. 'The light of the whole world had gone out'; he writes, 'the head of the Roman Empire has been cut down'; and, 'In Rome alone the whole world has perished.' And in his grief the sombre verses of the prophets are mingled with Virgil's plaint over the sack of Troy:

> *Quis cladem illius noctis, quis funera fando*
> *Explicet, aut possit lacrimis aequare delorem?*
> *Urbs antiqua ruit multos dominata per annos.*

But in the austere mind of St Augustine, the sack of Rome inspired the pages of *De excidio urbis* and the gigantic construction of the *De civitate Dei contra paganos*: a heroic attempt to free himself from tradition, to give a new interpretation and significance, in the plan of divine Providence to the whole history of mankind, sacred and profane, which was to become the model of all the historiography and the framework of all the political thought of the Middle Ages. And Paulus Orosius concluded his reflections on the universal ruin in the light of his faith:

'If it were only for this that the barbarians had come into the lands of Rome, that from east to west the churches of Christ should be filled with Huns, Swabians, Vandals, Burgundians, and the other innumerable tribes of believers, it would seem that we should praise God for His mercy, because, even though it entails our ruin, so many nations come thus to a knowledge of the truth which they could find in no other way.'

Let this for us too, though in a different sense, be the historical significance of the fall of the empire, and of the Germanic occupations and invasions. The death of imperial Rome was the triumph of the Rome of Christ; the empire paid with its life for its last and greatest victory of its century-old career, the inclusion of the barbarians in the civil orbit of Rome.

In this way a great experience had been completed. The alternating treaties and devastations did respond to the immediate day-to-day needs of the people and the ambitions of their leader; but at the same time they were something higher; the sign of an antagonism that could not be overcome without long suffering, and by other roads than those trodden by Honorius and Alaric. What else was the indomitable force that impelled Alaric to destroy Rome against his will, than the dim consciousness of the unbridgable gulf, the illusion that only this destruction could assure his full and total triumph? In his very hesitation before the city was there not perhaps also a religious fear, the idea that this sacrilegious weapon might break in his hands if he took hold of it? And in his march on Reggio, and his abandonment of the African expedition, was there not the sudden bewilderment of a man who has directed all his strength to one aim, only to see it vanish before him as he grasps it?

After fifteen years of struggle, Alaric had fallen, an unknowing hero of the vast battle for the rebirth of the world. The Rome that he had thought to tread down, to annihilate with his sword, he could not touch, because she was greater than he and his people, because she was not in the splendour of palaces and gardens, nor in the decadence of her citizens, but in the hearts of men, in the customs of civil life, in the tradition of thought and beauty, in the strength of a faith, and because to conquer her it was necessary to rise to her level and understand her, to bend to her discipline and be conquered.

CHAPTER 4

GERMAN ARIANISM AND ROMAN CATHOLICISM

THEODORIC AND CLOVIS

The apparent victory and actual defeat of Alaric was not unfertile. Its consequences were already seen under his immediate successor, his brother-in-law Ataulf, who married into the imperial family by his union with the emperor's half-sister, Galla Placidia, taken prisoner in the sack of Rome. He then served the empire faithfully, fighting with his Goths in Gaul and Spain against barbarians and pretenders. According to his own confession recorded by a writer of the time:

'He had originally had a burning desire to wipe out the name of Rome, to make and to call all the Roman territory the empire of the Goths, so that there should be, say, *Gothia* in place of what had been *Romania*, and that he, Ataulf, should become a new Augustus Caesar. But he had found through long experience that the Goths with their unbridled barbarity were quite incapable of obeying laws, and that at the same time the framework of law was essential to the constitution of any true state; he had therefore chosen to win glory instead by restoring and promoting the fortune of Rome with the strength of the Goths, and to be remembered by posterity as the rebuilder of Rome, as he could not be her reformer. Thus he abstained from war and strove to keep the peace, helped to wise counsel especially by his wife Placidia, a woman of strong intelligence and religious honesty. But just when he was making every effort to request and offer peace, near Barcelona in Spain, he was killed, as the story goes, by a conspiracy of his own men.'

There is perhaps no more eloquent testimony than this to cast light on the period of the Germanic occupations and domination. The projects of this single man, his actions, even his violent end, show in miniature the vast drama of the western world between the fifth and sixth century. The essential polarity of Rome and Germania, which had been dimly sensed and experienced by Fravitus and Eriwulf, by Alaric and the Goths, gradually comes up in the consciousness, and finally gives rise to the deep conviction that Rome cannot and must not be destroyed, that the invaders' task is to serve not their own blind impulses, but the renewal and greatness of the empire.

At the close of the fifth century the problem of co-existence between Romans and Germans was much more serious than it had been when the bands of Visigoths had been over-running Illyricum and Italy. There was no longer a single leader looking for honour, nor merely one people in search of battles, lands, gold and provisions. Germanic races had settled throughout the western world, large or small national societies of *foederati* or simply invaders, had superimposed themselves on the Roman society. Some of them, armed, powerful and insolent, reasoning only with the sword, had robbed the former owners of a third of their land, and now exploited it with slave labour; others were unarmed, or rather armed only with the weapon that was bound to win in the end, their culture, their civil experience, and their faith. The former were pagans, as the Franks and the Alemanni, or Arians, as the Visigoths, Burgundians and Ostrogoths; the latter were Catholics who had their place in the organization of bishoprics headed by Rome. And the religious creed was not merely a question of peaceable personal belief, or the empty habitual practice of a cult. For the word Catholic implies Roman, and suggests a whole tradition and manner of life and thought; the word Arian implies German—a culture completely opposed to and irreconcilable with Romanism. Religion is the basic principle in which all the values of the two societies are expressed and for which they fight and win.

In Britain, where the Roman influence had been more superficial, the conflict was immediately resolved in favour of the Germans, and it was centuries before the island was brought back into the European orbit. The Angles and Saxons founded their seven monarchies there in the middle of the fifth century, while the romanized islanders flowed back onto the continent to the Armoric peninsula which adopted the name of Brittany. But in Italy, Gaul and Spain, where the future of Europe was being evolved, the conflict was strong and strenuous, and the struggle was prolonged in all its severity for a whole century. In the end the elements that were irreconcilable with Catholicism—Arianism and paganism—were excluded. The invaders for their part yielded to the law to some extent, while the solemn edifice of Roman institutions gave place to rough and rudimentary codes which, in comparison with the past, seem barbaric and regressive, but which were nevertheless the only way to the foundation of a Christian Europe. Odovacar was dominant in Italy, where he headed the military federation of Heruli, Sciri, Rugians and Turcilingi; Euric ruled over the Visigoths in Spain and Aquitaine (Southern Gaul up to the Loire). The rest of Gaul was a mosaic of large and small kingdoms: here were the Salian Franks, the Ripuarian Franks, the Varni, the Thuringians, the Alemanni and the Burgundians; in the territory of Soissons, a Roman general, Syagrius, was holding back the further Germanic tribes. These Germanic potentates were kings by hereditary right and the recognition and election of their people who had raised them high on their shields in the assembly of the free; but they had nevertheless to apply to Byzantium, the official seat of the empire, for recognition of their power, which was in fact exercised over the Roman population; and it was here that they requested and obtained titles and official status of a varied and often ill-defined nature.

Two great figures can sum up for us the deep significance of this age, the dream of the past and the promise of the future, the triumph and fall of Ataulf's *Gothia* and the preparation of the new Christian *Romania* of the conquered and the conquerors: Clovis and Theodoric.

Clovis was born in 466 of royal line, in a tribe of Salian Franks whose capital was at Tours. At fifteen he was king, and at twenty started to war with Syagrius. He was a pagan, a worshipper of Wotan; and the nature and customs of his race were to survive in him in spite of the white robe of the catechumen, the lustral water and the purple cloak that were to make a Roman of him. His wife was a Catholic, the Burgundian princess Clothilde. He gave way to her prayers to have their first-born son baptized, but attributed his untimely death to this baptism, which was an insult to the gods of his fathers. Catholic too were the bishops around him; they were the defenders, protectors and representatives of the local peoples, and it was with them that he had to treat in his gradual conquest and ordering of his kingdom. And the Sicambrian Clovis, to use the words of the legend, humbly bowed his head before St Remigius in Rheims cathedral, and learned to burn what he had worshipped and worship what he had burned.

How and when his conversion came about is both too easy and too difficult to say. The traditional story set the scene on a battlefield, which reminds us of Constantine, the miraculous monogram and the victory of the Mulvian Bridge. We are told that in a battle against the Alemanni in 496, Clovis, seeing his Franks give way, looked up to heaven with tears in his eyes and cried, 'O Jesus Christ, whom

Clothilde claims to be the son of the living God, who is said to help the wretched and give victory to His believers, I humbly invoke your aid, and promise that if you will grant me victory over these foes, I will believe in you and have myself baptized in your name. For I have prayed to my own gods and seen that they have no power and do not help their worshippers.' No sooner had he pronounced these words, than the fighting is supposed to have taken a new turn; the Franks took heart, the Alemanni were put to flight and the day ended with their defeat and the death of their king.

The tradition has been denied by several authoritative critics, who have preferred to suppose that 'the conversion was the result of the miracles he witnessed at the tomb of St Martin in Tours'. Here too it is impossible to read the deep secrets of a soul, especially at such distance in time, in such complicated circumstances and in a society so different from our own. Doubtless the slow, diligent work of persuasion exercised on Clovis by Clothilde and the neighbouring bishops contributed to the change. Another factor was certainly his political experience, which taught him to yield to the conquered, it being impossible to bring them down to the level of their conquerors, and showed him how much easier conquest was made by a favourable attitude to the Catholicism of the Gallo-Romans, suggesting that only the sacrifice of his ancestral beliefs could give any stability to the new structure of king and people. Nor is it improbable that it was in the anguish of a decisive battle that this long preparation provoked the formal promise which was at once a desperate invocation to God, an encouragement to the Catholics, and the announcement of an intention that had been maturing for a long time, but whose fulfilment would depend on the outcome of the battle.

In any case, whatever the motives and whatever the occasion of Clovis' conversion, it is certainly an important date, in a way the date of the beginning of the formation of Europe. Because of this, there was now a Catholic king and kingdom among the Germanic peoples of the west which was to inspire a new friendliness, hope and faith in the Church and the Roman populations whose sufferings from Vandals and Visigoths were not forgotten. To increase their confidence, there was an exceptional condition of great importance prevailing in the territories conquered and occupied by the Franks: here, unlike the other Germanic kingdoms, the Romans were not left in a state of inferiority, as an unarmed civil society more or less exploited, oppressed and despised, at the mercy of an armed minority that was foreign in language, customs and faith. Instead they were without exception the equals of their conquerors and fought in their army. In 500 Clovis had thus raised himself from the petty kingship of a tribe of Salian Franks to the command of all the land between the Loire and the Rhine, and was now pushing with all his energy into the neighbouring states of the Burgundians and Visigoths, where he was invoked as a liberator by the local populations and where the very threat of his policy was accelerating the process of Romanization, promoting conversions, the drawing up of laws and a greater tolerance towards Catholics.

A few years before, Theodoric had appeared in the west at the head of the Ostrogoths. His career as a young man was as swiftly successful as Clovis', but very different. Born around 454, he spent his formative years, from eight to eighteen, in Constantinople, where he had been left as a peace hostage by his father, King Theodemir. At the age of twenty he became king himself, and found himself at the head of a warrior people settled in Lower Moesia as *foederati*. He was involved in the turbid dynastic vicissitudes of the Byzantine court, and fought both for and against the empire, now raised to the giddy heights of *Magister utriusque militiae* and consul, now a rebel intent on the sacking of provinces. Then finally the Emperor Zeno decided to turn his restless energy to the reconquest of Italy from Odovacar, who had recently, to Byzantium's dismay, occupied Dalmatia and defeated the Rugian invaders of Noricum. The operation took five years, from 488, when Theodoric set out to conquer the peninsula from Novae (now Sistova) on the Danube with his people (around 40,000 warriors and about 200,000 heads in all) until 493, when after forcing Odovacar to surrender Ravenna and making an agreement with him that they should rule together, he led him into an ambush in his palace, and seeing the assassins' hesitation, pierced him with his own sword, crying, 'Thus didst thou to my friends'.

Theodoric's reign opened with the blood of Odovacar and ended with the blood of the Roman martyrs, Boethius, Symmachus and Pope John. At one end we have the political crime which removes the most serious obstacle to the establishment of a new regime; at the other, persecution: the revenge for the revival of Romanism, the blind, hopeless epilogue to a great but unfulfilled dream. In between the two, this single dream was nurtured for thirty years; after being promoted with unremitting care and heroic self-denial, it was accomplished only to be undone; but in the king's mind it was to have been the final end, the definitive solution of the conflict between Germans and Romans. Unlike the Vandals in Africa and the Visigoths in Spain, where these Arian conquerors persecuted Catholicism and tried in vain to dislodge it, Theodoric professed the most impartial tolerance towards both cults, being content merely to keep the peace in his kingdom. He was tolerant even to the Jews, of whom he said, '*Religionem imperare non possumus, quia nemo cogitur ut credat invitus*'.

This tolerance and impartiality were born of no theistic indifference towards all creeds, nor were they founded on the assumption that all religions are the same, being all equally true and equally false with the worship of God at the bottom of each one of them. Rather they were the attributes of an Arian Christian educated in Constantinople, and facets of a clear government policy that aimed to ensure the peaceful co-existence of the conquered and the conquerors, and to restore and promote the civilization of the former with the strength of the latter. Goths and Romans were to constitute two separate societies, of which the one should be Arian, and reserved exclusively to the practice of arms, the other Catholic and concerned exclusively with civil administration.

The same ideal of peace and maintenance of the *status quo* was the principal element in his foreign policy towards the German potentates. Whatever the status whereby the king of the Ostrogoths governed Italy in the eyes of Byzantium, he exercised throughout the west a power not very unlike that of the old Roman emperors in its scope, though different in nature. He made marriage alliances with all the kings, Vandals, Visigoths, Franks, Thuringians, Alemanni and Burgundians alike, and devoted all his energy and vigilance to prevent or to smooth out their differences, and especially to bridle Clovis' enthusiasm for expansion.

But there came a moment when the policies of the two kings clashed in a decisive trial of strength. In the first years of the sixth century, Clovis attacked the Burgundians and, on being driven back because of their support from the Visigoths, he turned against the Visigoth kingdom itself, where he was looked to as a liberator by the Romans of Aquitaine. With all the fervour and eloquence at his command, Theodoric conjured the kings of the west to prevent the clash, which was a threat to his whole political system, and set his son-in-law, Alaric II, against his brother-in-law. But all in vain. He could not even rush to the aid of the Visigoths, because Byzantium was hand in glove with the Franks and had sent ships to plunder the coasts of Southern Italy. In 507 Alaric II fell on the field of Vouillé, leaving his crown to a child. The whole of Aquitaine down to the Pyrenees was conquered, and the very capital of the kingdom, Toulouse, fell into the hands of the victors; with it went the treasure of the Visigothic kings, the rich booty of Alaric and Ataulf. And Clovis, on his victorious return to Tours, received the purple cloak from the hands of the Byzantine ambassadors and was saluted as consul, a title which legitimized his power and received him into the vast unity of the empire.

Even after this Theodoric maintained his pre-eminence and carried on taking advantage of the misfortunes of others, as far as appearances went. He stopped a further expansion of the Franks onto the flowering Mediterranean coast between the Alps and the Pyrenees, annexed Provence and left Septimania to the Visigoths. Soon after Clovis died, at the height of his strength at the age of only forty-five, Theodoric's glory returned with a new period of flourishing economy, splendid public works and civil government. But nevertheless, he was beaten; his international system had failed. And soon before his death he could see clearly that all his efforts had been in vain; for, on the death of his son-in-law Eutharic, the succession fell to a weak child, his grandson Amalaric; the blook-stained throne of the Burgundians fell to a new, more fortunate attack from the Franks; and lastly, even the Vandal kingdom was drawn to Byzantium and Catholicism and deserted him.

More eloquently tragic, though essentially the same, was the failure of his policy of balance with his Roman subjects. There was a time at which Theodoric could have deceived himself into thinking that his dream had become a glorious, living reality: when he visited Rome in 500 and stayed there for several months. He was received at the gates of the city by the senate and the people, headed by the Pope, and went first of all to the Basilica of St Peter to pray at the tomb of the Apostle, and thence, always accompanied by a solemn procession, to the Curia of the senate and the Roman Forum. And there, before the senatorial aristocracy, the clergy, the people, the Gothic army and the throngs of foreign visitors, he pronounced his oration, inspired by memories of the glorious past, promising honour and peace to the city. The imperial palaces of the Palatine were opened again to the life and splendours of former days, commercial relations with Ostia and Portus were taken up with new energy, and the distributions of corn to the poor were increased. The Colosseum and the Circus Maximus, packed with the crowds, resounded once more to the sound of applause and the shouts at the chariot races, the struggles of the *venatores* and *arenarii,* and the wrestlers and athletes. The walls of Aurelian and Honorius and the crumbling old buildings were systematically restored with bricks from the royal works, marked with Theodoric's emblem, the sign of the cross, and the augural formula *Felix Roma, Bono Romae.*

But it was enough for the king to leave the city for the trouble that had been calmed shortly before his arrival to break out again. The Laurentian Schism, which split Rome into two camps, was not of course a simple question of rivalry between the two elected popes Symmachus and Laurence; nor was it an abstract doctrinal quarrel between the followers of the former, who were rigidly orthodox, and those of his opponent, who favoured the acceptance of the decree of union (Henoticon) issued by the Emperor Zeno in 482 according some tolerance to the Monophysites. The question was of the greatest importance both politically and religiously, in that it concerned both the integrity of the faith, the present and the future of the Church of Rome, and the intimate conscience of the Roman world in its devotion to the eastern empire. Theodoric, who between 497 and 498 had made his peace with Byzantium, was faithful to his governmental policy and refrained from intervening to stop the schism. Only in the interest of peace or at the invitation of the rivals, he did his best to encourage the Church to find within herself the remedy to the ills that troubled her. Then when Symmachus and orthodoxy had definitively triumphed, he not only recognized him as the legitimate pope, but threw all his strength into healing the breach that for over thirty years had divided east and west. The senate, the last refuge of imperial Rome, took an active part in the struggle for the papacy and then in the negotiations for reconciliation. These negotiations, with the frequent exchange of ambassadors they involved, rendered the relations between the old and the new Rome gradually more and more cordial; and, with Justin's accession to the throne (519), the ideal pursued in such different ways by the empire, the senators, the Church and Theodoric, was finally attained with Byzantium's return to orthodoxy.

Now Theodoric's historical situation is something of a paradox, in that he was destined to work for his ruin with his own hands. In other words, the result of all his conscientiousness and prudence in the healing of the schism, and his peace-making between Church and empire was merely this: that as long as the disagreement lasted, the Romans and the senate in Italy had adapted themselves to the Gothic dominion, but as soon as the empire returned to orthodoxy, they looked again to the east, as though expecting their liberation. Men like Cassiodorus could become familiars of the king and be excited by his passion, courtiers who were sincerely devoted or abjectly servile could teach their children the Gothic language, the conquered could bend with the wind and be silent. But nevertheless the Roman refugees in Constantinople spoke for them, and the very best intentions could not prevent the violence of the armed Goths, the interested acquiescence of the baser Romans, and the mute resentment caused by the repression of the Roman conscience that looked back to its old tradition. At a certain point Theodoric suddenly realized or suspected that his thirty years of wise, generous and tireless government had constructed nothing, that Rome had remained implacably hostile to him and was closing in on him in an ever narrowing circle, ensnaring him through the very men who were closest to him and to whom he had entrusted the high offices of his reign.

This is the drama of Theodoric, Boethius, Symmachus, and Pope John I. Its details are hazy, its historical significance crystal clear; a drama in which, as so often happens, it is the killer who loses and the victim who wins.

In 523, while Theodoric was in Verona, the *referendarius*, Cyprian, denounced one of the most important senators, the patrician Albinus, accusing him of carrying on a treasonable secret correspondence with Justin. Since the official counsel for the defence was silent, Severinus Boethius, the *magister officiorum*, alone took up his defence in the king's council. Boethius was a member of the noble family of the Anicii, one of the major figures of his time, deeply and widely cultured, exceptionally trusted and honoured at court, and inflexibly just in dealing with the dishonesties and prevarications of the Goths and their Roman imitators in the performance of his high office. 'Cyprianus' accusation is false,' he is reported to have said, 'but if Albinus were guilty, I and all the senate would be guilty as well: it is false O King.' The accusation was fully refuted and Albinus covered by the authority of the Master of Offices and of the senate; there were no proofs and the accused denied the charge. Under these conditions Cyprian ran the risk of being incriminated in his turn for bearing false witness, if he did not manage to stain the defender with the same crime as the original 'culprit'. For some time Boethius managed to thwart the plots against himself and the senate; but in the end, he too was denounced by compliant witnesses, and in spite of all his denials, was arrested and held in the baptistry of Ravenna cathedral to await trial. The king passed the trial to the senate, either as a mark of respect towards the authority of this body and the dignity of the accused, or in order to avoid the odium that his condemnation would incur and instead to compromise the senate before both people and emperor. No one had the courage to speak for him as he had for Albinus, and so the Master of Offices, stripped of his position, undefended and far from Rome, was condemned by the men for whom he had sacrificed fame and liberty. Not without reason did he write bitterly on the eve of his death: 'O worthy men indeed, that none can be condemned for a crime like mine.' He was killed by flogging after cruel tortures, *in agro Calventiano*, probably near Milan or Pavia, in autumn 524. A year later his father-in-law, Symmachus, of whom he wrote with such deep emotion and reverence in his last pages, was sent to his death for no other crime than that his desolate old age was a living protest against the crime performed.

In the meantime, the circle round the Gothic monarchy was tightening steadily. In 523 Justin had issued an edict against the heretics, especially the Manichees, though he excluded from it the Goths and confederates in the service of the empire, that is the Arians, perhaps as a mark of consideration to Theodoric. But over the new year of 525, when the empire felt itself injured in some way by Boethius' execution, these considerations were set aside and the persecution extended to the Goths; their churches were confiscated for the use of the Catholics and many of them were forced to forswear their faith. Deeply hurt and urged to action by his fellow Goths, Theodoric sent an embassy to Constantinople composed of Pope John I, the bishops of Ravenna, Fano, and Capua, the patrician Agapitus and various other senators.

The position of John I was a singular one indeed. No pope had ever been to Constantinople: he, the first, went there to plead the cause of heresy. But the situation was difficult, and a straight refusal might have had serious consequences for the Roman population; so the pope agreed to petition that the persecution should be stopped and the churches restored, but not certainly that the converts should return to their former faith, which his conscience could never have supported. He was given a triumphal reception at Byzantium. The emperor came to meet him twelve miles outside the city, accompanied by a vast crowd, and prostrated himself at his feet. On Easter Day, John said mass in Latin in the Basilica of Santa Sophia in the place of the patriarch, and once more celebrated the coronation the emperor had received from the patriarch John in 519. He was given everything, except for the favour he had been unable to ask. Nevertheless, on his return he was imprisoned; and a few days later, sick and broken by the voyage, he died in prison, on May 18, 526.

What was it that was held against him? That he had not performed his mission faithfully? No; it was something bigger and more serious, which did not involve the responsibility of an individual, and could not be avenged and blotted out with the death of one man. His crime was, we may say, to have found himself, his own tradition, his true country and his true sovereign in the city of Constantine, and not in the tutelary shade of the Gothic monarchy.

This threefold but single drama marked the failure, or rather the end of a compromise that had undeniably had its reasons and its utility, but which perpetuated the conflict that was troubling the social order instead of resolving it. The Roman consciousness had woken again, and Theodoric had felt himself betrayed, threatened by a danger that was the more menacing for its unexpectedness and ineluctability, because it was hidden in the hearts of men. Boethius, John and Symmachus are heroes and martyrs of Romanism in no rhetorical or sentimental sense, but as a matter of historical fact. We read the details of the trial, the baseness of the accusations, the courage of the defence, the torture of their last hours, with human curiosity and emotion; we follow the pope on his bitter pilgrimage. But here too there is in fact something that goes far beyond the narrow circle of individual passions and actions. The match is not being fought merely between Theodoric, Cyprian and Opilio on the one side, and Boethius, John, Symmachus and Albinus on the other; nor in a narrow sphere, between the over-weaning Goths or the cringing 'Gothic' Romans, and the unsubmissive Romans. The protagonists, representatives of Catholic and imperial Rome or of Germanic Arianism, bore within themselves an ineffaceable heredity, and their battle stations were determined for them. The monophysite question and the Roman orthodoxy, in the vast compass and depth of their action, rendered the clash inevitable, and enforced a definitive decision. Each took his own part: Cyprian with base servility, Theodoric with the blind desperation of betrayal, John with firmness and resignation, Boethius among them all with heroic drive and clear conscience of his mission.

It is not for us, artificially, to make a symbol of the figure of Boethius. His defence of Rome and of the senate, his end, and above all the words he wrote before his death, make him in truth what he was said to be: the last of the Romans. 'You and God are my witnesses,' he says as he addresses Philosophy who visits him in prison, 'that no other ambition than the common good led me to high office. For this my grievous and inexorable enmities with the wicked, my resolute opposition to the powerful in the defence of justice—the only way proper to a free conscience. How often did I not oppose Conigast, when he was making inroads on the fortunes of the weak, how often did I not repel Triquilla, the superintendent of the palace, from some ill-deed undertaken or already committed; how often did I not imperil my authority to protect the poor, who were incessantly persecuted with calumnies by the ever unpunished greed of the barbarians! Nothing ever led me off the path of justice. If the provincials' fortunes were lost, by private robbery or public taxes, I grieved as much as those who suffered.' 'You remember, I think, because it was you, always with me, who directed my every word and deed, you remember how, when the king, as if seized by a desire to ruin us all, tried at Verona to throw the accusation of high treason falsely levelled against Albinus onto the whole senate, I defended the innocence of all the senators, and with what consciousness of my own danger. You know that I speak the truth and have never boasted; because the secret satisfaction of one's own conscience is somehow diminished, whenever one gains the prize of fame by boasting of the good one has done. But you see the fate that has rewarded my integrity: instead of the prize for true virtue I bear the penalty of a false crime. What open confession ever met with judges who so agreed in their severity, that not one of them let himself be moved by the very weakness innate in human nature or by the capriciousness of fortune towards all men? If I had been accused of trying to burn down churches, slay the priests with an impious sword, plot the death of all good men, a sentence of punishment would have been passed on me, but in my presence, on my confession and conviction; but now, nearly five hundred miles away, dumb and undefended for the excess of my love for the senate, I am condemned to death and disgrace.'

And now, following the words of his great mistress, the narrow, personal anguish that tears at his heart and overflows in his lament is gradually purified and raised to a higher plane, transcending time and place, to acquire a quality of universality and eternity. This was the work that concluded a whole life-time and a whole civilization, the last exalted words pronounced by ancient wisdom on the problem of the world, the most living and beautiful fruit of a whole existence full of great experience, deep meditation, and exquisite sensibility. It was, under both aspects, an aspiration towards the heights, towards the supreme harmony in which all terrestial conflicts find peace.

'Our hopes and prayers are not given to God in vain, for when they are sincere, they cannot but be fruitful. Keep yourselves therefore from sin, cultivate virtue, lift your souls to high hopes, and raise your humble prayers to Heaven. If you do not want to be deceived, a great necessity for good is imposed upon you, because you act before the eyes of the Judge, who sees all things.'

This was the spiritual testament Boethius left to the whole Middle Ages; and this, the image of the Roman martyr, is what posterity has kept of him.

But, for an hour of madness, all the nobility of a thirty year effort, the uncorrupted devotion to the ideals that Rome had represented, fell to nothingness. And legend has enjoyed depicting Theodoric, now dismayed in the revelry of a banquet by a vile mortal illness as he makes ready for his final persecution of the Catholics, now carried off astride the black horse in the wild chase to eternal damnation.

Shall we see how he wrote, this barbarian persecutor of the Romans? How he wrote, that is, with Cassiodorus' pen, for, as is well known, his literary activity probably went no further than signing documents with the aid of a gold stencil, which guided his hand in tracing the four letters *Legi* or *Theo*, the first part of his name. But even through this erudite and mannered interpreter, the spirit is his own, and his the policy from the beginning to the end of his reign.

He wrote to the Emperor Anastasius:

'Most clement emperor, there should be peace between us, for there is no true reason for animosity. All kingdoms should desire peace, because in peacetime the people flourish and the common good is assured. Peace is the gracious mother of all the fine arts; she multiplies the race of men as they die and are renewed; she increases our power, and tempers our customs, and the stranger to her influence is deprived of all these benefits.' And further on,

'You are the fairest ornament of all realms, the safeguard and defence of the world; to you all other princes look justly with reverence, for they find in you something that exists nowhere else. But we above them all look to you with reverence, since by the grace of God it was in your state that we learned the art of governing Romans with justice. Our kingdom is an imitation of yours, which is the example for all good achievements, the only model of the empire. The more we imitate you, the more we excel the other nations.'

This is how he wrote to the Provencals, whom he had annexed to his kingdom:

'Here you are then by the grace of Providence back in the Roman society and restored to your ancient liberty. Take back then also customs worthy of the people who wear the toga; strip yourselves of barbarity and ferocity. What could be more beautiful than to live under the rule of the right, to be under the protection of the laws and have nothing to fear? Law is the guarantee against all weakness, and the fount of civilization; individual caprice belongs to barbarity.'

For Theodoric, the Goths were to be the example to all the other races for having succeeded in bending the violence of barbarity to the majesty of the law; the boast of the Goths was to be the *civilitas custodita*, that is the fact that they had kept the structure of Rome standing when collapse seemed imminent. Mutual love between Goths and Romans, peace between the princes, was the continual prayer of the king.

Shall we see now how Clovis spoke? The witnesses are not of course first hand; but Gregory of Tours and Fredegarius, who have kept his words for us, even though they may have embroidered them here and there, have probably not betrayed the essential nature of king and his people. The pages of the French chroniclers show us, if we are not mistaken, a typical picture of the barbarian people that had invaded Gaul. While Theodoric is occupied with the maintenance of peace and the triumph of law and culture, Clovis' world is one of war, conquest and booty. He follows the impulses of the great, and often the basest, elemental passions, in a rough, primitive, unclear manner, whereby the motives of his action and the action itself, remain wrapped in the darkness of instinct, without reaching the clarity, discretion and responsibility of consciousness.

The well-known episode of the vase of Soissons not only shows us the little Germanic king among his warriors at the beginning of his fortune, but makes the man himself known to us, as he suffers an insult in silence and cherishes his hate in his heart until the day of revenge. In one of his first expeditions a church had been sacked. Among the other sacred objects there was a precious urn of great beauty, and the bishop of the diocese, who was particularly fond of it, sent to Clovis to beg him to return it to him. When the campaign was over, the king invited the messengers to follow him to Soissons, where the booty would be divided; and there in the presence of the army, he asked that the urn should be given to him over and above his share, so that he could grant the bishop's wish. All except one consented, who, protesting against the injustice of the claim, shattered the urn with his axe, and told the king that he could have had it only if it fell to him as his share. Strictly speaking, the warrior was in the right, he was defending the interests of his fellows, and Clovis said nothing. But the next year, when he was inspecting the army, he stopped in front of the soldier and attacked him thus:

'No one here is as badly armed as you are: your spear, your sword and your axe are not worth a farthing.' He tore the axe from his hand, threw it to the ground, and as the offender stooped to pick it up, dealt him a mortal blow on the head with his *francisca*, shouting: 'That's what you did to the Soissons vase.'

During the war with Syagrius, Clovis had called a relation of his, Chararic, the king of the Salians of Thuringia, to his aid. Having noticed his ally waiting at a distance from the fight to see what would be the outcome, Clovis turned on him and his son after the victory and had them both tonsured and consecrated, as a priest and a deacon respectively. The story goes that, as Chararic was bewailing his lot, his son consoled him saying, 'The leaves of the green tree have been pruned, but soon they will sprout again; may the man who committed this crime die as soon.' On hearing these words Clovis had both father and son beheaded, and appropriated their treasure and their kingdom.

In this case his revenge, which didn't even respect the blood relationship, did nevertheless have some justification in the victims' defection on the battlefield, and the danger of a revolt; even the tonsuring of his two royal kinsmen, if we consider the man and the time he was living in, may appear as an act of singular generosity. But very often the only motive for the crime is greed for other men's dominion, and the crime itself is prepared by treachery, accompanied and concluded with a heavy cunning which gives to these bloody episodes the flavour of a vast cruel joke. In the case of a relation of his, Regnacarius, King of Cambrai, Clovis had begun by bribing the men in Regnacarius' service with gold coins and ornaments, then had declared war on him. When Regnacarius and his brother Richerius were brought before him in chains, after being captured as they fled, he said to Regnacarius, 'Why have you let our blood be disgraced, allowing yourself to be put into chains? It would have been better for you to die.' And split open his head with a blow of his axe. Then turning to Richerius: 'If you had helped your brother, they would not have bound him.' And he laid him out with another mortal blow. After this, the traitors found out that the gold that had been showered on them so generously was false and complained about it to Clovis, who replied, 'A man who voluntarily sends his master to his death deserves no better gold than this; be content that you are left your life and are not made to expiate your treachery by submitting to torture.'

Another episode, one among many of the same kind: Sigebert the Lame, the ageing king of the Ripuarian Franks, was lame from a battle wound, and thus less physically imposing and less respected by his people. When Clovis was in Paris, he sent a secret message to Cloderic, his son, which ran: 'Now your father is old and lame. If he should happen to die you would inherit his kingdom and become our friend.' Naturally before he could turn around Sigebert was put out of the way, and the good counsellor received the happy news: 'My father is dead and I am in possession of his treasure and his kingdom. Send me men whom you trust and I will gladly give them the part of his riches that is due to you.' Clovis sent back a message: 'I thank you for your good will and pray you to show your treasure to my envoys; afterwards you may keep it all for yourself.' As soon as the ambassadors arrived, Cloderic showed them the treasure, and, along with the rest, a chest where his father used to keep his gold coins. 'Plunge your hands in and take out all you can,' they said to him; and while Cloderic rushed to obey them, they broke open his head with an axe.

Clovis then went to Cologne, assembled the people, and spoke to them as follows:

'Listen to what has happened. While I was sailing on the River Schelde (Escaut), Cloderic the son of my kinsman Sigebert, was pursuing his father and spreading the rumour that I wanted him killed. And as the old man fled through the Buconian wood he sent assassins after him who killed him. He himself has been slaughtered, by whom I do not know, as he opened his father's treasure. As for myself, I have taken no part in these actions; I know that it would be a crime to shed the blood of my kinsmen. But as the harm is done, I will give you some advice, which you will not regret following: give yourselves up to me, and you will be under my protection.'

This may seem strange in a man of this nature, and it is nonetheless certain that Clovis was not insensible to religious suggestion; only his religion did not exclude either violence or treachery; indeed it was quite easily reconcileable with his qualities of warrior and conqueror. We have already mentioned his conversion on the battlefield, and it will be enough now to recall once more the exclamation of the royal catechumen at the story of the passion of Christ: 'If I had been there with my Franks, I should have avenged his wrong!' or the kind of proclamation hurled at his army before the struggle with Visigoths: 'I cannot tolerate that these Arians should occupy a large part of Gaul. Let us go and conquer them with the help of God, and put their land under our own authority.' In such utterances as these, the emotion felt before the human and divine drama of the passion, and religious intolerance and faith, are translated respectively into a thrill of revenge and a call to war.

The Visigoths defeated, Clovis goes to give thanks at the tomb of St Martin of Tours. According to the sacred tradition he gives his war-horse to feed the poor of the church, only immediately ransoms it with an offer of money. He offers a hundred gold pieces, and still cannot get the horse brought out of the stable; in short, he has to double the sum before he can get his way, at which he comments jokingly, '*Vere beatus Martinus est bonus in auxilio, sed carus in negotio*'.

And with this sample of his unpolished joviality we have perhaps said enough to illustrate the more significant aspects of the character of Clovis and his warriors.

To which of the two, Theodoric or Clovis, do our sympathies incline? There is no doubt in the matter: it is towards the loser, the king of the Ostrogoths, educated in Byzantium, who affirms the eternal values of civilization against the roughness and force of the barbarians, and pursues his dreams heroically for thirty years. His words about Roman law are valid for all time and even today sound live and solemn in our hearts.

But history has set the cultured Theodoric in the wrong, and approved the barbarian Clovis. And indeed, when we think about it a little, the culture of the former could not but stand in the way of the renewal to which the very lack of culture and even the paganism of the latter offered the best chances of success. Theodoric was looking to the past; his ideal was a static one, which aimed to keep

Romanism and Germanism stiff and sterile in their respective positions. He in fact devalued the civilization that he imagined he was exalting, and which from now on was known as Catholicism. His failure, and that of the Ostrogothic monarchy, show that the order he cherished had completed its mission, and new forces were pressing to the conquest of the west and the formation of Europe.

It was to these forces that Clovis opened the door with his baptism, with his levelling of the Franks and the Gallo-Romans, the battle of Vouillé, his consulship, and his many cunning, ambitious and bloody actions. Whatever his own consciousness of his work, he was the future. He destroyed an old world of compromises and stirred the energies of the new Rome, which wanted Romans and Germans moulded together within itself, fused in a single citizenship.

CHAPTER 5

MONASTIC LIFE IN THE WEST

ST BENEDICT

'Obscultа, o fili, praecepta magistri.' 'Listen, o son, to the precepts of the master, incline the ear of your heart and receive in gladness the teachings of the Holy Father, and practise them efficiently, in order that by an effort of obedience you may return to Him, from whom you had strayed through inertia and disobedience. To you then I now turn, whoever you may be, and enjoin you to give up your own desires, and put on the most strong and splendid arms of obedience to fight under the true king, Christ Our Lord.'

With these solemn words, imbued with the consciousness of a high mission, St Benedict began his *Rule*, and in these immortal pages rose above the confusion of his times, to set the seal on his experience and teaching. During their preparation; Rome and Italy had been going through a turbulent period, and as the saint wrote his spiritual testimony in his oasis of peace, the tempest was raging at the foot of the hill. The monophysite crisis and Byzantium's return to orthodoxy had provoked the final struggle in which the stability of Theodoric's Gothic-Roman system was balanced in the battlefield against the empire's ability to turn back up the course of time, and recompose and contain the ancient unity of lands and peoples. Gothic and Byzantine armies were camped in Latium and Campania, famine was rampant, Totila beating at the gates of Rome.

Benedict must have seen the turmoil of the schism with his own eyes. He was born in Nursia of a devout family of the provincial nobility, who had consecrated his sister Scholastica to God from her infancy. From there he went down to Rome in about 500, as a young man of eighteen or twenty, to attend to his studies. But he was not made for the rhetorical exercises, nor for the tumultous streets and the squares crowded with laymen, monks and priests, cheering for Theodoric, or for this pope or the other.

We cannot tell what his secret plan was after this; the fact is that he said farewell to Rome and his literary studies and retired with his old housekeeper to Affile, a little village in the Sabine hills, where he took lodgings near the church of St Peter. But he did not find peace here either. The very comforts of life, the love and devotion of the humble, pushed him on further. More than anything he needed to examine himself, to look for himself in solitude, to find himself a way of life different from all the ones open to him that he had refused; the pleasures of life, worldly success, the priesthood, the monastery. To do this he had to break the last ties that still bound him to the world and his family. So he fled secretly from his housekeeper and wandered alone over the hills, looking for a completely deserted place.

As the fugitive strayed over rocks and through scrub, he was found by a monk, Romanus, who asked him where he was going, and when he was told, promised to tell no one and to give him the help he needed for his new life. He then clothed him in the monastic habit, the *melote*, a cloak of goatskin worn by the monks of the east. Benedict passed three years at Subiaco in the narrowest of caves overlooking the Anio gorge, with above him a towering precipice. He remained unknown to all but Romanus, who lived in a monastery not far away under the discipline of the Abbot Deodatus, and on certain pre-arranged days would lower a little bread taken from his own mouth down to him on a rope, calling him out of his lair with a bell attached to the rope itself. The days passed, one no different from the next, without name or number; the anchorite, emancipated, unkempt, wasted by his fast, meditation and prayer, covered with animal skins, looked more like a wild beast than a man. Then suddenly, his solitude was broken by an unexpected visit. A priest from a faraway church had, by a truly divine inspiration, set out to look for him in caves and over precipices, and had finally found him in time to share with him the joy of the Easter Resurrection.

'And when, after praying and blessing the all-powerful Lord, they had sat down and talked sweetly of life, the priest who had arrived said, "Get up and let us eat, for today is Easter Day". To which the man of God replied, "I know that today is Easter, because I have been found worthy to see you". But the venerable priest insisted, saying "Today is truly the Pasqual day of the Resurrection of Our Lord: today you must not fast, for I have been sent to this end, that we may together partake of the gifts of the Almighty Lord".'

A resurrection indeed. A chapter of his spiritual life had ended, and he had concluded an experience that was not to be repeated.

Although his divine project was by now unshakeable, the great work towards which he was moving with all his strength was still being formed in the depths of his consciousness, and was not yet embodied in any concrete reality. However, from now on his work was to be in communion with men—human teaching of devotion and love, not the sterile asceticism of the oriental type, which degraded and annihilated man in solitude and suffering. Some shepherds who happened to pass that way found him, and were enlightened by his words; from then on the visits of the devout folk who came to find the master grew more and more frequent. Finally people flocked in from all the places around, where his fame had spread, to receive his training and instruction. Perhaps in that first new contact with the world, his sensuality, up till then tamed by the spirit and dulled by penitence, reawoke. A violent temptation, such as he had never before experienced, presented to him the image of a woman he had seen long ago, and so forceful was its seduction, that he actually considered escaping. But it was the last trial. With blind desperate energy he tore the skins he was wearing off his back and threw himself naked into the thorns and nettles; he got up with a torn body, but a purified heart. And from that time on, as he told his disciples, 'the temptation of sensual pleasure remained so wholly tamed in him that he never felt its prick again'.

He left his beloved solitude reluctantly at the insistent prayers of the monks of a nearby monastery who wanted him for their abbot. At first he had resisted because he knew he was made to command, to impose his own will fair and square, not to submit to others, or to bend himself to compromises. The monks soon realized this, and being undisciplined and dissolute, they felt they had chosen a tyrant instead of a father, and planned to poison him. So one day, when the abbot had just taken his place at table, they handed him the cup for him to bless it according to the monastic custom; but at the sign of the cross the cup fell, and their crime was clear to him. He then rose calmly, his face glowing with serenity, summoned all the monks and said to them, 'May Almighty God have mercy upon you, brothers; why did you want to do this to me? Well? Did I not tell you from the beginning that your habits were incompatible with mine? Go, and find yourselves an abbot of your own kind, for I cannot stay with you after what has happened'. 'With these words he returned to his beloved solitude, and alone, with only God's eye upon him, he lived with himself.'

We too may be momentarily confronted with the doubt that we find hovering in the very pages of St Gregory, from whom the whole story is taken: how was it that Benedict abandoned the care of the monks after having once accepted it; how was it that he preferred to go back to living alone, rather than staying there with the danger, where there was an evil to be fought and healed, where instead of quantities of vague possibilities, there was an absolute duty, a precise and immediate job to be done. St Gregory points to the depth of the general corruption in the monastery, where time and energy would have been wasted, the risk that Benedict would have been running, by staying, of losing 'his tranquillity and peace of mind, the light of contemplation and the vigour of his heart'. But this and another apparent desertion that we shall speak of shortly should definitely not be explained in terms of weakness, or non-resistance to evil. They were rather signs of strength, of faithful waiting for a new world that was to be different and all his own, but was biding its time; signs which show the rejection of one responsibility for a new and infinitely greater responsibility in the future.

The saint had run the risk of letting his mission be cramped within the narrow walls of a monastery, and get addled in the bitter struggle against inveterate vice. He had refused to, because he felt dimly within himself the spirit of the master and legislator of a new religious order. It was another way that was to take him to his goal. Now he set out on the way—not yet the right one—that he was led to by circumstances, by the wonderful fortune of his example and his words: in the good Goth who came to ask to be clothed as a monk, and was received with open arms, in the little Placidus, in young Maurus, his first real creatures, entrusted to him by the noble Equitius and the patrician Tertullus, to be brought up by him in the service of God.

A whole fervent and disciplined religious life now began to take form and nourishment from him. Twelve little monasteries, each one with twelve monks and an abbot, gradually cropped up in the nearby countryside. And now the scene, that is so far away and hazy for us, is peopled by figures, and quickened to life with touches of realism: the saint, armed only with his faith, going up over the crags with the little Placidus, looking for water for his monasteries; the saint in the attitude of severe teacher, beating a dissipated monk with a stick; the good Goth beside the lake working flat out to clear a patch of weeds and brambles and turn it into a garden, paralysed with fright when the scythe flies off its handle into the lake, leaving his hand in mid-air; Placidus, the little boy, going down to the lake for water and nearly drowning; Maurus rushing to the spot and saving him with his innocent faith in his master.

This time the hostility did not come from the monks, the family itself rebelling against its father and founder. The institution reflected the soul of its creator in its discipline, even if it had partly to adapt itself to the limitations and the possibilities of the place and the time. The clash, which was to have such immense consequences, was caused by a priest called Florentius, the rector of a nearby church, who was jealous of the saint, because all the faithful flocked to him, leaving his own church empty. He began by whispering here and there, trying to hinder his works, and finally tried to kill him wth a poisoned loaf. When the crime was discovered, he resorted, according to rumour, to the more subtle expedient of sending 'into the monastic garden, in front of the monks' as Gregory puts it, 'seven naked harlots, who, joining hands and dancing, gradually inflamed their hearts with a perverse passion'.

And here once again Benedict gave up. He felt that he, his own person and his fervour were the cause of this bitterness, he had an overwhelming need of other more virgin land to work on and make fertile, of men to enlighten, of a spiritual and material structure that would be all his, from roof to cellar, designed, inspired and governed by himself. So after setting the monasteries in order, he collected a few monks, perhaps his dearest pupils, and with them a few craftsmen, some men who would be tougher for the work ahead, and left. He probably went down the Sacco valley to Alatri, Veroli, Frosinone, and from there to Cassino by the Via Latina. According to the tradition this was in 529, which would be a memorable date, were there not several reasons to doubt its exactitude. The mountain 'on whose side Cassino stands' then rose thickly wooded from the plain; it was topped by an ancient temple to Apollo, and scattered with groves dedicated to the gods, where the peasants would climb with sacred victims and offerings from their fields. Here, with the well-known force and gesture of the martyr, Benedict had the image of the god destroyed, the altar overturned, the woods beaten down, and, 'on the site of the temple, he built an oratory dedicated to St Martin, and put an altar dedicated to St John in place of the old one to Apollo. Then with his assiduous preaching, he called the multitude of the surrounding villages to the faith'.

The woods resounded with the work of the monks, which he superintended. Trees were felled, stone cut, the earth hollowed out and levelled, the foundations were laid. A wall fell and buried a monk, a block of stone refused to move in spite of every effort made to dislodge it; and in this retreat of paganism, the certainty, even the vision of the enemy was aroused, sworn to prevent the holy work, eternally arrogant and eternally defeated. And then the monastery arose: the oratory, the library, the dormitory, the refectory, the guest house, the furnace and the mill, the kitchen and the wash-house, the workshops, the garden and the cemetery, and above and before them all the tower. From this tower the saint would watch over the entrance to the cloister, amid his work and his reading, prayer and meditation; from there he would have his visions of the whole world summed up in a ray of sunlight, and of the souls of the bishop Germanus and his sister Scholastica ascending into heaven.

And now the family was complete: the brothers, the deacons, to whom, 'for the merit of their good life and their understanding of true wisdom, the abbot entrusts a part of his responsibility'; the provost at his side, trusted by him and the brethren; the cellarer, a sober, brisk and wise monk, who administered and cared for everything; the prudent old doorkeeper; the novices, who had come into the monastery of their own free will or at the wish of their parents, and who before taking their final vows were instructed by the deacons in the monastic discipline. No one could leave the monastery without the consent or order of the abbot.

Men of all kinds knocked at the door: the poor man pursued by his creditor, looking for money; Zalla the Goth, 'an Arian enraged against all the servants of God', driving the miserable farmer he intended to deprive of his land before his horse; Agapitus the subdeacon, coming to ask for the gift of a little oil in a time of scarcity; the nobleman with his sick son hoping for his cure; the peasant with his dead son in his arms begging that he be resuscitated; the monk Valentinian's brother, or the Abbot Servandus, coming as pilgrims through their devotion to the saint.

This time there was no dispersion; the great light shone out steadily from the mountain and enlightened all the countryside around. When Benedict was begged by a believer to found a monastery on a farm of his near Terracina, he granted his wish; but he did not go down, as the farmer's sons had expected, to advise them on the design of the oratory, the refectory and the guest-house. The noise of the world, the ambition of kings, the anxiety of the war that was raging around Rome, all was remote, except in so far as it was brought near by the famine and by the news brought by pilgrims, such as the bishop of Canosa, or Totila himself on his march against Rome. The king sent to announce his visit and received the reply from the monastery that he would be welcome. But he first wanted to test the miraculous powers of the saint; he had his sword-bearer, Rigon, put on his royal robes, and sent him forward with three of the most prominent men of his retinue. However, they were hardly within earshot when, from the top of the tower, they heard the shout, 'Put off, my son, put off what you are wearing; it is not yours'. They fell on their faces, amazed that the deception had been discovered. They then went straight back to the king, who then went forward to the monastery himself. Totila knelt before the saint, who got up, came towards him, and asked him to rise; then he reproved him for the harm he had done and was doing, asked him to repent, foretold the capture of Rome, his sea crossing, his death. And the king went off in great confusion after commending himself to his prayers.

Benedict's life too was turning towards its close. His sister Scholastica had gone on some time ahead of him. She used to go to see him once a year and waited for him in a house near the monastery, where the saint would go down to meet her:

'Once her venerable brother went down to her with his disciples, and after passing the whole day in the praise of God and pious conversation, they took a little food together as dusk fell. And while they were still at table, having prolonged their talk of holy matters far into the evening, his sister started to beg him: "Do not leave me tonight, so that we can talk until morning about the joys of celestial life". Was there a presentiment in her prayer? But he, faithful to the law he had imposed on himself, replied, "What are you suggesting, sister? I cannot under any condition stay outside the monastery at night". The sky at that moment was so clear that not the slightest wisp of cloud was to be seen. On hearing the refusal of her brother, the saintly woman folded her hands on the table and bent her head over them to pray to the Lord, "with great tears falling from her eyes".'

When she lifted her head, they heard thunder claps and pelting rain outside.

'The saint realized that it was impossible to return to the monastery, was annoyed and started to complain: "May God forgive you, sister. What have you done?" and she, "I asked you and you would not grant my wish: I prayed to Our Lord and he heard me'.''

Love had prevailed over the law, and the whole night was spent in sweet conversation of the spiritual life. It was perhaps a premonition. A few days later, the seer was certain of the passing and the glory of Scholastica. He gave thanks to God with hymns of joy, and sent to fetch the holy body, so that it should be laid in the tomb he had built for himself in the oratory of St John the Baptist.

In the year that was to be his last, he foretold the day of his death to some of his disciples both near and far, enjoining them to keep the secret. Six days before it he had his tomb opened. Then in the grip of a raging fever, which rendered him gradually weaker and weaker, he had himself carried into the oratory, where he received the body and blood of Christ; and there, surrounded by monks who held up his failing limbs, he awaited his passing standing in prayer with his arms raised to heaven.

If we look, as is right and proper, for dates, references, precise circumstances and a logical progression of events in the stories of great men, we will in this case be bitterly disappointed. This account of the deeds of St Benedict is only the thousandth of the more or less altered and remoulded editions taken from the only source at our disposal, a book of St Gregory's *Dialogi*. This is a valuable source, because it was written only fifty years or so after the death of the saint and was founded on first-hand accounts of his immediate successors at Subiaco and Monte Cassino; but as it was intended to edify, to show Saint Benedict's miraculous and prophetic powers, it does precisely lack a logical progression of events, and is without dates or exact references. And yet when we have read the dialogue we do not feel that well-known torment of unsatisfied curiosity that we so often feel in the presence of the great figures of history, when, in spite of all our efforts, their true humanity and essential character seems to escape us.

Let us too, more than thirteen hundred years later, ask the same simple question as the deacon Peter, the interlocutor in Gregory's dialogue: 'But tell me, in plain words, what sort of a man this Benedict was.' We know nothing certain about his physical appearance; but he is such a lively and human personality that we hardly feel the lack. Gregory replies: 'He was a saint, Peter. There was no occasion on which even the most commonplace word fell from his lips without being fully weighed and pondered. If he threatened, even without ordering a punishment, the force of his words, completely without doubt or hesitation, was so great that they had the same effect as if the sentence had been carried out.' He does in fact arouse in us an image of deep inward concentration, of a busy and imperious will, not without human feeling, but free of any human weakness, strained towards the fulfilment of his mission, and completely devoid of egoism or self-indulgence. His eyes, lit by an inner light, must have been serious, regal and penetrating in times of solemnity; those eyes, which had perhaps made the poisoned cup fall from the monk's hands as he searched into the depths of his soul, which rising slowly from his book, had suddenly quenched the threats and insults in the mouth of Zalla, the enraged Arian, without the saint speaking a word; which had read on the face of the proud monk his secret resentment at having to stand holding the light at his table, whence he had reproved him: 'Cross yourself, brother; what are you saying? Cross your heart.' Only on one occasion is he too beaten, and he too suffers the common lot of grief, when the monk Theoprobus goes into his cell and finds him weeping desperately, because it has been revealed to him that, by the will of God, his whole monastery is to fall into the hands of the infidels.

And for us those tears, that single breakdown, are not so much human grief for work that has been done in vain, a momentary bewilderment in the face of the apparent contradiction of his mission by the divine will, as a sign of the force with which he had fulfilled this mission.

The most important reason for which we are thus satisfied and are sure that we possess the true St Benedict, is that his spiritual testament, the *Rule*, has been passed down to us. In this document we find all his life, with his consciousness of his high vocation, his experiences and his achievement; here is the whole man, as we have come to know him, with his steadiness and great heartedness. Gregory pointed this out in other words when he said: 'Apart from this, if you want to get a clearer idea of the life and habits of the saint, you have only to recall the single items of his *Rule* to find in them all his deeds as a teacher, because Benedict could only teach the life he himself lived.' If it could ever be said of anybody, it can certainly be said of Benedict that we have completely lost the physical man, and the successive moments and circumstances of his existence; but that nevertheless he lives in his full humanity, both individual and universal, filtered through to us in his last utterance and his creation. These reach their peak in Monte Cassino, but in the mind of its founder they have a wider scope, and a higher object.

In contrast with the rare perfection of the anchorites, who after instruction in the cloister, go out to the single combat of the hermit against the temptations of the flesh and of the spirit, and in contrast also with the dissolute life of the sarabaites and the wandering monks, he sets out 'with the help of God, to order the strong and steady band of cenobites'. And the 'authorities' of the *Rule*, the 'Holy Rule', are the continual reminder almost of a divine law that sets itself against all uncertainty and wanderings from the path.

This does not mean that his words take on a tiresome sermonizing tone, nor does the reader feel an inhuman weight of sin upon him. The solemnity of the prologue gives way to the dramatic liveliness of the dialogue between God and man, of the persuasion and exhortation that includes both master and pupil. The many 'instruments of good works' might dishearten rather than encourage the reader, if at the end he did not find these smiling words of hope: 'And let us never despair of the mercy of God.' The twelve steps of humility would perhaps be too hard to climb, were it not that here too, the teaching finally rises into a kind of hymn of liberation, picturing for us the monk who has finally achieved the perfect love of God: 'And through this love, he starts to perform all the actions that before he did with some trepidation, with no difficulty at all, as if they came naturally, no longer from fear of Hell, but for the love of Christ, and through the same good and delightful habit of virtue.'

The work is not developed on any rigorously organized plan, but has an ample, clear and generous style, treating of the big and apparently small things indispensable to a well-ordered community. It introduces variety—not deliberately, but because this is in the nature and experience of the author—by depicting figures and vivid realistic scenes among the practical advice and religious precepts. We are shown the monk who drops his work half done at the sound of the bell to hurry at once to divine office; another who is asking a guest for his blessing and leaves him abruptly because he is not allowed to stay; another who, being far away from the monastery and the oratory, kneels down to pray in the fields; the brothers in the refectory passing each other what they need to eat and drink in silence; then the fatherly abbot, the imperious provost, the good cellarer, the wise old doorkeeper, with their lifelike qualities, all observed with profound understanding of the human soul.

The monastic community is conceived as having two aspects which merge into each other and have as their common basis the love of God and man: it is at once a school of divine service and a family. Its master is called lord, abbot and father, and represents Christ; the old men who supervise are familiarly and affectionately known as grandfathers; the pupils are brothers. The brother who has to go on a journey recommends himself to every one's prayers, and is remembered daily in the last prayer in divine office. Anyone can be accepted as a member of the community, slave and freeman, Goth and Roman, provided that he shows himself to be worthy in his year of novitiate and binds himself by a solemn oath, recorded in a signed document that is laid on the altar and kept in the monastery archives. Such a family does not tolerate dispersion or desertion; the monk who has pronounced his vow has tied himself to perpetual 'stability', except, as has been said, in rare cases of the consent or order of the abbot. The law that governs their common life is a single and simple one, almost unattainable in its full perfection: love, all love, except self-love, which means the complete renunciation of the individual will, the self-abnegation before God and one's neighbour, before brothers, novices, lay-brothers, the guest who knocks at the door, whoever he may be, for in the guest it is Christ who is received. Age is of no consequence in the hierarchic order; it is the length of monastic life and the discretion of the abbot, that will promote or call to high responsibilities one monk or another, according to the deserts of his life and his wisdom. The monastery is, so to speak, an authoritarian republic which venerates Christ in the abbot, a republic where all can and sometimes must be consulted, where no one counts as a person, and where only one man may *will*. But there is no point at which this authority of the abbot is exercised, in which he can forget his formidable responsibility for the souls that are entrusted to him, and for which he will be called to account before God.

Since the cloister is essentially a family and a school of divine service, the centre of life is in the liturgical office, which is celebrated by the whole community night and day, at regular hours. Individual prayer, devoid of any noisy exterior manifestation, should be short, dumb language of the heart, an urgent cry rather than a sound of words; voluntary ascetic practices must be approved by the abbot. And since ease is the enemy of the soul, 'the brothers must busy themselves with manual work at certain times of day, and at others apply themselves to reading divine texts'.

This then is the life of the monk: prayer, reading, and work. A pale prospect, if we do not enliven it with the spirit that the saint wanted to instill into his creation. Remember the words of Benedict, when he restored the scythe fallen into the lake from the good Goth's hand, as he was clearing the bramble from the field. 'Here you are, work, and be happy'. It may be taken as a symbol. No one must be saddened by any one else's fault; no one must sadden his brother. The cellarer must provide enough and in good time, so that no one has occasion for complaint, and if he has nothing to give, let him at least reply with a kind word, for, 'as it is written, a good word is worth more than the richest gift'. Those who need help with their work must be given it, so that they do not become embittered. All impurities, all negative passions, must be removed from the monastery, all that can disturb the harmonious community of the divine family and school.

With a tone that is higher than usual, Benedict condemns, both the wandering of monks outside the monastery, the destructiveness of reporting what has been seen or heard outside the monastery, and the plague of possession: 'This vice before all others is to be eradicated: that anyone should dare to give or receive anything without the order of the abbot, or to possess anything of his own, anything at all, even a manuscript, a tablet or a pen; for the brothers are similarly forbidden to employ their own bodies or their own wills as they think best. Everything is held in common, as it is written, and no one must presume to say or to think that anything is his.'

But it is with quite exceptional energy and emphasis that he condemns 'muttering', the mute rebellion of the soul that is at variance with the expression that hides it. Even the monk 'who happens to have had an impossibly heavy task imposed on him' is not allowed to grumble. He must always accept the order of his superior with the utmost tranquillity and obedience. At the very most he may patiently explain the reasons for his inability to his superior, at the right time, and without showing any spirit of pride, resistance or contradiction. And if, after this, the order is not cancelled, he must know that it is best for him to perform the task and obey in love, trusting in the help of God.

In these pages we find a complex quality of serene and lofty harmony, a blend of practical and spiritual alacrity, of generous indulgence and severity, of a nobility and purity that triumph over all experiences. This is the spirit that animates the prayer, reading, work and the whole life of the monastic community. The love of God and consciousness of sin neither kill or debase man. He does not become brutish from his suffering. His habit is such as is necessary for decency and dictated by weather and environment; food and sleep are sufficient to ensure health, even wine is allowed. Everything is closely organized: the calendar and the daily timetable, the order of service, work, study, the amount of food and drink, and kitchen and wardrobe duty. Everything, without any pettiness or meanness, but rather with that sound judgment which, for those who can understand it, is a true source of enlightenment. Especially lenient measures are ordered for the old, the sick and the children; though in the case of the latter—I mention this incidentally and for the sake of accuracy—it is thought best to correct their mistakes in reading and their other faults with the rod rather than with reason.

Punishments are graded, from exhortations and warnings to excommunication (whereby the erring brother is excluded from the common life of the monastery), thence to flagellation, to prayers in common for his amendment, and finally to expulsion. The erring brother is by no means left to himself; on the contrary, 'the abbot must give all possible care and attention to the monks that have gone astray, because it is the sick, not the healthy, that need the physician'; 'He must send the older and wiser monks as secret comforters to console their lapsing brother almost confidentially, and lead him gently to humble repentance.'

Culture and devotion unite to prescribe the practice for communal singing and reading aloud, which are only to be entrusted, only indeed permitted, to those who are capable of discharging these duties to the edification and satisfaction of their listeners. The measured tone of voice, which is not *silentium* but *taciturnitas*, the sweet speech, the avoidance of all immoderate joking and laughter, the readiness of bearing and its entire serenity, the brotherly love between equals, composed of mutual love, obedience and respect, and the humility towards the father and the old men, the ready self-prostration at their feet the minute that they appear displeased, even for a trifle; all these precepts do indeed have a religious purpose, in the service of God and the attainment of individual purity of soul, but at the same time they leave a human imprint of dignity and nobility on the monastic community, such as one might look for in vain elsewhere in the world of this century.

Now, as we have clearly seen, this life without dates or precise preferences, this separation from men and affairs, from the political interests of the time, spring from no defect of the hagiographic source; they reflect the profoundest truth of the existence of the saint and his foundation. If he flees from experience to experience; if in Totila he condemns not the Arian and the King of the Goths, but the man who has sown death and destruction; if his prophecy of the end of Rome sounds cold, and the strife of peoples, the ambition of princes and the tumult of war reach his hill only as a distant echo, this is because he, like thousands of other cenobites and hermits throughout the Roman world, wants to flee from the world. To flee, but not to deny; and this is his great significance. We might even say that it was to affirm, to save the highest values of civilization, to create an oasis of peace amid the tempest, where faith can smile, where work and meditation, purity of life and brotherly love may be held sacred, where a man can lift his eyes up to heaven without shame, and life is free to assume a serene and industrious rhythm of its own.

It was both the negation and the passionate, unspoken invocation of the times. St Benedict felt this cry within himself, received it into his great soul, and made it the centre of his life. He received a response from every part of the west, and in every distant land conquered for the faith, the Benedictine institutions were the bulwark of Romanism and the instrument of the loftiest victories. Monte Cassino was reborn miraculously at Bobbio and Farfa, Corbie and Bec, St Gall and Reichenau, Westminster and Malmesbury.

Because the Order met a profound and widespread need, the monastery found itself going beyond its founder's ideals and even against its own intentions; it became a part of the world, conducting large-scale economic, social and cultural work which made the Benedictines the teachers and farmers of Europe, and finally widened its sphere to become a bank, laboratory, agricultural concern, school, and library. Because the value of its ideals was perennial and no slave of the times, the monastery was a reserve of healthy energy for the Church in times of bewilderment or battle. Disciples of Benedict were: Augustine, Wilfrid of York, and St Boniface; they carried the Message to England, Frisia and Saxony. When the Church, caught up in its feudal domains and chained to the earth, seemed to have forgotten her universal mission, it was from the great abbots of Cluny that the salutary reminder came. Then, amid the investitures and the crusades—that turbulent impetus of liberation, Christian Europe's impulse to conquest under the command of Rome—when men's spirits were assailed by a new desire for purity and self denial and the Roman hierarchy was in need of a disciplined and well organized force, Robert of Molesme and Bernard of Clairvaux went back with heroic strength to the primary source, the teaching of the *Rule*, for the foundation of the Cistercian order.

Thus it was with a sense of a mission accomplished down the centuries that the Benedictine chroniclers could in their narrative send two mysterious navigators against the Saracens who had destroyed the monastery, one in a priest's habit and the other in a monk's, St Peter and St Benedict, almost as though to compare Rome and Monte Cassino, the patriarch of the Western monasticism and the Apostolic successor of Peter, the two heads of the secular and regular clergy.

And it was the same consciousness that made a gentle Benedictine poet of the eleventh century sing:

> This hill is a hill like Sinai,
> for it holds the divine commandments.

CHAPTER 6

THE ROMAN CHURCH

ST GREGORY THE GREAT

'Rome will not be exterminated by the barbarians,' says St Benedict in Gregory the Great's *Dialogues*, 'but it will rot within itself, harassed by storms, thunderbolts, whirlwinds and earthquake.' And St Gregory comments, 'The mystery of this prophecy has now become clearer than daylight to us, as we see this city with its walls falling down, its houses in ruins, its churches destroyed by whirlwinds, and its buildings, worn out from sheer old age, continually collapsing into dust.'

In another part of his work, the fall of Rome attains the biblical grandeur of the sack of Nineveh or Samaria, and takes on the solemn and doom-laden tones of Ezekiel, Nahum, and Micah:

'There came to pass in her all that the prophet had once foretold. And indeed, where is the senate, and where the people? In her all the glory of the kingdoms of the earth has been put out. *Iam vacua ardet Roma.* Where are those who once exulted in their fame? Where is their magnificence? Where their pride? Show now your nakedness, o eagle, now that the feathers have fallen from the powerful wings on which you used to fly.'

There is no pity in this cry. Here the conquest that made the greatness of Rome is nothing but plundering and lust for glory, wickedness and vanity; and the continual scourges are the expiation for men's sins ordained by divine justice. And yet, beyond this religious motif that is so simple and so austere, we feel a tearing, a conflict in his cry, the past dying painfully within him. Indeed, there was no one more worthy than he to mourn this decline, for no one had clung to his Roman birthright more tenaciously, profoundly and, we might say, exclusively; no one else had stamped his work more clearly with the mark of the Roman culture.

He was born in Rome in 540 of a prominent family that owned vast domains in Sicily and Calabria, and had several houses on the

Clivus Scaevi, overlooking the Palatine, where the church of St Gregory now stands. We know little more of his parents than their names, Gordianus and Silvia. So it is all the more interesting to read in a late bibliography of the saint, that he had their portraits painted in his monastery of St Andrew. His father looked grave and solemn, while his mother had a pleasant expression, with delicately arched eyebrows and large blue eyes. His three paternal aunts, Tarsilla, Emiliana and Gordiana, had made vows of virginity and, like many other women of that time, had retired to lead a life of pious devotion in their respective houses. But, while the first two had persevered until death in their holy intention, Gordiana had allowed herself to be lured back by the temptations of the world, and had ended up by marrying the bailiff of one of her farms. Gregory later records this fact in the most scorching words, which reveal not only his condemnation of her broken vow and shameful indulgence of worldly pleasures, but his indignation at the family disgrace.

We know nothing in particular of his education, but it must have been much like that of all young noblemen of the time in a city like Rome, which was returning to its studious pursuits once more after the horrors of the Gothic war. Gregory of Tours claims for him that he outshone every one else in the city in his knowledge of grammar, dialectic and rhetoric. But in fact, in all his volumes of rather heavy writing we find only an occasional whiff of Seneca, Marcus Aurelius, and the Nicomachean Ethics, which can be traced to an early training in literature. What most concerns us is not to know what he formally studied, but what he made his own, whether from school or from his life, and also what he excluded, with his extremely strong character, the character of a religious and practical man, a Roman and a Christian, in the absolute sense of the word. From this point of view his education was in the main firstly legal, and then religious rather than literary. He was always more interested in facts than in words, as is shown by his own writing in general and by his declared contempt for rhetorical artifice: 'I have taken no pains to observe the norms prescribed for the art of writing,' he wrote to Bishop Leander of Seville, when sending him his commentary to the Book of Job, 'because I consider it truly unworthy to cramp the words of Holy Scripture into the rules of Donatus.'

The civic and religious strain of his family reappeared with new strength in this exceptional young man; *vita activa* and *vita contemplativa* were interwoven to form the web of his adolescence and his manhood.

As was customary for young men of good family, he embarked on the career of honours, and around 573 he held the position of praefect of the city. The Gothic war had ended twenty years before with the Byzantine restoration; but there were rumours of a new war from the north of Italy, where the Lombard invasion had been raging for the past five years. In spite of the decline of the importance of the civic magistrates before the authority of the exarch in Ravenna and the religious and civil power of the pope, the praefecture still put this young man in his early thirties into contact with the church and the exarchy. He was entrusted with ample duties in the sphere of the city—justice, the army, the police, provisions, the upkeep of aqueducts, of flour mills, and of public buildings—and had a load of responsibilities, an experience of men and things, an understanding and ability to act, which were in harmony with his inner nature and were to serve him as a school for more exalted leadership. He gained the same kind of experience, in all probability, from the administration of his property, both near and far, which demanded constant attention and vigilence, and was liable to reveal all sorts of ugliness, weakness and misery to him.

In the course of his praefecture his father died, and his mother retired to a life of prayer. The times were sad ones, what with the Lombards camping in the vicinity of Rome, the demands of the army, the raging famine, and the fugitives thronging into the city. In the midst of his high honours and worldly responsibilities, his soul opened itself suddenly to a thirst for liberation, and his plan to flee from the world slowly matured. Gregory himself has left a written record of how he had put off the grace of conversion for a long time, and even after the celestial inspiration, had decided that it was best to retain his secular garments. But at a certain point he realized that he had conceded more than he had intended, felt, that is, that the world, to whose demands he had submitted only in appearance, was causing him countless worries and occupying all his attention. He therefore hastened his decision, though without allowing it to necessitate any violent rupture with the past, or a complete rebuilding of his life.

So the patrician and magistrate who used to go out into the streets of Rome in silken garments laden with jewels, put on the Benedictine habit; the palace on the *Clivus Scauri* was turned into the monastery of Saint Andrew, and six more monasteries were founded and endowed from Gregory's possessions in Sicily. But his life remained unchanged in many respects, except for his strict separation from society and worldly cares, his beloved routine with the monks and his ascetic fervour, which was to leave his spirit permanently intoxicated and his body likewise bent. He had built himself his own world in what he was always to call *his* monastery, where his people had lived from generation to generation, and where he himself had grown up. He was poor and humble, yes; but the poverty and humility were such that they still allowed him to attend to his ancestral lands and use them for religious purposes, and to wield a degree of power in Saint Andrew's monastery never envisaged by the Rule, as a result of his position as founder and of his nobility of birth and personal gifts.

Later on he is always to turn back to those years with infinite longing, as to the time of his happiness, when, 'the soul, lifted above all transient things, conquered the prison of the flesh in contemplation and loved death as a beginning of life, as the reward for its labours, when, free of every earthly desire, he seemed to stand at the summit of creation, all his being breathless at the vision of God'.

It was Pope Pelagius II who took him from this peaceful existence. Being well aware of Gregory's abilities and of the Church's need for such a man, the pope had him consecrated as a deacon, and put him in charge of one of the seven city deaconships, which also placed him among his closest counsellors, and finally sent him as apocrisiary, that is, as permanent representative of the Holy See, to the court of Constantinople. The Lombards were threatening Rome once more and Gregory had to ask for help. Pelagius wrote to him, 'You must speak, and manage somehow to send help as soon as possible, because the state of affairs is reduced to such a pass that if God does not persuade the most pious emperor to grant us a general or a commander, we are completely without defence, especially as the Roman territory has not so much as a garrison on it, and the exarch writes that he can give us no help at all, as he has not even enough troops to garrison his own land. May God command him, then, to send help quickly in this time of danger, before, God forbid it, the lands now held by the empire are occupied by the army of these most wicked people.'

But the fate of the empire was then being fought out on the Persian frontier, and when faced with these new dangers which were threatening Italy and demanded immediate and energetic attention, Byzantium showed its inability to hold up the ancient edifice that Justinian had restored. The long drawn out negotiations bore no fruit. Being either unable or unwilling to send any troops, the eastern court resorted to an expedient that it was, indeed, not unaccustomed to using: employing barbarians to drive out other barbarians. King Childebert of Austrasia was engaged for a sum of money to attack the Lombards from the west. The only result of this was to put an end to their own anarchic independence of each other as their awareness of a common danger led them to strengthen their tribal organization by restoring the monarchy, under the kingship of Authari.

For a man who was more easily satisfied by mere appearances than was Gregory, the political failure would have been sufficiently made up for by the cordial relationship he established with the Emperor

Mauritius and the Empress Constantina, whose eldest son he baptized, and by the goodwill between himself and influential men and noble women at court, such as the doctor Theodorus and the *comes* Narses, also perhaps by his resounding victory over Eutichius, the patriarch of Constantinople, over the question of the resurrection of the body at the last Judgment. But he was not this kind of man. Instead, he found it more useful to learn to understand people, to experiment with the intricacies of Byzantine diplomacy, to confront the Lombard problem in all its desperate complexity, which only a few years later was to put all his strength and ability to the test; and finally it served him in that he discovered that he was more implacably a Roman than ever. In the six years that he was in Constantinople he never learned Greek; certainly not for lack of ability, but rather because it was too insignificant a matter to bother about, and because there was other more urgent business to be attended to. One day he was to declare that he had not replied to a letter from a certain noblewoman living in Byzantium, because although she was a Latin she had written to him in Greek; and he is to write to the *comes* Narses: 'We possess neither your cleverness nor your wiles.'

He looked for refreshment from this distressing experience to the one bit of Rome that he had brought with him in his exile—to the brothers of his monastery, who 'anchored him, as it were, with their example, to the peaceful shores of prayer', and to whom he would expound his commentary on the Book of Job. A storm-tossed Job he was himself; he had hoped for a safe port and had been driven back into the world's tempests, was born to prudent and straightforward action, and forced into the equivocations of politics.

He probably returned to Rome in 585, and naturally took a prominent place in the Curia. The Church was still agitated by the Schism of the Three Chapters, as it had been for the past thirty years or more. This schism consisted of the opposition of the bishops of Istria and part of the state of Venetia to the decrees of the Fifth Ecumenical Council of Constantinople in 553, in which certain works of Theodorus of Mopsuestia, Theodorus of Chios and Iba of Edessa had been condemned on the grounds that they were tainted with the Nestorian heresy. The doctrinal question was complicated by the political situation, which exposed the schismatic bishops' loyalty to the empire to the enticements of the Lombards. Gregory had already had to deal with the matter when he was praefect of the city, and had signed the act with which Laurentius, the archbishop of Milan, had returned to the Roman confession of faith. He now set to work to put an end to the dispute, although he could look for no help to Byzantium, and was hesitant to use force because of the risk of a defection on the part of the bishops.

Meanwhile, the three years truce made by the exarch Smaragdus in 585 expired, and the Lombards had started up the war again; fugitives crowded into the city in ever greater numbers before the fury of their advance. Then Byzantium finally disengaged itself from the Persians and decided to send some troops (in 589); but there were so few of them, and their pay was so meagre, that the measure was almost totally ineffective. Torrential rains and fearful floods wreaked havoc in Rome and Italy, and the famine and the plague raged even more implacably. At this point, in January, 590, Pelagius II succumbed to the plague and died. The clergy, the senate and the people elected the deacon Gregory to wear the papal tiara in his place.

We must of course recall the stories that have been told about the event. There was the letter he wrote to the Emperor Mauritius begging him to refuse his permission, which was intercepted by the praefect of the city, the temptation or the attempt to escape his fate by secret means. We repeat this out of respect for the tradition, and as a sign of the times which expected some show of humble resistance from the pope elect, and which often endangered not only his possessions but even his life with all the exultation and tumult. But in fact, this was no time to encourage ambition, and in any case Gregory has no need of our apologies, believing as we do in his profound humility. If officially he took a step, if the idea of evading this formidable weight of responsibility flashed into his mind, as it certainly did, he finally gave in and resigned himself to the accomplishment of human and divine will; for, as he said at the time, 'There is no hiding place that can save the soul without the grace of God'; and perhaps also because, 'the true humility is not obstinately to refuse the duty that has been usefully ordained for us'.

The new Pope was still to lament his lost peace from time to time; but Providence had assigned him his post; it was his, imposed on him by the emergency, and no one else could take it for him. So whatever his original hesitations may have been, he threw himself into his work with all the richness of his experience and energy. Even in the teeth of moment to moment contrasts, *vita activa* and *vita contemplativa* were reconciled in his lofty consciousness; and from the threshhold of his papacy he pronounced the warning words: 'The good shepherd is the man who does not forget the care for the soul in the midst of worldly preoccupations, or abandon his concern for the affairs of the world through his solicitude for the soul'; and later when writing about a pious monk who had become bishop of Ravenna, 'He must not imagine that a little study and prayer are sufficient virtues for a bishop. A bishop must not retire into the calm of his retreat; he must endeavour to win souls by action.'

The most important practical business of the pope consists of the administration of the Church's patrimonial lands, the solid economic foundation on which the magnificent edifice of St Peter rests. Ever since the Donation of Constantine the Holy See had been growing steadily richer, and divided its wealth into *massae*, and these in turn into *patrimonia*. The largest and richest patrimony was the Sicilian, but there were others in Calabria, Campania, Sardinia, Corsica, Africa, Gaul and the Balkan peninsula. A small amount of the land was granted to free farmers, but for the most part it was worked by settlers who depended on the contractors or *conductores*; but unlike the settlers on imperial lands, these had the opportunity to correspond directly with the pope. A subdeacon, sent by the Papal Curia with the title of *rector*, was in charge of the administration of each *patrimonium* and the countless duties of all kinds that were connected with it. He was assisted, by Gregory's express wish, only by churchmen, and was sometimes charged with the surveillance of the local population and clergy. All the economic and financial matters were co-ordinated in Rome at the *scholae*—which might be called colleges or guilds—of the *notarii* and *defensores* of the Holy see.

But the directing mind and soul was that of the pope. There was no question, however insignificant it might seem, that did not interest him. Thus he would order the rector of the Sicilian patrimony to sell the aging cows and bulls and use the money for something else, or to get rid of the mares, which were no use for anything, or to keep only 400 fillies for breeding, because the accounts would not balance if you paid 60 *solidi* wages to the herdsmen when the animals did not return 60 *denari*. His constant concern was that the administration should be scrupulous and profitable, that the Holy See should get all its due, nothing more and nothing less, through right not might, and that at the same time justice should be done to the poor, who must be given protection against pestering contractors and secular potentates. When he found out that the *conductores* in Sicily had cheated the settlers with false weights in their collection of dues in kind, he ordered that the settlers themselves be indemnified, and added, 'We do not wish the patrimony of the Church to be contaminated by dishonourable gains. You have heard what I want, now think what you must do'. Then in the instructions given to the subdeacon Peter, the interlocutor of the Dialogues, he wrote these words, 'Consider the majesty of our future Judge and return everything that has been taken sinfully, knowing that you bring me great gain if you collect blessings rather than riches'; and then, 'See that the secular nobles and the praetor love you for your humility, and do not abhor you for your pride. And at the same time, if you happen to know that one of them is committing some injustice against a poor man, rise suddenly out of your humility, so as to show them that you are always respectful if they do good, but hostile if they do evil. But endeavour that your humility does not err through leniency, nor your authority through severity, so that rectitude tempers your humility and humility softens your rectitude.'

In his every word and deed we recognize the same man, with his severity and his discretion. And should we be surprised at such detailed care for earthly matters, we must remember that he was once the proprietor of a great Roman family's lands, and the *praefectus Urbi*, and that these patrimonies were, as he points out, the inheritance of the poor, and this grain, this money, collected so scrupulously, went partly to relieve the poverty of an abbot who is 'unpardonably discreet', or to help old ladies who have fallen upon bad times, like *domna* Pateria, *domna* Palatina, and *domna* Viviana, who occasioned a severe reprimand from the pope to the rector for not having pointed them out to him. Mostly though, the revenue took the road to Rome, to bring succour to the hungry people and the fallen nobles, to the 300 nuns who were also registered in the books of the Curia Romana and to the citizens who had fallen into the hands of the Lombards and had to be ransomed. 'For twenty-seven years,' writes Gregory to the Empress Constantina, 'we have been living under the sword of the Lombards. There is no need for me to tell you how much the Church has had to spend in order to survive. In short, just as the Emperor has a *sacellarius* at Ravenna, who sees to the army's expenses day by day as the necessity arises, so in this city I am the Emperor's *sacellarius* on every occasion. Yet the Church has to support its clergy, its monasteries, its poor, its people, and on top of it all has to pay the Lombards.'

In order to understand the significance of the Lombard question for the whole future of the west, we shall do well to consider the position of the papacy in the old Roman world.

The primacy of the Roman Church was recognized in both west and east. But Gregory was not only the successor of Peter. He was also the head of one of the five patriarchates of the empire: Rome, Alexandria, Antioch, Jerusalem, and Constantinople. His was the western patriarchate which included Greece and the Balkan peninsula, Byzantine Italy with Sicily and Corsica, West Africa with Sardinia, and the small district of Spain that Justinian had reclaimed from the Visigoths. Finally he was at the same time metropolitan of Italy, that is chief of the bishops of central and southern Italy, Corsica and Sardinia, and recognized by them as their superior diocesan. As metropolitan and patriarch, the pope found himself incorporated in the empire, invested with important public functions and subject to imperial needs and requirements; he was in the unique position that the Byzantine Caesaro-papism had made for the bishops, a position that will help to explain to us his civil, military and political activity in Italy.

But in contrast to the old world there was a new one where the direct action of the empire no longer reached, and where there was a future full of promise for the Church: the Spain of the Visigoths, only very recently converted to Catholicism, after a long struggle, by Recared, king of the Visigoths; the Gaul of the Franks whose civil and religious organization had been deeply shaken, after Clovis' death, by the anarchic disturbances of the military aristocracy; Ireland, which was Catholic, but still not in touch with Rome; and lastly pagan Germany, Frisia and England.

In the middle, between the two worlds, were the Lombards. Before them, Gregory, as a bishop of the empire and subject of the exarch, was bound to the absolute obedience of a faithful citizen, but as head of the universal Church, as an Italian and a Roman in circumstances that were extremely critical for Rome and for Italy, he was inevitably compelled to develop his own independent policy, which often conflicted with the interests of the empire. In other words, there was a battle line stretched between the two worlds, on which the future of Europe was to be decided.

There is no doubt that Gregory was deeply convinced that the spiritual was superior to the temporal, and that the state must be inspired by the principle of the Church, and lend a hand in the struggle against the heretics. These are his words: 'Heaven has given power over all men to the emperor, so that those who seek after righteousness shall be helped, and the earthly kingdom shall serve the heavenly.' There is no doubt, on the other hand, that he professed himself and exacted from his clergy the most scrupulous fulfilment of their duties to their sovereign. But he was neither a theoretician nor a revolutionary; so just as he felt no need to organize his political credo into a doctrinal volume, so he never used his belief in this spiritual supremacy as a banner, as did Leo I and Gelasius I. He did not deny history to create a higher reality; he adhered to it tenaciously, moulding it into new forms.

As a devoted subject, experienced ruler and diplomat, and a wise and prudent man, he resisted firmly every time he felt that the integrity of the Church or the principles of justice were being compromised. When faced with the unjust taxation, impositions and corruption of the Byzantine officials, he was roused immediately, carrying the complaints of the oppressed to Byzantium. When an imperial edict forbade soldiers and lawyers to enter monasteries because of the serious military and financial loss that these desertions cost the state, Gregory at once registered this offence to religion, tendered his respectful objection, and would not rest until the provision was modified. As for the title of *oikoumenikos*, meaning universal, adopted by the Byzantine patriarch, he waged war without quarter against it. He wrote of it to the emperor, to the empress, to the patriarch himself, in a firm, serious, sorrowful tone, and to his nuncio Sabinianus with strong determination and even neglect of the normal conventions, terrifying him with the sudden outburst: 'We will beat out a straight path, fearing no one in this matter but Almighty God. Have no fear,' and 'Do what you have to do in this matter with all your authority and without respect, because when they refuse to give us protection against the Lombards, when for love of the State we have lost gold, silver, goods, and even the clothes off our backs, it is too ignomious that through their doing we should lose even the faith.' What offended him was this personal ambition, so unworthy of a priest, this boast of universality which belonged to the Church and all the bishops, not to one man in particular, and the ambiguity of this title which, if it was to signify a primacy, should have referred only to the pope. For himself Gregory assumed with proud humility the title, 'Servant of the servants of God', and replied to the Patriarch of Alexandria who had called him 'universal pope': 'I beg your most sweet holiness not to do such a thing. I will not hear of an honour that would be prejudicial to the honour of my brothers. The honour you pay me belongs to the universal Church.' 'If your Holiness styles me universal pope, you deny your own status as bishop, in supposing that I am universal. May God not will it. Far be it from us to use words which inflate pride and offend charity.'

The unity of the Church; this is the stable principle on which all his action in the field of the patriarchate is based. The pagans, the idolaters, who were still holding out in small or great numbers in various places, especially in Sardinia, had to be converted, not by persecution but by persuasion and forceful indirect pressure, such as increased taxes or reduction of civil rights. The heretics, on the other hand, Christians who had fallen back into pagan beliefs, had according to the Justinian law itself to be led back to the Church with direct coercive measures, which did not exclude recourse to imperial arms. Then, when duly reformed and repentant, they might count on the charitable indulgence of the pope. It was in this way that the last vigorous resistance of the Donatist schism was broken down in Africa; there was an attempt, though not a very successful one, to put an end to the Schism of the Three Chapters in Venetia and Istria; and the amicable connection with Queen Theodolinda was established, an association which with the enthusiastic help of the bishops, was to start the conversion of the Lombards to Catholicism.

But here, as we have said, the Church's politics were trespassing on imperial ground, representing the Church's own interests and assuming an individual position. And it was not merely a question of religious politics. Gregory had hardly risen to the papacy when the Lombard situation became desperate. Indeed while Arichis of Beneventum was bearing down on Naples, Ariulf of Spoleto was threating both Rome and Ravenna, the seat of the exarch and military centre of Byzantine Italy, by blocking the only direct route between the two cities. To invoke help from the exarch, to conjure them with a truce, all such measures were useless. Action was imperative, and Gregory, setting a precedent in the history of the Church, resolutely undertook the defence of the peninsula and the city, sending troops and officers to the places in danger, directing the strategy of the war, and inviting the bishops to watch and pray. Nor did he hesitate to descend to parleying, when, his efforts having proved in vain, Ariulf arrived at the gates of Rome.

In 593 the Lombard king himself, Agilulf, renewed the threat. Under the very eyes of the pope, as we know from his own writings, the citizens were killed, had their hands chopped off, were taken prisoner and tied like dogs by their necks, to be taken to be sold in France. Yet he succeeded, in an interview with the king, in getting him to withdraw by promising him on behalf of the Church an annual payment of five hundred pounds of gold. He then established more frequent and friendly relations with the court, and set to work as best he could to smother the Schism of the Three Chapters, convert the Lombards, and at the same time make every effort to induce the empire and its enemies in Italy to make peace, or, failing that, a lasting treaty at least.

These enemies naturally enough felt that it was no small success to have isolated the pope, and to have drawn him to a certain extent on to their side. Equally naturally, Gregory had found the behaviour of the exarch absurd, and obviously dictated by his impotence and ill-will. Surely he had an undeniable duty to defend *his* land and *his* fellow citizens, to establish civil and religious peace and help to convert the heathen. But the exarch's field of action embraced a larger territory of which Rome was only a part, and was geared to a policy that was not centred in Italy. To the emperor this bishop must have appeared as little more than a traitor, this loyal subject, indeed, who poked his nose into other people's affairs. He waged war; he negotiated treaties; he held out his hand to the enemy behind the empire's back; he presumed to pose as peace-maker between one and the other, for all the world as if they were not just a bunch of bandits to be wiped out.

Hence, in the course of these events, came the inevitable clash, an offensive letter from the emperor which has not come down to us, and Gregory's famous reply, in which we find all the majesty of an unjustly wounded conscience:

'In his most serene letter, his most pious majesty, while pretending to wish to show indulgence to me, has in no way spared me. In fact with the urbane word *simplicity* he calls me a fool.'

Then after various biblical reminiscences, designed to show that *simplicitas* without other qualification signifies imbecility, he continues:

'It follows that I, in the emperor's most serene letter, being deceived by the clever Ariulf, am referred to as simple without qualification, which means that I am called a fool. This I recognize to be true. Indeed, even if your pious majesty had not mentioned it, everything would shout it to the sky. For had I not been a fool, I should never have had to put up with the misfortunes I have had to undergo here in the midst of the Lombard swords. As for what I mentioned with regard to Ariulf, that he was prepared with all his heart to come to an agreement with the empire; since I am not believed, I am also accused of lying. But even if I do not deserve to be a priest, I know that it is a serious insult to accuse a priest who serves truth of being a liar.

'And indeed if the wickedness of this earth did not grow daily worse, I would be silent, rejoicing in the contempt and scorn that falls on me. But what hurts me so deeply is that from the place where I am accused of falseness, Italy is dragged daily further into subjection to the yoke of the Lombards; and while my words are being completely neglected and disbelieved, the enemy forces are increasing alarmingly. I would at any rate suggest this to the most pious emperor: that he think all the ill he will of me, but that when the good of the public and the devastation of Italy are at stake, he do not lent his pious ears to whosoever approaches him, but that he believe in facts rather than words. Then in his dealings with priests, let him not, because of his own temporal power, too hastily scorn Our Lord, but rule over them with the greatest consideration, out of respect for Him whose servants they are, so as to accord them the reverence that is their due. I say this not for myself, but for the priests. I, it is true, am a miserable sinner, and since every day I fail incessantly in my duty to Almighty God, I hope that it will be of some comfort to me in the fearful judgment that I am daily injured by incessant blows.' And again further on: 'As for the terrible judgment of Almighty God with which his pious majesty threatens me, I beg him in the name of the same Almighty God to speak no more of it. There are many facets of the divine judgment that men know nothing of, and He may condemn what you praise, and praise what you condemn. So amidst all these uncertainties, I return to my lonely tears, praying Almighty God to support our most pious lord with his hand, and to find him pure of all sin in his terrible judgment, and to let me please men in such a way as not to offend His eternal Grace.'

We must repeat it once more: this is not a question of a temporary clash of personal susceptibilities. There is no right and wrong that we can apportion with authority to the pope or the emperor. There was a great revolution in progress which marks the importance of the historical period. The empire was showing in practice its inadequacy for the maintenance of Justinian's conquests. The west was slowly and painfully beginning its final rupture with the east. The Church had found a man equal to the circumstances, and was being led, under his rule, to disentangle itself from the Byzantine Caesaro-papism, to rely on its own strength and use its own power, and to become to a certain extent a mediator in the contest between Byzantium and the Lombards. The road shown by Gregory was followed in the end; but the pope had closed his eyes long before the empire gave in to the sad reality of its defeat.

In this new world, which, being free of the Byzantine influence, offered such a wide field of action to Rome, there was another project left unfinished. It was one on which Gregory had lavished his most assiduous care, the restoration of the Frankish episcopal hierarchy under a papal vicar, and of ecclesiastical discipline by means of a council. The disorders of the France of Fredegund and Brunhild, the organization of their private church with all its economic and political complexities, effectively prevented the papal vicariate from achieving its ends, and the council from meeting and abolishing the abuses of the sale of spiritual benefices, and their apportionment to laymen by laymen, those whom Gregory was wont to call neophytes. But although the assiduously cordial relations with the Frankish potentates, and especially with Brunhild, were of no immediate use in the pursuit of these ends, they had immense importance for the present and the future as an example of the free enterprise and autonomous diplomacy of the Church in contrast to its subordination to Byzantium; furthermore, and above all, they were highly significant for the support they gave to the greatest conquest of the Church in this period, the conversion of the Anglo-Saxons, who were about to encircle pagan Germany from the north.

England's first historian, the Venerable Bede, relates that one day before Gregory had risen to the papacy, he saw some children in the market place with the most beautiful faces and bodies, with blue eyes and splendid golden hair, waiting to be sold. He asked where they came from; from Britain; whether they were pagan or Christian; pagan; what the name of their race was; Angles, he was told. And he replied, 'Nay, angels, for they have angelic faces and must be heirs to heaven with the angels.' This is said to have been the inspiration for his exalted project. We are told that he addressed himself to Pope Pelagius II for permission to go and preach the Gospel in those distant lands; and would have gone if the opposition of his fellow citizens had not detained him. It is a legend, one of the many voices of the new Christians' love and devotion to their true spiritual father. Indeed, although he had formerly turned his thoughts to Britain, as he certainly did, the first reference to the plan for its conversion was in 595, when he charged the priest Candidus, who was going to take control of the patrimony of Gaul, to find some young Angles of seventeen or eighteen to be dedicated to the service of God in the monasteries.

The next year a group of monks from St Andrew's left under the leadership of Augustine for the island, where King Ethelbert of Kent held out hopes of a successful enterprise, on account both of his influence over the local potentates, and his marriage to a Catholic princess, Berta, the daughter of the Frankish King Caribert. But they had not gone half their journey when they lost their way, and Augustine returned to Rome to bewail the difficulties of the journey and the ill-will of the people, and first among them probably the Frankish clergy themselves. Gregory's reply was stern, that it would have been better not to start the good work than to abandon it after once undertaking it, and that it must therefore be completed whatever happened. So Augustine could only start out once more to find his monks, though this time he was honoured with the title of abbot, and armed with warm recommendations to the kings Theodoric and Theodobert and the bishops of France.

Their way thus smoothed, the missionaries, there were about forty of them, landed on the Island of Thanet with their Frankish interpreters. A few days later the king came to the island in person and received them on a throne in the open air, being afraid, the historian would have us believe, of their sorcery. The monks approached him with a silver cross and an image of Christ raised aloft, singing the litany. They preached the Gospel, and obtained not only permission to teach their faith freely, but also a house to live in in the town of Doruvernum (Canterbury). Their work, which had probably already been prepared by the Frankish influence and was facilitated by England's attraction to the more advanced culture of the continent, was not to encounter any serious obstacles, so that after only a short time Gregory could write exultantly to Eulogius, the patriarch of Alexandria:

'As the race of the Angles, situated in a far corner of the world, were still unbelieving, worshipping trees and stones, I saw fit with the help of your prayers to send a mission there, according to God's will, headed by a monk from my monastery. He was consecrated bishop by the Frankish bishops with my leave, and with their help reached the very edge of the world. As for his safety and his work, we have already heard that both he and his companions are shining with such great miracles that they seem to approach the virtue of the Apostles. Furthermore, our brother and fellow bishop is announced to have celebrated Christmas with the baptism of over 10,000 Angles.'

To translate the conversion into practice must have been a considerably harder task than the official conversion. And here, more than in any other field, Gregory was able to show his never failing prudence, knowing how to act, adjust and wait according to the circumstances. His first care was to see to the organization of the Anglo-Saxon church and its bishoprics, both for the present and the future, in case of further expansion. But as far as we can see, Augustine had allowed himself to become somewhat elated by the patent welcome with which his mission had been received. The comparison of his own stern and successful effort and the disintegration of the Frankish Church had tempted him to intervene in the latter to restore discipline. He had perhaps brought a casuist strictness and a dangerous intransigence to his high calling as a result of his monastic education and his own temperament. The pope was therefore duty bound to recall him paternally to humility, and suggest that he correct the straying sheep by his example rather than by force. He refused him all authority over the bishops in Gaul and indicated case by case, following the detailed questions Augustine sent him, what he considered necessary and expedient in the organization of a growing church. 'Since in our time,' as he says, 'the Holy Church corrects some things strictly, tolerates others mildly, and others again it deliberately ignores and suffers in silence, in such a way that by thus appearing to tolerate them it often succeeds in curbing their evil.'

In his last years the raging storms died down. With the assassination of Mauritius and Foca's assumption of the throne, the empire's policy towards Rome became milder, while the Lombard rulers, Agilulf and Theodelinda, became more and more devoted and close to the pope. A sweeter and more human tone, tenderer and more sorrowful, crept into the letters that Gregory wrote to his old friends.

Eulogius of Alexandria and Leander of Seville, his good monk Marinianus, now bishop of Ravenna, and the noble Rusticiana. If his body was tortured with pain, his spirit was still lively, though longing for rest. Invocation of the end was the insistent note of these years. 'All my consolation,' he wrote, 'is in my expectation of death. This is why I ask you to pray for me, that I may soon be released from this prison of flesh, and leave behind the pain that has tormented me too long.' Still in December of 603 he promised to reply to Queen Theodelinda if he were to recover. But the great comforter probably received him before he could fulfil his promise (March 12, 604).

The unknown versifier who composed his epitaph, after first celebrating his leadership and example, his works of charity and the conversion of the Angles, exclaims, 'And now, made consul of God, you enjoy your triumph, since the reward for your work is without end.' *Consul Dei*; perhaps the expression goes beyond the intentions of the writer in arresting us like a flash or light; for it seems to capture Gregory's true essence, and express with the most simple directness the Roman and civic flavour of his religious activity. We have known the praefect of the city, and the monk; but the man himself is there at every moment of his life; under the magistrate's cloak there is already the soul of the Benedictine, and the soul of the magistrate remains under the Benedictine's habit. There is no sudden enlightenment, no violent crisis, to mark the passage from one state to the other. An almost stoic severity seems to be in control of both experiences, which appear so remote from each other; his conversion and farewell to the world, nay, his abnegation of the world, lead only to a deepening of his former way of life, and soon impose on him an earthly service that is harder and more demanding than the other that he had tried to flee.

This pope combined as could no other, the exalted and vital inheritance of Romanism and the *Rule*. He was suited by his own nature and the times he lived in to govern men with Roman efficiency and with the spirit of St Benedict, though without achieving the sweetness and joy with which the saint had been able to permeate his creation, on account of the intrusion of the world with its chaotic impositions and its refusal to be reduced to the concord of the cloister. The *rectitudo*, which recurs so often in his writings, belongs to the old magistrate, and may symbolise for us his respect and guardianship of the law, his scrupulous fulfilment of duty, his good administration with his practical experience and precise reports; his strong sense of reality, his strength in action and suffering, his generosity and perseverence belong to Rome. From St Benedict he gets the *discretio*, which inspires the now loving, now indulgent, now severe tone of his letters, and makes him patient or vigorous in action, according to the men or circumstances he is dealing with, 'like a good father to the family of Christ'. Lastly from his civil and religious formation, and above all from his consciousness of his exalted mission, he acquires his absolute intransigence when faced with the most trifling impairment of the Church's prerogatives. In such cases he does not hesitate to write to the emperor: 'I have faith in Almighty God that a man who through swollenness of vain glory lifts up his head against Him and against the statutes of the Fathers of the Church, will not be able to make me bow my head to him, even with his swords'; or to his nuncio 'You know how these things affect me: I am prepared to die rather than see the power of the Church of the blessed Apostle Peter weakened in my lifetime. You know my character well—I will be tolerant for a long time, but if once I decide to put up with no more, I go ahead gaily, whatever the dangers.'

Let us turn back our thoughts for a moment to the heroes we have spoken of so far: Constantine, Alaric, Stilicho, Clovis, and Theodoric. They fought and suffered; but still there was for them a day of sunshine, the joy of victory, the rest after work well done. Even St Benedict could rejoice and rest among his brothers, in his refuge of peace. But the greatness of Gregory has something truly stoical and desolate about it. The joy that had been his, his call to the spiritual life, his lonely striving towards God, was lost for ever; he was chained to the earth, and stayed manfully at his post even when his tortured flesh rebelled. He did not rise on the crest of any movement of his times, had no triumph and no fall. He is a great workman of history, who lives, suffers, and works in his age, enlightened by faith, guided by experience, and supported by a heroic inner control.

His work was gradual preparation rather than initiation or fulfilment. Before closing his eyes for the last time he saw the Angles converted, Donatism stamped out, the son of Agilulf and Theodelinda given a Catholic baptism. These were his victories and his joys; but he certainly had no idea of the far-reaching consequences of his actions, even those that had been the most slow and laborious, and those that had been left far from accomplished. *His* undefended land, that Gregory cast in the teeth of the exarch and Byzantium, his intransigeance against unjust taxation and bureaucratic corruption, his intolerance of vanity, sophistries, and deceptions, all reveal an antagonism that was to go deeper and deeper, and that heralded the formation of a new western Catholicism, or in other words of Europe. His civil and military provisions in the struggle with the Lombards were a preparation for the temporal rule of the Church, and the precedent for its aspirations to the inheritance of Byzantine

Italy. The assiduous relations with the Frankish potentate and the missionary activity in England were signs of the political axis shifting from east to west. The Church's supremacy, liberty, hierarchy and discipline, may all have been more or less violated or outraged in the years to come, but they were the basis on which the edifice of Nicholas I, Gregory VII and Innocent III was built.

It will be most suitable to consider Gregory's literary work also, in this broad historical perspective. His *Moralia* and his *Regula Pastoralis* especially enjoyed much praise in the centuries that followed him. It has been said that with St Gregory the real Middle Ages begin, in the sense that the sad decline of art and thought begin in his writings and his lifetime. It has been said that the poverty of his prose corresponds and is proportionate to the spiritual poverty of the people around him, a credulous and superstitious humanity that has returned to its childhood.

Now, there is no doubt that there is a chasm between Gregory and the classical world. His nature and his temperament separate him appreciably even from Christian writers who are nearer to us, like St Augustine and St Ambrose. His style is generally clear, correct, severe, with little light, but with a more popular flavour in the *Dialogues*. It must also be said that the heavy symbolico-doctrinal apparatus of what we may call the great theological and moral encyclopedias, the *Moralia* and the *Homilia* on Ezekiel, is as far as it could be from our habits of thought and feeling. And the thaumatology of the *Dialogues* presupposes an extreme, sometimes almost infantile, credulity. When all this is said, we must still remember that although this cumbersome scriptural exegesis may indulge lengthily and excessively, and without any true warmth, in a play of frigid cerebral intricacies, it does initially come from a sincere inspiration, in as much as it sees in the Old Testament a symbol of the New, in the Holy Scriptures the model of thought and accomplished Truth, and in all things a single image, the secret of God, of life and death, of sin and the Redemption. Then as for the *Dialogues*, it will be as well to remember here that Gregory is a believer speaking to believers, his monks, and is met half way by their faith and their need for the fantastic, the imaginative, the poetic, within the sphere of their keenest spiritual interests. And moreover our demand for rationality is weakened or completely quietened in us, when we read the pages that are religiously and artistically the greatest, as, to quote only one of them, the last conversation between St Benedict and Scholastica.

All this means quite simply that, although Gregory quite often shows the temper of a writer, he is not a man of letters writing for the learned, but a preacher who is instructing, warning and exhorting the multitude of his faithful, who are uncultured but not degraded, and that therefore the true importance of his works should not be looked for in any abstract cultural or literary merit. Gregorian prose, all introspection, moral teaching, redemption, and at the same time life as it is lived, practical and direct advice, shows in itself the spirit of Rome taking on a new stoic and Christian severity, a new tone of command, a new grace of affections. It is a clear mirror of an age that had faith and courage, and found only in God a refuge from the desolation of the world.

CHAPTER 7

THE ICONOCLASTIC STRUGGLE

ROME AND BYZANTIUM

I

In the seventh century the revolution which we have seen signs of in St Gregory's time and which lays the foundations for the history of Europe, develops and draws to a close. The link that since the restoration of Justinian has reunited east and west, Rome and Byzantium, is gradually loosened in a series of dramatic crises.

The Byzantine seventh century was an age of great emperors and great exploits: Heraclius and his proud descendants, Constans II, Constantine IV and Justinian II; the military and agricultural organization of the *themi*; the reconquest of the eastern provinces from the Persians, and, immediately afterwards, their disappearance under the Arab tide, which advances as far as Egypt and the African exarchate; the vigorous defence of Byzantium and the memorable defeat of Muawiya in 678; the alternating victories and defeats in the wars against the Avars, Bulgars and Slavs who were advancing down the Balkan peninsula.

There were brave captains and glorious campaigns; but all in all, there was no longer any question of power or prestige after the victories over the Persians. The empire, though cut in two, showed exceptional vitality; but from now on it was fighting for its very existence.

It does not occur to any of the emperors, even Constans II when he transfers his residence from Byzantium to Syracuse, that they might sacrifice the east for the safety of the west, or abandon the west to save the east. The Roman, universal conception and aim of the empire remains unchanged; nevertheless, almost imperceptibly through old and new circumstances, it is changing from Roman to Byzantine, it is beginning to withdraw towards its capital, to enclose itself in a more restricted circle of interests. In public documents and announcements, Greek now takes the place of Latin, the Imperator, the Caesar, the Augustus, of the official titles, give place to the

Greek *Basileus*, and the entire political and religious system may be summed up in the growing co-operation of the emperors and the patriarchs, who become increasingly subordinate to them.

Such a state of affairs could not but have its effect in the west. The decline of the empire in Egypt and the African exarchate was chiefly felt in Ravenna, Rome and the Byzantine provinces of Italy. The news of the periodic dynastic crises, the triumphant victories, and the humiliating surrenders, arrived in the west as though muffled, like echoes from a strange and faraway world, simply because of the distance and the slowness of communications.

But their effects were disastrous. The trouble over successions upset the local government, the wars required support and the Italian subjects were called upon to contribute to an ever larger extent; the soldiers were left unpaid, and there was no adequate defence left against the Lombards, with the result that Rothari was able to take possession of the whole of Liguria encountering hardly any resistance. The empire was in effect remote and practically non-existent, or rather, it existed only for the inconveniences it imposed and the harm it caused by its unfulfilled obligations. It should be added that the armies of which the sources tell us, stationed in Rome, Ravenna and Naples under the command of Byzantine officers (the exarch at the top and under him chartularies, dukes and tribunes), were conscripted more and more from the local residents, men who were tied to their own interests, to their homes, their land, their family and friends more than to their duty as subjects and faithful soldiers.

This situation gave rise to the progressive estrangement of the local populations from the life and political organization of the empire, and to the participation of citizens and soldiers in the great and small struggles of the time, the development of different factions, and the formation of a new consciousness, the affirmation of a new will to rule. Hence the periodic rebellions and the peculiar position in which the exarchs found themselves, caught between the fierce impotence of the empire and the threats and wheedlings of the local politicians.

The first risings and the first attempts to usurp the empire, on the part of the exarch Eleutherius in 619 and the *cubicularius* Mauritius between 640 and 643, are motivated by the question of military pay, by personal ambition, by the difficulties with which the empire is struggling, and perhaps also in the long run, in the case of Mauritius, by the religious conflict between Rome and Byzantium.

They are sporadic almost incidental symptoms, movements that reveal an uneasiness and a breaking away, rather than a constructive effort, signs of the formation of a new consciousness, of an obscure and undiscovered need trying out ways of translating itself into reality. The mark of their inconsistency is that the insurrections are rapidly put down and the usurpers killed, with no other consequences than a pair of severed heads, one sent to gladden the eyes of the 'most pious prince', the other stuck on a spike in the circus, to instil suitable terror into the people of Ravenna.

The fundamental and permanent cause for first the opposition and then the separation of Rome and Byzantium, is a religious one. The main object of dispute is the definition of the person of Christ, an essentially doctrinal question which nevertheless is an expression of opposing tendencies of civilization and culture in the controversy between the two sides; and in as much as it questions the basic rights of papacy and empire, it jeopardizes the whole system of Christian administration.

Although the Council of Chalcedon had under the guidance of Rome dogmatically defined the dual nature of Christ in 451, the empire continued to be troubled by the christological problem. The ideal which it held in view, indeed its innermost image of itself, was the universality and indissoluble unity of government and faith. But in actual fact it was divided in two: the eastern half consisted of Asia Minor, Syria, Palestine, Armenia, Mesopotamia, where the Monophysite creed was widely accepted and which had its own ecclesiastical organization; the western side was orthodox, and contained the Roman patriarchate—Greece, the Balkan peninsula, Italy and the African exarchate.

The consequences of this dangerous dualism had appeared only too clearly when in the Persian wars the Monophysite populations preferred to surrender to the invaders rather than remain faithful to the orthodox Byzantium. When Heraclius had reconquered the eastern provinces from the Persians, he had to face once more the problem of religious pacification and unity. He took the route of compromise, which had been tried before by Zeno and Justinian, and in 638 promulgated the *Ekthesis*, which made Monotheletism, the doctrine of the double nature and single purpose of Christ, obligatory for all his subjects.

This *Ekthesis* was a fundamental dogmatic definition, which was claimed to have been approved by Pope Honorius I (625-638) himself, but which had in fact been composed by the Byzantine patriarch and approved by a Byzantine synod appointed by imperial decree, which violated the decrees of Chalcedon. The compromise, as compromises often do, had only the effect of exciting a lively and mutual hostility between the Monophysite and the orthodox, and more particularly ran into the obstacle of the Roman Church, which, devoted though it was to the empire, was still inflexible in its defence of the tradition of the Fathers and the Councils, and in affirming the supreme authority of its doctrinal teachings.

Thus began the struggle of Monotheletism. It was revived in 648 by Constans II's ill-fated attempt to silence the disputants with a new decree, the *Typos*; and after that dragged on for over forty years.

A prominent part in the struggle was taken by the anti-monothelete priests, who, on fleeing from Syria with the Arabs on their heels, had found asylum in Italy and Roman Africa. Stephen, the Bishop of Dora in Africa, Maximus, the Archimandrite of Chrysopolis, and his disciple Anastasius were tireless leaders of the movement.

The climax of the struggle was marked by the enormous crisis in the time of the popes Theodore I (642-649) and Martin I (649-655), when it really seemed that east and west were about to muster their forces against each other for the final and decisive battle.

Gregory, the exarch of Africa, supported Pope Theodore against Monotheletism, and through his mediation and the fruitful intervention of Maximus at Chrysopolis, the patriarch Pyrrhus was brought back to orthodox respectability, after his arbitrary deposition in the dynastic crisis at Heraclius's death and his flight to the African exarchy. The next year, 646, the pro-Roman enthusiasm of the exarch gave rise to an open rebellion against the emperor. Now, we do not know if any agreements were made between the pope, the exarch and the patriarch, or if so what they were; but we cannot disregard the probability that the coincidence of the two events was not entirely fortuitous, and that some agreement between them must have been instrumental in the development of the rebellion, and that the weak Pyrrhus, solemnly recognized by the Holy See as the legitimate patriarch of Byzantium, played his part in it as a tool in the game.

However it happened, the rebellion had no future, as in 647 Gregory was killed by the Arabs, who after conquering Egypt had raided Roman Africa. Pyrrhus himself put an end to the intended manipulation of the patriarchy by abandoning Rome to the imperial forces, denying his change of faith, and declaring that it had been forced from him by heavy material and psychological pressure.

Through the energy of Theodore and Maximus and their successors, the battle was still kept going in the doctrinal field with the excommunication and deposition of both Pyrrhus and his successor, and the firm condemnation of the *Typos*.

Martin I, who had been papal nuncio in Constantinople before the last crisis and succeeded Theodore in the papacy, was led by his strength of character as well as by circumstances to repeat the policy of his predecessor with an even clearer and more threatening challenge. He died a martyr, witness at one to his faith and to a great historical necessity, a dogmatic principle which was at the same time a manifestation of a whole world of civilization and culture.

Though elected according to normal procedure, Martin I was consecrated without the approval of the emperor or his representative being either requested or granted. He was thus treated by Constans II as an intruder in the Apostolic See. His first action in 649 was to hold a council in the Lateran to discuss the Monothelete question. It was attended by twenty-five bishops from Lombard and Byzantine Italy, from Sicily, Sardinia and the African dioceses. Maximus, Archimandrite of Chrysopolis, Stephen of Dora and the Greek monks who had fled to Rome all attended and held firmly to an attitude of complete intransigence. Maurus, Archbishop of Ravenna, excused himself on the grounds of the imminent danger from the Lombards; and though this conduct might give rise to some suspicion of political wariness on his part, we must nevertheless remember that in his letter to the pope he makes an avowal of his anti-monothelete faith, and undertakes to accept the decisions made by the council.

The outcome was as was to be expected: Monotheletism condemned, the doctrine recognizing the two wills and operations of Christ defined and declared an article of faith, the Byzantine Monothelete patriarchs and the *Ekthesis* and the *Typos* anathematized, and not a word on the person or function of the emperors. But what is most important for us, because it shows with what deep conscientiousness, what fervour and resolution the battle for the integrity of the faith and the primacy was fought, is the fact that the decisions of the Council were made known in every part of the Catholic world, east and west, and were accompanied with words of warm exhortation and warning; that the pope sent the acts of the Council particularly to Amandus, the Bishop of Mastricht, asking him to have them confirmed by an episcopal synod of the Franks, and soliciting through him the co-operation of King Sigebert, to send a delegation of bishops to Rome, who should then take the emperor the deliberations of both assemblies.

The acts were delivered to Constans II in the Latin text and the Greek translation accompanied by the most ingratiating letter from the pope, asking that the condemnation pronounced by the Council should be made effective by the passing of a new law. But this formal homage was not enough to heal the offence rendered to the imperial majesty by Martin's consecration, or to change the prevailing state of affairs revealed by the acts of the Council, namely the infringement of the *Typos*, the condemnation of the two imperial edicts and the three patriarchs who had acted under the direct influence of the emperors, and—here we get to the bottom of the matter—the

D*

affirmation of the Roman primacy and the refusal to recognize the imperial right to dictate in matters of religion.

When the news of Martin's assumption of the papacy arrived in Constantinople, Constans had sent the *cubicularius* Olympius to Italy as exarch, with appropriate instructions suggested by the patriarch on the one hand and on the other by certain high-placed experts on Italian affairs. The patriarch, to whom violence was unbecoming, had supposed that it was possible that the people resident in the exarchy would consent to the *Typos*, and, working on this hypothesis, he suggested that the bishops and the clergy should be compelled to endorse it. The experts had spoken with greater clarity and sense of reality: if the army could be counted on, Martin should be immediately taken into custody and the clergy then worked upon; if this was not possible, the best thing would be to temporise until the loyalty of the army was assured and then strike the final blow as quickly as possible.

The trouble was that when Olympius arrived in Italy, he found a state of affairs that was far worse than anything imagined by the experts. Public opinion was excited, the army was in near mutiny, the pope was openly at war with the empire, at the height of his prestige in the Council he had convened, and surrounded by the very bishops that the exarch had been told to reduce to obedience. He had the forces congregate beneath the walls of Rome, tried the spirit of the soldiers and their leaders, and finally had to admit to himself that any thought of following his instructions was quite out of the question. His situation was a repetition, in even more obvious circumstances than Gregory's, of the Byzantine governor given the choice of remaining loyal to the Empire at the risk of his own life, or saving his life at the price of making common cause with the local inhabitants, thereby breaking his sworn promise.

And Olympius broke his word. He had soldiers and their captains swear allegiance to him as sovereign, had the few imperial officials who opposed him hounded from the palace of the Palatine, came to an agreement with the pope, and for two years ruled the exarchy quite independently of Byzantium, without the latter finding the power to bring the rebels to heel.

Its help, here as in Africa, came, at least indirectly, from the Arabs, who had just invaded Sicily, the granary of Rome and treasure house of the Church, which received a constant stream of revenues from its rich patrimony. On this occasion the invasion of the Mohammedans was only a temporary one which turned into a mere pillaging and slave-hunting expedition; but Olympius, who had hurried to give battle to the intruders, lost the greater part of his men, many of whom belonged to the Roman army, in a tremendous epidemic, and died in Sicily himself.

It had been a brave attempt, and one that the papacy, with the forces now left at its disposal, was no longer equal to. With Olympius gone, the army disheartened, in the bitterness of mourning and the consciousness of betrayal, Martin was now left alone and undefended to face the anger of Constans II.

The new exarch, Theodore Calliopas, a great expert in Italian affairs, was given the responsibility of arresting the culprit, and the *cubicularius* Theodore Pellurius, was to co-operate in his arrest and conduct him to Constantinople. The calvary of Martin I lasted more or less from the beginning of June, 653, until the day of his death, December 16, 655. What with the doubts and fears of the people, the exarch had no trouble in reawakening the rivalry between Rome and Ravenna, and soon reduced the Ravenna army to obedience. He then led it against Rome.

In one of his letters, Martin has left us a most vivid account of those days in which he had been 'snatched from the seat of St Peter the Apostle like a lonely sparrow from a building' where he has made his nest. It was customary, when the exarch visited Rome, for him to be received in the imperial palace by the members of the clergy with the pope at their head. But this time the pope was not there, and the exarch, who could ill conceal his annoyance, said repeatedly in an ambiguous tone, that he wanted to go and pay homage to him. The encounter took place, in fact, when Martin was lying on a sick bed in front of the great altar of the Basilica Constantiniana: Theodore Pellurius accused him of having hidden arms and catapult stones in the Lateran. Its every corner was turned upside down, and after half an hour of fruitless search, the basilica was invaded by soldiers with lances, swords, bows and shields, and soon resounded to the clash of arms and the crashing of candelabra as they fell to the floor. The last scene he describes occurred in the imperial palace, a little while before his departure. The pope asked if he could be accompanied by his own men, and, when the exarch refused, he replied proudly, 'The clergy is at my command', almost as if he did not realize the extent of his present downfall, or the fate that awaited him. And the clergy raised the cry; 'With him we live, and with him we die!'

To a devout and faithful friend who had written to him about the calumnies that were being circulated about him, the pope replied from Constantinople, with the assurance that in life and death he would defend the faith on which the world's salvation depended. And nothing that he promised did he then go back on. But in his trial, in that single session of the senate, which had been convened after much delay as a high court of justice under the presidency of the emperor's *sacellarius*, the issue of faith was not considered; the charge was one of high treason. Indeed, when he tried to refer to the precedents for the rebellion and the religious question, he was rudely interrupted and reminded of his charge.

His body was broken, but his conduct was firm and dignified. The *sacellarius* inveighed, 'Tell us, wretch, what harm has the emperor done you? Has he stolen anything from you? Has he done any violence to you?' And he was silent. The whole matter was so much greater than his own person, so much wider and more complex than his accusers liked to think, that he could not speak. The most vehement witnesses for the prosecution were of course the high ranking Byzantine officials who had taken part in the rebellion and had no other means of escape than to throw all the blame on the pope. He in his turn begged the senators not to make them speak on oath, so as to avoid burdening their consciences with yet another sin, but to listen to their evidence without swearing them in and then to do what they would with him. But even though his sentence had been decided a good time before the judgment was announced, he had no difficulty in pointing out, against the accusations of treason of his judge, that he had not been able to show any resistance to force (an inability for which the impotence of the empire itself was largely responsible), or in asking what sort of behaviour the senate had displayed when Valentine Arsacides, the protagonist of the *coup d'état* that had brought Constans II to the throne, had successfully requested to be appointed co-regent.

He was sentenced to death by quartering, the legal punishment for traitors, and, the sentence heard, he underwent the humiliating ceremony of deposition, the torture of being dragged in chains through the streets of the city to prison. But thanks to the intercession of the patriarch Paul, who was on his death bed, the sentence was not carried out. Three months later, in March, 654, Martin I left for Cherson, at the outermost limits of the Roman world where it yielded to paganism and barbarity. Occasional ships would put in there to restock their supply of salt, but everything necessary to the most frugal existence, wine, corn and oil, was unobtainable, and one literally died of hunger there. He begged that he should be sent something, and marvelled that his relations, his friends, and even the people of his church should have forgotten him as if he were already dead; he asked what fear could have taken hold of them, so that they could no longer obey God's commandments, and asked if ever he had seemed to them to be an adversary, an enemy of the Church. At last the storm within him calmed itself in his expectancy of death and in the stability of the orthodox faith, which he commended to his friends and to all Christians, 'because,' he wrote, 'the Lord himself is the keeper of this poor body of mine, and may treat it as he will, with ceaseless tribulation or with some refreshment. The Lord is indeed with me, so why am I afflicted? Now I hope that, in His mercy, he will not delay to bring the course of my life to an end'.

Unfortunately historic justice is no respecter of persons. The bestial cruelty and low passions of Constans II and his associates, and the atrocious suffering and strength of Martin I and Maximus, Abbot of Chrysopolis, have a value and a significance which far transcend their transitory and individual responsibilities. On the one side there was the unitary ideal of the empire, universal power, both political and religious; on the other there was the primacy of Rome and the new Europe which was gradually coming into being around it. Even taking all extenuating circumstances into account, Martin had in effect betrayed, or, as the fiercest of his accusers, the patrician Dorotheus, had declared at his trial, 'subverted, destroyed and sent to its ruin the entire west, and had been, in full agreement with Olympius, the deadly enemy of the emperor and of Roman civilization'.

And for this very reason he deserves to be numbered among the martyrs of nascent Europe.

The exarch Theodore Calliopas had declared to the Roman clergy that Martin had taken over the Holy See in an irregular and illegal manner, and that therefore a new election must be held. The pope naturally shrank from any such idea; he openly nourished the firm faith that as long as he lived this would never happen, and he wrote as much, even several months after his arrest, from Constantinople. But he was deceiving himself. Indeed while he was languishing in Cherson, in August, 654, the Roman Eugenius I was appointed as his successor.

This drama of the pope being condemned for treason and sent to the outermost limits of the empire to die of privation, had in actuality the effect of teaching the virtue of prudence both to Rome and Byzantium. Once the crisis was over everything appeared to return to normal, and it seemed that the battle for the primacy and for Europe, fought with a varying degree of consciousness of its existence, had been lost. Both sides seemed to be in favour of reconciliation; indeed the attitude of Eugenius I looked so conciliating that it alarmed the abbot Maximus and his disciple Anastasius, imprisoned as they were, and it was only through their capable propaganda, through pressure from the clergy and the people, that the pope was induced to send back the synodical letter from Peter, the Patriarch of Constantinople, which contained the customary announcement of his appointment and his profession of faith. And from this time on, such a rejection became the normal practice for every new successor, without it causing any disturbance in the relations between the Holy See and the empire. Constans II sent gifts in return for the synodical letter of Vitalianus (657-672), which announced to him his assumption of the papacy, and Vitalianus in his turn, not only received Martin I's assassin with devotion, but gave a final proof of his unshakeable loyalty by siding with Constantinus IV, the son and successor of Constans II, against the Armenian Mezezius, who had been acclaimed as emperor by the imperial troops stationed in Sicily.

As is obvious, this relaxation of tension between Rome and Byzantium was not the solution of the problem. It was rather, on the part of the empire, a decline of interest in the religious question, since the majority of the monophysitically inclined provinces had been taken by the Arabs, the consciousness of a victory over the papacy which could not be taken to its logical conclusion without putting the empire into mortal danger, and the need of conserving its forces; on the part of the papacy it was a cautious loyalism, which was only the cover for its radical opposition. On both sides there was the inability to find any means of reaching mutual agreement, and also a weariness of the strain, and a need to get on with the business of living.

But by this way of reconciliation they also arrived much further than they knew or intended, so as to reach the very roots of the conflict. And there came a time, around 680, in which, to judge by the broad sweep of appearances, one might delude oneself that Church and empire, Byzantine and Lombard Italy had finally arrived at a peaceful arrangement. 'There followed a perfect peace in east and west,' writes the historian Theophanes, after recounting the memorable liberation of Constantinople from the grasp of the Arabs in 678. Constantine IV actually went to the trouble of convening a Council at Constantinople (the sixth Ecumenical Council 680-681), in which, under the chairmanship of the emperor himself, the unity of the faith according to the Roman doctrine of the two operations and the two wills was re-established. At the same time a new, more formal and more lasting agreement was made, probably with the support and encouragement of the pope, between Byzantium and the Lombards.

But in spite of all the hopes and good intentions, the remedies were only temporary ones, which did not change the deeper truths of the situation. The peace made with the Lombards was qualified by their ambition, their vital need to conquer, and the defensive capacity of the empire. They were a wedge driven into the body of

Italy, and before long, while believing that they were working merely for their own aggrandizement in the peninsula, they were to strike the final blow to the great separation of east and west.

More illusory than anything else was the unity of the faith and of imperial prestige in the whole Christian world. Rome and Constantinople spoke different languages, even literally. We have already noticed it. The Roman Empire of Justinian had turned into a Byzantine empire, the Latin of the official documents had been substituted by Greek, the Imperator, the Augustus, by the Basileus. But there was a deeper diversity of language than this, of which this was only the most obvious manifestation. Nothing is more revealing, when considering this question, than to compare the acts of the Council with those of the Synod held in Rome by Pope Agatho in preparation for the Council itself, and the demeanour of the emperor and his advisers with that of the pope and his bishops.

When Constantine IV invites the pope to send his delegates to the Council, he insists on his absolute impartiality towards the contendents; the Council itself is convened and customarily presided over by him and at the end of their labours the emperor is applauded: 'Thou hast made clear the identity of the two natures of Christ Our Lord! Protect, O Lord, the luminary of peace! Thou hast put to flight all the heretics! Protect, O Lord, the scourge of the heretics!' Finally, in the *sermo prosphoneticus*, the closing address of homage to Constantine the emperor appears to be invested with a supreme religious mission, connected by a direct and intimate link with the Divinity, who has conferred the diadem upon him, and whom he rewards by procuring peace for his churches.

To put it briefly, however explicitly and devoutly it may have been declared that the dogmatic definition adopted by the Council was the one formulated by Pope Agatho and the Roman synod, it was made clear by small actions of the emperor and the Council, and by the general tone of the correspondence and the acts of the Council, that the *Basileus* held in his own person the supreme political and religious power over the entire Christian world, and that he was pre-eminently responsible for the guardianship of the faith.

From the papal viewpoint matters looked quite different. Agatho replied to Constantine IV's invitation to send his delegates to the Council in a spirit of self-congratulation, pleased that the emperor should wish to learn the true faith from him, the 'truth', pure and simple, 'of the orthodox Catholic faith', which 'from the Fount of true light, through the ministry of St Peter and St Paul, the leaders of the Apostles and of their disciples and Apostolic successors, had been gradually passed down to his humble self'. What, to him, made the *respublica* of the empire supreme to all nations, was the fact that in it 'had been founded the See of the blessed Peter, the chief of the Apostles, whose authority was an object of veneration and worship among all Christian peoples'. His confidence in the primacy was bound up with the example of the popes who, to the eternal disgrace of the empire, had, 'persistently defended the limits of the faith that it was impious to transgress, even with their last breath, without letting themselves be seduced by flattery or frightened by imminent danger'. The most immediate and vivid example of all, was of course that of Martin, 'of Apostolic memory' and of his Roman synod.

The reader could not miss the deliberate emphasis of the Synod on the contrast between 'flowing words' and 'false loquacity' of 'the eloquence of secular learning', the 'pomp of style' and the misunderstandings that arise from it, the Byzantine subtlety which had offended St Gregory and given rise to the christological heresies, and the 'simplicity of heart' and 'gentleness of speech' with which the Gospel was preached to the barbarian nations, and the 'perfect knowledge' which is understanding of divine truth. This was all that the bishops who met in Rome with Pope Agatho were able to offer Constantine by way of a reply to his invitation. It was useless to look for one among them who might take pride in his worldly learning, for in the places they came from (and here we may perhaps detect an ill-concealed reproach) 'every day one or another people were stirred to anger, with wars, raids, and plunderings as a result'. In their toil-worn lives 'even their food was the fruit of their own labours', because the Church's material support had been discontinued amid all the calamities. 'Their only wealth was their faith, to live with which was their supreme glory, and to die for it eternal gain'; their 'perfect knowledge' was to keep the Catholic and Apostolic faith uncorrupted, as it was professed by the Church of Rome.

This was where the strength of the pope lay, and he made no bones about it. About him there sat a hundred and twenty-five bishops, among them Theodore, archbishop of Ravenna, several bishops from the Lombard territories, two from France and one from England. The points that they mentioned in justification for their delay in sending their delegates to Constantinople were at the same time a demonstration of their power, or rather a token of the penetration and organization of Rome, which in those years found its most fertile ground among the Lombards, the Franks and the Anglo-Saxons. They wrote in fact that 'a large proportion of their number lived in lands that were washed by the Ocean and a long time was needed for the journey', that 'they had waited in the hope of being able to relieve their insufficiency with the presence of Theodore, the archbishop and philosopher of the great island of Britain', the learned

Greek monk who was archbishop of Canterbury, and their other brothers living out there or in various other parts of the world, among the Lombards, the Slavs, the Franks, the Gauls, and the Goths, so that the entire episcopate might participate in their deliberations. For all of them took a vital interest in the questions of faith and all of them were in agreement with the Church of Rome.

So to be brief: contrary to Constantine's assumption, there was no question of setting up a trial in which the emperor should make a show of his impartiality. There were no two sides, of which one or the other might be right, or between which it might be possible to find some way of compromise. There existed only one Truth, which was founded on the evangelic and apostolic tradition, on the writings of the Fathers, and on the decisions of the five Ecumenical Councils. And the Church of Rome was the one and only guarantor, depositary and interpreter of that one Truth, on account of the mission entrusted by Christ to Peter and his successors in the See of Rome. The power of orthodoxy was in Rome, and in those barbarians who had received from Rome the light of truth.

Byzantium's treaty with the Lombards, its official recognition of their kingdom, and the religious unity formally re-established by the Council were able to make peace between east and west for a short period, but they could not stop the *respublica* of the Christian empire from gradually fading away, leaving its two halves to go on working and developing according to the forces inherent in them. Thus Byzantium was left to enclose itself in the strength of its patriarchy, its culture and its *Basileis,* good generals invested with a supreme religious mission, and Rome to found its own empire in the western and northern parts of Europe.

Before long the two worlds, the two irreconcilable universalities of papacy and empire, had yet another collision on the line that so irremediably divided them. Ten years after the sixth Ecumenical Council, the last descendant of Heraclius, the 'servant of Christ' as he called himself on his coins, the pious and sanguinary Justinian II (685-695 and 705-711) convened a synod at Constantinople that was known as the *Trullan* because it was held in Trullus, the domed hall of the imperial palace, and also as the *Quinisextine*, because it was intended to integrate the decisions of the fifth and sixth Ecumenical Councils (691-692).

This council did not in fact deal with any doctrinal questions, but was concerned with making provisions intended to regularize the liturgy and to check various moral disorders of the clergy and the laity. The trouble was that some of these provisions, which incidentally offer us a well coloured picture of Byzantine customs, went against the discipline of the Roman Church, among others, the concession to members of the secular clergy to contract marriage. The papal apocrisiaries were present at the synod and endorsed its resolutions. But when the acts of the synod were presented to the pope, Sergius I (687-701), he refused to confirm them, in spite of the fact that they had met with the approval of the patriarchs of Constantinople, Alexandria and Antioch, and of the emperor and his own apocrisiaries.

The reaction was not slow to come. In the hope of thus overcoming the resistance of the pope, two of his most authoritative advisers were arrested and taken to Byzantium. When this expedient did not obtain the desired effect, the *protospatharius* Zacharias was given the task of seizing Sergius and accompanying him to Constantinople.

Could there be anyone who had forgotten the fate of Pope Martin?

But at this point a new chapter in the relations between papacy and empire began. The local armies of Byzantine Italy came into the picture with a greater autonomy. They were rather a confused force, in the process of groping their way towards Rome and the West, and they put the Holy See in the difficult position of having both to use them to support its own intransigence and to curb their excesses in defence of its loyalism.

No sooner had the *protospatharius* arrived in Rome to execute his imperial orders, than, whether by spontaneous impulse or in response to an appeal, we do not know, the armies of Ravenna, the Pentapolis and the surrounding regions all rushed to the defence of the pope. Fearing the worst, Zacharias had the city gates closed and the pope detained. 'But the army from Ravenna entered through the gate of the blessed Apostle Peter, armed and to the sound of trumpets, they came straight to the Lateran, in burning anxiety to see Sergius, who was said to have been taken away and put on board ship in the night. And while the doors of the patriarchal residence were still shut, with the crowd threatening to break them down if they were not opened immediately, the *spatharius* Zacharias hid under the pope's bed, in an agony of desperation and fear for his life, such was his state of witlessness and confusion. But the pope reassured him and told him that he need have no fear. The same most blessed pope then left the room named after Pope Theodore, and sitting enthroned at the open doors under the image of the Apostles, he ceremoniously welcomed the multitude of soldiers and people who had rushed to his defence, and sweetened their temper with well-chosen and gentle words.' However he did not manage to get them to leave the palace until the emperor's messenger had left the city, evidently under the protection of the Pope.

This was the first victory of the new local forces which were now coming into action on the side of the Church and against the empire. It was a victory of a kind too for Sergius I, who, at least according to appearances, had been obliged to give way to force and had, within the limits of possibility, given proof of his loyalty without deserting his religious duty. As for Zacharias, he had found a way of compromise between the two extreme alternatives which Byzantine officials in Italy had to choose from in times of stress, loyalty and death, or betrayal and life. Under the papal aegis and in wholly novel circumstances, his course of action for the moment prejudiced neither his life or his honour.

The rebellion was followed by no retribution, as in 695 Justinian was deposed, mutilated (whence his nickname *Rhinotmetus*, the noseless emperor) and finally relegated to Cherson, where Constans II had had Pope Martin deported. But a smouldering rebellion was seething beneath the surface of Byzantine Italy. For some years, if the silence of our sources reflects the actual situation, there had been no more mention of an exarch. Now the news that the exarch Theophylact had arrived in Rome from Sicily under orders from the Emperor Tiberius II (698-705), was enough to make 'the armies of all Italy march tumultuously to Rome, with the intention of making life difficult for him!' And in this case, too, the pope, John VI (701-705), 'intervened to mediate, had the gates of the city closed, and sent a delegation of priests to where they were gathered, and calmed their wild commotion with salutary words of warning'.

The revenge for Zacharias' sudden and unexpected rebuff and the rebellious spirit of the army and the two great centres of the peninsula fell on Rome and Ravenna a few years after Justinian had reconquered Constantinople, and put Leo, who had usurped his throne (695-698), and Tiberius II who had overthrown Leo, to death.

The ground was probably prepared by stimulating a renewal of rivalry between Rome and Ravenna, so as to break up the unity of the Italian forces. Then while the pope, Constantine I (708-715), was sailing by order of the emperor to Constantinople, with an entourage of members of the senior clergy and the top ecclesiastical administration, and being received at every port of call with imperial honours, Justinian had a number of high-ranking churchmen and papal functionaries, evidently suspected of being leaders of the anti-Byzantine opposition, murdered behind his back. The new exarch, John Rizocapus, was responsible for the arrangements. Pope and exarch had met *en route*, each travelling to his own destination. Rizocapus, having dispatched his business in Rome, set out for Ravenna, probably with the intention of completing his mission there. But the inhabitants had heard of the happenings in Rome, and so, suspecting his intentions, they gave him no chance to carry them out. The reaction to the assassination of the exarch was a fearful one: the Archbishop Felix and the elders of the city were dragged to Constantinople in chains, where the former was blinded and deported to Pontus, the latter mostly executed.

In the meantime the most solemn and cordial entente between papacy and empire was being celebrated:

'On the day that they (pope and emperor) met, the most Christian Augustus, crowned with his diadem, prostrated himself before the pope and kissed his feet, then they fell into each other's arms, and there was great rejoicing among the people, for they all saw such humility in their good prince. On Sunday the pope celebrated mass for the emperor, who, after receiving communion from his hands and asking him to pray for his crimes, renewed all the privileges of the Church and gave the most holy pope permission to return to his See.'

And here we must consider the situation for a moment. We should not be surprised that Justinian II, one of the most notorious murderers of all time, has gone down in the official ecclesiastical records with the title of 'most Christian and orthodox emperor', for he was entitled to it by his religious fervour, the peace he made with the Church, his violent death, and his succession by a Monothelete emperor, Philip Bardanes (711-713).

Nor should we certainly reproach Constantine I for his devotion to the empire. There are several more or less obvious reasons ready to explain why it was that the popes in these years observed an out and out loyalty to the empire, why they resisted the tumultuous pressure of army and people, scrupulously avoided interfering in any political questions and limited themselves to defending the doctrinal and disciplinary teachings with more or less intransigence. Martin I's fate, as we have already said, was an example of some importance, especially when dealing with a man of prompt action like Justinian. Another point was that the Greek and Syrian churchmen, who for sixty years almost without interruption were enthroned in the chair of St Peter, probably brought with them a strong feeling of loyal citizenship of the empire and felt less intimately tied to the feelings and revolts of the local inhabitants. This was probably the result of their more inclusive cultural background and their familiarity with the east, their respect for Byzantium, which it was unfitting to suspect, and the powerful influence exercised by the orthodox refugees in their Roman surroundings. Finally, apart from the force of tradition, there was no compelling necessity to induce the papacy to break the link that connected it with the other universal power, to turn the risings into a revolution, and to set up a new political régime in the Byzantine territory of Italy, which still had no foundations on which to build one; especially as the only result of the insurrections of army and people had been to inspire the duke of Beneventum to start gnawing at the borders of Roman territory.

Nevertheless, in this case, the papal loyalism, the scrupulous non-interference in the political sphere, does reach a point which cannot but give us food for thought and may well cause surprise. Although it is indeed rash to mention the word 'connivance' with reference to the pope and the emperor's part in the John Rizocapus enterprise, it was no longer merely a case of a military disturbance, but of a departure of the pope, his large entourage of privileged churchmen, his meeting with the exarch, could all have occurred as they did without Constantine and his intimate advisors having at least some faint idea of what was in the offing; and if they did not, it does seem strange that the pope, when told of the misdeed which touched him so closely, should have had no adverse reaction against the man who had arranged it.

The fact of the matter is that the zeal of Justinian II and the religious peace he made had brought the Holy See to a halt, and indeed forced it to go back in its tracks; it had shattered its solidarity with the Italian forces, and made of them, in their obscure confusion, an enemy and a threat to both papacy and empire.

At the accession of Philip Bardanes, what with the dragging on of the old vendettas and the reopening of the religious conflict, the people of Byzantine Italy were once more up in arms, and the papal loyalism was put to a hard test. There were risings in both Rome and Ravenna in 712, for different and, in a way, directly opposite reasons. The people of Ravenna were mourning their dead and cursing Justinian, and rose against Byzantium under the command of the son of Johannitius, a recent imperial victim. The Romans—and here it was no longer merely a case of a military disturbance, but of a real civil and religious revolution—decided not to recognize the Monothelete emperor, not to date their acts with his name, to refuse to use his coinage, and insisted that his effigy should not be allowed inside the churches, nor his name mentioned in the celebration of mass.

Philip Bardanes reconciled Ravenna to the empire with the joyful and instructive spectacle of the severed head of Justinian (and why not?) and with whatever reparation of their wrongs was possible, above all with the repatriation of the unhappy archbishop, laden with honour and riches. In Rome he tried to confront the hostility of the laity and the greater part of the clergy with the appointment of a new duke, Peter, nominated by the exarch, in place of Christopher, the duke currently in office. Christopher and Peter are little more than names to us, but the biographer of Pope Constantine tells us enough for us to understand that the former, appointed by Justinian, was supported by the rebellious majority of the citizens, both lay and clerical, and the latter by an accommodating minority, who were either afraid of the consequences of a rebellion or over mindful of the crimes of the 'most Christian emperor'. And what, in these circumstances, was the course taken by the pope? An evasion of anything irreparable, even in dealing with a heretic who had risen to the throne by a crime, as had Philip Bardanes. So when the partisans of the old and the new duke came to blows in the Via Sacra in front of the imperial palace, and a good number of them had been killed in the fighting, Constantine, seeing that the supporters of Peter were getting the worst of it, gave them an opportunity to retreat by sending some priests to the spot, carrying the Gospels and the Cross, to separate the combatants.

This semi-victory and semi-defeat must have left both sides equally discontented. If, to make an abstract hypothesis, the circumstances had not changed and the popes had continued to follow the policy of prudence and loyalism to the death, as had Constantine and his oriental predecessors, they would have perpetuated the revolutionary ferment in the Byzantine territory of the peninsula, isolated the Holy See from the deepest aspirations of the Italian peoples, and sterilized the most fertile seeds of future development.

But it was not so. The reappearance of old troubles and the appearance of new ones brought the long process to its final conclusion and pointed to a new road which led to a sudden change in papal policy. The knot tightened for the last time, and was then undone, when Leo II was occupying the imperial throne, Gregory II and Gregory III the chair of St Peter, Liutprand and Aistulf were ruling the Lombards, and Charles Martel and Pippin III the Franks, all of them great figures at a decisive moment in world history.

2

A great historical task brought east and west together in the first half of the eighth century—the Arab wars, which came so near to submerging the whole Christian world in these decades. The victory of 718, which marks the end of the Moslem attacks on Constantinople, is balanced by that won by the Franks under Charles Martel at Poitiers, and Leo III's campaigns in Asia Minor from 726 to his death, by the campaigns of Charles and Pippin in central and southern France. The final blow had been struck both in west and east, the spreading flood had been dammed up and began, very slowly it is true, to subside.

But not even the common task of saving Christianity had the strength to create a common consciousness, a solidarity of interest and purpose, or to stop the gulf between the two worlds widening and each one going its own way according to its own needs and nature. Indeed while Byzantium, under the Isaurian, was checking its enemies, organizing its defence, and remoulding its domestic legislation, but still focussing its attention upon itself and withdrawing into its centre, Rome was exercising a growing attraction and power of command on the Byzantine region of Italy. And the wave of expansion, conquest, and civil and religious organization spread in an ever-widening circle from the Holy See, the masters of the palace and the Anglo-Saxon monks.

The unity of the exarchate was broken, and there emerged from it, under the papal aegis, the Roman duchy, with at its head the military authority of the duke. From the end of Gregory III's papacy, the duke was the patrician Stephen, whose conduct and the circumstances of the time made him look more like a locally appointed commander than a Byzantine official, or at any rate entirely a Roman politician by adoption. Gregory II and Gregory III set to work, with an authority and responsibility that increased daily with the growing impotence of Byzantium, to restore the walls of Rome and *Centumcellae* (now Civitavecchia) on the Tyrrhenian border between the Roman duchy and Lombard Tuscia, to defend these cities against all possible kinds of enemies, the Arabs at sea, the pious Lombards, and the sacred emperor himself. The very distance of the Byzantine sovereign, the proximity of the rival potentates of Pavia, Spoleto and Beneventum, and the fatal attraction that the ill-defended lands of the empire held for them, set in motion, through a series of small skirmishes and crucial choices, a new political autonomy on the part of the popes. Their policy grew more and more independent of the empire until the decisive moment in 739 when the papacy made its first plea for non-imperial assistance. The situation was one in which Liutprand was already encamped with his army in the fields of Nero, at the very gates of Rome. Gregory III sent for help to Charles Martel, the ruler of the Franks.

There had been no other way of salvation, no other choice than than between subjection to the Lombard king and the patronage of the Frankish *subregulus*. But it was in this direction, to the north and west, that the new life, the great vital breath of missionary and military conquest lay. The sons of the Germanic invaders, those Anglo-Saxons with their strange sounding names, Ceadwalla, Cenred, Offa and Ine, left Britain and came to weep, pray, and die at the tomb of St Peter. What was it that made them do it? What passion ruled their hearts? Less than a century after its evangelization, the island had become the most fervent field of cultural and religious activity. The converted Anglo-Saxons came back to the continent, bearing the Christian message to their brother peoples in the lands of their origin. Wilfrid, Benedict Biscop, Ceolfrid, the Venerable Bede, Willibrord, Wynfrith, brought to Rome the treasure of their manuscripts, sought in Rome the word of justice, the true teaching, the authority of the Apostles, and took from Rome the very names of piety and battle: Clement and Boniface. Through their work, and also the agreement of Rome and the sons of Pippin, the Frankish church was reformed, the Anglo-Saxon church organized, and the Gospel preached, in competition with the conquests of the Frankish army, to the Bavarians, the Alemanni, the Saxons, the Frisians, and the Thuringians.

Thus, while the empire was hardening in the structure of its old laws and closing in upon itself, a whole new world, the Europe of the future in embryo, was expanding westward from the edge of the Byzantine sphere. And a new structure, basically religious, secondarily both political and religious, was being formed, with its focus in Rome and the court of the sons of Pippin.

It may seem strange that the evidence for a historical fact like the iconoclastic struggle, the exceptional importance and revolutionary consequences of which were recognized even by the people living at the time, should be full of uncertainties and contradictions. But still, the fact is that, although we may succeed in making out the general significance of the events, as soon as we try to find out any details, such as the origins of the conflict, or the chronology of particular events, we come across a great number of difficulties, which scholars have only partly succeeded in resolving in spite of their miraculous patience and insight.

It would appear, then, but we cannot be sure, that the first clash between Leo the Isaurian and Pope Gregory II was the result of a fiscal, not a religious, dispute. The taxes on the Italian provinces were increased and they were further extended to the Church institutions themselves, which had until then been traditionally exempt. The empire was asking the Church and its Italian subjects to pay their share of the great financial sacrifices that had been necessitated by its wars, by natural disasters and by the need for reforms. It met with a vigorous opposition, led by the pope. This was not so much because the ecclesiastical privilege was being violated as because the political responsibility and the leadership of Italy had fallen naturally into the hands of the pope, and it was absurd to exact a sacrifice from them which would have no recompense, a tangible sign of a solidarity which by now had become almost nonexistent.

To Leo III, Gregory II was a rebel, and either with the emperor's consent or by his express orders an attempt was made to remove him by force. A conspiracy was formed, which included the duke Basilius, the chartulary Jordanus and the subdeacon John Lurion. The *spatarius* Marinus was sent from Byzantium to Rome to join it, and to take command in the Roman duchy. But first the conspirators were unable to find the right moment, then the *spatarius*, who was to be, if not the actual perpetrator, at least the life and soul of the plot, was struck by an attack of apoplexy and obliged to leave the city. The exarch Paul took his place to direct proceedings, but had no better luck, as the Romans got wind of what was in the offing, and put Jordanus and John Lurion to death and forced the duke Basilius to become a monk. In the end the exarch and the new *spatharius*, who was destined to the command of the Roman duchy, intervened openly in an attempt to seize the pope, and order the election of another in his place. But the bid to move the army of Ravenna against Rome only had the result of inducing the Romans on the one side and the Lombards from the duchies of Spoleto and Tuscia on the other, to join forces to bar the road to their common enemy.

This, or something like it, we seem to be able to gather from the only piece of evidence that is at all contemporary, the *Vita* of Gregory II in the *Liber Pontificalis*, which, confused though its account is, tells us clearly how great was the power of the pope, how vain the presumption of the emperor in attempting to do violence to him and bend him to his will, and how great the danger of an alliance between Rome and the Lombards.

The religious clash between Church and empire occurs around this time. The *Liber Pontificalis* puts it a little after the events we refer to above, and describes it independently of the fiscal question. The Byzantine Theophanes, writing nearly a century later, puts it just before, and sees Gregory's resistance to the fiscal measures as a reaction to the emperor's religious innovations.

In 726, a violent earthquake threw up a new island between Thera and Therasia, and was reputedly interpreted by Leo III as a sign of divine anger at the idolatrous cult of the holy images, with the result that he decided to start an energetic campaign for their abolition. He began by discreetly mentioning the question in public meetings, continued with propaganda and moral pressure, and finally gave the first formal example of his intentions: at the beginning of 727 he gave orders for the icon of Christ above the great bronze doors of the imperial palace to be destroyed. But at this point the repressed popular discontent broke out in open violence. The crowd, which contained many women, threw the *spatarius* responsible for the execution of the order off his ladder, and massacred several courtiers who were helping him. The culprits were condemned to flogging, mutilation and exile, and the campaign was continued with inexorable energy. Serious measures, we gather from Theophanes, were taken against the professors of the imperial university of Constantinople, who were evidently hostile to iconoclasm. The forces of the *Thema* in Greece and the Cyclades, showed a much greater violence and hostility, and in April, 727, proclaimed a new emperor and arrived with their fleet before Constantinople. But their ships were set on fire and the leaders of the revolt seized and put to death.

Our sources obviously insist on the personal character of the struggle against iconoclasm, on the initiative of Leo III and the reaction of his great antagonists, the patriarch Germanus, Gregory II and Gregory III, and John Damascene. And indeed, it is only the clearly defined political and religious position of the emperor and the intransigence of the orthodox leaders that give the conflict its substance and configuration, right up to the ultimate consequences of the conflict between east and west.

But the sources also tell us that iconoclasm is to be seen in a broader setting, beyond the limits of Rome and Byzantium, and beyond the personalities of its protagonists, and they thereby help to clarify its significance for us.

The orthodox writers inveigh against the σαρακηνοφρων Leo, the disciple of the Arabs, and against Beser, who was converted to Islam and then returned to 'the Roman way of life' to fight at the side of the emperor, winning his favour by his physical strength and his agreement with the Iconoclastic error; and in doing so they are not merely giving vent to their anger against the enemy of the holy icons, they are pointing to a serious fact. The whole Hebrew and Islamic east is hostile to the cult of sacred images. The Jews cling to the Mosaic precept and use it as a weapon to accuse the Christians of idolatry. The Musulman iconoclastic tendency appears at the beginning of the eighth century, and gives rise to the violence of the caliph Yezid, who is said to have had the sacred images destroyed in the Christian churches in 723 just before Leo III's campaign, on the advice of a Hebrew of Tiberias. Thus Moslems and Jews come together in a common intolerance of any material representation of the Deity or anything related to the spiritual world, in a common horror of any manifestation that might be idolatrous.

A similar tendency appears, as if by contagion, in the eastern provinces of the empire not long before the disturbance caused by Leo III. The two leaders of the movement, apart from Theodosius, Archbishop of Ephesus, who is mentioned by Gregory II as one of the emperor's principal advisers, are the bishops Constantine of

Nacolea and Thomas of Claudiopolis. Constantine visits the patriarch Germanus and confided his doubts about the images. Germanus unravelled his difficulties, and was so confident of having convinced him that he actually entrusted him with a reassuring letter to deliver to his metropolitan, John of Synnada, who had written to him in a state of great apprehension about his bishop. But the patriarch was wrong, and not for the last time. Constantine did not deliver the letter, and stood out against the orders and threats of Germanus, who was later to accuse him of being 'the initiator and leader' of iconoclasm. Thomas's case was different. He too, came to Constantinople and conferred with the patriarch, and did not so much as open his mouth on the subject. But on returning to his see, he had the holy images removed, and consequently set serious trouble in motion in Asia Minor.

We do not know what degree of collaboration there was between Leo III, Constantine of Nacolea and Thomas of Claudiopolis, though it is most unlikely that there was none. It has been assumed, perhaps with good reason, though again we have no proof either way, that the fact that the emperor was born in the eastern provinces, on the borders between Syria and Cilicia, contributed to the development of his iconoclastic tendencies. The precedents of his religious policy, to which we may well look for enlightenment of the outbreak of the controversy, show us ten years of peace with the Holy See, a decree for the compulsory baptism of the Jews in 722, and its application to the Montanists, or as some say, to the Manichees or the Paulicians. As so often happens, we should like to have more precise details available, to satisfy our curiosity and help to clarify the development of events. In any case, the sources being as they are, it is unlikely that we shall manage to get much further, or penetrate the secrets of the emperor's conscience more deeply than this. And perhaps what we already know is enough.

It is not easy to conceive such a difficult and dangerous undertaking as the Isaurian's without strong religious feeling and a clearly planned policy. It has been too uncompromisingly stated that the controversy over the images does not touch on questions of dogma, at least in the early period of Leo III, but only the customs and traditions of the Church. For in actuality, there is a fine but unbroken thread connecting the christological polemic of the Monophysites, the Monourgites and the Monothelites, with the development of iconoclasm. Even though the iconoclasts condemn every kind of sacred representation, their attitude is based, on the one side, in general, on the horror common to most of the east at the material representation of the Deity, and on the other, in particular, on the inability inherent in the greater part of eastern Christianity to conceive the dual nature of Christ or to accept the Catholic doctrine of the Incarnation.

So whatever its personal origin (and this we cannot determine), the emperor's religious sentiments are the expression of an exigency that was strongly felt throughout the eastern world. His action is not substantially different from the *Henoticon*, the *Ekthesis* and the *Typos*. In starting an open fight he was following the propensities of his times, seizing an effective instrument of propaganda and conquest from the Arabs, and attempting once more, under a new flag (and perhaps this, too, is the explanation of the decree for the baptism of the Jews) to pacify his perpetually divided empire.

His greatest difficulty lay in making the leaders of orthodoxy, the pope and the patriarch, submit to iconoclasm: his greatest danger in the particular political, military and religious conditions obtaining in Byzantine Italy. Leo tried to compel Germanus to do his bidding, and in the heat of the discussion had no hesitation in accusing both his own predecessors and those of the patriarch of idolatry. To Gregory II he sent a letter informing him of his decisions with regard to images, 'since they were accursed things', and promising him his favours if he acquiesced, and threatening deposition if he did not.

The quarrel that develops between the emperor on the one side, and on the other the pope, the patriarch of Constantinople and John Damascene, is quite simply a confirmation, even a final clarification and deepening of the conflict between east and west. Apart from his threat to bring the pope to the same end as Martin I, the points made by Leo III are basically two: that the worship of images is forbidden by the Old Testament and constitutes idolatry, and that he, as 'emperor and priest', has authority to enforce their abolition. His opponents live each in a different world, one in Rome, caught between the Byzantine hostility and the unreliable friendship of the Lombards, one in the very heart of the empire, at Byzantium, and the other in Damascus, as a high-placed official in the service of the Umayyad caliphs. The tone of their arguments may vary from one to the other, according to their nature and their circumstances. But they all reason similarly and all use the same weapons, which are those that were forged in the course of centuries under the guidance of Rome.

On the question of idolatry, they are easily able to point out that there were sacred figures decorating the Holy Ark and the temple of Solomon, and that the Mosaic prohibition, though valid with regard to idols, cannot be applied to the images of Christ, the Virgin mother of God, the Apostles, saints and martyrs. These figures, as the Greek and Latin Fathers of the Church taught, express devotion towards them, a desire for their presence, and are useful for teaching and instruction, for, as St Gregory says, 'the Church uses pictures in churches to this end, that people who are illiterate may yet read, by looking at the walls, what they are incapable of reading in books'. The worship, the adoration, is not directed to the image, nor to the material of which it is made, but through the suggestion of the image to the Deity and the divine teaching.

But the material also comes into the arguments of the orthodox for a more subtle reason. It is here that the doctrinal theme which is the more or less explicit implication throughout the iconoclastic dispute comes in. 'If the prophecies have not been accomplished,' writes Pope Gregory II, 'then let no facts be written down to demonstrate what has not yet occurred. That is, if Our Lord has not been incarnate, let not His holy image be formed according to the flesh. If He was not born in Bethlehem of the glorious Virgin, the mother of God, if He, who rules the universe, was not carried as a babe in the arms of His mother, if He, who feeds all flesh, did not stoop to feed on His mother's milk, let not His be shown either. If He did not raise the dead, or loose the limbs of the paralysed, or purify lepers, or give sight to the blind and words to the dumb, let not His miracles be shown. If He did not voluntarily submit to His passion, if He did not descend into Hell, if He did not rise again and ascend into Heaven, He who shall come to judge the quick and the dead, in that case let no letters or colours be used to represent these things. But if all this did happen, and it is a great mystery of mercy, then would it were possible for the sky, the earth and the sea, the plants and the animals and every living thing to tell of it with voice, with writing and in painting.'

The patriarch Germanus echoes the pope's words: 'We allow the image of Our Lord Jesus Christ, represented in a human body, according to his visible Theophany, in perpetual memory of His life in the flesh, of His passion, of the salvation of His death, and the redemption it brought to the world, since through this image we come to understand the supreme humiliation of the divine Word.' 'Since the only begotten Son of the Father deigned to become a man, participating in flesh and blood in our likeness, we yearn to represent these beliefs, to show that He made Himself one with our nature in no fantastic or shadowy way, as some of the ancient heretics claimed, but that He really and truly became a complete man in every aspect, except that He was sinless.'

In short, the pope, the patriarch, and John Damascene suspected, not without reason, that the iconoclastic horror at the representation of Christ and the Mother of God, was the manifestation of a return to the christological heresies, which only a few years later were to find a keen interpreter in the very heart of iconoclasm, in the son and successor of Leo III, Constantine V.

To the Isaurian's proud claim to be 'emperor and priest' the great voices of Catholicism reply with one accord: 'You, know, o emperor, that the dogmas of the Holy Church are not in the care of the emperors, but of the priests'. It is not for the emperors to make laws for the Church, their responsibility is the good government of the state'. 'We will obey you, o emperor, in everything concerned with normal life, in taxes, levies, and trade, for in regard to these, you have been given the guardianship over our affairs, but in the constitution of the Church, we have the shepherds, who speak to us of the Word and shape our ecclesiastical law'. To the overweaning pretensions of the emperor, Gregory II opposes the firm principle of the Roman primacy, and the divine power of binding and unbinding.

Unanimous, too, is the cry of alarm at the arbitrary tyranny of one who presumes to make legal innovations, to plunge his hands into the treasure of ecclesiastic tradition, and at the danger that, if one stone is removed, the whole edifice may tumble to the ground. The patriarch warns: 'If you repudiate the venerable images of the saints as idols, you come close to dislodging the very foundations of the faith. Indeed, not merely the Gentiles, but the sons of Christians, will say that the traditions of our Church can have no solidity, since we reject our most ancient customs'; and 'We must protect ourselves at all costs from innovation, especially when it is accompanied by confusion and cause for scandal among Christian people, for in churches, time-worn custom has the force of law'.

And John Damascene, with his warm eloquence: 'Listen, all peoples, tribes, tongues, men, women and children, old, growing and young, holy seed of the Christians, if any one tries to teach you anything contrary to what the Catholic Church has received from the holy Apostles, the Fathers, and the synods, and that it has kept to this day, pay no heed to him. Even if an angel, even if the emperor tells you something other than what you have received from the tradition, close your ears to him'. 'We beg the people of God, the holy race, to hold firm to the ecclesiastic traditions. For to abolish little by little what has been handed down to us will soon make the whole structure fall to the ground, just as would a house whose stones were removed one by one.' 'Let us stand firm, brothers, on the rock of the faith and on the traditions of the Church, without moving the limits that the Holy Fathers laid down for us, or giving in to those who want to make innovations and destroy the structure of the Holy Catholic and Apostolic Church of God.'

Caesaro-papism, then, on the one hand, and the distinction of the two supreme powers and their union in peace and charity on the other; the restless spirit of novelty set against faithfulness to tradition, form the ideal antithesis of east and west.

In practice, Gregory II, on receiving the emperor's letter, in the words of his biographer, 'despising the profane command of the prince, immediately armed himself against the emperor as against an enemy, condemning his heresy, and writing to Christians everywhere that they should be on their guard, for an impiety had been let loose'.

The consequences were not long in coming. We have already mentioned the rebellion of the *thema* in Greece and the Cyclades, which were included in the scope of the Roman patriarchy. It is not unlikely that the first impetus to resistance came from Rome. The armies of Venetia and the Pentapolis rose at the same time, marshalling their forces in defence of the pope against the exarch and the emperor. On their example, the movement spread throughout Byzantine Italy, the *duces* appointed by the exarch were chased hither and thither, and their posts were occupied by elected officers. Even the choice of a new emperor and his transportation to Byzantium was considered.

In Rome and Ravenna, the commander of the Roman duchy and the exarch did attempt to make some show of resistance to the insurrections. The duke, Exilaratus and his son, Adrian, who was notorious for having married a deaconess and consequently being excommunicated by a synod in 721, retired into Campagna in the hope of leading the local troops and populations back against the pope. But the Romans followed close behind him, seized him and his son, and killed them, charging them with 'having written against the pope to the emperor'. The fate of Exilaratus' successor, the duke Peter, was scarcely less tragic; he was blinded.

In Ravenna the conflict broke out between the supporters of the Isaurian, led by the patrician exarch Paul, and those of Pope Gregory; and the exarch lost his life in it. His successor, the eunuch patrician Eutychius, landed in Naples in 727 and sent orders in writing to Rome for the assassination of the Pope and the Roman dignitaries. The only result was that the messenger escaped the fate intended for the pope by some miracle, and 'all men, high and low, committed themselves on oath', even if it should cost them their life, 'not to allow the pope, the zealous defender of the Christian faith and of the churches, to be hurt or removed'.

This was more or less the state of affairs in Italy. But by setting out the facts in this way, emphasizing only the brave reaction of the pope, the religious loyalty and the rebellious spirit of the Italian people, we run the risk of falsifying or misunderstanding the character of the iconoclastic revolution, as though it were a battle won almost before being fought.

In actual fact the chain of events was much more complex, and the struggle was one of extreme anxiety and fateful decisions for the Holy See and for Italy. Gregory II had replied to the emperor's first threat with an even more serious one. As if he had a clear premonition of future events, he had written that the bishops of Rome, 'set like a dividing wall between east and west,' were the arbiters of peace, that in spite of his lack of power, all the west looked to him, as the successor of St Peter, and that it would have sufficed for him to go only three miles out of Rome to foil all plots made against him. This too was true. His greatest political and religious strength lay now in Roman and Lombard Italy, in the lands conquered and ruled by the sons of Pippin, and in the great islands of the north. And it was a sign of the ripeness of the times, that he had such a clear consciousness and precise definition of the problem.

The trouble was that the subsequent behaviour of the pope was less bold than his first words. It was one thing to commit himself to the hilt in the defence of the dogmas, the traditions, and the prerogatives of the Church, and quite another to withhold his loyalty to the empire, which meant jeopardizing the ecclesiastic patrimonies, and what was more, radically changing the structure of Byzantine Italy, and indeed, the whole political and religious system of the Christian world. Once Gregory II had thrown down the glove, he could not but congratulate himself on the prompt response of the military forces and the Italian peoples. Nevertheless, he had to backtrack quickly to stop the movement getting out of his control. It was the pope who stopped the plan for the nomination of a new emperor, who, remember, was to set sail for Constantinople, it was the pope who saved the life of the exarch Eutychius' messenger. What he wanted was not the ruin but the conversion of the culprit. Nothing was further from his thoughts and those of his supporters than what we might call a national sally against the emperor under papal leadership. It was no easy matter to overcome the deep influence of time-honoured tradition, and in any case, the papal supporters could not give free rein to any impulsive actions. Gregory II had to watch over the course of events with all the old political wisdom of the papacy.

One of the most important factors that made caution advisable, and which indeed contributed more than anything else to the increasing show of papal loyalism to the empire, was the political situation of the Lombards—the same situation that in only a few decades was to bring the process started by the iconoclastic struggle to its conclusion in creating the States of the Church.

The first consequence of the upheavals around Ravenna and the insurrection in the Pentapolis was a new move on the part of King Liutprand. Partly by force and partly through their spontaneous surrender, he took possession of the Byzantine castles intended to defend the exarchate, beyond the borders of his kingdom along the Panarus, and also of the cities of Osimo, Numana, and Ancona in the Pentapolis. This expansion was a clear indication of the alternative fate of the papacy if the power of Byzantium were to be weakened to an excessive degree, and was at the same time an immediate threat to the rebellious duchy of Spoleto, which was in the process of emphasizing its actual, though not nominal, independence of the Lombard kingdom by making common cause with the Romans against Byzantium.

All this resulted in a paradoxical state of affairs. The king and the exarch, who were enemies, had in common the pressing need to break up the alliance between Rome and the duchies of Spoleto and Benevento. Gregory II, for his part, needed the help of Spoleto and Benevento, help which he was somewhat overwhelmed by and would have been happy to have done without, so as to keep out of the dangerous Lombard game and keep his opposition to Byzantium within the limits of the purely religious conflict.

The king and the exarch applied themselves, each for himself, to the destruction of the alliance. Liutprand started with the pope. In 728 he occupied the castle of Sutri, which belonged to the patrimony of the Holy See, and only after four months of protests and negotiations could he be persuaded to give it back, still keeping his hold on its rural dependencies. Eutychius, in his turn, lavished gifts and promises upon the rebellious Lombards to convince them to abandon the pope. But Spoleto, Rome, and Benevento could only count on their own forces, so instead of giving in, 'they drew together like brothers in a pact', declaring that they were ready to die in defence of the pope. He, for his part, caught in the inextricable contradictions of the situation, while thanking them for their good intentions, exhorted them all with gentle words to progress towards God by virtue of their good actions and to stay firm in their faith, but warned them not to relinquish their love and loyalty to the Roman empire.

The events that follow suggest that at a certain point the coincidence of immediate interests prevailed over the fundamental political and religious opposition between king and exarch, and that Liutprand and Eutychius came to an agreement to reduce the duchies of Benevento and Spoleto to obedience to the kingdom, and Rome and its duchy to obedience to the empire. What is more, we may even suspect, though this suspicion is not supported by any explicit testimony, that the pope himself did not stay completely aloof from the understanding, and that the impunity of the rebels was the result of his intervention.

What happened was that in 729 Liutprand occupied Spoleto and received oaths of obedience from the Duke of Spoleto, Transemund II, and the Duke of Benevento, Romuald II, and then proceeded to Rome, to camp in the so-called Fields of Nero nearby. Here he was joined by the pope, and peace was made, with great marks of devotion on the part of the king, between Gregory, Liutprand and Eutychius.

It was a case of compromise rather than peace. The time was not ripe, and the pope's best course of action was simply to hold firm in his loyalty to the empire and to thus ensure the impunity of Rome and her duchy, which in effect he represented. He had the opportunity of demonstrating this loyalism anew not long after, when, in Roman Tuscia, where the fire of the rebellion was not yet burnt out, a certain Tiberius Petasius forced his way into the castle of Manturiano, near the Lake of Bracciano, and proclaimed himself emperor, having all the nearby inhabitants swear an oath of allegiance to him. Thanks to Gregory II's material and moral help, Eutychius was able to put down the rising, and capture and do justice to the pretender, whose severed head was sent to Constantinople, according to the custom.

But the papal loyalism was fraught with too many implied reservations for it to be above suspicion. The pope's biographer writes that, in spite of the clear proof of his loyalty, 'the emperor never entirely renewed his favours to the Romans'. Nor could it have been otherwise. If, indeed, the run of events had suggested to him or to his exarch that a truce was possible, the problem of the relationship between empire and papacy, between caesaro-papism and primacy, east and west, was now once more an immediate and urgent one. And the emperor himself saw to it that their separation was made inevitable.

After having tried in vain to make the patriarch Germanus submit to iconoclasm, Leo III summoned a solemn conference of senators and high lay and ecclesiastic dignitaries. The conference was held on January 17, 730, in the triclinium of the nineteen couches, one of the largest rooms in the palace, and there he promulgated the edict that forbade the cult of sacred images. The patriarch refused to sign the act, and took the alternative of retiring. He was succeeded by his disciple and Syncellus, Anastasius, a man who was as ready to compromise as he had been inflexible. According to the normal procedure, he sent the synodical to the pope with his profession of faith. But the pope returned it, telling the new patriarch not to consider him as a brother, and threatening to exclude him from the ministry if he did not return to orthodoxy.

Thus, while in the east legal persecution was beginning, in the west the cycle was starting up afresh. Just as if nothing had happened—threats of deposition and death, the disturbances of wars and insurrections—Gregory II, shortly before dying (on February 11, 731), firm in his faith and in the solidarity of the west, repeated, as if for the first time, as always, that the successor of Peter had the supreme authority to bind and to loose, that the tradition of the Church was sacred, and that it was no concern of the emperor's to interfere in ecclesiastical matters.

The official and irreparable act which proscribed the cult of sacred images throughout the empire marks the break in diplomatic relations, lively though they were, between Rome and Byzantium, and had the effect of provoking a clear official explanation from the Holy See. On November 1, 731, Gregory III, who had been consecrated on March 18th in the same year with the approval of the exarch, or at least without his opposition, summoned a council 'istius Speriae partis', in other words of Italy, in St Peter's, to discuss the question of iconoclasm—a clear sign, if it were needed, that the separation was in force. The council was attended by ninety-three bishops, among them the Patriarch of Grado and the Archbishop of Ravenna, both of them with their assistants, all the clergy of Rome, and the dignitaries and people of the city. This showed that the pope could count on the political and religious solidarity of both the Roman laity and the most important ecclesiastical representatives of Byzantine and Lombard Italy in making his final decision.

The acts of the council are lost, but the final decree is enough for us. It has been preserved for us by the biographer of Gregory III and we find an eloquent echo in the speeches of John Damascene: 'If, from now on, any one holds those who remain faithful to the ancient customs of the Apostolic Church in contempt, and hating the sacred images of God and Our Lord Jesus Christ and of his mother Mary, ever virgin, immaculate and glorious, of the holy Apostles and all the Saints, tears down these images, destroys, profanes and blasphemes them, let him be denied the blood and body of Christ, and excluded from the unity and company of all the Church.'

The emperor was not referred to in person, but the condemnation was aimed at him before anyone else, and with him, at the patriarch Anastasius and a multitude of lay and churchmen. Nevertheless, in spite of the exceptional gravity of the measure, there was no sign before, during, or after the council of any reaction on the part of the exarch Eutychius or any other Byzantine officials. In Byzantine Italy, and perhaps also in the Lombard territory, there was a state of unusual suspension and expectancy. Peace reigned everywhere. The pope appeared to be acting in absolute safety and complete freedom, but the question of what the emperor might do remained. His only hostile actions had, one might say, a negative character; they consisted of intercepting all correspondence addressed by the pope to himself or to the patriarch and in imprisoning the messengers. The same lot befell an embassy, by means of which the Italian subjects appealed for a repeal of the decree of iconoclasm.

It is obvious that Leo III had no intention of treating with the people he considered rebels, especially with the pope, whose words of warning and threats of excommunication he was not disposed to receive. Besides, if he and his predecessors had been unable to get satisfaction from the papal intransigence and pacify and stabilize the Italian provinces with the normal means at their disposal, it is exceedingly unlikely that he was under the delusion that he could now achieve his end by intercepting letters and imprisoning the messengers. Thus we may conclude that these measures constituted a waiting game, the concentration of energy that precedes and prepares for an action, a change of direction, dictated by the conviction that in the present state of affairs the harm was irreparable and must be dealt with by other means.

The action began with an act of force, the dispatch of a powerful fleet to Italy under the command of Manes, the admiral of the maritime theme of the Cibyrrhaeots. But a tempest scattered and destroyed the ships in the Adriatic, and the expedition came to nothing. According to Theophanes, Leo III's exasperation was such that he increased the poll-tax in the themes of Calabria and Sicily by a third, and confiscated the patrimonies of the Roman Church, by making arrangements for their enormous revenues to go in future to the imperial treasury. Another important measure which Theophanes does not mention, was in all probability taken by the emperor on the same occasion: the dioceses of the Balkan peninsula, Southern Italy and Sicily were detached from the Roman patriarchy and annexed to that of Constantinople.

Now if we consider these facts carefully and reflect on the sequence of events and of the relations of Rome with Italy on the one hand and Byzantium on the other, we realize that this is no impulsive reaction or vendetta, but a carefully meditated plan, which is not just one among many in the struggle for and against holy images, but that of its conclusion, indeed of the end of the century-long political, religious and cultural conflict between east and west.

All the efforts to force iconoclasm onto the Roman Church had failed and now no further attempts were made. The imperial rights over Venetia, the exarchate, the Pentapolis, and the duchy of Rome remained unchanged, but these Italian provinces were now more or less left to themselves and practically lost. The loss was compensated for by the confiscation of the ecclesiastical patrimonies and the impositions inflicted on the strongly hellenized populations of the themes of Calabria and Sicily. The field of the Byzantine patriarchy was adjusted to coincide with the effective boundaries of the empire.

Thus east and west were separated, exponents as they were of two distinct traditions and two different ways of life, the world of the primacy and the world of Caesaro-papism, Rome and Byzantium. And at the same time the faith in the unitary government of Christianity through the co-operation of the two supreme powers was torn apart.

For more than a century after this time, the empire was still agitated by the iconoclastic struggle, between the alternatives of orthodoxy and iconoclasm. But the west was left untouched by it, and the later polemic between Adrian I and Charlemagne, which is recorded in the *Libri Carolingi*, was more an academic discussion than a substantial religious or politico-religious conflict.

As the imperial authority grew ever weaker, another important problem was to occupy the attention and the forces of papal Rome, Italy and the west: the question of the inheritance of the Byzantine exarchate, the Pentapolis, and the duchy of Rome.

Once iconoclasm was a thing of the past, the Holy See maintained its fidelity to the empire, and received an occasional sign of recognition in return. According to the opportunities offered by the general situation, and with ever-increasing liberty of action, Rome alternated her alliances with the duchies of Spoleto and Benevento against the kings of Pavia, and with the kings against the dukes, always to the end of countering the powerful pressure from the Lombards, which threatened to take the old place of Byzantium and to cancel out the lofty patronage and guidance that she exercised in particular in the duchy, and in general over all the peoples of North and Central Italy.

Only when her ruin appeared imminent, did she turn for aid to the sons of Pippin, the great promoters of the papal missions among the Germans (the first time, with no effect, in 739 to Charles Martel, the second and the third time, successfully, in 753 and 755 to Pippin III). She thereby favoured their ambitions and resolutely moved her political axis from east to west, from Byzantines to the Franks, from the past to the present and the future.

In this way the last contradictions of the dying Romano-Byzantine system were resolved, and the period of compromises between the impotent empire, the firm authority of the papacy and the adventurous policy of the Lombards, drew to a close. The Church, which had led the west in the struggle against the east, established itself as the heir of Byzantium in the duchy, the exarchate and the Pentapolis, in affirmation of its prestige and in defence of its liberty.

CHAPTER 8

THE FOUNDATION OF EUROPE

CHARLEMAGNE

Students of history are in a way physicians of the soul. History fills us with sorrow; and they try to bring a measure of comfort to this sorrow, by showing that it was necessary for the further development of mankind. History is absurd with its alternating creation and destruction, triumph brought by one day and downfall by the next; and they try to show that this is an illusion, and that history, far from being arbitrary and fortuitous, is reason itself in its perpetual process of creation, and that, however unlikely it may seem, every moment in history presupposes all the past, whether it denies it or confirms it, and carries it forward spontaneously. They are physicians, then, who endeavour to create an austere faith in history and in life, which otherwise, in appearance and in practice, seem nothing but a fearful succession of hierarchy and anarchy, hard-won peace and destruction, and inexplicable victories and defeats.

We mention this in speaking of Charlemagne, the only individual, it has been remarked, whose name has the attribute of greatness indissolubly attached to it. This greatness seems to tower, unique and hugely disproportionate, in a historically absurd fashion, over the dynastic scandals and gruesome horrors of the Merovingians and the boldness and ability of the sons of Pippin which went before it, and the quarrels of the successors and the feudal anarchy of the empire that followed it. To bring Charlemagne back into the framework of history means detracting somewhat from the values of imagination, and renouncing many suggestive literary reminiscences for the sake of truth. But at the same time the importance of the man is in this way better revealed, and he will continue to excite our admiration, even though, or rather because, he gives form to and ennobles a secular tradition, and prepares a fertile though turbulent future by his work in the present.

There was probably no principle of government, no important political problem or broad plain of conquest that Charlemagne did not inherit either directly or indirectly from the Franks and the masters of the palace, later kings, from whose royal stock he was born. The unity of his kingdom had been re-established and defended with the arms of Pippin the Younger and Charles Martel at Tertry (687) and Vincy (717) respectively. The conversion of his church from the east to the greater Catholic power of the west, under pressure from the Lombards, was already an accomplished fact. With the pope's hand, Pippin III had put on the crown of kingship, and his sons Charles and Charlemagne had assumed the title of patricians; a vague title, but not exclusively an honorific one, it suggested a relationship with the city and the empire, and a supreme protectorship over the most meaningful part of the empire to remain in the west, Rome and the Church itself. Another fruit of the alliance as we have already seen, had been the recognition of the Holy See's right to the Byzantine territories that had been the object of Liutprand's and Aistulf's ambitions. But the Lombard problem still remained the focal point of western politics on account of the monarchy's fatal urge to make a single state of the whole peninsula, and the inevitable recourse of the popes to their beneficiaries and protectors beyond the Alps.

Charles Martel and Pippin III had conducted no less than ten campaigns in order to keep their boundaries intact and to support the work of the Anglo-Saxon missionaries. And it was with Pippin's help that the greatest of these missionaries, St Boniface, had accomplished the dream of Gregory the Great, in carrying out a reform of the hierarchy and the discipline of the Frankish church.

When the Arab tide had already engulfed North Africa and Visigothic Spain, and began to threaten France and the entire western world, it was Charles Martel at the head of the *Europenses*—(this meaningful word is used by a contemporary chronicler)—who blocked its way at Poitiers, and drove the infidels back beyond the Pyrenees, conquering the whole of Aquitaine in the process.

The result of all the labours of the sons of Pippin had been the establishment of an immense kingdom that was territorially compact, though organized in a most elementary fashion. For the sake of clarity, we might define its boundaries as, the Pyrenees, the Mediterranean and the broad sweep of the Alps, the Atlantic Ocean, the English Channel and the North Sea, the higher Danube and the course of the Elbe, except that within these boundaries there was the independent Armoric peninsula in the north-west, parts of Frisia and Saxony that were still pagan in the east and north-east, and the vassal duchy of Bavaria in the south-east.

An inheritance less obvious to our eyes but in fact of greater importance, which had been developed in the course of incessant wars and negotiations with the Church, the Lombards, and Byzantium, was the formation of a lively military and diplomatic tradition which raised the Frankish monarchy above all the other powers of the west, and destined it to its place in the world.

Such was the inheritance that Charlemagne received in its entirety when he was between twenty-six and twenty-nine years of age, as a result of the death of Pippin in 768 and that of his brother Carloman in 771. His greatness was to consist not in creating something out of nothing, but in realizing to the full the potentialities developed by his ancestors and his people, and in spending the first thirty years of his reign, inexhaustibly youthful and impervious to the blows of fortune as they were, in stimulating the bellicose faith of the Franks to such an extent, that he shaped their kingdom into Europe, the new empire, which was the concrete expression of the Christian consciousness of the west, in contrast to the Arabs and the Byzantines.

Just as the iconoclastic period seemed harsh, confused and tormented, so the age of Charlemagne seems designed to satisfy our imagination, and our natural desire for serenity and grandeur. The man commands our sympathy even with his physical presence itself: tall stature, sturdy body, manly bearing, and a happy face lit up by large lively eyes. Contemptuous of foreign customs, he dressed in the normal style of the Franks, and always wore a sword; but on ceremonial occasions, and in the presence of foreign ambassadors, his head was surmounted by a crown, decorated with jewels and precious fabrics. There was much of his simple and robust ancestry in him. His favourite food was game, and the recreations he most delighted in were hunting and taking hot baths. He had an open mind, and a clear, easy and fluent manner of speech, he spoke Latin, Frankish, and Romance and understood Greek rather better than he spoke it. Such was his lifelong passion for learning, that he had his daughters, as well as his sons, trained in the liberal arts. At meal-times he had *De civitate Dei* or stories of antiquity read aloud to him, and kept a stylus and tablets under his pillow at night, so that he could learn to write and practice through his frequent wakeful nights. His faith was keen and sincere, but quite unscrupulous. His spirit showed generosity in its ready forgiveness, its deeply felt friendship and its liberality. Complete master of himself, he hid both ill-will and grief, except that he could not disguise his bitterness at the Spanish defeat, or his tears for the death of his sons in his old age.

With this exceptional temper of body and spirit, and the tireless energy that emanated from it, he was to dominate the world scene for more than forty years, with wars on the distant boundaries of his kingdom, universal civil provisions, and far reaching diplomatic relations.

This man, so open, direct and generous in his actions, yet presents us with a mystery that still remains unsolved in spite of all the diligence scholars have lavished upon it. It concerns his first great political move, and touches on the fundamental problem of the west. How was it that Charles denied the tradition of his family, which had won Pippin the throne and him the patricianship? How was it that he divorced his wife Imiltrude (if we are to believe the story, it was at the suggestion of his mother, Bertrada), to enter into the family constellation of Desiderius, King of the Lombards, by marrying, as had the dukes of Bavaria and Benevento before him, one of the king's daughters, the unknown princess whom historians have not even bothered to name, but who is immortalized for us in the figure of Ermengarda?* One explanation that has been considered is that it was part of a scheme of general pacification, conceived and carried out by Bertrada. However this may be, if we reflect for a little on Charles's temperament, on the hostility that existed between him and his brother, and the geographical position of their respective kingdoms, Carloman's bordering on Italy and the Lombard kingdom and Charles's being peripheral to it, with no way of direct communication with the peninsula, it occurs to us rather that the matrimonial alliance may have been designed by Charles himself as a form of threat or defence against his brother, and a safeguard to his Italian interests.

In any case, what happened subsequently was that once his brother was dead, and his authority was diminishing in Rome on account of Desiderius' attacks, he lost no time in repudiating the Lombard princess and promptly substituting the thirteen-year-old Hildegarde. Then a few years later he saw to it that the matter was definitely settled by conquering the Lombard kingdom, sending the king to end his days in pious seclusion in a monastery beyond the Alps, and making the pope an enormous grant of land, consisting of almost all the Italian peninsula, which, incidentally, he never respected in the future. The whole enterprise had been accomplished with such ease, thanks to the weakness of the kingdom, and even more to the resolution of the attack, that Lombard treason has been suspected, but wrongly.

This, then, is the image that we have of Charlemagne, energetic, resolute and thoroughly great, a warrior king, who from year to year moves at the head of his army against Arabs and Lombards, Bavarians and Saxons, Avars and Slavs, not infrequently with his wife and small children. But we must establish the nature of this military activity before going any further. The army was no long-standing body of troops with an organic identity and hierarchic

* In Manzoni's play *Adelchi*.

organization. Before each campaign a proportion of the population would be called to arms, usually those who lived nearest to the theatre of war, and ordered to assemble with arms and provisions at a prearranged place and time, under the command of the same officers who were set over them in time of peace. The only innovation worthy of note was the substantial increase in the numbers of the cavalry, which was in line with a general tendency of the time, and was also intended to prevent a repetition of the unfortunate experience of Poitiers, in which the Arab cavalry had stopped the Frankish infantry reaping the last and best fruit of the victory. We have to deal, then, with an organization that is primitive and rudimentary in character, and whose strength lies in the undivided will of its leader, the force of its dynastic and national tradition, and in the extraordinary unity of its impulse, which shines through the inextricable tangle of its wars.

With the destruction of the Lombard kingdom, the most serious problem of the past was solved, and the Church left with almost no possibility of pursuing an independent policy. At the same time, if Charlemagne were not to jeopardize his gains, he now had to accept responsibility for the civil and religious organization of the Roman world, a task that was not only the most jealously guarded prerogative of the Church, but also the most pressing and permanent exigency of the Christian west. There were still dangerous Lombard outposts resisting him: Benevento, which was capable of siding with Byzantium and harbouring Desiderius' son, who had fled to Constantinople, and Bavaria, a wedge driven into the Frankish territory, where Liutperga encouraged her husband to oppose him. Both these threats were quickly annulled. The conquest of Bavaria and Carinthia threw up the curtain on a race of Mongol plunderers, the Avars, who were settled on the eastern borders. They were great sackers of churches and monasteries, and were only tamed after eight years of war, by the destruction of their entrenched circular ground, the famous *Ring*, and the confiscation of their treasure and baptism of their leaders. Aquitaine rose and had to be reduced once more to subjection right at the beginning of his reign. Then, on account of the continuous danger constituted by the presence of the Arabs in the Pyrenees, the complaints of the Spaniards subjected to the infidels, and the generous promises of assistance given at Paderborn in 777 by the governor of Barcelona in defiance of the emir of Cordova, Charlemagne embarked on the campaign that has remained famous for the slaughter of the retiring rearguard by the Basques.

So terrible was the defeat that the king vowed never to set foot in Aquitaine again. In any case, he was temporarily prevented from avenging his loss by bad news from Hesse and southern Westphalia.

He had been under the illusion that in five years of bold and insistent work he had succeeded in building up a solidly organized defence against the Saxons in these regions. But they had taken advantage of his absence to make their way up the Rhine to its confluence with the Moselle, destroying the Frankish settlements on its right bank with fire and the sword. The campaigns against the Saxons, as is well known, went on for more than twenty years, and were the toughest undertaking of the whole reign. They were pagans, and worshipped fountains, woods, trees in leaf, believed in charms and sorcerers, burned their dead, and adored idols shaped like trunks, roughly fashioned from wood or stone, to which they offered precious objects and human and animal sacrifices. They were jealous of their liberty and their beliefs, and had repeatedly resisted the military and religious penetration of the Franks, with ambushes and sudden attacks on towns, churches and monasteries. The bellicose nature of these people made the struggle tough enough as it was, but it was rendered even more wearing by the trackless swamps and forests of the terrain, and the lack of any kind of political entity or national army which could be challenged to a decisive combat. There was a Saxon leader, Widukind; but he was an elusive enemy, who had the authority and the energy to stir up a sudden rebellion or revolt and then flee to the Slavs beyond the Elbe or the Normans in Denmark, but was not obliging enough, or perhaps sufficiently powerful, to bring the scattered Saxon tribes together into a single force to resist the invader.

The most famous revolt of all was that of 782, which appeared to cancel out all the work of the missionaries at a single blow. It was perhaps on account of the over-hasty reaction it provoked in the local forces and their officers that it led to the disastrous battle fought near the Süntel Hill. Charlemagne arrived, had the culprits, who had broken their oath of allegiance, handed over to him, and (the example is probably unique in Western history) had all 4,500 of them beheaded together at Werden. He was back the next year at the first hint of trouble, as soon as Queen Hildegarde's funeral celebrations were completed, and stayed there winter and summer almost uninterruptedly until 785, dashing up and down the country in a wild rage. He even had his new queen and his children sent out to join him, as if to show how strong was his resolution to bring the war to an end. He left only when he was satisfied that all resistance was thoroughly broken, when Widukind himself, being assured of impunity, was baptized, only to disappear without a trace from the historical scene.

But it was an illusion. In 793 the rebellion was raging once more, partly because of the severity of the clergy and the strictly enforced collection of tithes, as Alcuin himself affirms. Charlemagne returned to the fray for another six consecutive years, from 794 to 799, and harrowed the whole country, laying it waste far and wide, until it was finally subjected.

And here again, the Christian west, as it advances with its armies and missionaries, announces the dawn to new peoples, who, though enemies today, tomorrow will live one life with Europe: the Normans, who will attempt to make a landing on the islands off Aquitaine for the first time in 799, and the Slavs from beyond the Elbe, who, whether they were allies or were beaten in the war with the Saxons, will end up as Frankish subjects one way or another.

We may be disturbed by the death of the 4,500 prisoners, by the twenty year long devastation of a country and its people in the name of civilization and conversion. But the great judgments of history are not measured with the yardstick of our sensibility. A conflict occurred between the Franks with their bellicose faith on the one hand, and the wild and untamed strength and superstition of the Saxons on the other. Clashes and provocations were inevitable, and peaceful coexistence impossible. The struggle between the two peoples was a struggle to the death, and both sides waged the war with the utmost energy and ferocity, until civilization finally triumphed.

As for Charlemagne, he certainly had no compunction and no hesitation in taking this step, as the men responsible for the revolt had broken a sacred bond, the oath of allegiance sworn to him, and also because there was no doubt in his mind that it was incumbent upon him through faith, tradition and his divine consecration, to exterminate the threat and provocation of paganism with his Christian army and his missionaries.

This spirit of simultaneously military and religious conquest is shown clearly by the famous *Capitulatio de partibus Saxoniae*, the exact date of which is unknown, but was perhaps 782. Among many other regulations, this document forbids the worship of springs, woods and trees, and prescribes that the same honour formerly paid to the pagan temples, or rather more, should now be paid to the Christian churches built in Saxony. It further makes the baptism of babies within a year from birth obligatory, under pain of heavy fines, and finally ordains that the death penalty shall be exacted from any who, according to the old customs, burn their dead, make human sacrifices, or burn 'witches', and similarly from all who betray their allegiance to the king, neglect to fast in Lent, refuse to be converted, or commit the crime of breaking into, robbing or burning a church.

And yet Charlemagne has gone down in history with a reputation for magnanimity that is no lie. He puts the art of diplomatic negotiation before that of war, and understands and carries it further.

He wreaks no wrath on the fallen, such as Desiderius, Queen Ansa, Tassilo of Bavaria, Widukind, Campulus and Sergius, the assailants of Leo III, and his eldest son Pippin, who conspired against him, provided that they will bend themselves to his absolute will, and are willing to renounce the world for the pious seclusion of a cloister. His method of accepting the surrender and assuring the obedience of the conquered, the oath of allegiance and taking of hostages, is at once simple and deeply religious. He is a great assimilator, and tries to reconcile the peoples he has subjected by his generosity, showering single individuals with gifts and favours, to make out of them his faithful vassals, be they Lombard, Saxon, Avar, or Bavarian, to frequent his palace and form the backbone of the administration of the conquered countries. Civil penetration either accompanies the military or follows it closely, with the institution of counties and bishoprics, and the foundation of palaces, churches and monasteries. And we find Arno of Salzburg and Paulinus of Aquileia going to preach among the Avars, the old Sturm, who has the soul of St Boniface, Willehad, and Lindger, doing likewise all over Saxony amid wars and insurrections; and the episcopal sees of Bremen, Münster and Paderborn are created.

For the spirit of his conquests is first and foremost Christian, and aims at the defence and propagation of Christianity. And we must realize fully that in this profession and practice of Christianity, there is no duplicity, no question of any base use of the faith to further political domination. Likewise we must not confuse Charlemagne's healthy conscience with the fear and trembling of the sinner, the ecstasy of the mystic, or the impassioned martyrdom of the ascetic. Nor must we be too surprised to find that this adorer of relics and founder of churches, this king of missionaries and great ecclesiastical legislator, should consider himself personally an exception to almost every rule, and refuse to tolerate any obstacle to his despotic will, and should be so far from being able to control his own exurberant vitality, that after repudiating two wives and being widowed by three, he brings four concubines in succession to share the royal bed. This king holds within himself the great forces of his age and develops them further; and the creation is still full of gravity and grandeur, even though it is inevitably the work of men, and has to give way to the demands of the men and of the times. Here the struggle was between Catholicism, or western Romanism on the one hand, and Byzantinism, Islam, and paganism on the other; and Catholicism was victorious.

Charlemagne was called David by his friends at court; and he must have been pleased with the name. He was a David indeed, with his divine mission, his love of poetry, and his human weaknesses; but he was less exalted than the King of Israel, and more calmly confident in himself and in the God who had called him to rule over the peoples of Europe. According to the biblical model, he had been anointed as both king and priest, so that he could write: 'Having received the government of our realm from the Lord in the bosom of the Church, we must struggle with all our might and with the help of Christ for its defence and exaltation, in order to be worthy of being called a good and faithful servant by Him, we, to whom this Church has been confided, amidst the stormy billows of this time, that we may govern it'. Thus it came about that the law-giver not only ruled that all his subjects should learn the *Credo* and the *Pater*, attend mass with compunction, pray, observe church holidays and fast days, and obey the Ten Commandments, all on pain of severe penalties for non-observance, but he also ordained that the clergy must explain to the faithful the nature of the pains of Hell, the joy of Paradise, the sins that lead to eternal damnation, and the virtues that open the gates of Heaven.

He considered it strictly within his province to watch over the conduct of the clergy, whether secular or regular, and to organize the ecclesiastical departments of his realm, to summon councils, and even to lay down their subjects for discussion, and to make a personal intervention with his friendly authority even beyond his own boundaries, in England, at the court of King Offa of Mercia, to forward the reform of the Church. Counts, bishops and abbots were all equally his officers of state. Peace and unity were the order of the day, and the western world of old invasions and new conquests had to be marked with the lasting stamp of Romanism and Christianity; for this purpose all possible forces had to be called into the fray. Charlemagne's mission did not even stop at the threshhold of St Peter's where he could send the Abbot of St Riquier, Angilbert, to warn Leo III (much is made clear when we consider the character of the man and the particular circumstances) to lead a pure life, observe the holy canons, rule the Church piously, and to remind him that his job was to pray to strengthen the Church internally by the teaching of the Catholic faith, and to leave the king to worry about the external defence of the Church against the pagan attacks.

The understanding of the faith was one of Charles' most lively spiritual interests. It was on his suggestion that the learned churchmen grouped around him helped him in his search for knowledge, which in this case was a question of belief and action. And he, secure in himself of his own possession of the truth, of his own omnipotence, had no hesitation, as might any Byzantine autocrat, in legislating on religious questions, quarrelling with Rome on matters of doctrine, and imposing his own will, especially when important political reasons were involved along with his deep conscientiousness and the purity of his faith. Thus, he had it stated in the *Credo*, in contrast to the dogma of the Church, that the Holy Ghost proceeded from the Father and the Son. He had the Spanish heresy of Adoptianism, which was threatening the integrity of the faith and the peace of Aquitaine at one and the same time, first discussed, then combatted and quashed. He attacked iconoclasm and image-worship with equal violence, when the repeal of the iconoclastic decrees by the Empress Irene had temporarily brought Byzantium and Rome near to reconciliation.

Among those who frequented his company and competed in singing his praises, Theodulf saw in Charlemagne the great protector of the Church:

Sit dominus et pater, sit res et sacerdos.
Per te pontifices iura sacra tenent.

but Paulinus of Aquileia described him with greater truth and accuracy when he wrote:

Arma es pontificum, spes et defensio cleri.

In this new infancy of the west, as in a patriarchal society, in which both civil government and priesthood reside indissolubly in the head of the community, the universal provisions of the king regulated not merely the peace, purity of customs and the welfare of the souls in its care, but also every moment of earthly life. There was no matter, it may be said, that was not covered by his ordinances, general or particular, and by the legislation of the Capitularies: law and army, activity of *comites* and *missi*, weights, measures and coinage, industry and commerce, agriculture and management of property, all ordered with a variety, generosity and care for detail that yet reveal a primitive and elementary quality far removed from the norm of Roman Law.

For many years the king's own life was marked by this simplicity. He had no capital where he resided permanently. He was rich in villas and forests scattered all over his kingdom, managed by the Queen, with the help of the high court officials. When he was not at war or travelling, he retired, like his Merovingian predecessors, to one or another of his domains, at Quierzy, Attigny, Compiègne, Verberie, Héristal, Thionville or Worms, in the company of his vast and splendid family, his trusted friends, who were favoured by his company and his generosity. And there he gave himself up to his favourite pastimes: hot baths, hunting, conversation and lessons from the scholars of his court, Peter of Pisa, Paulinus of Aquileia, Paul the Deacon, and Alcuin, who discussed theology, grammar, and dialectic with him, and read him the classical authors along with their own poetry. But in time he felt the need of more spacious, permanent and luxurious surroundings; so in the last years of his reign he began the construction of the palaces of Nimes, Ingelheim, and Aachen.

This last, from Christmas 794 on, was more or less the habitual residence of the king. He had been present at the construction of the palace himself; under his eyes the octagonal chapel had gone up down below—the shrine of St Martin's cloak—with its pilasters, its rounded arches, its columns and capitals, and the bronze balustrades, whose pattern and materials had been furnished by the old Roman buildings of Francia and Italy. Higher up on a hill, was the *aula regalis*, which is almost entirely lost to us, except for what we read of it in the writers of the time, who speak glowingly of the huge reception room with the throne, the apartments of the royal family, richly equipped with furniture, draperies and carpets, with precious objects, gold and silver tables, views of Rome and Constantinople and a map of the world, the treasure room, the wardrobe for materials, clothes, arms and tapestries, the library, the archives, and the baths with the enormous fish pond and its marble steps. Between the chapel and the palace there was a vast courtyard with porticos and pavillions, and in the centre an equestrian statue of Theodoric in gilded bronze that Charlemagne had brought from Ravenna. All around there were flowering gardens, and the park reached as far as the eye could see, with its old trees, meadows, running water, and everywhere deer, wild boar, stags and does. It is not surprising that what with the devotion of his courtiers, the faithfulness to the classical and biblical tradition, the sincere admiration for the creation, and the unusual beauty of the place, that it inspired in the poets' minds the comparison with the temple of Solomon, and Virgil's account of the foundation of Carthage.

Around the king there were grouped the apocrisiary, who superintended ecclesiastical affairs and the chancellery, the Palatine count, who presided over civil affairs, in particular the administration of the law, and all the high officials dedicated to his personal service, in his treasury, kitchens, cellars, stables, household and hunting field. A whole world was in animation around the palace. Christian and Jewish merchants came to do business there. *Missi dominici* and counts came and went, as did ambassadors from all over the known world, from the King of England and the Emir of Cordova, from the Pope and the Caliph of Bagdad, Aaron the Wise, from the Khan of the Avars and the Augustus of the Eastern Empire, all with their gifts, overtures and exotic garments. Tribute of gold and silver flowed in from the subject peoples, and the money collected in his kingdom from fines, taxes, tolls, and the income from the royal demesnes. And here conquered chieftains would be baptized, great banquets and solemn ceremonies held, in which the king of the simple life and homely Frankish habits, appeared surrounded by all the lavish display of his court.

The greatest minds from all over the kingdom and the western world flocked to the school, or academy, at the palace, Adelhard, Theodulf, Angilbert, and Alcuin among them. Conquered, conquerors and foreigners all shared in the cult of beauty and knowledge, both Roman and Christian, and in their devotion to a man who was almost the symbol of Romanism and Christianity; and those of them who were far away were present in their letters and their verses. It was not from any scholarly quirk, adulation or ambition that Charlemagne was known as David, Alcuin as Horace, Angilbert as Homer, Moduin as Ovid, and Eginhard as Beseleel, the wonderful craftsman of the Old Testament. It was rather because in the fervour of their spiritual life they felt that they were lifted right out of time, and could commune with the great men of all ages. In this breath of new life, with the richness and serenity of mind that was theirs, they turned once more to the ancients, and found there the clear and polished expression that they sought. And in this new spirit the undecipherable muddle of the old texts was sorted out from codices and parchments, and the shining model of the minuscule, a reflection of the regained serenity that was theirs, was substituted. Prayerbooks illuminated in purple and gold were created in all their incomparable beauty. And, by the king's will, this love of beauty and learning was spread from the palace to the churches and monasteries, even in the remotest towns.

In the court circle, where all the highest intellect of Europe was gathered, and in Rome itself, a need had already been expressed, and a name pronounced, to designate the priest-king, who had broadened the boundaries of the Christian world, and assumed its temporal, civil and spiritual government at one and the same time. The name was 'emperor'. In this title and the need for it, the old and the new were merged and the consciousness of the Christian and Roman unity of Europe was expressed. Its actual fulfilment was accelerated by two events at this time. A woman, the Empress Irene, had first blinded her son, and then laid claim to the throne of the Caesars. A pope, Leo III, a man of humble birth and no great spirit, had been kidnapped, accused of immoral conduct, violently attacked, and had fled to Paderborn to his natural protector, Charles. Then, when the pope had cleared himself by oath and been fully exculpated before a synod summoned and presided over by the king, on December 25,

800, the renewal of the empire was accomplished in St Peter's, by papal consecration and the acclamation of the people: 'To Charles, most pious Augustus, crowned by God, great and peaceful emperor, long life and victory'. The final seal had been set on the arduous century-long creation of the Merovingians, the sons of Pippin and Charlemagne.

Two days before the coronation a monk of Saint Saba and another from the Mount of Olives in Jerusalem had presented the king, on behalf of the patriarch, with 'the keys of the Holy Sepulchure and those of the Mount of Sion with a banner'. It was a symbolic act of homage, a new halo of sanctity bound on the brow of the king, who had extended his protection beyond the seas and who was to protect the Christians of Palestine, Syria, Egypt and Tunisia, in a generous spirit of co-operation with Aaron the Wise.

With the coronation, the great period of his work may be considered closed. There is no rest for the army: the fighting continues on the frontiers, and the defence of the border lands is organized; a long war in the Adriatic finally forces even Byzantium to recognize the empire. But the time of heroism is over. Shadows great and small darken the splendour of the sunset; the corrupt life of the court, and of the very daughters of the king, who were forbidden to marry because he could not do without their company; the death of one daughter and two sons, Charles and Pippin; his weakness in his declining years for Madelgarde and Gersuinda, whose fate after his death he worries and chafes over continually; and above all the threat of the development of private vassalage, which becomes more and more marked as the great wars draw to a close, of the free men who have lost their position and attach themselves to men in power, without regard to their duty to the army, and of the military aristocracy, who, having made their way to the top in the field, now put the resources of the state to their own uses.

Then came the end. Now old, and of uncertain health, Charlemagne sent for Louis, King of Aquitaine, the only son of Hildegarde's left him, and in the presence of the great he took him into partnership in the empire, and established him as heir to his title and crowned him with the imperial diadem. After sending him back to Aquitaine, he left, as usual, to go hunting not far from Aachen, and stayed there until the end of autumn. While wintering in the palace he was attacked by a violent fever, which he tried in vain to get the better of, as he had others, by rigorous fasting and occasional drinks. He died after seven days of illness on the morning of January 28, 814, at the age of seventy-two.

Although long before he had expressed the wish to be laid in St Denis beside his father Pippin and his mother Bertrada, his body was buried instead, in an old magnificent marble sarcophagus, in the basilica that he himself had built near the palace. The inscription read simply as follows: 'In this grave lies the body of Charles, great and orthodox Emperor, who nobly enlarged and gladly ruled the kingdom of the Franks for forty-six years. He died a septuagenarian in the year of Our Lord DCCCXIV, in the seventh indiction, five days before the calends of February'.

When the great man was gone, an unknown poet raised this lament for all men:

A solis ortu usque ad occidua
litora maria planctus pulsat pectora.
Heu mihi misero!
Ultra marina agmina tristitia
tetigit ingens cum merore nimio.
Heu mihi misero!
Franci, Romani atque cuncti creduli
luctu punguntur et magna molestia
Heu mihi misero!
Iam iam non cessant lacrimarum flumina,
Nam plangit orbis interitum Karoli.
Heu mihi misero!

A great light had gone out indeed, a word been spoken for always, and an eternal and irrevocable time in history was accomplished. And what was its significance? Reflecting upon this period, we are struck by an unusual contrast. From one point of view we see a whole world full of exalted spiritual interests: religious fervour, passionate study, love of beauty and thirst for conquest, and together with these, the speedy and enlightened provision of civil ordinances. From the other side, the political, social and economic angle, we see a rudimentary and natural world that was all the circumstances of the time would permit. In the whole of Gaul there was probably no town with more than ten thousand inhabitants, and ninety per cent of the population worked in the fields. The king's life, as we have already noticed, was patriarchal, moving as he did from one residence to another, from district to district, with his women and children, his archives and his treasure. The organization of the state was completely elementary and personal, with the two independent kingdoms of Aquitaine and Italy, the apocrisiary and the count of the palace, the officers of court, the counts and the *missi*, the royal council, the synods and assemblies. The oath of allegiance and the consignment of hostages by the conquered took the place of good armies and fortifications. The national and universal laws, and the detailed provisions of the capitularies, revealed the primitiveness rather than the maturity of the legal system. And yet, because of the presence and vitality of the spiritual values, because of the talk of empire, almost unconsciously, and wrongly, we ascribe a stable political foundation to this time in history, and weep for the fall of the Carolingian empire, as though a thing of beauty and greatness had been lost.

The unknown poet could weep, as he looked into the future:

Vae tibi, Roma, Romanoque populo
amisso summo glorioso Karolo.
Heu mihi misero!
Vae tibi, sola, formonsa Italia,
cunctisque tuis tam honestis urbibus.
Heu mihi misero!
Francia diras perpessa iniurias
nullum iam talem dolorem sustinuit,
heu mihi misero,
quando augustum facundumque Karolum
in Aquisgrani glebis terrae tradidit.

The Patriarch of Europe was dead, and the west was faced with the most difficult of tasks. The converted pagans were being assimilated. The military aristocracies, who had come to the fore through decades of war, prepared to reconstruct the whole structure from the foundations up, amid enormous upheavals and disturbances, to transform the mass of summarily Christianized and romanized peoples into a civil society with local and national states. New invasions were threatened by the Norman, Slav and Hungarian pagans, who had by now begun to recover from the Christian conquest, but were finally to be brought into the orbit of Christian civilization.

This was the world created by Charlemagne's reign and his empire. It is no stable political entity, but a *regnum Christianitatis,* as Alcuin wrote of it, a *Christiana religio,* as we read on the coins of the new emperor. It is the end of the old west of invasions, of Germanic appropriations, and of attempted oppression by the eastern empire. It is the expression of those civil and religious values that gave Charlemagne his title. It forms the foundation of Europe, the first conscious manifestation of the united Christian and Roman West.

CHAPTER 9

MEDIEVAL PARTICULARISM

ALBERIC II

Certain great concepts, such as the sovereignty of the state, the compass of public and private law, of civil and religious life, are by now so thoroughly a part of the modern consciousness, that we find it almost impossible that they were not equally clear in times other than our own. The time in our history in which such an awareness hardly existed was the period roughly between the close of the IX century, or the end of the Carolingian empire, and the second half of the X century, more particularly the coronation of Otto I.

Charles' empire, as we have seen, was the first great manifestation of united Christian Europe against Arabs, Byzantines, and pagans from beyond the eastern and northern frontiers. It was a kind of a rough draft of Europe, a provisional arrangement of nations, or rather of military Germanic societies, distinct among themselves but not yet properly integrated with the old Roman populations, superimposed, not rooted, on the countries they had conquered. Now in the course of the ninth century, the empire was subjected to a process of disintegration due to difficulties with the line of succession, the local military forces, and the threat of new invaders. To one who cares to look at the political picture of that time, this disintegration of the empire is clearly shown by the emergence of new kingdoms from its very heart: France, Germany, Italy, Upper and Lower Burgundy, and by its own progressive dislocation from Italy to France and Germany.

With the abdication of Charles the Fat, the last illusion is gone; the principle of authority, on which the Christian world has been ruled until now, has failed; and the last descendants of the Carolingians, Arnulf of Carinthia, Berengar of Friuli, the Spoletans and the Burgundians, all plunge into a desperate struggle to snatch the crowns of the Italian kingdom and the empire from each other's hands. And we must note that the empire is no longer pervaded by the noble spirit and intention to serve the Christian government of the world. It is now coveted for reasons of prestige and power, that are more or less well-founded, and for the opportunity that it offers to influence Rome and lay hands on its Patrimony.

This is the beginning of the most ill-famed period of the Middle Ages, that of feudal anarchy, the age of lead, or iron, as it was called. Once the veil of the Carolingian empire is torn aside, and the papacy that consecrated it and received its support has declined, the profound transformation of European society that has taken place in one century is discovered. Personal bonds and beneficiary concessions have taken the place of the almost nonexistent authority of the state. Positions of national power are more and more frequently usurped or transferred. Thus the political reality of the time, and the protagonists of this period, are not the kingdoms or the empire, but the great feudatory lords, who compete for the various crowns.

In the absence of satisfactory leaders, the mutual agreement between the organs of civil and religious life comes to an end, and these two aspects of life, needful of each other as they are, interpenetrate and grow together into an inextricable tangle. The laity sets its hands on the ecclesiastical institutions and patrimony, founds churches and monasteries privately and uses them for its own ends, either for money or by nominating bishops and abbots with no regard to age, vocation or preparation, but merely according to their own family and political convenience, and further by endowing them with power over the public and claiming feudal homage from them. In a word the prestige and the riches of the Church are caught in the secular net, put to the service of the feudal system and absorbed into the feudal world. Towers, castles, and walled enclosures shoot up everywhere, ready to receive the Arabs, Hungarians, Slavs and Normans, who overrun Italy, France and Germany, periodically sacking towns, churches and monasteries as they go with impunity.

Small wonder then, that in such conditions the whole of Europe has the same spectacle of small scale and unceasing war to offer everywhere, that all the basest passions are let loose and nourished to the full, and that even the clergy, the depositary of the faith and of culture, is so secularized that it becomes barely distinguishable from the laity.

To be shocked or horrified by such a state of affairs is as far from our task as it could be. To understand the development of the Middle Ages we have had to chase from our minds the illusion of a vast, solid and powerful Carolingian empire, organically constituted, that collapses at the death of its founder through the ignorance and inertia of kings, the ambition of princes, and the pressure of foreign races. Just so, in reverse, we shall have to make ourselves look with sympathy even at this tragic age, so full of tumult and suffering, to decide whether we are witnessing in it some kind of universal madness of mankind, and the loss of all noble moral and civil principles, or whether this particularism, this rise of small local powers that obtains all over Europe, feudal and non-feudal, between the ninth and tenth century, is not rather the expression of a desperate and heroic effort to rise out of the darkness into the light, to create something new and great.

For obvious reasons this crisis of authority had its most violent repercussions and more serious consequences in the very centre of Catholicism. Rome was harassed in the ninth century by two great evils: externally, by the attacks and the pillaging of the Arabs; internally by the confused ferment of local activity, in particular the aristocracy of the Curia, who wanted to seize power, to ensnare and dominate the very authority from which they derived their strength.

A shudder of horror spread throughout the west when in 846 the Arabs made their way up the Tiber and, flooding through the country, sacked the basilicas of St Peter and St Paul. The blame was laid at the emperor's door, for failing in his obligation to defend the Church and the Christian republic; and in a solemn diet presided over by the Emperor Lothar himself, it was decided to fortify St Peter's with a sum to be levied from all the subjects of the empire. This was the beginning of a recovery. But it was no vague recovery of the empire and the Christian west, but a particular, localized Italian and Roman one. Towers were built on both banks of the Tiber, and the river was made unnavigable with chains. The burden of the construction of the Leonine City was shared between Rome, the lesser regions of the territory, the *domuscultae* or papal estates, the public funds of the Romans, and the ecclesiastical institutions. And when in 849 a Saracen fleet put in an appearance at the mouth of the Tiber, it was confronted by the ships of the Italian league in battle array, from Rome, Amalfi, Naples and Gaeta. These ships, which had shortly before received the papal benediction from Leo IV, quickly moved to the attack and scattered the enemy fleet in confusion.

For the first time in centuries, the city saw prisoners of war toiling within her walls to make the seat of the Apostle more beautiful and more invincible. A triumphal hymn rises from the inscriptions that adorned the gates of the Leonine city:

Qui venis ac vadis decus hoc attende, viator,
Quod quartus struxit nunc Leo Papa libens;

'You who come and go, look traveller, at this glory that Pope Leo has just built so gladly.'

Romanus, Francus, Bardusque viator et omnis
Hoc qui intendit opus cantica digna cantet;

'Roman, Frank, Lombard, and every passer-by who sees this work, sing worthy canticles.'

People of all races who crowded around St Peter's in a surge of faith were called to witness the noble enterprise in which she exalted:

Roma, caput orbis, splendor, spes, aurea Roma;

'Rome, golden Rome, the head, the glory and the hope of the world.'

But the hymn was premature. Throughout his twenty-five years as emperor, from 850-875, Louis II laboured in vain to put an end to the conflagration in Southern Italy, which was continually breaking out afresh. He tried to bind into one alliance, which would have been an inflexible one, those Southern potentates who were the first enemies of both themselves and Italy, being perpetually at loggerheads with each other, and anything but unwilling to make alliances and to trade with the Saracens. Worse was to come, when under Charles the Bald and Charles the Fat, the empire was reduced to a distant dream. Pope John VIII, who had formerly announced his naval victory at Capo Circeo triumphantly to Louis and his Queen, Engilberga, could now do no more than send desperate letters pleading for help and describing the pitiable state of the deserted countryside, and the destruction, pillage, and abandonment of the churches and monasteries right up to the gates of Rome.

The most tragic moment was when Docibile, the Duke of Gaeta, called the Saracens of Agropolis to his aid, to defend himself against the outrages perpetrated by the Count Paldolf of Capua. The infidels, to use the imperfect Latin of the monk Benedict of Saint Andrew's of Mt. Soracte—'*veniente ad fluvium qui dicitur Garinganu, apprehenderunt turres et facta est eorum habitatio*'; in other words, they camped at the mouth of the Garigliano, on its right bank, and made a fortification on a hill, perhaps the Monte d'Argento of today, where they kept their wives and children, their prisoners and plunder, and whence they could move freely over the sea and the river, which they scoured with their ships, or over the beautiful countryside around them, which they ravaged with their raids and fires. There followed years of unprecedented violence. In Benedict's words again: '*Regnaverunt Agarenis in Romano regno anni XXX; redacta est terra in solitudine, et monasteria sancta sine laudes*'. Amid flames and plundering the great lights of civilization, the monasteries, were put out: Saint Vincent's at Volturno, Saint Clement's of Casauria, Farfa, after seven years of courageous defence on the part of the abbot Peter, and Monte Cassino, where the abbot, Bertarius, fell to a Saracen's sword before the altar of St Martin. Several regions of the Roman duchy and the Sabina were firmly occupied, their countryside devastated and deserted, and Rome was isolated in a pitiable and fearsome solitude. Rather than any organic conquest dominated by some political and military principle, this was systematic brigandage with nothing but booty in view. What rendered it so disastrous was the atomism, the particularism, so characteristic of the times, the lack of any consciousness that went beyond the narrow sphere of personal and local interests.

Now between the wane of the ninth century and the beginning of the tenth, the first signs of recovery appear. There is a raid by Guy of Spoleto, who is tempted by the imperial crown, against the Saracen lair on the Garigliano. There is an alliance of the princes of Benevento and Capua, Naples and Amalfi, though it is put on the defensive by Gaeta's obstinate alliance with the Saracens. There is a sporadic, but unplanned, action here and there in Tuscia, the Sabina, and the Roman duchy, that dislodges the Arabs from the places they have occupied and sends them running to their last post of defence on the Garigliano. Then, through long and difficult negotiations, we come to the formation of the great league that was to put an end to the conflict. It was the Capuans who took the initiative, by turning to Byzantium for help. A powerful fleet arrived in the Tyrrhenian Sea under the command of the imperial patrician Nicholas Picingli. The imperial patricianship, which was conferred on Landolf of Capua, Gregory of Naples, and John of Gaeta, was well used in rewarding the former for his devotion, and in tearing the other two away from their Saracen alliance. Guaimar, Prince of Salerno, joined the league also; and at the beginning of the summer of 915 the allied army, its ranks swollen with Apulians and Calabrians, encamped on the left bank of the Garigliano. Meanwhile, there were more negotiations going on in Rome. To be more precise, as the celebrated document of Monte d'Argento allows us to be, they were between the pope and the Roman aristocracy, who were officially at his command, principally Theophylact and John, both of them Roman senators, and then the dukes Gratian, Gregory, and Anthony, the high officers of the Curia, and various other members of the nobility.

When the rewards had been fixed and the agreements made, the Romans, at the command of the pope, swore the solemn oath: 'We swear to you that we will never have peace with them (the Saracens), until *we have exterminated them from all Italy*. Again, we promise to all those named above, by Christ Our Lord and by the virtues of the saints and by all the sacraments of the faith, that we will fight the Saracens with all our might and in every way we can, and we will try to destroy them; and we swear that from now on we will not be at peace with them in any way.' It is possible, as some people think, that *donec illos deleamus de tota Italia* is merely a rhetorical amplification. But we like to read this robust expression and the name of Italy in the oath with which the people from a large part of the peninsula overcome their old rivalries to come together for a while to fight their common enemy. Immediately after this treaty, in June, 915, a powerful army under John X and Alberic, Marquess of Camerino and Duke of Spoleto, went down to the Garigliano and set up camp on the right bank of the river, taking the Saracens in a grip of iron, while the fleet of Nicholas Picingli, probably flanked by the ships of Naples, Gaeta and Rome, shut off the escape by sea. For three months the enemies faced each other. When battle was joined at last, the Arabs were forced to take refuge in their citadel, then to set fire to their houses and attempt a desperate sortie. The Saracen lair, which had spelt destruction to so much of Italy, was finally destroyed. The Marquess Alberic, according to Benedict of St Andrew, *factus est leo fortissimus inter Sarracenos*. John X, writing some time after the battle to Herman, Archbishop of Cologne, was still trembling with pride at having exposed his breast to the enemy swords and having led the soldiers to the attack twice in person.

This then, was the first mark of recovery of Italy and the west. These were the men of the time, great laymen and priests, who stood side by side in worldly government and the use of arms.

In the treaty that precedes the battle of Garigliano we meet the protagonists of the new history of Rome. All the disintegration in the city that for nearly a century had followed on the death of Charlemagne—what with the Saracen attacks, the ambitions of the Church with regard to Southern Italy, the disputes over the papal and imperial succession, the violence and assassinations—still had a constructive significance that was quite clear and truly elevated. It was the endeavour, confused, unconscious and instinctive, as you wish, to found in the universal disorder a more limited and stronger principle of order. It was the creation and the progressive conquest of civil and political consciousness. In Rome this new awareness was personified in the name and the offspring of Theophylact, *senator Romanorum, vestararius et magister militum*, the highest officer of the papal curia, who took the oath against the Arabs at the head of the Roman aristocracy, and immediately after him, in his daughter Marozia, the patrician and senatress, as our sources call her.

It is impossible to pronounce Marozia's name without thinking of the unambiguous expression that the Bishop of Cremona used to describe her a few decades later: '*Scortum impudens satis*'. We cannot speak of her without remembering all the great women of the ninth and tenth centuries: the Empress Engilberga, wife and counsellor of Louis II, Ageltrude, the widow of Guy of Spoleto, who saved Rome for her son Lambert, and had the corpse of Pope Formosus brought to trial, Bertha, the wife first of Theobald of Provence, then of Adalbert of Tuscany, her daughter Ermingard, the beautiful Marquess of Ivrea, and lastly, shining in the light of her defenceless youth that was so atrociously misused, and then with the splendour of the imperial crown, Adelaide, the tragic widow of Lothar, who was deceived by Berengar II and set free by the Saxon Otto I, King of Germany.

We must confess that these figures have always inspired sharp curiosity in our mind. Was the number of these women, and the dominant part they played in the history of the west a mere casual coincidence? Or was it not rather intimately linked with the life of the times, to their wild exuberance in which passion and vigour were intensified? And related to a particular time in history when women, trained as they were beside men to face action and danger, and perhaps more prodigal of their love than they could have been in their place as wives and mothers, were able by a gift of nature and the favour of circumstances to impose the rule of their own ambition in a masculine fashion. There is perhaps some truth in this hypothesis. In any case, we have no faith in the chroniclers who make the fate of the world depend on the despotic and corrupt will of a woman. This too is simple pragmatism, which looks, very humanly, for a single idol for its devotion, a single target for its hate, and a convenient expedient to recount and to judge. But it does not take into consideration all the forces, noble and ignoble, that are all the time pushing, supporting and influencing the hidden will of those in power. And when the same chroniclers tell tales of these heroines having the most scandalous love affairs, we can be sure that they are lying. Not that we can in each and every case be guarantors of their chastity, which at bottom is no concern of ours; but because, firstly, theirs is the voice of a new age in politics and religion, which judges the past with the exaggerations and falsifications expected of all new conquerors; and secondly, they are working from a too shakily legitimate conception of history, and therefore find the causes of the most serious political reversals in the frustrated sensuality of a woman.

According to the contemporary sources, Benedict and Liudprand, Marozia was the concubine of Alberic of Spoleto, the youthful mistress or the adulterous wife in the arms of Pope Sergius III, and was married three times, through ambition for power, and in open contempt for every law, human and divine. Certainly, we know that she had three husbands in succession, that she had no less than six children, and that she died when little more than forty years old no later than 937. All her marriages were political in character. Her first husband, Alberic of Spoleto and Camerino, was a man new to power, who by agreement with the part of the Roman aristocracy led by Theophylact, had taken Sergius III, panting for vengeance, back to Rome, and was to fight beside John X on the Garigliano only a few years later. When Theophylact and Alberic were gone, Marozia found herself at odds with John X, who nevertheless owed his tiara to her family, and with his brother Peter, who was a member of the nobility. The pope was seeking his own emancipation, and trying to save himself from the Hungarians, under the protection of Hugh of Provence, who had recently landed in Italy. Marozia wanted to consolidate her own power by giving her hand in marriage to Guy of Tuscany, Hugh's half-brother. So with the help of the Tuscan army, amid uproar from the citizens, the Lateran was invaded, Peter killed in front of his brother, and the pope himself thrown into prison and suffocated with a pillow. In his vigorous and ungrammatical lament, the monk of St Andrew's exclaims: *'Subiugatus est Romam potestative in manu femine, sicut in propheta legimus: "Feminini dominabunt Hierusalem".'* The Church, too, was subjugated, and saw popes created at the will of the senatress, the last of them being her own son, John XI.

It is here, not in her love affairs, that the historical interest lies; this that makes the greatness and importance of Marozia. And it is true greatness, even if her methods of government were, according to the circumstances of the time, somewhat remote from our own political norms. In this capable, ambitious and energetic woman we find the personification of the noble family tradition and the political will of the Roman aristocracy, and indeed of Rome herself, as centre of the west and fount of the imperial consecration. She paid her debt to fame continually with her vigilance, audacity and strong will. So far was her domination from being tied to womanly vanities and lusts, that it remained intact, indeed stronger than ever, in the time of Alberic II, the creature of her blood and of her spirit.

The end, we are told, came about in a violent manner. Being widowed for the second time, Marozia was careful to take precautions against the dangers that threatened her, by offering her hand to Hugh of Provence, King of Italy. A royal bride, the mistress of the papacy, she opened the way to the empire for herself and her consort. A daughter of hers was about to marry a son of the Byzantine Emperor Romanus Lecapenus. The new dynastic foundation was reaching its full strength just as the Carolingian tradition was fading out. The new Rome was to be united once more to the Roman greatness of the Orient.

But the reply from Byzantium came too late. According to Liudprand the wedding celebrations were in process in the powerful fortress of the Castel Sant'Angelo, Marozia's home, when Alberic was slapped in the face by his new father-in-law. Infuriated by this insult, he is said to have gathered the Romans around him and harangued them thus: 'The dignity of the city of Rome has been brought to such a pass of stupidity as to obey the commands of prostitutes. What is there, indeed, more shameful or more base, than that for the incest of a single woman all the citizens of Rome should be destroyed? Shall those who were once the slaves of Rome, the Burgundians, now give orders to the Romans? If he has slapped me, his son-in-law, the minute he is received as a guest, what do you think he will do to you as time goes on? Do you perhaps know nothing of the greed and pride of the Burgundians?' The bells rang by their hundreds, the citizens rushed to arms, raised the battle cry, and stormed the castle, whence a terrified Hugh escaped by letting himself down to earth on a rope. It has been suggested that the king intended to blind his son-in-law. However, there is something larger and more complex at the root of this Roman revolution. The speech that Liudprand puts in Alberic's mouth has all the marks of a modest rhetorical exercise; but this does not mean that it echoes the deep, substantial motives for the revolt any less accurately. Whatever idea we may have of the way of life of the Romans in the tenth century, it is clear that this mature woman, who was marrying for the third time through lust for power, and marrying in spite of the Church's condemnation of the union as incestuous, was repugnant to their religious and moral conscience. The Roman spirit was not extinguished. Here it came into its own again and gloried in its resistance to the woman's rule, which was made the more humiliating by the violent and cunning complicity of the Burgundian foreigner and intruder. Rome herself was struck to the heart by the insult and the atrocious designs of the king.

With his flight, the revolution was accomplished. The *patricia*, the *senatrix*, was closely guarded by her son, and disappeared mysteriously several years later. The pope, John XI, was relegated to obscurity by his brother, and was only allowed to re-emerge to die. The young man, who in the hour of danger had spoken the word that all Romans had in the bottom of their hearts, though none knew, dared, or were able to pronounce it, took the title of *Prince and Senator of all the Romans*, and took the government into his own hands.

He represented both the dynastic tradition and the revolution.

His blood was that of Theophylact and Marozia, the flower of the Roman aristocracy that had acquired both understanding and power in the offices of the Curia, in the hardship of the struggle against the Arabs, of the imperial successions and the Formosian ordinances. But he no longer took his title, as had his maternal grandfather, from the offices he exercised in the papal administration, treasurer, master of the army, nor did he use the honorary appellation, *Senator Romanorum*. The chain was broken. He claimed for himself as senator to represent and have effective power over all the Romans. He was the prince who, without constitutional definition, derived his power from himself, from his own dynastic tradition, and from the Romans who had heard his words and followed him in the uprising.

The apparent anarchy, which was in reality a fruitful exercise of force, a deepening of consciousness, an attempt at a political creation at the dissolution of the Carolingian empire, had given rise to a hierarchy of narrow limits, that had yet grown from the ground, was well rooted to the earth and resistant to every disturbance. The nobles wearing the robes of judges and assessors, who met with Alberic in his palace at the Holy Apostles, where Piazza Colonna now stands, and who by his will ruled over the Sabina, or one or another part of the Roman duchy, were all lords of castles in the Roman territory. And the people of the alleyways, stirred by his assiduous and energetic appeal, took up arms with confidence, and began once more to work and trade with a will.

When in the solitude of Mount Soracte the monk of St Andrew's went over the happenings of a few decades before, he did not know whether Alberic should be more execrated for his tyranny and oppression of the popes, or admired for his active and devout spirit; and with indiscriminate simplicity he juxtaposed the one attitude with the other in alternate accents of hate and praise. He celebrated him as a worthy successor to his father in his personal valour: '*Vultum nitentem sicut pater eius, grandevus virtus eius*', and condemned him for the harshness of his despotism: '*Erat enim terribilis nimis, et aggrabatum est iugum super Romanos et in Sancte Sedis apostolice. Electus Marinus papa non audebat adtingere aliquis extro iusso Alberici principi*'. And yet this was the same '*gloriosus princeps*', who by inspiration of the Holy Ghost gave his help to Odo of Cluny to reduce the corrupt monks to the discipline they had once known, and enriched the monasteries with large donations as well as founding new ones. Nor could it have displeased this writer, who was to close his chronicle with an invective against Rome in her oppression by Otto I, to record that at Alberic's command, the city gates were barred against Otto's Germans and the

Burgundians of Hugh of Provence: '*A regibus terre Langobardorum seu Transalpine nullus robore suis temporibus in Romanae finibus non sunt ingressi*'.

All these manifestations, his religious piety, his despotism, his oppression of the popes, his unshakable firmness against foreign potentates, which excited such contradictory feelings in the breast of the chronicler, are now illuminated for us by a single light, and help to explain the significance of the figure of Alberic to us.

The most terrible stories are told about religious life in general and monastic life in particular in the tenth century; nor will our systematic optimism dare to deny the tradition. Indeed we read of monks and abbots who lived a secular life, of their wives or concubines, of the property of the Church being split up and becoming a family inheritance, of feasts and debauchery, hatred and quarrels ended by swords or poison. Perhaps the most scandalous example of this dissolution was given only a few kilometres from Rome, in the imperial monastery of Farfa. After it had been destroyed by the Saracens, its huge estates had fallen into chaos and fallen prey to the rebellion of serfs and the usurpation of the powerful. About twenty years after the battle of Garigliano, it looked as if it was being revitalized by the work of Abbot Roffred, when he was poisoned by two of his monks. Their names were Hildebrand and Campone, and the latter, born of a good Sabine family, had entered the convent as a young man and had been taught grammar and medicine by the abbot himself. Once the ground was cleared, Campone obtained the position of abbot, by dint of large 'gifts' to Hugh of Provence, and had taken to ruling like a real feudal lord, surrounded by his wife, one Liuza, his ten children, and his vassals. Hildebrand did the same for his part, when, after coming into too close competition with Campone, he had established his own seat in the castle of Fermo and had appropriated the lands of the March. What became of the rest of the land, the splendid fabrics and the treasures and the imperial charters with their gold seals, it is all too easy to imagine.

There is no doubt about it: the war had turned the monastic orders unside down, and violated the sanctity of the cloister and holiness of hearts along with the walls of the monastery. The world in which the monks and priests had had to penetrate to exercise their ministry, the almost elemental world of personal ties, defence and attack, had overwhelmed and ensnared them, reduced them to themselves, and stimulated and let loose in them too the primitive forces of instinct. Alberic was clearly neither an ascetic or a reformer; and yet, he had more than the universal kind of piety he shared with the lords of the time, which on the one side reflected their faith, on the other their tendency to lay their hands on the

Church. For his policy coincided in quite a special way with that of the greatest reformer of the age, Odo of Cluny, in that he aimed to hamstring anarchy, re-establish peace and order with a firm hand, and guarantee the city safety and adequate provisions through efficient administration of the surrounding territory. Hence come the donations, foundations and reforms entrusted to the fervent work of the Abbot of Cluny, of which the chronicler of St Andrew's tells us. Hence, too—and the coincidence is not a fortuitous one—the reform he imposed on the monastery of Farfa by force of arms. The monks of Cluny, who had been sent there to re-establish discipline under Campone, had fled terror-stricken when they had just escaped being murdered. Alberic then intervened in person with an army. He chased out the abbot, put a certain brother Dagobert of Cuma in his place, took back the fugitives, and had the stolen goods restored to the monastery. This was the final action in his conquest of the Sabina, which he had accomplished a few years before; an action in which political and religious interests, pressures within the principality and the universal exigencies of religion were interwoven and merged together.

His demeanour towards the Holy See and the more or less declared aspirants to the empire was analagous in a way, and dictated by analogous necessities. It was a demeanour completely the opposite of Marozia's, when she had dreamed of dominating the Holy See, and at the same time binding to her dynasty the greatness of the Italian kingdom and the universality of the empire. If one looked back, at that time, at events in Rome over the past century, Church and empire, in their successions and their reciprocal relations, must have appeared as permanent breeders of disorder. And Alberic struck at the root of the evil: he shut the gates to Hugh and Otto, he chose men for the papacy who were worthy of it and devoted to him, giving the liberty to exercise their spiritual ministry in the Catholic world, but cutting them out of all political interference. What seemed to Benedict of St Andrew's a yoke of tyranny was, for the moment, the indispensable condition of proper civil organization in Rome and in the duchy.

We can see the way the times were developing, and the plan matured in Alberic's mind over the years, in his last political action. A few years before, John X, the victor of the battle of the Garigliano, had tried to introduce a system of papal government supported by the lay military force of his brother Peter, and he had seen him fall to the assassins of Marozia's and Guy of Tuscany's army. Now the tendency was to reverse the procedure: instead of a lay principality, the absorption of the supreme ecclesiastic power. Alberic had a son, who he had named Octavian, perhaps prophetically. When he realized that his last hour was come, he had himself carried to St

Peter's, called all the Roman nobles round him, and made them swear to him that on the death of Agapetus II they would elect his son as pope. And in the middle of December, 955, Octavian brought together in his own person the supreme religious and civil powers of Rome, according to the promise. Medieval particularism had thus reached its zenith; the universal power of the Apostle, and the government of *aurea Roma,* of the *caput mundi,* were for reasons of heredity put into the hands of a youth, who, according to the undoubtedly biased tradition of the conquerer, Otto I of Germany, was a weakling, and who was proved by events to be inferior to his most exacting task.

There is perhaps no time in history that has been so universally abominated as the tenth century, especially in Rome. Catholic and Protestant historians have for once agreed in their judgment, the *Annales Ecclesiastici* being of the same opinion as the *Centuriae* of Magdeburg. They have spoken of the deep sleep of Christ in his boat, of the century of lead or iron, of the Roman *pornocracy* (this delicate expression is still in use today among certain German and Italian writers) and of the brutalization of political, religious and cultural life. Then in more recent times, a few decades or so ago, doubts began to spring up, and cautious reservations were advanced. In effect, it was said, the Latin written not far from Rome by the monk of Mount Soracte certainly had very little to do with the classics or with true Latin; but this did not mean that all trace of the ancient culture was lost. The life led in Rome, Farfa, and Monte Cassino, was anything but a model of purity; crimes of blood, a common method of opening up one's way or keeping oneself in power, did not apparently provoke profound or lasting moral reactions; but this did not mean that it was a good thing to have blind faith in all the libel that the slanderous and well-bribed pen of the bishop Liudprand of Cremona lays at the feet of Theodora, Marozia, and the popes, Sergius III, John XI, and John XII.

Now, no one would wish to dispute the expediency of such a revision or the desirability of substituting life as it was really lived for the vain constructions of fantasy, of showing that the society was less corrupt, its customs less violent and its culture less primitive, than they were commonly thought to have been. For a sound historical judgment, it is useful, indispensable even, to keep in mind in as broad a manner as possible, that the picture we have been given of the women, popes and princes who occupy our attention until after the middle of the tenth century, is a condemnation of the conquered by their conquerors, by reformers pronouncing against the feudal church, by the empire, resurrected to its former vitality by Otto I, against the potentates who had opposed its triumph. But we must nevertheless confess that, however great an effort we may make to re-evaluate the tenth century in this way, the night still remains dark, and that in spite of our fine distinctions, restrictions and reservations, the age of Marozia, within Rome and without, speaks a language that is almost incomprehensible to us, and will always remain terribly remote, and estranged from our civil and moral consciousness.

Indeed if, as we believe, a re-evaluation is possible, it must not come from any *more* or *less* in the morality and culture of the age, but in the way we have tried to indicate above. During the crisis of authority, the city that was the centre of the universal powers did not escape the common lot, it had to rely on its own inherent strength to save it. And so, from the turbulent vicissitudes of the Church in the decline of the Carolingian empire, there emerged an aristocracy of the Curia, a local dynasty and prince, who with strength of action and their capacity to rule, freed Rome from the grip of the Saracens, removed her from the ambitions and oscillations of kings and emperors, and restored her to security and greatness.

Analogous situations develop contemporaneously in many different ways all over the west, and are given the collective name of feudalism, or medieval particularism. When transferred to our modern consciousness, this may seem chaotic and inglorious. Yet, when we reconsider feudalism in the context of historical development, we see that it was the superhuman effort with which the military societies, created by the great wars of Charlemagne's Franks, rebuilt their church and state from the foundations by means of the progressive acquisition of local power. And this they even accomplished amidst the tumult of new invasions, amid violence and ugliness of every kind. This was the laborious process by which men of different history and descent took root, laid their foundations, created a political, social and economic order which was at once uniform and subdivided to infinity, and gave birth to most intricate hierarchies based on personal devotion, possession of land, and exercise of political functions.

Then slowly but surely the light of the new dawn appears. From the blind confusion of war and ambition, political entities that are ever stronger and more vast raise their heads throughout the west, until we come to the German monarchy of the Saxons. From the worldly life of the clergy, and the absorption of the Church into the secular world, there is born, along with the revival of the state, the Cluniacensian movement of redemption. The alarm cry of Atho of Vercelli and Ratheri of Liège rings out, as they give vigorous expression to the inviolable moral exigency and faith in the salutary power of the Church, which had appeared to be buried beneath arms, assassinations and debauchery.

CHAPTER 10

THE FEUDAL EMPIRE

OTTO III

In considering the figure of Alberic II today, we can reiterate the opinion expressed several decades ago by Ferdinand Gregorovius, that most highly regarded student of medieval Rome, who recognized him as one of the foremost leaders of his time and the first of the great Romans of the Middle Ages who was not a pope. Alberic was in fact not just generically the final heir to a family tradition, and the inflexible founder of a state that was in opposition to the political papacy, the ecclesiastic empire, feudal ambitions and local factions. He was the mouthpiece of the citizens, the champion of long cherished Romanism which had now taken root again and flowered in the letters of John VIII and the poetry of Eugenius Vulgarius, in the revival of the senate and patricianship. He had succeeded in transplanting it in time to the small area of the Roman duchy, and in transplanting the ideal into a concrete political creation and policy.

And yet there was an intrinsic defect in the very foundations of his edifice. This marvellous feat of reconstruction that he had accomplished in the name of Rome, by closing the gates of the city to Hugh of Provence and Otto I of Saxony, was in effect totally sterile and contradictory, because it struck at the very roots from which the power and vitality of Rome grew. If, by an absurd hypothesis, the regime created by the son of Marozia had been perpetuated by a long line of successors, continuing in its local character, with the political subjection of the papacy and the strong resistance to all Italian or foreign potentates, the duchy and the Sabina would have enjoyed peace and tranquillity, but Rome would have forfeited its right to speak to the world, the seed of power and priesthood that made Rome the mother of nascent Europe would have shrivelled up. In other words, in Alberic's time, by virtue of his political foundation, the conflict that was to be Rome's tragedy for centuries began. It was the conflict between her local needs and her universal mission, between the consciousness of her citizens, which was indeed nourished by their memories of the glorious past, and another consciousness of Romanism, that was also closely tied to the 'ancient walls', but was the mouthpiece of the whole Catholic west.

The clash between the two forces came about a few years after the death of Alberic II, when Otto I of Saxony, King of Germany, was drawn down into Italy by hopes of the imperial crown held out by John XII, who in his turn was disturbed by Berengar II's policy of aggression against the lands of the Holy See. The human ambition of the one thus met the human weakness of the other half-way; but their temporary agreement and their subsequent rupture sprung from a far deeper root and went much further than any small personal passions. Otto and his contemporaries had before their eyes the image of Charlemagne, now transfigured into the symbol of the Christian emperor. In the same Saxony that Charlemagne had devastated and converted, he created the first great, solid monarchy of the west out of the feudal chaos. He took over the stern campaign of civilization against the Normans in the north and the Hungarians and Slavs beyond the Elbe; and these peoples he so welded to Europe, and adapted to her civil legislation, that for several centuries they constituted the Catholic bulwark against the Byzantine east. All the threads of European history, from England, France and Burgundy and especially from Italy, came together at the court of Otto. Sovereign of nations, general of conquering armies, missionary of the faith, supreme influence in the politics of the west, Otto was in the minds of princes, army and people, the new Charlemagne. 'Father of the country and emperor' he was hailed on the battlefield, according to the Roman custom, by the soldiers he had led to a decisive victory over the Hungarians in 955. But only consecration could make him the legitimate successor of Charlemagne, and could effectively set himself, his office and his authority apart from all the European potentates, and especially from his former peers, the dukes of Germany whom he and his house had subdued. The very constitution of the monarchy, founded as it was on the great bishoprics and abbeys of royal nomination, which had been granted enormous riches by the crown so that they should act as a counterbalance to the fickle lay feudality, made it necessary for him to go to the focal point of the faith. By doing this he hoped to bring about an alliance between Church and kingdom, or preferably the subjection of the Church, so that the ecclesiastic discipline on which the state depended should be guaranteed, and at the same time he could satisfy that moral and religious conscience which deplored the abasement of the papacy and the corruption of the clergy.

The call of Rome was historically inevitable, as are all powerful living traditions which men serve with youthful vigour and devotion without hesitating to risk and to sacrifice. Otto I marched down into Italy and had himself crowned King of Italy in Pavia and Emperor in Rome. Then, turning against John XII, the weight of whose protection he found unbearable, he deposed him in contempt of court with the most horrible accusations made in front of a great gathering of laymen and ecclesiastics over which he presided himself. In his place he elected Leo VIII. When, a few decades later, the monk of Mount Soracte remembered the destruction inflicted on the city by the emperor and his soldiers, he could not restrain his contempt and broke into the famous invective:

'Woe to you, Rome, oppressed and down-trodden by so many peoples, now you are taken by the Saxon king, your people transfixed, and your strength brought to nothing. You were a mother, now you are a whore; what you had you have lost, you are stripped of your ancient virtue. Proudly you triumphed with your peoples, you trampled on the world, you strangled the kings of the earth, you held the sceptre and the supreme power; now you have been stripped by the Saxon king *et menstruata fortiter.*'

But it was a voice from the grave, echoing in its unpolished Latin the lament of the prophets over the destruction of Samaria and Jerusalem, the lugubrious plaint of St Gregory over the city attacked by hunger, plagues, floods and the Lombard armies. The Rome that St Benedict had wept for was in the distant and irrevocable past; the significance of these events was a new one. The limited, though heroic, local Romanism founded by the house of Theophylact and Alberic, was in conflict with the universal Romanism of the European tradition. When Otto I deposed John XII and elected Leo VIII, it meant, among other things, that the papacy, and Rome herself, were universal institutions, not the prerogative of a single man or of one Roman family. Many other things resulted from the imperial coronation and the new papal election: the assumption by the German Caesars of the large-scale politics of the Catholic west, that is the desperate effort to purify the Church and incorporate it in the empire, to sweep the Arabs and Byzantines out of the peninsula, and to legitimize the imperial crown against that of Byzantium, which was now claiming more and more forcefully to be the sole heir to Rome, and finally to hold safely in check both Germany and Italy, in spite of all their repressed hates and ambitions and their untidy and exuberant vitality. For if they looked to Charlemagne as an ideal model, this was no longer his Europe, no longer a summary aggregate of catholic peoples with elementary legislation. With the rise of the feudal monarchies the first traces of a European political system emerged: Germany and Italy, these great creators of history, were united, the former with its Caesars, sleeplessly pursuing the mirage of Rome, the latter with its popes, its bishop-counts, and its cities. Before Germany, there stood the France of Hugh Capet; between them, the object of centuries-long contest, Lorraine.

In our everyday, admittedly superficial, historical perspective, the three Ottos look to us each one less important than his predecessor. We see a decline from the greatness of Otto I, who for nearly forty years played the central role on the stage of Europe, to his son, Otto II, the luckless adversary of the Arabs and Byzantines, who scarcely escaped the battle of Stilo with his life, and was lost to the world before his youth was spent. From him we may observe a further decline to Otto III, a fantastic character, at once religious autocrat and vindictively ambitious ascetic, who died at the age of twenty-two after witnessing the failure of his dream of a *Renovatio*. And yet if we wish, as we do, to examine the anatomy of heroism in the Middle Ages at its critical points, we cannot but stop before Otto III. For in the contradictions of his own life he illustrates the deep-seated turmoil of the age: heir to the dynastic tradition of his line, he leads it on to its ultimate disastrous conclusion, and harbouring Europe's longing for unity, purity and peace in his own soul, he accomplishes the fulfilment of its hopes.

He was three years old when his father died. After some degree of uncertainty about the succession, which was threatened by the ambition of Henry of Bavaria, he was crowned in Aachen with the help and favour of the great ecclesiastics of the kingdom. There were three women, all endowed with exceptional intelligence and political experience, who watched over his career. The first was his mother, Theophano, the sweet princess from Greece, niece of John Tzimisces. She had come to Italy in 972 when she was sixteen years old as Otto II's bride and as a pledge of peace between the eastern and western empires. Next, after Theophano's untimely death in 991, came his paternal grandmother, the very Adelaide of Burgundy who, as the young widow of Lothar, had called Otto I into the peninsula to defend her against the siege of Berengar II. Then finally came his aunt Matilda, the abbess of the convent of Quedlinburg. His mother, perhaps the meekest and most tender of the three, was assisted by two noble Saxons, the Count Hoik and Bernard, who saw to his chivalric and spiritual education respectively. The child grew up amidst army encampments beyond the frontier of the Slavs of Brandenburg where he learnt to write (an unusual accomplishment for royalty) and learnt Greek, Latin and German. With this training and experience, he naturally developed into a precociously mature young man, well served by a sturdy body and a lively mind. In 995, at the age of fifteen, he became his own master. He celebrated his majority in two ways; the first was a new expedition against the Wilsi and the Abotrites of Mecklenburg, in which he was supported by the subject dukes of Bohemia and Poland; the second was the opening of negotiations for his marriage with one of the three daughters of Constantine VIII, the Emperor of Byzantium. This, according to traditional Saxon policy, was the only worthy match for a prince destined to the empire, who might thereby look to the possibility of a succession which would put an end to the centuries old conflict between the dynasties of the east and west and re-establish the unity of the Roman Empire of old. The negotiations lasted for six years, and were brought to a happy conclusion only when it was too late, when the Gordian knot had already been cut by his death.

Rome meanwhile was once more in the grip of her own invincible disease. The dynasty of Theophylact was gone, and a new line, which was in fact related to it, and was known as the Crescentii, had succeeded to its hegemony in the city. This family had the same political consciousness, but less force of determination than Alberic had had, and soon came into collision with Pope John XV (985-996). The pope, faced with the oppressor at his door, found no better solution than to invoke help from afar, and sent an embassy to Germany to offer the young king the imperial crown. The actors may change, but the same scene is repeated century after century, always apparently the same. So we expect to find the usual journey south, the solemn incoronation, the return, and then the rebirth of the conflict between the territorial and universal aspirations of the Church on the one hand, and the dynastic, secular consciousness on the other. But this time, only for a short while perhaps, but with the most serious consequences for the future, events developed differently.

When six years before, in 991, a solemn synod of the French clergy had met in the church of Saint Basle de Verzy to pass judgment on the Bishop of Rheims as a traitor to his sovereign Hugh Capet, one of those present, Arnulf, Bishop of Orleans, had spoken more or less as follows:

'Most reverend fathers, we in truth consider that the Church of Rome should always be respected, in memory of St Peter, and we do not intend to go against the decrees of the popes of Rome. But, oh unhappy Rome, who brought our forbears the splendid light of the Fathers, and in our own time spread monstrous shadows, what an object of infamy you will be to future generations! What have we not had to witness in these times? Has it really been decreed that countless priests of God throughout the world, whose knowledge and virtue shines out for all to see, must be subjected to such monsters,*

* John XII and his successors.

ignominious as they are, and devoid of all knowledge be it divine or human? What is this, most reverend fathers? By what depravation are we to believe that the first of the churches of God, which was raised up to Heaven and crowned with honour and glory, has been thus flung in the mud, and covered with ignominy and disgrace?' If the disputes of kings had not prevented it, he would have asked the bishops of Belgium and Germany, who were true priests of God, for their judgment, 'rather than (asking) this city, which is now put up for sale to all comers, and dispenses its justice according to the quantity of money offered.'

Beneath the dispute of the bishopric of Rheims, there were great political interests at stake. The crown of France might fall to Carolingians or Capets, and the possession of Lorraine to France or Germany.

Yet Arnulf's invective went further than either of these questions; and it was not merely the view of one man, inspired by personal hate or ambition, or subservient to the political designs of his lord. It was the national pride and religious consciousness of the French bishops that spoke through his mouth, and with it the revolt of a great part of the western clergy and laity against the decadence of the Church, isolated as it was by the aristocratic families of Rome and entrusted to hands unworthy of its name.

Arnulf's tirade at the synod of Verzy sets Otto III's first act of greatness in its true perspective. Only a few days after he set foot in Italy, John XV, the pope who had summoned him, and who had been so severely censured by Arnulf of Orleans, died. An embassy of the Roman aristocracy arrived in Ravenna to invite him to choose his successor. The man on whom his choice, or rather the court's choice, fell was his own cousin, Bruno of Carinthia, the first German to rise to the papal throne. He assumed the auspicious name of Gregory V. It has been said that this election reduced the See of Rome to the level of any German bishopric. It would be truer to say that the particularism of the feudal reconstruction had in fact ensnared and debased even the Church of Rome, with all the others. Now the revolutionary violence of this election wrenched the papacy out of the hands of both clergy and aristocracy, and freed it and lifted it high above the tumult of local passions. This, more than anything was his purpose. He established a new solidarity between kingdom and priesthood, founded on tradition, common blood and interests; and vindicated the Transalpine clergy in their complaints of the venality of the Curia, holding themselves up as an example of knowledge and probity in contrast to the unworthy ambition of the popes.

In the spring of 996 Otto entered Rome for the first time. On the twenty-first of May he received the imperial crown from the hands of Gregory V, while the patrician John Crescentius, an old enemy of John XV, paid homage and was pardoned. Here in Rome the young emperor went through some of the deepest experiences of his life. Most important, he met the Czech Weitech who had been baptized with the German name of Adalbert. He was one of the great individuals of the time, had been Bishop of Prague, and then became a monk at St Boniface and Alessio on the Aventine. The adventurous life of Adalbert, full of both personal and public agitation as it is, may well serve us as one example among many—some of which, equally illustrious, we shall meet shortly—of that turbulent ferment of renewal which spread throughout the Catholic world at the close of the tenth century.

There is in fact no corner of Europe that is not shaken from top to bottom by the religious struggle, there is no place that does not hear the words or see the example of the hermits, the preachers of reform, and the missionaries. The rigid ascetic ideal which so inspired many of them, seems to us instinctively to be something abnormal and inhuman, a crude exercise in endurance, with no relief and little hope, and in a word a voluntary annihilation of the individual. But apart from the excesses of cruelty which in a way reflect the ferocity of the time, the ascetism of this century springs from life, not mortification. It provides the solace of a haven removed from the tumult of the world, a return to the peace of one's own soul and to intimate communion with God, and a restored hope for salvation.

Then when the new ideals triumphed, hagiographers and chroniclers were to leave us a desolate picture of the old society both lay and ecclesiastic, and were to pronounce a ringing moral condemnation of it. In actuality it was not a question, as they thought, of a struggle between good and bad men. If we translate it into human terms and bring it back to earth, we see that it was in fact a war between the force of tradition and a strong revolutionary urge. The words of the reformers, apparently so innocent and simple, peace, purity of life, disinterest in worldly things, were actually a universal provocation and reproof. What constitutes their greatness is precisely the fact that they struggled with such spirit against the exigencies of history, which only those with a heroic will to sacrifice could hope to change.

Adalbert was all his life torn between bishopric and monastery, between the ascetic ideal and his pastoral duties. Dispirited by the futility of his struggle against the corruption of clergy and laity, he fled from Prague and set out on the difficult search for a refuge. He went first to Rome to consult the pope, then to Monte Cassino and to St Nilus at St Michael of Barrea. Mansone, the Abbot of Monte Cassino, wanted to keep him at all costs, especially as in his capacity as bishop he would be able to help the monastery by exercising his pastoral offices of consecration of cells and ordination of the monks. But he was given this reply: 'Do you think I am a man or an ass, that you expect me to consecrate your churches as a bishop, when I have abandoned my flock and stopped being a bishop?' After this, St Nilus avoided accepting him, as his monastery was a cell of Monte Cassino and he was afraid, for the sake of his monks, of being dismissed. However, he sent him with the warmest recommendations to the monastery of St Boniface and Alessio in Rome, where he finally enjoyed a short period of peace. When recalled to his episcopal ministry by his diocesan superior, Willigis of Mayence, he obeyed; but he could not stand the test and once more returned to his refuge in the religious solitude of the Aventine.

It was at this time that Otto met him first. They then saw each other again a few months later at Mayence (at the end of 996) where the emperor had been recalled by his duties to the German state, and the bishop to his diocese by the inflexible Willigis. Here they delighted to spend their time together in intimate conversation, absorbed in thoughts of humility and justice. This was not merely the encounter of two men and two souls. We are reminded of the reformers of the preceding generation, of Ratheri, the eternal innocent and tireless petitioner, ill-used, scorned and expelled; or of Odo of Cluny, who spoke with popes and princes and thus won the battle for his monasteries. But we feel also that here, as indeed later on in Otto's intimate relationship with St Romuald and St Nilus, there is something more: the whole vast religious impulse of the west confronts the young emperor and his empire with a new immediacy and a new depth of emotion and understanding, almost as though to charge them with their sacred mission. Otto himself is to remain wounded by this contact all his life, yearning like his teachers for his final release, even amid the sensual allurements, ambitions and violence of his court. And the empire, with the ghost of Charlemagne ever-present, holds the Catholic world together in a new synthesis, with a consciousness of the unity of the divine and human, with its primacy in Rome, and its thirst for purity in peace.

In Germany Otto and Adalbert's ways parted, as it turned out, for ever. Otto marched into battle against the Slavs, Adalbert moved on to his own fate. He should have returned to Prague, but was prevented from doing so. The people of his diocese had killed his parents, whom they suspected of treachery with Poland and Germany, and drove him out for fear of his revenge. The invocation to Christ which the hagiographer puts in his mouth may never actually have been spoken, but it certainly expresses this troubled soul's joy at his liberation with convincing humanity and historical accuracy:

'On hearing these words, the holy bishop gives way to a laugh of such happiness that his accustomed severity is somewhat softened: "Thou hast broken my chains," he cried, "I offer thee a sacrifice of praise and glory, because their rejection has lifted the weight of my pastoral duties from my shoulders. I proclaim that from this day, good Jesus, I am all yours; to see, Lord of eternal virtue, be praise, honour and glory. Thou hast rejected those who do not want thee, and whose desires lead them far from the path of truth." '

He embarked at Danzig, and set out to convert the Prussians; but he was killed by the spear of a pagan priest and his followers on April 23, 997. His body was taken to Poland and buried at Gniezno.

In Otto's first expedition to Rome there was no more than a faint hint of what was to come. This lay in the election of Gregory V, and perhaps the brief formula *Romanorum Imperator Augustus*, which from now on appeared without fail on all his documents and affirmed the true Roman origin, and hence the legitimacy, of the western empire in the face of the Byzantine emperor, who was pleased to call himself *The King of the Romans*. Otto III was indeed different from his predecessors in an important way: on his mother's side, in character as well as blood, he was Greek, in the full Roman sense of the word. Now, in Rome itself, the young emperor had happened to meet Gerbert, the disputed Archbishop of Rheims, a mature man of fifty, with long experience of people, places and affairs. He was of humble birth, and had been brought up in the monastery of Aurillac in the Auvergne. Gripped by an insatiable desire for knowledge, he had learnt mathematics, music and astronomy at Ausona in Spain, and logic in Rheims; he had visited Rome and the court of the Ottos. Apart from a short and unhappy monastic interlude, spent as abbot of the rich monastery of Bobbio, Rheims had been the great centre of his life, the fertile field of his political experience, the place of his studies and his teaching as master and director of the cathedral school, and finally his cross, when the synod of Verzy called him to succeed the archbishop Arnulf, when he was deposed for treason. To call him the most cultured man of his time is not enough. What we wonder at today when reading his letters and his treatises, is not so much the occasional classical quotation, the vastness of his knowledge or his subtlety of argument, as the sphere of his spiritual interests and the extraordinarily unique tone of his writing, the Roman spirit living once more in the serenity of thought and word, measured, limpid and pure.

In February of the year 997, Gerbert was summoned to the court in Germany by a famous letter in which Otto, disdainful of the '*Saxona rusticitas*' around him, appealed to him to instruct his '*graecisca subtilitas*', so that the west should not be bereft of '*Graecorum industriae aliqua scintilla*'. In this case too, history was born as the result of the fortuitous encounter of two men, men who were destined by some deep necessity to search each other out. Gerbert brought the highest and purest part of the Roman heritage to the imperial court, and with it excited in the young man of Saxon and Grecian blood a consciousness of empire which showed itself in his successful emulation of the Caesars of the east. Between the cares of war, in Aachen, now resplendent with new churches and monasteries devoted to the religious cult of Charlemagne, he listened, like Alexander to Aristotle, to the lofty speculations of Boethius on the tongue of Gerbert. From 'the dearest of masters', 'the most devoted of disciples' learnt, in Roman accents, what was the true reward of victory pursued in arms: 'What glory is greater for the prince, what virtue more praiseworthy in the general, than to gather his legions, break into enemy territory, withstand the impact of the foe with his own person, and face the greatest dangers for his fatherland, his religion, his men and for the common weal?' For his young pupil, the spiritual heir of Rome became the interpreter of the undisputed superiority of the west over Byzantium; 'Ours, ours is the Roman Empire. We are given strength by Italy, fertile in crops, by Gaul and Germany fertile in soldiers, and ours are the mighty kingdoms of the Scythians. You too; Caesar, are ours, Emperor of the Romans and Augustus, who, being born of the highest Grecian blood, excel the Greeks in empire, rule the Romans by hereditary right, and outdo both in intellect and eloquence'.

This, at a distance of thirty years, was the reply and retaliation to the insult of the Emperor Nicephoros Foca, who had scorned the western peoples for their pretence of Romanism, calling them Lombards, and also against the servile insult of Otto I's own ambassador Liudprand of Cremona, who had replied by saying that they, Germans of all races, were in the habit of referring with a single word, Roman, to all the basest things in the world; '*quidquid ignobilitatis, quidquid timiditatis, quidquid avaritiae, quidquid luxuriae, quidquid mendacii, immo quidquid vitiorum est*'.

But, as always, while the emperor was campaigning in the north, Rome slipped out of his hands. John Crescentius was in control again, and Gregory V, who had been forced to leave the city, had been unable to do more than pronounce a severe condemnation of his action, and impatiently await and solicit the absent Otto's return. At just the right moment, John Philagathus had arrived back in Rome from Byzantium, where he had been to negotiate Otto's marriage. He was a Greek from Calabria, a fellow-countryman of St Nilus, who had risen from lowly beginnings to the dizzy heights of the bishopric of Piacenza and the Italian chancery. If it was his greed and ambition or his weakness that was responsible we shall never know, but the fact remains that the patrician Crescentius had drawn him into his game, and had him elected pope, with the obvious intention (not a novel one in the politics of the city) of escaping the Germanic pressure on Rome by means of an alliance with the east.

So Otto was obliged to cross the Alps once more and hurry down to Rome. When at the beginning of 998 it was known that he was approaching the city, the antipope fled and Crescentius shut himself in the Castel Sant'Angelo. But this time the revenge was implacable, and even tainted with the smell of perjury. Resentment for the dangers encountered, for the betrayal and ingratitude, and the need to thoroughly deracinate the evil and so prevent its recurrence, prevailed over all other considerations. The pope, being a resolute man by nature and having suffered the offence most directly, was the most fierce in his reaction. Crescentius, induced to surrender probably by a promise of mercy, was beheaded, his bloody head thrown down from the height of Castel Cant'Angelo, and his body hung from the gallows on Monte Mario along with those of twelve other citizens. And it was by this scene that the victory was remembered, for an imperial letter to the monastery of Einiedeln fixes in its date the great day '*quando Crescentius decollatus suspensus fuit*'.

John Philagathus was run to ground and captured in his hiding place in the Campagna; his nose and tongue were cut out, he was blinded, and thrown into prison. St Nilus had written to him in vain to warn him of the risks his pursuit of power was leading him into. Now the failing old man came down in person from his hermitage near Gaeta, to plead to be given custody of the wretched antipope. When the pope and the emperor sat him between them and kissed his hands, he said, 'In the name of God, you must pardon the greatest of all sinners, this poor old man so near the grave, for I am unworthy of the honour you pay me. I have not come in search of your grace and favour, but to ask you for the man who has done much in your service, who held you both at the baptismal font, and whom you have deprived of his sight.' The emperor agreed, on condition that he moved, if not to Rome as he would have liked, at least to the monastery of St Anastasius nearby. But the pope still put his captive, whose face was horribly deformed and his clothes in rags, through the torture of an opprobrious procession through the streets of the city. St Nilus was irreconcilable. To the imperial messenger sent to placate him he said, 'Go and say to the emperor and the pope, "This is what the old fool says: You gave me this blind man not out of any fear for me or for my power, but solely for the love of God.

Now all the evil you have done him since that time you have done to me, not to him, nay, you have done it to God Himself. Know that just as you have had no pity for the man God put into your hands, so God will grant you no remission of your sins."' And with that he fled, silent and inflexible, back to his Gaeta hermitage with his monks.

The censure and condemnation of the saint wounded Otto so deeply that he never recovered; his name was indelibly branded, perhaps in a way he did not deserve.

Whether or not Crescentius was in fact the victim of a breach of oath, and whatever the exact nature of the tortures inflicted on John Philagathus, Otto's second stay in Rome and Italy, which lasted for two years, 998 and 999, bears witness throughout to his clear thinking and resolution in political matters. Thus there was little scope for the frivolity of the Roman aristocracy's dynastic ambitions, for Church acquiescence to local interests, or for interference from Byzantium. This is the second period of greatness in Otto's reign. The inscription that appears on his seal at this time, *Renovatio imperii Romanorum*, is an indication of the well-considered policy, behind his actions. The tradition started by the donation of Constantine was decisively abandoned; the Caesars no longer left their city and the west out of reverence to St Peter. Now Caesar himself built his palace on the Aventine, and in conjunction with the pope demonstrated the strength of the Roman Empire in the face of Byzantium. The ceremony and the offices of court were restored, and the emperor's counsellors, the inspirers and supporters of his policy, were promoted to higher positions. The chancellor for Italy, Heribert, was appointed to take over the German chancery as well, given the title of arch-chancellor and archlogothete, and finally made archbishop of Cologne. Leo was made first chancellor and then bishop of Vercelli. The toilworn Gerbert was appointed to the archbishopric of Ravenna, that Byzantine corner of Italy so dear to the emperor's heart and so important for relations with Byzantium. Then after the death of Gregory V in 999, he was raised to the papal chair, with the significant appellation of Silvester II, a new Silvester to a new and different Constantine. Finally, Otto restored the imperial jurisdiction over the principalities of the centre and south of Italy, after the example of Otto I.

But there is something more important than all these single actions, which transcends and explains them all. The west at this time was presented with the unique phenomenon of an emperor and a pope who together were undisputed masters of Rome, who shared the same interests, and were firmly united beneath the aegis of the imperial power. In the city and throughout Italy they discussed

Church and empire in solemn assemblies of prominent laymen and ecclesiastics. They forbade the alienation of property by churches and monasteries, struggled against the corruption of the clergy, and condemned the impious rebel, Ardoin.

In a document written in the hand of Leo of Vercelli Otto III expressed his idea of the spiritual and temporal renewal he had in mind:

'Liberty and security for the Church of God, prosperity of the empire, triumph of the armies, propagation of the power of the Roman people, restoration of the republic.'

This was a plan which enabled him to hope, "*in huius mundi hospitio honeste vivere, de huius vite carcere honestius avolare et cum Domino honestissime regnare*'. This was the miracle that the same Leo celebrated when he wrote in his verse:

'Christ, hear our prayers, look down upon your Rome, let Rome rise to the empire under Otto III. Let there be great jubilation in Rome, let its palace rejoice; under the power of Caesar, the pope purifies the world. You, like two stars, enlighten the churches and dissipate darkness throughout the world, so that one may prevail with the sword, the other make his word resound.'

There is a note of inspiration in these and other utterances of the court circle, which goes beyond the bounds of a project that is merely political. In these two years there was room for more than the struggle against traitors and rebels, and the watchful care needed for the restoration of Church and republic. Otto's heart was heavy with guilt, he felt himself accused before man and God for the murder of Crescentius, the torture of the antipope, and perhaps for his youthful indiscretions in Rome, where he apparently fell in love with a certain Stephania, who belonged to the Crescentius family itself. He confessed all this to St Romuald and, in accordance with the penitence allotted him, he went on a humble pilgrimage to the monastery of St Michael at Gargano, he begged the Beneventans in vain for the relics of the apostle Bartholomew, which he wanted for a chapel in honour of St Adalbert on the Isola Tiberina, and finally he visited St Nilus in his hermitage near Gaeta, an experience which brought back the most unhappy memories of his life and his triumphs. In bidding him farewell, the saint, his hand placed on his heart, replied to the solicitous gifts of the emperor as follows: 'I ask nothing more from your reign than the salvation of your soul, for, emperor though you be, you are still a mortal man, and as such you are destined to die, and to stand before the judgment seat to answer for the good and the evil you have done.' And the young man, in tears, had put his crown into his hands and received his blessing on it.

The whole of the last period of great imperial policy was animated by this deeply felt religiosity. What started as the private affliction of a penitent sinner seems now to be sublimated and opened out so as to embrace the universal aspiration to conquest, renewal and faith, and to be transfused into a new religious mission within the empire itself. We find no longer a juxtaposition of Church and empire, even united under the aegis of the empire, but the empire itself rising into a sphere of pure spirituality, and in full awareness of its right, taking on the great responsibilities of the Christian republic. Grandiose schemes must have been discussed at the assembly '*pro restituenda republica*' held near Farfa in 999 and attended by the pope, Hugh of Tuscany, and the dignitaries of the empire. The existence of ambitious plans for Catholic penetration into eastern Europe with the support of Byzantium is hinted at by the imperial connections established at this time with Hungary, Dalmatia and Russia.

But meanwhile, with the death of Mathilda of Quedlinburg in February, and of Adelaide in December, 999, Otto was urgently needed in Germany. At the beginning of the year 1000 he crossed the Alps again, taking with him his Roman court, cardinals, Roman aristocracy, a representative of the pope, and the patrician of Rome, who was now a Saxon chosen by the emperor. He reached the land of his fathers and set his eyes on Aachen once more, as though to refresh himself at the stream that fed his own roots. He went from one end of the kingdom to the other, to pray at the tombs of St Adalbert and of Charlemagne. He took the relics from them with a furtive, superstitious veneration, as though he hoped to reassure himself of their thaumaturgical power, and take the essence of the two great models of his life into himself. Under his auspices, Poland and Hungary were definitively brought into the orbit of Catholic organization, and by an unusual kind of bond these new subjects were annexed to the Rome of the Caesars and of Christ rather than to Germany.

As a pilgrim in Germany, and on his return to Italy after six months, the emperor liked to be addressed by his own formulas, as '*Servus Iesu Christi et Romanorum imperator secundum voluntatem Dei Salvatorisque nostrique liberatoris*', as '*Sanctarum ecclesiarum devotissimus et fidelissimus dilatator*', and as '*Romanus, Saxonicus et Italicus, Apostolorum servus, dono Dei romani orbis Imperator Augustus*'. In other words he was the apostle of Christ who spread the Gospel, the servant of St Peter and St Paul, who had reminded his people of their subjecthood, and embraced them in the sovereign unity of the faith.

In a document of January, 1001, drawn up by Leo of Vercelli and adorned with a little leaden bull inscribed *Aurea Roma*, one of the most singular testimonies of the Middle Ages, Otto III solemnly reaffirmed his political and religious credo. After making his profession of faith: '*Romam caput mundi profiemur, Romanam Ecclesiam matrem omnium ecclesiarum esse testamur*', he went on to inveigh with equal vehemence against the synod of Verzy, against the popes who had dissipated the property of the Church, within the city and outside it, to satisfy their own licentiousness, and then made up their losses deceitfully from the riches of the empire. He then denounced the falseness of Constantine's donation and the invalidity of the Ponthion donation to John VIII from Charles the Bald. The entire juridical foundation on which the power and territorial policy of the Church had been based for more than a century was nullified, and the empire was restored to its full rights. And having thus vindicated his rights, the emperor, for love of Pope Silvester his master, gave to St Peter, whose faithful servant he was proud to be, eight counties of the Pentapolis, which had already been contemplated in the former donations, 'for our common safety, and as an increment to the apostolate and the empire'. This was at once the spiritual and temporal triumph of Rome. Never before and never again was there such close co-operation between Church and empire, such a concentration and coincidence of the two powers, such a renunciation on the part of the Church of her terrestrial politics, or a more complete dedication of the empire to religious ideals.

This was Otto III's last political action of any significance. His imperial edifice threatened collapse on every side. The German nobility, even the bishops, prop of the empire though they were, bewailed his desertion of his kingdom, and the favours he bestowed on Italians and Romans. Rome in her turn might well accept his bounty, serve him and be silent, but she could not forget her past struggles and the glory of her citizens, her princes, her popes and her dead. And there were probably men in both camps who had their doubts about the exalted monks who knew the emperor's heart and enjoyed his favours, and about the blind mysticism of a man who claimed to rule the world.

The trouble began with the insurrection of Tivoli, which was put down almost immediately through the mediation of the pope, Bishop Bernard of Hildesheim, and St Romuald. Then came Rome, mindful of the Crescentii and resentful at the leniency with which her neighbour had been treated. Otto himself was encircled by the rebels, and had to be rescued by Henry of Bavaria and Hugh of Tuscany, who managed to get through to him. Deeply hurt, he spoke to his Romans, with the bitterness born of sudden disappointment:

'Listen to the words of your father, pay attention, and hold them carefully in your minds. Are you not my Romans? It was for you I left my country, and even my family. For love of you I have set aside my Saxons and all Germans, though they are my own blood. I have led you to distant parts of our empire, where your forefathers, when they ruled the world, never set foot, all with the purpose of extending your name and your glory to the ends of the earth. I have adopted you as my sons; I have preferred you to all men. For your sake, on account of this preferment, I have excited universal envy and hatred against myself. And now in return for all these favours you have repulsed your father, and cruelly done away with my companions; you have excluded me, and yet you cannot exclude me, for those whom I embrace with my paternal spirit, I can never allow to be exiled from my affections.'

On February 16, 1001, Otto III leaves Rome for the last time, accompanied by the pope. His whole structure has fallen, and for a year he has been floundering among the ruins. The harmony of his lofty creation is dissolved into its human, individual elements. The man comes closer to our human understanding in his bewilderment and his sorrow, in the fever of provisions and contradictory plans, and in the final peace that soothes his indomitable youth. His heroic effort to reconcile the principles of heaven and earth has turned out to be nothing but a dream. He is defeated, and the conflict between worldly passions and thirst for renunciation reopens implacably in his own heart. St Romuald, whom Otto visits in Ravenna, hoping for comfort, can only tell him to take refuge in God. And perhaps he promises: he will correct the errors of his rule, he will entrust the government to better hands, he will strip himself of all riches, and set himself with all his heart to follow barefoot in the steps of Christ. But first he needs soldiers to save Rome, or rather to avenge the offence to himself and to save his life's work. Finding no peace, he begs for reinforcements to be sent, he visits the Doge of Venice, Pietro Orseolo II, in secret for no one knows what purpose—his marriage, the possibility of abdication?—he rushes to settle the riots that have broken out at Benevento, returns to Ravenna, incapable of either keeping or forgetting his promise. He hides his anguish behind the impeturbable serenity of his expression; but in the silence of his sleepless nights he breaks down into tears and prayers.

Finally the time comes and he sets off for Rome. He is told that Heribert, Archbishop of Cologne is coming too with an army. More, the Byzantine princess whose hand he has been promised is about to land in Italy. But it is too late. On 23rd or 24th of January, 1002, the emperor breathes his last at Paterno, at the foot of Mount Soracte, aged twenty-two. His body is carried back over the Alps by his followers, who open their way through the riots throughout Italy with considerable difficulty. He is buried in Aachen beside Charlemagne.

The old legend depicts the dead emperor, clad in purple and propped up on his horse, leaving Rome, as he had willed it, as though to war. And the ghostly rider and his fantastic undertaking seem to offer us the symbol, which history has made its own for centuries, of squalid vanity and a life passed in a dream, haunted by thoughts of death. His defeated youth could only be a chastisement from on high, and Bruno of Querfurt, the chronicler of the time, lists the sins that caused it: the sin of having cherished only Rome and the Romans, and forgetting the land of his fathers, the '*desiderabilis et delectabilis Germania*'; the 'puerile game' in which he imagined he was reviving the ancient splendour of Rome; the sin of leading his army against the city of St Peter.

But perhaps it was not a sin; rather it was his cross, the part assigned to him on earth, to obey the call of his time and to try to bring about the overall synthesis of the Christian west in the name of Rome, to actually *serve*, in the only way he could, 'servant of Christ and the Apostles' that he was, the propagation of the faith, the liberation and elevation of the papacy and the clergy, and the triumph of the ideals of the reformers. He was fated to expend his life in the effort, and to die in the disappointment of defeat; and to leave behind him instead, a new consciousness of Church and empire, of Germany and Italy, which was to provoke the most terrible and the most fertile revolution of the middle ages.

'*Mirabilia Mundi*' was the phrase with which Otto III was referred to not long after his death; a wonder of the world perhaps on account of his dream, his brief and adventurous life, his refinement of culture, his ambitions, exaltations and terrors, and for that element of the spectacular that hung about his person and his palace. A wonder of the world in our eyes too, not only for his singularity of character and his lot, but for the liveliness and heroism he has lent to the history of the foundation of Europe.

CHAPTER 11

THE RECOVERY OF THE CHURCH AND ITS RESISTANCE TO FEUDALISM

GREGORY VII

Looking back on the historical developments that we have examined so far: the crisis of the age of Constantine; the antagonism and the subsequent reconciliation and fusion of the Germans with Rome, through which Alaric, Theodoric and Clovis lived their troubled lives; the foundation of St Benedict, that master of wisdom and learning in the dark ages; the Roman and western creation of St Gregory; the separation of east and west; Charlemagne's expansion and his affirmation of Europe as an entity; and Otto III's attempted *Renovatio;* we can see that each one of these episodes of history derives its primary significance and its force from the religious factor. This is the dominant characteristic of the Middle Ages, in this lies the greatness of their history, this drama of the human and the divine, in which there is no flutter of thought, no impulse to conquest, and no passion high or low, that need not be answered for to God and to the Church, and no aspiration to God that does not leave a lasting mark on society and on the state.

From this fundamental viewpoint, the eleventh century, or the age of Gregory VII as we shall consider it, can only be compared with the Christian *mutatio* of Constantine's reign, on account of the importance of the problem and the seriousness of the consequences. The so-called Struggle of the Investitures is in fact, more simply and radically, the crisis of the Middle Ages. Although, from the Germanic invasions on, kings and popes wove the fabric of events with their harmony and discord, pronounced words and did deeds of incalculable import for posterity, there was still something now superficial, now incomplete or episodic about each development. Never before this time was the contraposition of the temporal and spiritual powers so central and absolute, sprung as it was from the innermost principles of their existence, and disseminated in every section of the Catholic world, expressed and then implacably and systematically translated into the reality of everyday life. Never before did strength of faith, high principles and firmness of decision establish so formidable a judgment of God upon men and nations.

Otto III had done boldly the task that his time demanded of him. He had centred the empire on Rome once more, and enriched it with all the highest spiritual values. Finding the church in a state of decline, he had taken it over and given it the support of his own devotion, strength and prestige. At the risk of excessive systematization and with some exaggeration, one might say that he developed feudalism to the ultimate by incorporating the whole of the Church into its structure.

Before the final defeat of death, Otto had been beaten by two other forces: the feudal barons of Germany in their displeasure at his activities in Rome; and the Roman aristocracy in their pride, ambition and jealousy of their Roman tradition. He was defeated, in a word, by the tragic dualism which from Otto I onwards condemned the emperors to sustain their universal task only to see either Germany slip out of their grasp for Italy, or Italy for Germany, or sometimes both at once.

What did not die with Otto III was the link between papacy and empire, the tutelage exercised by the German monarchy over the papacy, the struggle against the sale of church benefices and the marriage or in general the immorality of the clergy. With the exception of the reign of Conrad II (1024-1039) who was openly simoniacal and heedless of Roman interests, we find that throughout the first half of the eleventh century the emperors appoint the popes, almost always with happy results, and the two powers co-operate to promote reform.

This was an enterprise of truly grandiose and fearful dimensions, whose breadth, depth and difficulties it is not easy to describe. Such words as reform, simony, lay investiture, concubinage, nicolaitism,* moral corruption, and crisis of the Middle Ages are choice, well-sounding words, and very useful ones for discussing these events; but they have the drawback of reducing history to a collection of empty formulas, without human substance. Let us leave aside the usual example of the abbey of Farfa with its murders, the concubinage and debauchery of monks and abbots, and the dissipation of the abbey's property for women and children. For our problem the seriousness of the evil does not lie in these exceptional scandalous cases. It is the placid normality with which married ecclesiastics and

* Nicolaitism=concubinage of the ecclesiastics.

their family business are referred to in many medieval documents that is serious; and similarly the simple reply (which is not without foundation) that the clergy of Verona gave to their bishop Ratheri of Liege in the middle of the tenth century, that without women they would not have been able to manage the elementary routine of feeding and clothing themselves. Serious again are the invectives of the German clergy a hundred years later against Gregory VII: 'that he wanted to force men to live like angels, and by going against nature, to encourage fornication and immorality; that if the pope stood by his decrees, they would renounce their priesthood rather than marriage, and since the pope of Rome held men in such horror, he would do well to find himself some angels to look after the Church of God.'

The same may be said for simony. The most scandalous cases of church benefices openly conferred for money to persons unworthy of them will serve to show, as examples can, to how great an extent the religious conscience had been dimmed. But if we want to understand how hard the battle the reformers undertook was, we must once again start with everyday normality, in this case with the immense and exceedingly intricate network of relations between the clergy and the laity: with the countless monasteries that were privately owned and run and administered in the interests of the proprietors; the bishoprics, abbeys and all kinds of livings, which were controlled by feudal lords, and the bishops and abbots who were great feudal lords themselves. We have to remember a king and emperor of Germany who drew his counsellors, diplomats, chancery officials, and the captains of his armies mainly from the higher ranks of the clergy, and the money for his military expeditions from church institutions, who considered it completely legitimate to choose the men who suited him best, and to extract the greatest possible gain for himself from the riches that he and his forbears had apportioned to charity and to the needs of the state.

To reform such a world as this meant offending universal interests and partialities, it meant tearing down the whole fabric of contemporary society. It was at once a gigantic and a unique enterprise; for while the only possibility of reform lay in the co-operation of the two powers, the completed reform was bound to give rise to an irreparable rift between them. In other words, there was an implicit contradiction in the task the empire had undertaken in answer to the complaints of the masses and the pleas of the reformers, and this contradiction, clear as it is to us, was less obvious at the time. And it was a contradiction which could only be resolved by force. The Church, which was put under the tutelage of the empire in order that it should be reformed, could only demonstrate the recovery of its conscience by vindicating its independence, its liberty, its primacy, its universal mission, and consequently it would strike a heavy blow at the empire whose power was now based on its freedom to dispose as it would of the papacy, and the great abbeys and bishoprics.

There is already much that is new towards the end of Henry III's reign (he dies in 1056) and during the minority of Henry IV. One can sense that the two ways are beginning to part, and that the period of agreement is drawing to a close. While Leo IX, the last pope but one to be nominated by the emperor, considers the approval of the Romans a necessary condition for a legitimate papal election, only five years after his death, and three after that of Henry III, Pope Nicholas II decrees quite simply that the pope must be elected by the cardinals and confirmed in office by the clergy and the people. This is a clean break indeed, which divides the future sharply from the past, in the shape of the last hundred years' tradition, and cuts the Gordian knot of papal subordination, in theory at least.

For a long time simony is discussed and fought against; by simony of course we mean, the practice of selling positions in the church, parishes, bishoprics and abbeys, the practice by which at one time in Milan the subdeaconship was rated at twelve denars, the deaconship at eighteen, and a priesthood at twenty-four. But one fine day the nature of the problem changes. People begin to realize (some had understood this right from the beginning) that the downfall of the Church does not lie merely in the shameless traffiicking of the sacred, but also in the very fact that spiritual benefices should be conferred by a layman, and that the Church, together with its laws and practices, has been set into the feudal framework and used for terrestrial ends. Once this discovery is made, all collaboration between the two powers is rendered impossible, and all lay investitures of ecclesiastical benefices, and indeed the vast majority of dealings between clergy and laity are deemed simoniacal and therefore null and void. In 1049, in the presence of the French clergy—this was before the war against the empire was declared—Leo IX begins by forbidding anyone to assume an ecclesiastical office unless he has been elected according to canon law, that is by the people and the clergy. Ten years later, in 1059, Nicholas strikes straight at the root of the matter by declaring that no ecclesiastic may receive a church from the hands of a layman.

Nicolaitism has been written and legislated against *ad nauseam*, along with solemn statements of principle, prohibitions and threats. Now punishment arrives on the scene. And since severe disciplinary sanctions are not enough to eradicate the evil, the Church introduces a completely revolutionary, subversive way of dealing with it. One can only hope to understand this extremely rich and complex century if one looks beyond the great protagonists to the middle and lower strata of the society: the *ministeriales* of Germany; the knights of France, poor, and eager for conquest and adventure; the Italian vavasours; the agricultural populace in its revolt against its feudal servitude; the townships, which had developed under the immunizing control of the bishops and were subject to thrills of evangelic purity which led them to the brink of heresy, working with fervour and darkly hating the rich and powerful, as those who intend to rise from their misery always do. It is to these local forces that the Church now turns for help in discovering and punishing the simoniacs and concubinaries. The great leaders of the Milanese Pataria appear: Landulf Cotta, Ariald, Anselm of Baggio, Erlembald, the standard-bearer of the Church. The city streets and the countryside are spattered with blood. On the one side are the 'married' clergy and the imperial bishops with all their family and feudal following, on the other the men who at the time appear as the soldiers, heroes and martyrs of the religious movement inspired by Rome, and who in the long run are destined to be the precursors of the commune, the champions in the fight against feudalism and the Middle Ages.

The new Church has already found her men—they are Peter Damian, Hildebrand, Humbert of Silva Candida, Anselm of Baggio and Hugh of Cluny. They serve her with absolute devotion, with their writings, their words and with legations to all parts of the Catholic world, wherever the need is most urgent or the struggle most fierce. After a century of passivity and subjection to the empire, the Church now makes the Roman primacy felt and seen with a succession of councils in France, Italy and Germany, presided over by the tireless Leo IX. The old territorial policy towards southern Italy is revived and the Norman invaders challenged; William the Bastard's invasion of England is given the papal blessing in the name of reform; the designs of the empire are foiled by the matrimonial alliance between the houses of Tuscany and Lorraine; on its own initiative the Church calls men like Stephen IX and Alexander II to the papal throne. In the lay world Alexander II was Anselm of Baggio, one of the leaders of the Milanese Pataria, and Stephen IX was Frederick, the brother of the threatening Geoffrey, Duke of Lorraine and Marquess of Tuscany.

To sum up, if we are to understand the importance of the Gregorian reform, we must remember the following points:

The historical creation of Otto III, the incorporation of the Church in the empire, the imperial election of the pope, and the sharing of the struggle against simony and concubinage, survives his death.

The reform which the two supreme powers have undertaken is a gigantic task which threatens to undermine the entire society; and it is also a contradictory one, because it aims at the purification and elevation of the Church, which, once achieved, can only result in an irremediable conflict between the Church herself and the empire.

The partnership lasts for the first half of the century more or less; from then on the consciousness of the rift becomes ever clearer and action is taken accordingly: the decree on papal elections, the condemnation of simony on all investitures of ecclesiastics performed by laymen, the revolutionary struggle against nicolaitism, the renewal of ecclesiastical cadres, the reaffirmation of the primacy, the political revival and the open challenge to the empire with the papal elections.

On April 22, 1073, Hildebrand, the archdeacon of the Holy Roman Church, was elected pope, with the name of Gregory VII. Alexander II having died the day before, he had prescribed a fast of three days, with almsgiving and prayers, in preparation for the decision on the new election. But although at first the citizens had stayed quiet, as they normally did on such occasions, suddenly during the burial ceremony (the story is one related by Gregory himself), a great throng appeared and threw themselves on him like madmen without giving him a chance to speak or think, and set him on the papal throne by pure force. After this, the cardinals, clergy and populace met in the Basilica of St Peter in Chains and formally repeated the election, and the ritual questions were answered by the customary acclamations: *'Placet vobis?' 'Placet.'*; *'Vultis eum?' 'Volumus.'*; *'Laudatis eum?' 'Laudamus'*.

Hildebrand was well prepared for the papal crown, and his accession was not unexpected. We know little of his early years, and it is hard to know how much credit to give the tradition that he was a native of Sovana near Siena, and the son of a peasant by the name of Bonizone. It is known that an uncle on his father's side was the Abbot of Santa Maria sull'Aventino, and various indications suggest that he was from his youth familiar with the Roman society of the time, and was on intimate terms with the powerful family of the Pierleoni, who had been converted to Christianity for several decades and were partisans of the reform. After being educated in the monastery on the Aventine, he had left the city to accompany the pious, austere and unhappy Gregory VI, who was deposed and exiled at the Synod of Sutri, to Germany. He may have been attached to him by a blood relationship as well as by the patent affinity of their ideals. After his death he returned to Italy in the train of Leo IX, under whose papacy he was made abbot of the monastery of St Paul outside the Walls, and subsequently subdeacon and cardinal (in 1050). In twenty years and more dedicated to the service of the Church he visited Italy, Germany and France, and spoken in person with the great men of the time: the foremost lay potentates, including Henry III and the Empress Agnes of Merania, and popes, cardinals, bishops, abbots, and reformers of every kind. He acquired first hand experience of all the most important ecclesiastical problems, the state of the Catholic clergy and the conditions of the empire, the Milanese Pataria, the Norman problem in Southern Italy, the Norman conquest of England. And he had first supported papal policy, as abbot and legate, and then directed it from the time of Alexander II, as archdeaçon of the Holy Roman Church, and done so vith Cluniacensian strictness and lively faith in the Roman primacy. as is usually supposed, he was born between 1015 and 1020, he now already over fifty years old; he was small of stature and epossessing to look at. His greatness lay elsewhere.

ketch the life of Gregory VII is a more difficult task than ne is to follow contemporary evidence faithfully, give short ne's imagination, and at the same time explain where the tness of this man lay. There are plenty of moving and dramatic incidents which historians have exploited to the full: the pope being torn from the altar by a band of armed men when he was celebrating the Christmas mass in Santa Maria Maggiore in 1075; his subsequent imprisonment in a tower where he was insulted and threatened, until he was rescued by the people and returned to the church to finish the interrupted service; the scene at Canossa, in the depths of winter, with the emperor begging for absolution at the gates of the castle and the pope first resisting and then finally giving in to the pleas of his retinue and pardoning his former and future enemy; his delivery from the hands of Henry IV by Robert Guiscard, who sacks Rome with his Norman army; his exile in Salerno, and the biblical pronouncement from his death bed, *'dilexi iustitiam at odivi iniquitatem propterea morior in exilio'*, the last attestation of his completed work, his bitterness and condemnation of the injustice of the world. Burdened as he was by the weight of the whole world, this man was also granted the friendship and solace of gracious noblewomen, such as Agnes of Merania, Beatrice of Tuscany and her daughter, Mathilde, the great countess who was the object of contempt, ambiguous remarks and open insinuations from the mouths of her early enemies and later adversaries.

But try as we may, the story of Gregory's life remains extraordinarily austere and resists all attempts at romanticization, encompassed as it is by a handful of synodical decrees, the twenty-seven propositions of the *Dictus papae* and a few hundred letters. At certain points it reminds us of the severity of Gregory the Great. He too trembles when the shouting Romans call him to the papal throne. He writes to Desiderius, the Abbot of Monte Cassino, 'The death of our lord, Pope Alexander, has fallen back onto me, and so shaken and disturbed are my very entrails that I can say with the prophet: "I have come into the deep of the sea and been submerged by the tempest; I have made hoarse my throat with crying",' and, 'Fear and trembling have come upon me and hidden in the darkness'. The monastery has formed his character permanently with its discipline; he too, like his namesake, but with far more serious consequences, wants the clergy divorced from the secular world, and the Church freed from its bonds.

Humble, charitable and pious to the point of tearfulness, Gregory clings before all things and all men to his profound and all-consuming conscience of his mission. Already in the first few months of his papacy he states what he takes to be his duty in a letter to the faithful of Lombardy, which echoes the *Regula Pastoralis* of St Gregory:

'I want you to know, dear brothers, and many of you know it already, that we have been put in such a position that we are compelled, whether willing or no, to announce truth and justice to all men, and especially to Christians, for the Lord said: "Shout and do not tire, lift your voice like a trumpet and announce their sins to my people"; and elsewhere He says: "If you do not announce his sin to the sinner, I shall hold you to account for his soul"; and the Prophet says: "Accursed be the man who holds back his sword from blood", which means who witholds the word of predication from censoring the things of the flesh.'

His small body is animated by enormous strength and a tireless spirit, but even he is sometimes overcome by 'a fearful grief and universal sorrow', he feels himself imprisoned and prays for deliverance. When he tells Beatrice and Mathilde of Tuscany of his recovery from a serious illness, Gregory adds: 'We feel we have more cause to grieve than to rejoice. Indeed our soul was already approaching and yearning for that homeland where He who weighs our labour and sorrow prepares rest and comfort for the weary. Instead, being restored to our usual labours and our endless troubles, we suffer with every hour the pains and anguish of a woman in childbirth, not knowing how to save the Church from being wrecked before our very eyes.' And in his hours of unhappiness he commends himself with the most tender, confident abandon to the prayers of his friends and of the faithful, for only this can obtain the salvation of the Church, or, if nothing more, his own peace.

Although the desolation and tenderness of St Gregory and of Hildebrand are equally profound, there is still a substantial difference in their characters. In the former the suffering is somewhat personal, it is the weight of worldly cares set against the leaping of his soul in its aspiration to be united with God. But however great his thirst for eternity, purity and peace, he clings with a will to reality, suffers, supports and fights it. The Roman primacy is the unshakeable principle of his faith; but it is not yet the measure and the norm of the world. Gregory VII, on the other hand, can repeat the words St Gregory wrote to St Augustine in England, to justify his leniency towards the French bishops: 'It is the practice of the Holy Roman Church to tolerate some things and even to ignore some others' and so on. But his basic character is not that of a man of action, or as some have said, of an astute politician; he is, in complete faithfulness to the tradition, a great revolutionary, with just that much of the abstract theorist in him to make a good innovator. There is a lack of contact between the interminable, contradictory involutions of politics and his simple and absolute conception of the government of the world, which transcends history and is both human and superhuman at the same time. This, in his hour of dejection, is the cause of his mortal sorrow that he cannot transfer to reality the warm and lucid certainty of his faith.

The truth and justice which Gregory VII, to use his own words, had to announce to men, are contained in the twenty-seven propositions of the *Dictatus papae*, written two years after his assumption of the papacy, in 1075, the fruit of thirty years of experience and meditation in the service of the Church. Together with two famous letters addressed to Herman, Bishop of Metz, the *Dictatus* is the original source of what we may in spite of authoritative objections still refer to as theocracy or papal theocracy. The whole structure rests on the principle of the Roman primacy, that the Roman Church has been founded by God alone, in virtue of the words of Christ to St Peter: 'Feed my sheep', and: 'I say unto you that you are Peter and upon this rock I shall build my church, and the gates of Hell shall not prevail against it. And I will give unto you the keys of the kingdom of Heaven. And all that you have bound on earth shall be bound also in Heaven; and all that you have loosed on earth shall be loosed also in Heaven'. It must be noted that this is not a question of a simple doctrinal statement but rather one of positive faith, which finds its most efficacious and human expression in the confidence with which Gregory refers to the Apostle in his actions and even identifies himself with him. From this principle are descended the doctrines of the infallibility of the Roman Church and the exclusion from Catholicism of those who are not in agreement with the Church; from this the attributes of the pope: 'The only man who may by right be called universal', whose feet all princes must kiss', 'whom no man may judge', 'who, once ordained according to canonical law, becomes indubitably holy by the merit of St

Peter', 'name unique in the world', 'the only one to be pronounced in all churches'. And hence finally the pope's absolute power in the government of the Church, and in the secular world, the authority 'to depose emperors', and 'to release subjects from their duties to the wicked'.

Being established in this manner, Gregory's position is a formidable one, for he has raised himself above the earth and above mankind, outside history, in a region where no human arguments can reach him. He is vindicating the divine right which gives him supreme judgment and power in the government of the world. His position is formidable particularly in his conflict with the empire; because Henry IV and the German clergy, bound as they are to the tradition of a kingdom founded on the election and conferment of the great ecclesiastical benefices by the king, are presented with the dilemma of either making peace with the pope and sacrificing the cornerstone of their power, or maintaining their power but being thrust from the bosom of the Church; in other words they will be deprived of their power one way or another.

This consideration, in addition to the knowledge of their personal characteristics, helps to explain the varying attitudes of the two adversaries throughout the course of their struggle: the hesitant, contradictory and temporarily impolitic actions and attitude of Gregory, alternately patient and impulsive, indulgent and stern, pacific and impetuous, condemned as he is to witness the contradiction between harsh reality and his own divine ideal; and the complete humanity of Henry IV, so much in harmony with his age, so bound to circumstances, hunted to death, abandoned, betrayed, yet untamable, crafty and heroic in the defence of his rights.

Gregory VII's work is concentrated as much on the east as on the west. The Byzantine Empire, which had been divorced completely from Rome since the schism effected twenty years before by the patriarch Michael Cerularius, was now in grievous straits, being mutilated by the Normans in Italy and dangerously threatened by the Turks in the east. The pope considered it his most urgent duty to bring the eastern world back to orthodoxy, and in order to achieve his religious ends he proposed to attack the Normans and to personally lead an expedition of succour to the east with forces provided by William of Burgundy, Godfrey of Lorraine, Raymond IV of Saint Giles, and Amedeus II of Savoy. The plan was a great one, but it placed too much trust in the good faith of the princes and the facility of the enterprise in southern Italy; and when put to the test Gregory's hopes proved completely illusory and he was outmanoeuvred politically as well. As a final stroke of irony, far from imposing his own will, he ended up by coming to terms with the greatest of the Normans, Robert Guiscard. He encouraged his plans for expansion in the Orient at a time when his presence in Italy was really indispensable to him; it was to his soldiers that he owed his deliverance at the time of his greatest danger, and it was in his territory that he found his last refuge and his tomb.

In the west, Gregory VII conducted a universal war against particularism, both lay and ecclesiastic. From this point of view, he was the greatest destroyer of the old feudal world and the greatest creator of the new order. His reform was a struggle against simony and nicolaitism, and at the same time it was a levelling, and a monarchic centralization of the whole ecclesiastic structure in Rome. The bishops lost more and more power over the monasteries, and with the institution of exemption, they were subordinated directly to the Holy See. Much the same happened to the secular clergy: the local powers, primates, metropolitans and bishops, were divested of their ancient prerogatives in favour of the papal legates; all dignitaries of the Church were obliged to come to Rome after their election to receive their pallium, and every effort was made to increase the subordination of the episcopate, and the frequency of its contact with the pope. One of the most significant phenomena of this time was the extreme mobility of the church dignitaries, from the centre to the periphery and vice versa, all beneath the command of a single will, which could grant no rest, either to others or itself. The whole of the vast field of Catholicism was cleared, every clod of earth broken, and the surface levelled. The regime of local particularism gave way to one of powerful centralization, which, though developed piecemeal in order to communicate the orders from Rome in the fight against simony and nicholaitism, grew into a great system which mirrored in its totality the fundamental consciousness of unity of the *Dictatus papae*.

Gregory VII's reform thus consisted of the struggle against secular influence in the Church and for papal centralization. And although the former usually claims the lion's share of our attention under the title, 'The Struggle of the Investitures', we cannot really draw a dividing line between them, or subordinate the one to the other in importance. The reason for our preference lies rather in the heroic and spectacular character of the fight, in its immediate success, and in the profound human interest it arouses in us.

The first skirmishes started in the years 1074-5. Henry IV was just recovering from a dual crisis, and had to proceed with great caution. On the one hand he had tried to dispossess the dukes of Bavaria and Saxony, who constituted a serious threat to his crown, and had been forced to make peace and to renounce his claims; on the other, after being excommunicated by Alexander II, he had had to cease all relations with persons out of favour with the Church and declare his devotion to the Holy See, the pope and the movement of reform, all this in order to obtain the pope's pardon. Gregory VII appeared to be personally disposed to allow the emperor greater indulgence and kindness. But, as has been pointed out, this was not an issue that could be solved by a personal agreement of two men, or one that could be sorted out with a modicum of good will on both sides.

When the condemnation of simony and concubinage was repeated, and worse, when all church and monastery investitures by laymen were unequivocally forbidden, and lay potentates and the faithful as a whole were called to take part in the campaign by seeing that the decrees were obeyed, the conflict and its dire implications finally became horribly and unambiguously clear. The German king and clergy who were opposed to the reform found themselves closely allied in the defence of their common interests. On January 24, 1076, Henry held a council of twenty-six bishops at Worms, at which they drew up a solemn document containing all the charges against Hildebrand. He was a usurper, who had succeeded to the papacy against his own solemn promise. With his worldly ambition, his cruelty and his pride, he had stripped the bishops of all power, assigned the government of ecclesiastical affairs to the mob, conferred church offices to the basest flatterers, and savagely ruined all the churches of Italy, Germany, France and Spain. He had filled the Church with scandal '*convictu et cohabitatione alienae mulieris familiori quam necesse est*',—the woman whose familiarity was in question was naturally Mathilde of Canossa, the wife of Godfrey Gibbosus; and had excited comment and complaints from all over Europe with his 'new council of women, to which he had given the right to administrate the whole ecclesiastical world'. Hildebrand was therefore declared an unlawful pope, and obedience to him unwarranted. Henry himself supported the council with two letters, one to Gregory charging him to relinquish the papal throne, the other to the Romans, telling them to force him to do so and to hold a new papal election.

The reply came about three weeks later from the Roman Lenten synod (in 1076). In answer to the insinuations, the personal resentment, the picayune attack of Henry and his followers, all perfectly understandable in human terms, this reply, with its controlled dignity, its decisiveness, and its gravity of expression, was one worthy of the writer of the *Dictatus Papae*. The decree reads:

'Blessed Peter, prince of the Apostles, lend your pious ear, we pray you, and listen to me your servant, whom you have nourished from infancy and have to this day delivered from the hands of the wicked who have hated me and hate me still for my faithfulness unto thee. Be thou my witness, and Our Lady the mother of God, and the blessed Paul, your brother among all the blessed, that the Holy Roman Church drew me, against my will, to its government, and I did not rise to your seat as a thief; that I would have preferred to end my life as a monk and a pilgrim, rather than occupy your office through worldly vanity with a profane heart. And therefore, by your grace, and not in virtue of my own deeds, I believe that it was and is your will that the Christian people that were committed particularly to your care should particularly obey me in your stead, as it has been entrusted to me. And that grace that comes to me from you is the power given by God to bind and to loose in Heaven and on earth. Thus supported by this confidence, for the honour and protection of the Church, on behalf of Almighty God, the Father the Son and the Holy Ghost, with your authority and power, I interdict the rule of the Germans and of Italy by King Henry, the son of Henry the emperor, who has risen with unprecedented pride against your Church, and I release all Christians from the bond of the oath which they have sworn and will swear to him, and I ordain that no one shall serve him as their king. It is indeed just, that he who tries to diminish the honour of your Church, should himself lose the honour with which he has been invested. And since he has disdained Christian obedience, and has not returned to God, from whose ways he had departed, by associating with the excommunicated and rejecting my warnings (which, thou art my witness, I sent him for his salvation), by separating himself from the Church, and by attempting to divide the Church itself, in thy name I now bind him with the chain of the anathema, and in virtue of thy faith I constrain him in such a way that all men may know that thou art Peter, and upon thy rock the Son of God built his Church and the gates of Hell shall not prevail against it.'

Until this time, whatever the affirmations of principle and the struggles in which the Holy See had had to exert itself, the Roman primacy had never before had to take the extreme step of striking at the heart of the greatest political organism of the west with the weapon of the excommunication and deposition of the sovereign, and of the liberation of his subjects from their oath of loyalty. A few months later (on September 3, 1076) Gregory VII went even further. In a letter addressed to all those 'who defend the Christian faith in the German kingdom', while expressing the hope that Henry 'might be converted with all his heart to God', and be reconciled, he still warned them of the possibility of a new election if this should not happen, and made the legitimacy of the result conditional on the promise of the electorate to consider the Church, 'as a mistress not as a slave' and to do all that was necessary for 'the well-being of the Christian religion and of all the empire. He reserved the right to make the final decision on Henry's restoration, and also, in effect, on the preparations for the new elections and on the person elected.

Henry had allowed himself one last action of defiance. On March 27, 1076, in Utrecht where his followers were grouped around him, he sent the pope another offensive letter, repeating the same accusations, and opposing the Gregorian doctrine with that of temporal monarchy and the divine right of kings. The letter ended with the well-known words, 'I Henry, king by the grace of God, and all my bishops, say unto thee: "Abdicate, abdicate, thou accursed for all time".' This was his last spark of spirit, after which he gave way to dejection. The pope's threat was leading his followers to desert him, his old enemies were gaining strength, and Rudolf of Swabia's fingers were itching for his crown. The deposed king found himself forced in the presence of the princes to make the humiliating promise that he would obey the Church in all things and put an end to his wrongdoing; if he were not reconciled with the pope within a year and a day he would be replaced (Treviri-Oppenheim, October 16th onwards, 1076).

But as we know, while Gregory was on his way to Germany to pass judgment on the king there, the latter surprised him at Canossa; and by dint of his repentance, whether true or false, and the resulting absolution from his excommunication (an act of extreme forbearance on Gregory's part, which it would nevertheless have been difficult and imprudent to refuse) Henry demolished the whole laborious construction of papal policy at a single blow. He returned to his kingdom reconciled with the Church, no longer in the garb of the humble penitent begging for mercy. The partisans of the pope felt themselves cheated, or in any case were disconcerted by the sudden *volte-face*. The power of initiative now slipped through the pope's fingers, and he could only watch the dynastic struggle which now broke out in Germany.

On March 15, 1077, at Forchheim the Saxon nobility elected Rudolf of Saxony king; and in accordance with the orders from Rome which were supported by the papal legate present at the diet, they asserted the elective principle of the German monarchy as against the hereditary, and affirmed the liberty of ecclesiastic elections. We would have expected Gregory to lose no time in recognizing Rudolf. Instead, by one of these contradictions which can only be explained by a certain insensibility of his to the immediate exigencies of the struggle and the prevalence in his policy of his high ideals, he now went on for three years announcing that he was coming to Germany to act as arbiter between the two contendents. He only finally decided to recognize Rudolf in 1080, when Henry's victorious army was pushing him from defeat to defeat and he was threatened by death, which in fact caught up with him three days after the battle on the Elster on October 15, 1080.

So Henry triumphed. Germany was once more in his hands, and he was able to go down into Italy, have himself crowned by his antipope, take possession of Rome, and blockade Gregory VII in the Castel'Sant'Angelo. Then as we know, came the liberation, and his exile and death.

'We have established nothing new, and nothing of our own invention, but leaving error behind us, we have held it imperative to seek out and follow the first and only discipline of the Church and the way trodden by the saints.' Words of this kind recur constantly in Gregory's writings, and they are reply enough to the accusations whose echo we have found in the letters of the king and clergy of Germany. He could proclaim his absolute loyalty to the catholic tradition in good faith. It was not in relation to the traditional principles which had been enunciated in the abstract, or partially and sporadically followed by his predecessors, that Gregory VII was a revolutionary; it was rather in relation to the Europe of the eleventh century, in as much as he took the principle of the Roman primacy to its ultimate conclusion and translated it systematically into action.

Although we have as usual been speaking almost exclusively of the conflict of Church and empire, we must remember that the crisis concerned all or nearly all the Catholic world, not excluding England; for William the Conquerer was devoted to both the Church and the movement of reform. But while, in the greater part of the Christian world, all errors, accusations, and condemnations remained circumscribed as it were in the immediate local or personal sphere, in Germany the very constitution of the state and the imperial power meant that the opposition to Rome, the disobedience of the king and of the leading laymen and ecclesiastics immediately became important political issues which radically affected the government of the world.

Feudalism had meant particularism: for the most part there had been tiny endless wars between districts and feudal lords. The movement of reform that culminated in Gregory VII did not bring peace; it brought more fearful and more universal war. The difference of this period, and the greatness, lay in this: that at a word of command from Rome, all the infinite, diminutive local interests were united and raised to the height of a single great political, religious and moral problem. Beneath the fervent, militant activity of the

Roman centralization, a second Europe was being moulded as a successor to Charlemagne's. It was more stable, larger, and more conscious of itself; the masses who pushed to get to the light, the protagonists of the morrow, were called as witnesses to the struggle.

The world did not become as Gregory had wanted it by magic. He died a disappointed man. When, after a few more decades of wars, we come to the stipulation of the Concordats between England, France, and finally the empire and the Holy See, when, that is, bitter experience had led to the conclusion that it was both possible and necessary to separate the temporal benefice from the spiritual, to leave the bestowal of lay honours to the lay potentates and the liberty of election and ordination to the Church, we might think that the agreement was one of simple compromise. But in fact an extremely serious and irretrievable step had been taken. The empire, once deprived of its ancient ecclesiastical privileges, of its religious substance, was mortally wounded, and forced to look for new claims to legitimacy in Roman law. The entire feudal system was dealt its death-blow too, on account of the recovery of the lower orders, the democratic and constitutional principles put out by the Church and translated into practise in the course of the struggle, the agitation of the great interests over and against particularism, and finally the deep-seated revolution that had taken place in society. For the Church was free at last; after nearly two centuries of desperate effort, it had succeeded in reforming the clergy, disentangling them from the tentacles of the laymen and the world, and was now moving forward with its army of a hierarchy, immense and compact, all answering to one command, towards the conquest and hegemony of Europe. The laity too was moving on its way; it served both Roman and European greatness, and in the meantime was developing within itself a new civic and political consciousness which was to put both feudalism and Church to trial; it was progressing towards the ends which were to be the first great abnegations of the Middle Ages, the commune, and the sovereign state.

When we think what interests were at stake, how much history (all the history up to the present day) was being prepared in the Roman synods, and in the diets and on the battlefields of Germany, we cannot but smile to remember that the polemics between the apologists and supporters of the two protagonists of the time have continued to this day, Gregory's holiness being contrasted with his ambition, and Henry's heroism with his cunning. For our own limited purpose, we have said enough.

There is not a butcher and a victim, a guilty and an innocent party, between whom it is our duty to judge. Our concern here is not with virtue and vice, but with the past and future of Europe, with the greatest revolution of the Middle Ages, and the deepest political and religious faith. Henry is the champion of his dynasty, of the imperial tradition, and of the entire west; he uses every weapon at his disposal to maintain the order of the past and to fight an unarmed but invincible foe. Gregory stands for revolution and the future. And our admiration for his lofty idealism must not blind us to the humanity of his adversary.

On the tomb of the emperor we should like to see engraved the words written four hundred years or so ago by a German historian:

'Supreme and valiant defender of the majesty of the empire,' who when excommunicated, abandoned by his followers and betrayed by his familiars, 'still was able to withstand despair, to retain his strength, and to stand by the principles on which the majesty of the empire had been built by his fathers.'

On the tomb of the pope we would not like to repeat the desolate, '*Dilexi iustitiam et odivi iniquitatem, propterea morior in exilio*', but to reread the lines in which Alfanus of Salerno linked the work of Hildebrand, the archdeacon of Rome, with the greatest exploits of the ancient Roman republic, the deeds of Marius, Caesar and the Scipios; we should like to see too the last solemn profession of faith made by this exiled and broken man not long before his death, in a state of complete detachment from all worldly passions:

'Since by divine disposition my mother Church has put me, in spite of my unworthiness, and, God is my witness, against my own will, in the seat of the Apostles, with all my strength I have attempted to act in such a way that the Holy Church, the bride of Christ, our mistress and our mother, should be honoured as of old, and should remain free, chaste and Catholic. Now, dear brothers, listen carefully to what I say. All those who bear the title Christian and know the obligations of their faith, know and believe that the blessed Peter, prince of the Apostles, is the father of all Christians and the first shepherd after Christ, and that the Holy Roman Church is the mother and mistress of all churches. If you have this faith and are untouched by any doubt, in the name of Almighty God I ask and command you, whoever your priest may be, even if he is unworthy, to help and succour your Father and your Mother, in order that you may obtain from them the absolution of your sins, and their blessing and grace in this world and in eternity.'

CHAPTER 12

THE EXPANSION OF THE CATHOLIC WORLD

THE FIRST CRUSADE

A historian has recently posed the question whether a third aspect of the life and work of Gregory VII, as significant as the political and the religious, should not be considered alongside them: the military. He asks whether we should not put alongside the images of the saint and the founder of the papal theocracy, that of the man of arms and war, indeed the most bellicose figure of the century. He is not thinking of the proverbial: 'Accursed be he who withholds his sword from blood', which he enjoys repeating, after the example of the Prophet and Gregory the Great, nor of the warlike phrases which we find in his letters and the decrees of his councils: 'victory over the enemy'; 'the standard of St Peter'; 'the army of Christ'; words and mental attitudes which re-echo an old tradition and reveal the fiery nature of the archdeacon and pope.

War in this context is no metaphor. When the chronicler, Landulf, writes that 'while residing in the palace he ruled the Roman forces like a captain' he is referring to actual military activity. And we may recall the mercenaries he enlisted, the great feudal barons of France and Germany he caused to rebel against their respective sovereigns, his threat to Philip I of France that he would *modis omnibus* lose his crown if he did not make amends for his sins, and the expeditions he planned or accomplished in Spain and England, southern Italy and the east.

Gregory VII's warlike attitude and action are not an original part of his character. In this aspect he reflects the life of the whole of Europe and of his own times. We have seen how the west had been nibbled on its borders, milked of its riches, and invaded from all sides by Normans, Arabs, Hungarians, Slavs and Byzantines. And now, between 900 and 1000, it shows the first signs of a miraculous youth, generous and fierce, adventurous and clever. This is the recovery of Europe, the decisive moment in which fortunes are reversed. Hungarians and Slavs have been halted in their territories, and civilized by imperial armies and missions. The Normans have settled on the continent and emigrate from the extreme west of France as merchants and pilgrims to the east and to the south of Italy. The Byzantine dominion in Italy has been shaken by rebellions. The Arabs, after being dislodged from the Garigliano and Frassineto, are now feeling the pressure from the Christian states in Spain, they clash with the Genoese and Pisan fleets in the western Mediterranean and are compelled to evacuate Sardinia. Finally Venice bars entry to all Moslems and sweeps the Croatian and Narentine pirates out of the Adriatic.

It is no good looking for a clear feeling of European unity in these events. Europe has little self-awareness as yet, and no consciousness of superior power, greater dignity, or moral obligation to make truth triumph over error. The impulse is local and multiple in character; it has something involuntary about it, which makes it look like a crisis of growth. And yet we feel that there is a profound design of history which brings a unity to these efforts. Their contemporaneity, far from being a coincidence, corresponds to the maturing of a fixed point in the history of the three worlds of the Mediterranean, the Roman, the Byzantine, and the Arab. In the west, there is a whole new society of sea-faring cities, both mercantile and warlike, of great feudal lords, heads of their own armies, who at the same time command and obey the impulse which comes from below, from the huge multitude of their vassals, a complex of more or less confused and obscure forces, of powerful virgin energy, hungry for war, conquest and adventure.

The Church, being the soul of the west and having grown together with it, does not abstain from this martial ferment. The movement for peace and the truce of God, started by the Cluniacs at the end of the tenth century and universally accepted in the first half of the eleventh, made it necessary for all local churches to organize arms very much of this world under their command, in order to enforce the observance of peace, and to punish the transgressors. A severe reformer such as the bishop Vason of Liege did not hesitate, in spite of being unarmed himself in obedience to Canon Law, to lead his knights to the defence of the city and its church property. The whole reform is war in the literal sense of the word, from the Church's return to temporal politics in its contest with Byzantines and Normans in the south of Italy, to the restoration of discipline, the struggle against ecclesiastic feudalism, and the affirmation of papal theocracy.

We may be surprised by the aggressive words which accompany Gregory VII's action; but our wonder is far greater, and the testimony a far more significant one, when a follower of St Benedict, Amatus of Monte Cassino, celebrates in his prose the mighty undertaking of Robert Guiscard and his companions, with the exultation of conquest and adventure; when another mild monk of Monte Cassino, Alphanus, who later becomes an archbishop, shows Gisolphus and Guido of Salerno that their goals must be victory over Arabs, Byzantines and Normans; when at the mere sight of Hildebrand, Roman hearts thrill with the ancient pride of the Scipios, of Marius, Caesar, the Via Sacra and the Via Latina, and the Capitol, the powerful seat of the empire; and they fling out their invective against the enthroned barbarity which must once more and this time for ever be subjected by the ancient arts of Rome and the burning sword of the Apostle Peter.

If the Church does not hold itself aloof from the military spirit that pervades the west between the tenth and eleventh century, so inversely, but more significantly and much more effectively, the religious spirit of the Church penetrates and imbues the warrior society of the time. This is shown by hundreds of small indications, the cries of 'St George', 'St Peter' and 'St Benedict' that resound on the battlefields; the banners with their symbols of the faith, the cross, pictures of the saints, fluttering from one end of Europe to the other, the *standards of St Peter*, bestowed by the Church to her champions with an indeterminate significance of benediction, consecration and feudal investiture; the armies of vassals and vavasours who respond with devotion and concern to the call of Rome, the churches and the monasteries; and finally the spiritual remuneration, the remission of sins promised to the combatants.

There is a simple expression which by the change in its meaning indicates the profound transformation which occurred in the western world during this period. *Militia Christi* had for centuries been life itself with its suffering and temptations, and *miles Christi* the man who by means of his faith had fought and triumphed over all the baser passions, had set the spirit above the flesh with self-denial and sacrifice, the priest, the monk and the hermit. Now the man who fights in the service of the Church is called, *knight*, or *soldier of Christ* or *of St Peter* in a literal sense.

The benediction which had formerly been invoked on the head and the arms of the sovereigns, is now given to the knight's sword, and to the ranks and standards of the new armies.

'O Lord, hear our prayer by your grace, and deign to bless with the right hand of your majesty this sword which your servant desires to wear, in order that it may be a defence and protection of churches, widows, orphans, and all who serve God, against the cruelty of the pagans an object of fear and terror, and of dread to all others who plot to ensnare us.'

'Almighty and everlasting God, who art the benediction of all men and the strength of the victors, turn your propitious glance to the prayers of our humility, and sanctify this standard, prepared for war, with your heavenly blessing, so that it may be strong against hostile and rebellious nations, and, furnished with this protection, it may be terrible to the enemies of the Christian people, and the salvation of him who trusts in Thee, and his certain faith in victory. For Thou, O God, art He who provokes wars and grants the aid of the heavenly host to those who put their trust in Thee.'

'O Lord, assist with Thy mercy this our army and beneath the brightness of the sky grant the help they desire for their voyage, and just as Thou gavest defence and safety to Israel in flight from Egypt, so now to Thy people moving to battle, send an angel of light who shall defend them against all adversities, both day and night.'

Towards the close of the millenium when Europe was on the verge of the crusades, the knightly rule, imbued as it was with the religious spirit, became the common conscience of the entire West. It was set down by Bonizo of Sutri in his *Book of the Christian Life*:

'The duty of a knight is to show himself subservient to his lord, not to seek for booty, not to spare his own life to save that of his lords, to fight to the death for the safety of the state, to overwhelm heretics and schismatics, to defend the poor, widows, and orphans, not to violate their promised faith nor in any way break their oath to their own lords.'

From the middle of the century on, the whole of the west is, so to speak, an immense theatre of war, Roman and Christian, a unique and infinitely varied scene. There are Italians and Germans moving with Leo IX to the battle and defeat of Civitate; Spanish kings and Aquitainian and Provencal nobles attacking the Arabs in the Iberian peninsula; Normans in the north, bringing reform with their victory to England, and Paterines making it triumph in Lombardy. There are alliances made by the Church between Tuscany and Lorraine and Tuscany and Bavaria, both to the detriment of the feudal empire; Normans in the south who have thrown themselves into the struggle and are hounding the Byzantines and the Moslems to the very tip of the Italian peninsula and into Sicily and the east; and finally seafaring republics taking possession of the Mediterranean and bringing war to the coasts of Africa and Asia. With the religious impulse, the petty feudal wars are ennobled and unified, the confused brute forces of Europe wake up gradually, discover their own purpose, take on a soul and a meaning, which is that of a Roman and Christian Europe, mistress of her own boundaries, teeming with power, and intolerant of all foreign interference.

Our reference to ennoblement and unity does not of course mean that we are assailed by nostalgia for that religious and heroic age, nor do we believe that the west at that time was transformed into a compact army pledged for life and death, with the tremendous austerity of a mission, to the extermination of schismatics and infidels and the triumph of Catholicism. This is a historical opinion and should be understood as such. Although the poetry of a later age presents us with the wisdom of Godfrey of Bouillon as the sublime model of the time, in point of fact, the stage of Europe was now for the first time peopled with a mass of great, well-defined figures, their feet firmly on the ground. They were a heroic generation, full of humanity, and subject in good circumstances and bad alike to all the passions of man. Without a predestined path or goal, they created a new consciousness in this time of trial, and, by their boldness constructed the present and future greatness of Europe.

Eja! letando, populi caterve,
Campidoctoris hoc carmen audite!

Spain is animated and exalted by the exploits of the Cid, the hero of her recovery, who yet, when banished from his homeland, has no hesitation in fighting with the Moors of Saragossa. Around him stand William, Count of Poitiers and Duke of Aquitaine, the Normans William of Montreuil and Robert Crispin, and the Provencal Raymond of St Gilles, Count of Toulouse, later the commander of the Crusaders of the East.

The whole of the action of Gregory VII is flanked by the virile strength of Mathilde of Canossa, the great countess, mistress of men and land, who puts armies in the field and contrives the intrigues for the whole of Europe. The Pataria follows the warrior Erlembald who has received the standard of the Church from Alexander II and falls in the streets of Milan while leading the people in the hunt for anti-Gregorian ecclesiastics and their supporters.

William the Conqueror too is armed with the banner of St Peter; but he gains his crown at Hastings, where he checks the flight of his men with blows, threats, and the display of his own bare head amid the tumult of the battle. He is to have no scruple in refusing to swear allegiance to the pope or stopping the primate of England, Lanfranc of Canterbury from visiting *ad limina Apostolorum*.

Robert Guiscard, nick-named the Cunning, looks on Calabria with his mouth watering—its rich cities, its many villas, its great pastures crowded with flocks. He is poor and takes to living by thievery. He trespasses onto Church property and is excommunicated; but this does not stop him becoming the champion of Christianity against the Arabs in Sicily, and champion of the reform against the supporters of Henry as they besiege Gregory VII in Rome, nor finally from dying on an expedition to the east that was blessed by the pope. And around Robert there stands the great generation of the Normans, mercenaries and brigands, conquerors and founders of states, Roger, Tancred, and Bohemond.

Men of all lands and all kinds are brought together and uplifted by their religion in a calling to war that does not admit desertion. But in this exercise of individual strength and courage, in the bravery of the warriors and merchants, so remote from the earlier world of local loyalties, in the new capacity for generalship and government, in the broad Mediterranean atmosphere that Europe now breathes, there is something more than religious unity, which points to a multiplicity of interests, to new and different horizons, and to the history of the future.

The epic of Charlemagne, the champion of Christ against the Moors of Spain, and the thousand voices of the chroniclers and biographers, the *Gesta* of William the Conqueror, the *Historia* of the Cid, the *Vita* of Mathilde, and the Lombard chronicles of Arnulf and Landulf, of Amatus, William Apulus, Godfrey Malaterra, are all signs of the adolescent consciousness of Europe. This is expressed sometimes with a prose which itself borders on the epic style in the fresh impetus of creation, sometimes with a rough assonant verse which feels the nobility of the theme and tries to become poetry. Memories of Rome, re-emerging from the depths of consciousness, while Rome returns, changed in spirit, to the Mediterranean, inspire the famous Pisan song of victory for the capture of Mahedia in 1087:

Inclytorum Pisanorum scripturus historiam
antiquorum Romanorum renovo memoriam,
nam extendit modo Pisa laudem admirabilem
quam olim accepit Roma vincendo Carthaginem.

The first crusade is framed in this universal movement which is at once military and religious. The single elements which go to make it up can be found scattered over all the history of the tenth and eleventh centuries, and even earlier, yet the period still retains its unique character of greatness and originality.

The first warlike reference to the Holy Land is perhaps contained in a much discussed letter which is included in the epistolary of Gerbert, the future Silvester II. It appears to come from his pen and to have been written at the close of the tenth century. It is in fact a kind of literary exercise, in which the Church of Jerusalem asks for help from the universal Church of Rome, and breaks into the fervent exhortation: 'Forward then, soldier of Christ, take up your standard and fight, or if you cannot fight with arms, help with your council and your wealth.'

It would be disastrous to try to twist these words, to search them for meaning they do not contain. This invocation of the Holy Land is a new cry, destined to re-echo with time and to acquire a vaster and more profound significance in the future. But in spite of all the discussion for and against that has taken place up to the present, we shall probably never know whether this *miles Christi*, this *signifer et compugnator* really wears armour, holds a lance, sword, and banner, or whether it is instead the old soldier of Christ for whom life itself is a war, in which virtue fights with temptation, or whether, finally the expression is intended to remain in religious and literary ambiguity.

All ambiguity, however, disappears and the call from the Holy Land becomes pressing and resolute when in 1010 the caliph Hakem destroys the Church of the Holy Sepulchure. This was the period at which throughout the Mediterranean basin, by land and sea, the conflict between the Christian and the Moslem worlds was becoming clearly delineated. The profanation of the temple, an object of universal cult, which for centuries had been the goal of pilgrims from every part of the world, was felt to be a provocation which demanded revenge, and had the effect of making the movement of Christian recovery more rapid and intense. The initiative came from Pope Sergius IV, in conjunction with the maritime cities of Italy, in particular Genoa and Venice, who now needed broader scope for their bursting vitality and were clashing at every step with Saracen merchants and pirates. The Holy See took up once more the tradition of the great warrior popes of the ninth and tenth centuries, Leo IV, John VIII and John X, who in the face of enormous difficulties had organized the first Italian alliances against the Arabs and had defeated them at Ostia, Capo Circeo and on the Garigliano.

But the *bannum pontificale* by which Sergius rallied the Christian forces had a much wider range, and revealed a new spirit in the papacy and the Christian west. His call was directed to the whole of the Catholic world, to the kings, the high and low clergy, and to all vassals, great and small. A universal peace declared by the Church and enforced under pain of heresy, allowed all of Europe to concentrate its forces on the common end. Those who could not participate in person at the *proelium Domini*, the battle of the Lord, were to help with the preparation of the arms and the ships. From the seafaring cities came the news that the work was being rushed forward and that many men were preparing to leave their former life to go to sea. For the pope intended, with the help of Venice and Genoa, to arm a fleet of a thousand ships, gather soldiers from Rome, Tuscany, Italy and all over the Christian world, and lead them to Syria 'to avenge the Redeemer and His tomb', and 'to kill the whole race of the infidels'.

But this grandiose plan, powerful as it was as a personal expression, and a presentiment of Europe obedient to the command of Rome, did not perhaps take sufficiently into account the actual state of Europe and the Mediterranean, the former being still too divided, and the latter too much encumbered with Saracen ships. And the great fight of Sergius' dream was split up into single episodes, with Genoa, Pisa and Venice as their sole, though victorious, protagonists. The early simplicity of line, and clarity of ends and means, could no longer be a part of Sergius' plan.

The church of the Holy Sepulchre was restored by the Caliph Mustapher in 1037, as a result of the intervention of the emperor Michael the Paphlagonian, and continued to attract pilgrims, who, perhaps partly for reasons of security, came in ever-increasing numbers, so that, in spite of all the difficulties, the crowds of Europe became familiar with the roads of the Orient. In 1064 the total number of pilgrims led to Jerusalem by the Archbishop of Mainz and the bishops of Bamberg, Ratisbon, and Utrecht was as high as seven to twelve thousand, a real army. They were men and women of every age and condition who faced discomfort and danger to venerate the tomb of Christ.

But the adventuring warrior spirit was by no means divorced from this piety. Indeed it was not unusual for penitents to enlist as soldiers in the service of the eastern empire after fulfilling their vow, as did the Norwegian king, Harald Hardrada, who acquired the reputation of a great commander there around 1040, and later the Normans, Hervé, Robert Crispin, Ursel of Bailleul, and the German Robert the Frisian, Count of Flanders, each of them naturally with his own following of mercenaries and adventurers.

For this and a thousand other reasons—curiosity, travel and defence—Jerusalem drew Constantinople into the limelight. There was one condition above all others, from the middle of the eleventh century onwards, which turned the eyes of the Church anxiously to the east. This was the Turkish advance, which as it spread through Syria and Asia Minor, was suffocating the Christian communities and threatening the capital of the empire itself.

The situation created an eastern problem, based on the one side on Byzantium's desperate pleas for help and on the other by the obligation felt by Rome to send help to the communities of the east and to heal the schism dividing the two Churches. Gregory VII, with his universal spirit and his feverish energy, felt the sufferings of his brothers as an agonizing wound, and the danger as an immutable command to sacrifice; and he sent his appeal to every corner of the Christian world, to the Emperor Henry IV, to William the Count of Burgundy, and 'to all Christians who have the will to defend the faith'; 'to all the faithful of St Peter, especially those beyond the Alps'.

To the emperor he wrote:

'Moreover, I would have your majesty note that the Christians of the lands over the sea, of whom the majority have been destroyed by the pagans with unheard of slaughter, and are being butchered like cattle every day, so that the Christians are almost reduced to nothing, have sent humbly to me, impelled by their excessive hardship, imploring me to help them, our brothers, in whatever way I could, so that the Christian religion should not become utterly lost in our time, which God forbid. And I, being overwhelmed by infinite sorrow and made even to long for death, in that I would rather give my life for them than, by ignoring them, have the whole world to do my bidding, I have endeavoured to encourage and exhort all Christians to be willing to give their lives for their brothers, by defending the law of Christ, and showing the nobility of the sons of God to be brighter than the sun. Italians and ultramontanes, by divine inspiration as I believe and indeed affirm, have received the exhortation favourably, and already more than 50,000 are preparing themselves, with the intention, if they can have me in the expedition as captain and pope, of attacking the enemies of God, and under His guidance reaching the sepulchure of the Lord. Moreover, the consideration which above all impels me to this undertaking is that the Church of Constantinople, which differs from us as regards the origin of the Holy Spirit, is prepared to come to an agreement with the Apostolic See, and also the greater part of the Armenians who have deviated from the Catholic faith and almost all the Orientals are waiting to hear what the faith of the Apostle Peter will decree concerning their different opinions.'

The grief was so piercing, the duty so absolute and the hope so fervent, that the pope was an easy victim of the illusion that the means were ready and the goal at hand. But in the event, nothing came of it, and when hope itself was gone, he felt himself, in his own words, in the grip of 'a mortal desolation'. This too was a preparation and a foretaste of the future. But Gregory could not fight at one and the same time, and with the same resources, both the battle for liberty against feudalism and the empire, and the battle for the safety of the east. So the former was pushed forward with every reserve of energy and the second quietly abandoned. Worse still, as a final triumph of irony, the pope, as an ally of the Normans, was obliged to approve Robert Guiscard's expedition against Byzantium, an undertaking which, if conducted to a definitive victory, could have changed the whole fate of the eastern empire and eastern Christianity, and which, halted as it was in mid-course by Guiscard's death, merely stimulated the ambition of the Normans, and weakened the empire's resistance to the Turks.

Victor III and Urban II, the successors to Gregory VII, inherited both his tasks. On the one hand they continued the negotiations for the unification of the churches and the relief of the east, and on the other pressed on with the campaign against simony and nicolaitism, and the fight against Henry IV and Clement III, his antipope, who together had occupied part of Rome and barred the pope from the Lateran and Castel Sant' Angelo. The only difference was that, although the Gregorian programme for the reform remained unchanged, and Urban II repeated the principles of liberty, purity and subordination to the pope indefatigably from council to council, the pursuance of the struggle had dampened much of the primitive warrior spirit in the Church itself, and the pope regained the Lateran in 1093 and Castel Sant' Angelo in 1095 not by force of arms but by payment, and Henry found himself abandoned by his own family, his wife Prassede and his son Conrad, who were drawn into the orbit of the papal politics.

This is the point at which Urban II held the famous councils of Piacanza, between the 1st and 7th of March, 1095, and Clermont, from the 18th to the 27th of November in the same year. This involved him in long journeys and many contacts with the most influential lay and ecclesiastical figures of Italy and France. The main subject of the meetings was still, as always the reform. And yet not without reason, at the very sound of the word Clermont, our minds turn to the famous scene of the announcement of the Crusade, to the last, or penultimate assembly held at Clermont on November 27th in the public square, the only place that would hold the crowd, when Urban vividly described the horrors inflicted on their brothers of the east by the infidels, the ruin of the churches, and exhorted all Christians to go and fight for their safety. The crowd, shuddering with horror and anger, burst into tears, and gave voice to the formidable cry that was to resound on the battlefields of Asia Minor and Syria: *'Deus le volt'*, 'God wills it'; and Ademar of Monteil, the Bishop of Puy, was the first to kneel before the pope, to beg to be allowed to take part in the expedition.

Urban II took up Gregory VII's plan and carried on with the talks started in 1089 for the unification of the two Churches. So he created nothing new or exceptional in this field either. Nevertheless we are given food for thought by the failure of Gregory VII, and the surprising response Europe made to Urban II; and further by the papacy's sponsoring of an undertaking on a world scale, while it was still engaged in the fight against simony and nicolaitism, and in establishing the theocracy in the face of the sovereigns, and when it did not even have undisputed control of its own seat, which was partly occupied by the antipope and by German forces.

But problems such as these no doubt arise from some preconceived idea which clouds our vision. Although the undertaking did in fact take on the character of a world conflict, it was probably conceived in much more modest terms, rather, on the model of the mercenaries in the service of the empire, as military aid to eastern Christianity, undertaken in view of the reunification of the Churches, and it turned out that in the event it surpassed the hopes and expectations of the pope. No detriment could come to the Church from a favourable reaction to Urban's preaching, that is from the removal of her military support overseas, for her aggressive policy towards the empire had been abandoned and the fortunes of Henry IV were on the wane. On the contrary, she could not but gain prestige, and consequently power. Nor should we allow ourselves to be deceived by her uncertain possession of Rome; for the papacy of Rome was not a bit of property that could be lost by an enemy occupation of long or short duration, it was a principle, a tradition, which, as was shown at this time and many others, could triumph even, or rather all the more, in exile. Urban II continued the work of Gregory VII and came into the better part of his heritage, for it is only by the implacable energy poured into the hierarchical struggle which called the Christian world to obey Rome, that we can explain the response made by Europe to the call of the crusade.

And yet, to judge by this overwhelming response to the pope's words, it seems probable that we are focussing too firmly on him and on the Councils of Piacanza and Clermont, instead of looking also at the people, near and far, who heard his words; and that there are now two protagonists, linked by a single bond, but still with interests that are substantially different and in the last analysis conflicting, the theocratic Church, and the powerful Europe of the eleventh century. According to a writer of this time, Foucher of Chartres, in his *Gesta Francorum*, the Council of Clermont was convened to remedy both the disasters and dangers of the east, and, even more, the disorders of the west, since Urban saw, 'the Christian faith being destroyed by every one, as much by the clergy as the people, with every sort of enormity. The princes were engaged in incessant wars, property and land robbed alternately by first one and then another; men were taken prisoner and driven into hideous dungeons, ransomed for enormous prices, or quietly put away when the pangs of hunger, thirst and cold had done their worst; the holy places were violated, monasteries and houses burned, not a mortal man was spared, and all things divine and human were made mock of'.

We who stand at a distance from these hardships can take such laments with a judicious pinch of salt, and can look at the western society of this time with a clearer eye and a more objective spirit. But Foucher of Chartres' remarks did have some truth in them. The troubled, greedy, violent Christianity that he depicts, was the young, exuberant Europe, which was troubled within itself, had proved itself here and there, in Spain, in the islands, on the open sea, on the coasts of Africa, and in Asia; it had developed its own self-awareness, or was in the process of doing so, and was ready to grapple with all obstacles in order to conquer land and sea. There was only one way of imposing a Christian peace on a Europe of this description, and that was to offer it another war in exchange, or better, its own exclusive war.

From one point of view the Church yields to this exigency in Europe, and becomes the enlightened and active mouthpiece for it. Its greatness and its power at this point lie in having spoken to the masses face to face, without using the monarchs as intermediaries, in having pointed to a goal, and ennobled and unified the European restlessness by setting the seal of religious sanction upon it, making a single peace from a thousand treaties and a single war from a thousand quarrels, both of them under the aegis of Rome. Small wonder that the masses, whatever their motives, responded to the appeal with such keen enthusiasm.

The question of what the crusaders intended to do and where they wanted to go, where Urban II was sending them, is not as naïve as it may seem. The answer is less clear than it might appear at first, and given the right one, we shall be able to understand the meaning of the crusade even better. Did they, in short, intend to go to Constantinople or to Jerusalem? To reclaim the lost lands of the empire from the Moslems, or to snatch the Holy Sepulchre from the hands of the infidels? A hymn which must have been heard at the time along the roads of east and west alike went like this:

Illuc debemus pergere,
nostros honores vendere,
templum Dei acquirere,
Saracenos destruere.

The most authoritative documents in fact speak indifferently, some of one, some of the other destination, and the crusade itself goes in its general course to both of them; it goes through Byzantium, fights the Turks, and aims finally at Jerusalem. It is therefore clear that it is only we who feel this need of so much precision and definition, not the people of the time, who instinctively looked on the expedition for the relief of the empire and the Christian communities of the east as a pilgrimage, this time an armed and universal one, which could have no other objective than the tomb of Christ.

In accordance with the decisions of the Councils a universal peace of God was declared. The property of the crusaders was taken under the special protection of the Church and entrusted to the bishops, who were to restore them when the owners returned. Those who fulfilled their crusader's vow through pure devotion, and not for the sake of honour and riches, were granted absolution for their sins. A married man was not allowed to take up the cross without the consent of his wife; and participation in the crusade by laymen and clergy alike, was conditional on the approval of the Church. The Bishop of Puy, Ademar of Monteil, was elected as leader of the expedition, and the departure was fixed for August 16, 1096.

The movement seemed to slip out of the hands of the Church right from the beginning. It was as if at the word of the pope a Europe-wide contest was unloosed to see who could be the first to avenge the outrages, to reach the fabulous treasures of Byzantium and the Orient, to free and venerate the Sepulchre. Peter the Hermit, a little man with an ardent spirit, his face ugly and thin from fasting, started to preach in Berry. He went from place to place on a donkey, barefoot and wearing only a rough tunic. He visited Orleanais, Champagne, and Lorraine, he went down the Moselle and Rhine valleys to Trier and Cologne, drawing behind him crowds of several thousands of men, women and children—a pilgrimage with all the confusion of an army, and an army with all the vulnerability of a pilgrimage. Several thousands more French and Germans gathered around Gottschalk, a German priest of unfortunate reputation. Yet another group of German crusaders collected around Count Emich von Leiningen, a brigand by profession, who taught them to make ends meet and scrape together a little money by systematically robbing and massacring the Jewish population of the Rhine basin.

While these ill-organized vanguards made their way east to be exterminated by the Hungarians, the Pechinegians in the service of the empire and the Turks, the crusading forces were flowing towards the Orient by land and sea from all parts of France, from Flanders, Lorraine, England, Italy, Denmark, and Norway. Ademar of Monteil left, perhaps a little later than had been planned, in the autumn of 1096, accompanied by Raymond of St Gilles, Count of Toulouse, the veteran of the Spanish wars. They were preceded by the brother of the King of France, Hugh of Vermandois, Godfrey of Bouillon, Duke of Lower Lorraine, his brother Baldwin of Boulogne, the son of Robert Guiscard Bohemond and his nephew, Tancred. And they were followed by the son of the Conqueror, Robert Courteheuse, Count of Normandy, and his brother-in-law Stephen, Count of Blois and Chartres, each with their own following.

To conclude—none of the sovereigns took up the cross. Those who did were a few princes of royal blood, a few of the great feudal lords, many of the middle and lower vassals, and the vast crowd of the nameless. The great majority of the crusaders came from France, the country of the pope, the field of his most fervent preaching, the land of indivisible inheritance, swarming with younger sons athirst for land. The Normans of Italy left in great numbers, being proficient in the use of arms and well-acquainted with the routes of the Orient. The Norwegians, the Danes, the English and above all the Genoese were the most enterprising at sea; they were quick to support the advance into enemy territory by supplying workmen, arms, instruments of war, and provisions. The Germans were few, even hostile, perhaps by nature, or perhaps on account of the ill-feeling caused by the reform and the quarrel of the investitures.

While Urban's preaching had limited itself to arousing the energy of Europe and pointing vaguely to a goal, the accomplishment of the crusade imposed the necessity of confronting and resolving serious military and political problems. It was a hard lesson of experience, which put to the test, in a quite exceptional manner, physical and moral strength, initiative, capacity for government and in fine all the best and worst gifts of man. The intentions of the few or the many may have been the most noble, but the Christian armies that passed through the lands of Hungary and the empire appeared to be and often were, especially in the early days, real bands of invaders and scoundrels, bereft equally of resources and discipline. Thus they found their way barred, their supplies cut off, and their stragglers killed; they had to negotiate and fight to open up their road and secure their provisions; the most fortunate were obliged merely to march in formation under the surveillance of the soldiery of the king of Hungary or the emperor.

The accusation of duplicity levelled at the Byzantine emperor Alexius Comnenus, seems to be totally without foundation, in spite of the testimony of the western historians of the time. To his eyes the whole enterprise was simply an attempt to reconquer the provinces of the empire seized by the Moslems; the great leaders of the western forces were in a way entering his service and thus were bound to pledge him their faith; on this condition they could be assured of his splendid generosity and the best possible arrangements for the troops. The trouble was that the crusade had been understood in quite different terms in the west, by Urban and his councillors, and differently again, indeed in a thousand different ways, from man to man, high and low, among those who had joined the crusade.

And here it would be appropriate to consider briefly the spirit in which these soldiers and pilgrims set out on their mission. But it would be difficult to add anything to what we all know by common experience of mankind and great movements of the masses. There was the austere strength of Ademar of Monteil, and the inflexible loyalty of Raymond of St Gilles, who refused to swear because he did not want to recognize any other lord than Him for whom he had left his country and his home. There was the piety, courage and able diplomacy of Godfrey of Bouillon, the cunning, enterprising and lawless ambition of Bohemond and Tancred, the cupidity, pride and political ability of Baldwin of Boulogne, the complacent avidity and simple marital affection of Stephen of Chartres, who in his correspondence with his wife Adela, the daughter of William the Conqueror, exulted, amid his account of the action of the war, in the generosity of the emperor and the treasures he had acquired; he wrote, 'Know for certain, O my beloved, that I now have twice as much gold, silver and other riches as I had when I left you', and closed his letter tenderly, 'Indeed few of many are the things that I write to you, dearest, and since I am unable to express all that is in my heart, I hope that you are well, dearest, and that you are looking after your land well, and treating honourably as is fitting for you, with your sons and your men, for as soon as it is possible for me, you will certainly see me. Keep well'. There are those who dream of returning, and those who have burned their boats behind them to make themselves a new life and a new fortune elsewhere. And there is the multitude which re-echoes, from man to man, in ever smaller and humbler circles, the passions of the leaders. It is a restless and changeable multitude, sensitive to miraculous inventions and visions, alternately heroic and bewildered, greedy for booty, and eager to be pardoned at the tomb of Christ. It is an obscure and powerful force, which pushes the captains, who have strayed among their own ambitions and rivalries, on towards the goal.

After accomplishing the concentration on Constantinople, the crusading armies moved against Nicaea. And here they met their disappointment. When they were about to unleash an attack on the city, the Byzantine flag appeared atop the towers and the walls. The emperor had obviated the damage that the capture and sacking of the town would have involved and the risks of a Latin occupation, by obtaining the citizens' surrender (June 26, 1097).

So they left Nicaea and marched towards Phrygia. It was perhaps for reasons of provisioning that the Normans of Italy and France led the way, in the command of Bohemond, Tancred, and Robert Courteheuse. They were followed at a distance by the legate Ademar of Monteil, Godfrey of Bouillon, Raymond of St Gilles and Hugh of Vermandois with their divisions from Lorraine and Provence. On the morning of the first of July the Normans, on arriving in the plain of Dorileus, found themselves suddenly surrounded on all sides by the Turkish army, and the encounter would have resulted in complete slaughter had it not been for the readiness and the courage of Bohemond and his men, and for the rapid arrival of first Godfrey of Bouillon with only fifty horsemen, and then one by one the other detachments, who had been warned of the desperate danger that threatened them. By two in the afternoon the entire Christian army was in the field, and the tide of battle turned. The battle of Dorileus marked the end of the Turks' threat to Constantinople and the first great affirmation of the military strength of Europe.

But it was not long before the union began to fall apart. After passing through Iconium and reaching Heraclea towards the middle of September, Baldwin of Boulogne and Tancred left the body of the army for the fertile plains of Cilicia to do their own private conquering there. They took possession of Tarsus, Adana, and Mamistra, and received reinforcements from the Flemish, the Frisians, and the Danes, who had arrived by sea aboard the ships of a famous adventurer and pirate, Guynemer of Boulogne. They came to blows over the division of the spoils, and Tancred, who had less soldiers to back him, got the worst deal. Towards the middle of October, Baldwin returned to the main army, in time to see his wife, who was dying or dead, for the last time. He left it again two days later, going east towards the Euphrates valley and Edessa. And here his real crusade ended. After having himself adopted as the san and heir of the Armenian Thoros, the governor of the city, he allowed him to be massacred by an enraged mob, and then stepped into his rightful inheritance and with it the title of count.

In the meantime the crusaders, after taking a long loop round by Caesarea and Marash, had arrived at Antioch on the border of Syria. The capture and defence of this city were the great achievement of Bohemond, and for leaders and troops alike this was the severest trial of the whole campaign. The siege lasted seven months, from October, 1097, to June, 1098, and the bloody encounters and severe deprivations attendant on it served only to dishearten the combatants and encourage defection. Bohemond was at the ready with every trick in the book to accomplish a single end—to make himself master of Antioch. He brought the deserters back by force, among others Peter the Hermit himself, he rid himself of the Byzantine reinforcements, who were liable to prove embarrassing, by a clever ruse, and he threatened to abandon the whole undertaking in order to make the worth of his help felt and thus win over the opposition. He then came to a secret agreement with a traitor, one Firuz, perhaps an Armenian converted to Islam, for the surrender of a tower, and with the confidence this gave him amid the general despair, he managed, under the threat of the approaching Turkish army commanded by Karbogha of Mosul, to force his fellow commanders to let him have his head. And so, on June 3rd at about four o'clock, in the morning, he scaled the tower of the Two Sisters with his men; then while the city was invaded by the rest, he rushed to plant his flaming banner on a hill not far from the citadel. The only irreconcilable enemy left him was Raymond of St Gilles, who, by a supreme stroke of irony, while Bohemond was breaking his oath to Byzantium, now appointed himself defender of the rights of the empire.

Their quarrel was set aside for a short time under the stress of Karbogha's siege, but the hardships and desertions started again. Bohemond's heroic energy, which went so far as to set fire to the city to force the soldiers to leave their houses for their posts on the walls, was still not enough to deal with such a crisis. What his resolution could not accomplish was left to the pious fraud of the Holy Lance, in the hands of a Provencal pilgrim, Pierre Barthélémy. On June 28, 1098, after discovering the presumed relic in the church of St Peter on the directions of the visionary, the crusaders, in a state of religious ecstasy, sallied forth from the city in battle order, attacked the enemy, and routed them completely. The best move would probably then have been to take advantage of their victory and move on Jerusalem immediately, but the resumption of the march was delayed by the desire to make good the losses they had suffered, the need for rest and reorganization, the negotiations with Alexius, and above all by the rivalry between Bohemond and Raymond.

In the end, the indignation of the crusaders, who could see the fulfilment of their vows being sacrificed to the personal ambition of their leaders, forced the Count of Toulouse to give in and continue the march. They left towards the middle of January, and after many trials and tribulations, reached Jerusalem on June 7, 1099.

All the chroniclers have depicted this arrival as a moment of unparalleled ecstasy and impulsive good will, when the years of endurance and longing broke from every heart in shouts of joy, in tears, sighs and prayers, and when everybody, at the sight of the towers and the walls, lifted their hands up to the sky, and then unshod themselves and bent to kiss the earth.

But it was the joy of a moment only. In the power of the Fatimites of Egypt, the city had been strongly garrisoned, and in the surrounding area the wells had been blocked, the fountains poisoned, the canals cut off, and the livestock removed, all this at the peak of a fiery summer. Luckily a Genoese fleet arrived with a cargo of provisions, other supplies, and workmen: so they were able to start on the construction of two great mobile towers made of wood. Their last attack on the city was preceded by a solemn procession around the walls, amid the jeers and insults of the defenders. Then finally, after a series of futile attacks, in the night between the 14th and 15th of July, the towers were brought up to the walls, and Godfrey of Bouillon, with his brother Eustace, was among the first to leap onto the ramparts. Only an hour or so later, Raymond of St Gilles succeeded in opening a breach with his tower, just when the Saracens were fleeing towards him with the Lorrainians on their heels. They resisted him fiercely and the butchery lasted until the evening, when the crusaders, exhausted from the slaughter and covered with blood, went in procession to give thanks at the Holy Sepulchre. The next morning they started the massacre again with unprecedented violence: an ineffaceable crime—it was perhaps a mistake—which caused a setback of many years to the conquest of Syria.

Although Jerusalem was the final goal that the crusading pilgrims longed to reach, its capture was only an episode in the story of Latin expansion in the eastern Mediterranean. Nevertheless, we can well stop here, since, for the problem which interests us, the characteristics of this epoch have now been clearly sign-posted.

Between 150,000 and 200,000 men abandoned Europe and poured into the east; and of these numbers no more than 50,000 arrived at the border of Syria; the others went home early, were deflected from the route, or fell by the wayside. We no longer believe simply in the miraculous influence of Urban II's words, or of Peter the Hermit's; nor in the force of superstition pushing the masses to the conquest of the most venerated of all relics. The crusade was rather the expression of European awareness, of the exuberance of the military and conquering spirit that the hierarchical warrior Church of Gregory VII, Victor III, and Urban II, had trained under its command, unified and thrown into an enterprise of global dimensions in the name of the Faith.

Although this great and unforeseen migration did not perhaps radically change the economic and social structure of Europe, it certainly gave a strong impetus to the commercial and industrial centres, especially the sea-faring cities, and it lightened the burden of feudal disorder alike for monarchs, city-dwellers and the common people of the land.

Perhaps the military aspect of the expedition was spoilt by all sorts of mistakes and weaknesses; but the rough-hewn Europe of the eleventh century could give no more. Certainly we find the brutality and baseness that spotted the crusades repugnant. But we must not forget on this account the privations the crusaders suffered, the dangers they ran, their sacrifices of blood, their fortitude in the most desperate moments, their readiness and courage, their love of risk and adventure, and the will and ability to rule men shown by their leaders. For it was the sum of all this marvellous energy and experience that put an end to the Turkish threat, it was through this that Europe gained possession of the Mediterranean for three centuries, and gave life to another Europe in miniature. And it was this that sent a fertile breath of civilization running from the Arab and Byzantine east to the west, bearing the great elementary forces and poetry, which first with the help of the theocratic Church, and then in spite of it, prepared the development of a new consciousness.

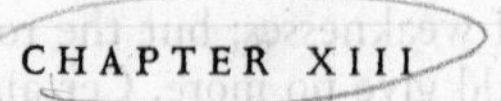

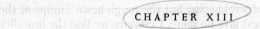

CHAPTER XIII

THE LAST BID FOR POWER OF THE MEDIEVAL EMPIRE

HENRY VI

I

The Struggle of the Investitures and the Concordats agreed by the Church with England in 1107, France in 1108, and the empire in 1122, are signs that the political and religious *unity* of the west—the word is of course used in a relative sense—is a thing of the past, and the Holy Roman Republic on its way to dissolution. Thirty years after the Concordat of Worms, a thirty years in which the papacy reaps the fruit of the Struggle of the Investitures in the triumph of her candidates for the imperial crown, Lothar II and Conrad III, the old conflict is renewed with unprecedented violence by Frederick Barbarossa. Empire and papacy remain loyal to their universal principles and fight for them, and to the superficial observer it would appear that Europe relapses into one of the usual crises that have ravaged it in the course of the past three hundred and fifty years. But in reality the whole world is changed. The knot that had bound the two supreme powers so intimately together for centuries has been untied; and the empire, bereft of its religious substance, is obliged to look elsewhere, in Roman law, for the titles to its legitimacy, and to insist on a principle of sovereignty which the monarchies of France and England are soon to invoke as a basis of their power, and with better results. The struggle still shows traces of its earlier phases, for the past is not dead. The link of the papal coronation of the emperor continues as before, and the empire tries to regain by force the power it lost at the Concordat of Worms, by means of the election of the bishops, the bestowal of the regalia on ecclesiastics, and the exercise of the imperial *ius spolii*. But the object of the contest is no longer the Christian government of the world; essentially it is the domination of Italy, in which the empire competes against the powers promoted by the Church during the period of reform, the communes and the Kingdom of Sicily.

Indeed, we can go further than this. Although the protagonists are in name still the papacy and the empire, and our attention is mainly focussed on them, in relation to the decline of the Middle Ages, the truth of the matter is different. The relations between the two universal powers are no longer of a size to comprehend and dominate either the whole or the greater part of the new Europe, which shows itself in the increasingly powerful and organic political structure in the Kingdom of Sicily, in the sea-faring republics and communes of Italy, in the German Guelfism and Ghibellinism, in the Capetian and Anglo-Norman monarchies of France and England, in the states reconquered by the Spaniards, and on its furthest borders, in Hungary, Denmark and Norway. There are too many particular problems, France and England for example, that break out of the world of medieval universalism. When the conflict between papacy and empire is at its height, the whole of Europe, directly or indirectly, by old-established tradition or interests of the moment, takes part in the struggle under one banner or the other, as its changeable alliances dictate; in other words the politics of papacy and empire are completely entangled, one might almost say submerged, in the complexity of European politics. The pope may support his own theocracy, and the emperor fight with sword and pen for the restoration of his former rights; but in both cases the results are the same and equally remote from the intentions of the two rivals, for while they look nostalgically into the past, they are working with their own hands on the inevitable construction of the new Europe. The same facts that strike to the heart of the Catholic consciousness, like the schism between Alexander III and Victor IV or the crusades, when they too are taken into the world of Europe and subjected to its differences, acquire as much political breadth and importance as they lose religious significance.

An integral part in western politics, and one of the greater importance than in the past, is played by the Byzantine Empire. This is because from the eleventh century on, beginning in particular with the first crusade, Europe's interests have become wider and its field of action changed. Its life now is essentially Mediterranean. On the reconquered sea, princes, cities, and nations compete for riches and power. The most memorable date of the twelfth century is the coronation of King Roger II, Count of Sicily and Duke of Apulia, by the antipope Anacletus II in 1130. And if we have to speak of a protagonist in this period, it can be none other than the kingdom of Roger, William I, and William II, not as a hegemony controlling the political fate of Europe, but as the centre of attraction for the entire Mediterranean world.

Though papal and feudal in its origin, the Sicilian monarchy has a spirit of independence and conquest, and it dominates by its position and its ships the routes from east to west in the Mediterranean. Faithful to the memory of the old navigators of Amalfi, of Robert Guiscard and the Normans, and of Bohemond and Tancred, it looks towards Africa, the Balkans, and Byzantium, and is in its turn the object of the eternal Byzantine longing for revenge, and the eternal imperial ambitions of the Germans. It is in Sicily that the diplomatic threads running from both empires, from renascent Spain, and above all from France and the related Anglo-Norman monarchy meet and intertwine. From the latter states there come numbers of ministers, courtiers, political refugees, and recommendations from Louis VII and Thomas à Becket for English exiles, or the pleas of Henry II, that William II should intercede for him with the pope. Just as the Sicilian enemies of Roger plot and intrigue at the German court, so the king works with the German Guelphs against the Ghibelline Conrad III.

From year to year, according to political circumstances, the most distinguished royal brides were offered to the last legitimate heir of the Normans—a daughter of Barbarossa, or of the Emperor Manuel Comnenus, or of Henry II of England. And in the end it was the English princess Joan, sister of Richard Coeur de Lion and John 'Lackland', who was married to William II in 1177. This was an important victory for the papacy, which thus succeeded in avoiding a dangerous union between the empire and its feudal kingdom in Sicily. For as matrimonial negotiations show which way the political wind is blowing, so this marriage is the seal set on an alliance, and the true final object of the competition is the inheritance of Sicily. These are all questions of unique and exceptional importance. Indeed by virtue of its central position the Sicilian kingdom attracts the most immoderate desires of the European potentates, and by playing its alliances cleverly it can alternately put the Church and the empires of east and west in peril, and thereby overturn the most subtly woven and universal conspiracy for its ruin.

Barbarossa had been defeated by the marriage of William II to Joan; from this time on his military and diplomatic fortune was on the wane; and yet he could resist Sicily's lure. It exercised an almost fatal attraction on him, understandably enough, as for the emperor, more than for any other sovereign in Europe, Sicily was a question of life and death. In this connection we have often referred to the repeated attempts of the German emperors to conquer Sicily, beginning with Otto I, or even with Ludwig II and Charlemagne; and there is no reason to doubt that this ancient tradition contributed to some extent to the formation of the imperial attitude of which Barbarossa's great Sicilian project was the logical outcome. But the magnetic attraction of Sicily for Barbarossa and Henry VI was a condition of their own time, a response to the exigencies of the day, to be explained in the light of new circumstances.

Rather than looking back to previous centuries for precedents we must look a few decades before Barbarossa's assumption of the throne, when Lothar of Supplinburg and Innocent II had joined forces to snatch Sicily from the hands of Roger and his antipope Anacletus II. In spite of a successful beginning, the expedition had been scattered to the four winds by the Sicilian king, who nevertheless then took the precaution of having his crown reconsecrated by the legitimate pope.

But even if we leave this immediate precedent out of consideration, the possession of the kingdom, or at least the linking of its fortunes with his own, was indispensable to the emperor for two reasons. Given control over Sicily, he would be able to bend the papacy to his will, by pressing hard on it on both sides and depriving it of all freedom of movement in Italy. He would also be able to put an end once and for all to the Byzantine pretensions to the peninsula, and resolve the renewed conflict between east and west by means of a German triumph. The presumed universal power of the empire would become an illusion if within the extended boundaries of Europe, in the heart of the Mediterranean there was a state that was superior in wealth, in naval force, and colonial expansion, and a centre of international relations in which conspiracies against the emperor could be engineered with the pope or the communes or Byzantium, or with England and the German Guelphs who were his own allies. If the universalism of the empire were not to betray itself, it was mercilessly condemned to the Herculean labour of repressing the states within its territorial sphere and subduing those beyond it, all this in the new Europe which denied imperial supremacy.

The very constitution of the Sicilian kingdom justified Barbarossa's hopes and ambitions. The dynasty had always been a fragile plant, what with the premature death of all Roger's legitimate sons except William I, and the long regency of Queen Margaret for William II in his minority, and it was now in danger of complete extinction if William and Joan's marriage continued to be infertile. The kingdom's economic prosperity, splendid culture, and vital impulse to conquest, could not dispel or hide its inherent weaknesses. It betrayed at every turn the incomplete and complicated process of its formation, and the harm done it by foreign influences: in the revolts of the Arabs; the intrigues of the exiles; the periodic violence and disturbances among the feudal nobility who disliked the court bureaucracy, both lay and ecclesiastic; and finally in the disagreements between the ministers themselves, who differed widely in both origin and interests.

In these circumstances, when the treaties of Venice and Constance, in 1177 and 1183 respectively, had ratified the military and diplomatic defeat of the empire in favour of the Church, Sicily and the Italian communes, Barbarossa returned to his old policy by offering the hand of his son Henry VI to the heir presumptive to the Sicilian throne, Constance, the daughter of Roger II. Frederick thus made the alliance that he had hoped to make by the marriage of one of his daughters to William II in another form.

Little information has come down to us about the negotiations that preceded the contract of marriage, which appears to have been agreed at Augusta on October 29, 1184. There is some controversy about the dates; the part that a contemporary source would have Pope Lucius III play in the proceedings has been understandably questioned. It is, moreover, difficult to determine exactly in what light the problem was considered by the three antagonists, pope, king and emperor, and whether the pope acted of his own volition, in accordance with a deliberate policy, or was not rather compelled to approve what he had no power to prevent.

In any case, there is no doubt about the nature and the importance of the act itself. After seven years of infertile marriage William II felt that it was in the interests of his kingdom and of the monarchy to provide for a successor; he also needed to settle the agreement with the empire once and for all, so as to be able to return to the traditional pursuit of Norman expansion in the east with greater security and greater compliance from Barbarossa. The very disparity in the ages of Henry VI and Constance, the former nineteen and the latter thirty, pointed to an important political design behind the union. This impression was backed up by the dissension that broke out at the court in Palermo between the supporters and opponents of the German marriage, by the ill-humour of the Roman Curia and the election of a rigorous defender of the rights of the Church, Hubert, Archbishop of Milan, who adopted the title Urban III, as successor to the weak Lucian III, at his death on November 29, 1185. That the assumption of the Sicilian throne by Constance was considered a serious possibility is shown by William's action at the assembly of Troy, at which he made his vassals swear the oath of allegiance to his aunt, and promise to recognize her as his rightful heir, in the event of his dying without legitimate sons.

For the moment there was no change apparent in the kingdom. There was merely a new possibility for the future, whose consequences the people of the day could only glimpse at, with no understanding of its deep significance. But in fact the marriage of

Henry VI and Constance, Barbarossa's deed of political genius, marked a point of history that affected the whole world. It put the medieval empire to its final test against the new Europe, and was the prelude to one of the most serious turning points in the history of the west, the downfall of the Holy Roman Empire, drawn into the fatal vortex of the Sicilian inheritance.

The moment of truth arrived sooner than anyone could have expected: on November 12, 1189, the question of the succession was laid open by the death of William II at the age of thirty-six. The grief caused by his loss was made all the more bitter by the uncertainty of the future. A contemporary poet of a simply prophetic spirit, Richard of San Germano, after celebrating and weeping for the 'most Christian king', 'the prince sublime among all princes' in his verse, turned to lament the strife-torn kingdom, open to enemy attack on all sides:

Lacet regnum desolatum,
dissolutum et turbatum,
sicque venientibus
cunctis patet hostibus.
Est obhuc dolendum
et plangendum
omnibus.
Regni filii,
tempus exterminii
vobis datum flete;
hoc verbum: 'Gaudete'
vobis est sublatum.

The 'hour of extermination' was drawing near. The diplomatic agreement between the royal houses of the empire and Sicily, and the oath sworn to the daughter of Roger II was one thing, the immediate threat that the hereditary enemy, in the person of Henry VI, should lay his hands on the crown, and the kingdom become the prey of foreign soldiers, was quite another. In the face of this danger personal ambitions were revived, factions of the court reborn, and all hearts invaded by an indeterminate national feeling, made up of love for the Norman monarchy and hate for the Germans, whom they knew as soldiers, and pictured as barbarians, fearfully celebrated for their roughness and cruelty, greed and luxury.

Henry VI and Constance, who were in fact supported by the Archbishop of Palermo, Walter Ophamil, were challenged by two rivals: Count Roger of Andria, one of the foremost feudal vassals of the crown, the great chamberlain under William II, who was the candidate of the barons of the mainland; and Tancred, Count of Lecce, the high constable and chief justice of Apulia and Terra di Lavoro; he too was of royal blood, being an illegitmate son of Duke Roger, the son of Roger II, and was supported by the vice-chancellor Matthew of Ajello and the people. In the end, as a result of the energy and ability of the vice-chancellor, Tancred prevailed and was crowned, probably in January, 1190.

Pietro Ansolino of Eboli, the courtier, and the illuminator of the manuscript of his *De Rebus Siculis Carmen* took delight in caricaturing the physical defects of the new king, who was ugly of face and small of stature. He was spared no insult: 'Dwarf, monster of nature, crowned monkey, embryo, half man, boy from behind and old man before'. But his moral stature was of the highest order. Of this he had given proof in the wars in the east under William II, and he showed it again at the beginning of his reign, when although he needed peace and quiet to prepare the resistance to the inevitable German attack, he found himself instead having to deal simultaneously with a Moslem insurrection, the rebellion of the nobles who supported Roger of Andria, and the invasion of the kingdom by the marshal Henry of Kalden in agreement with the rebels (at Rieti on March 8, 1190). No sooner were these dangers out of the way, than he was compelled to take up the threads of the traditional Norman policy, under pressure from the kings of England and France, whose fleets were anchored in Sicily on their way to the east (September, 1190).

After the defeat suffered by the Christians at Hittin on July 4, 1187, and the capture of Jerusalem by the Saladin on October 3rd, Barbarossa, Philip Augustus II, Henry II (d. July 6, 1189) and his son Richard Coeur de Lion took the cross. But while Frederick, being inspired by the warrior spirit and his conscience of his imperial mission, hurried to fulfil his vow, the two kings, insecure on their thrones and at war with each other, Henry being both the vassal and rival of Philip, had pledged themselves unwillingly, hoping to evade the fulfilment of their vows, and thus the departure of both French and English was delayed until Easter, 1190.

William II had tried to take advantage of the crusade for his own eastern expansion without actually taking part in it. He intended to control it from Sicily, harbouring the two fleets in his ports and contributing to the expedition with a large quantity of ships, money and provisions. But in the troubled dawn of Tancred's reign this ambitious project came to nothing; the English alliance was abandoned and the widowed Queen Joan was held prisoner, and her dowry, which consisted of the county of Monte St Angelo and its dependencies, was withheld from her. Now Richard Coeur de Lion arrived, both to ask for his sister's release and the restoration of the dowry, and to lay claim to a rich legacy left him by his brother-in-law, William II, clearly with a view to his participation in the crusade. It was composed of a golden table twelve feet by one and a half, a silk tent that would house two hundred soldiers, twenty-four gold goblets, a hundred galleys equipped for two years, sixty thousand cargoes of barley, corn, and wine.

Although Joan was released and a large indemnity paid her, the quarrel became so bitter that Richard took Messina by force and it was rumoured that he intended to make himself master of Sicily. But instead, to the disappointment of the King of France, who at one point had thought he would be able to draw Tancred into his game against his rival, the dispute was smoothed over with an agreement by which both claims were settled by a money payment and a family marriage sealed the bargain. Richard also undertook to give Tancred any military help he needed for as long as he was in Sicily, obviously against his only dangerous enemy, Henry VI.

For us it is this resolution of the quarrel that is interesting, for through it Sicily was drawn back into the old Anglo-Norman, anti-Swabian alliance, and the first strands of the enormous net in which the son of Barbarossa was soon to be enveloped were tied. In the meantime, the good relations between the Church and Tancred had been preserved, so this too pointed to a reprise of the struggle between papacy and empire, and greater scope for the formation of an anti-imperial front.

The young twenty-four-year-old whom Frederick Barbarossa had left to govern in his stead on his departure for the crusade on May 11, 1189, was completely different from his father: small of stature, thin, no lover of warfare, but a devotee of hunting and falconry, a good speaker, cultured, with Roman and canon law at his finger-tips, carefully generous in giving little to many, cunning, implacable, and vehement. The same excessive ambition for power, which was to make its mark on world history, was not to be upheld by faith, or redeemed by dying in the defence of the Holy Sepulchre, but animated by a personal overwhelming will to power, coloured by the new fancy that had the line of Roman and German kings and emperors descend directly from Priam of Troy. He had been elected king of Germany at the age of four, crowned King of Italy at Pavia by the Patriarch of Aquileia in 1186 and acclaimed as Caesar, in affirmation of the rights of the empire and as a challenge to Pope Urban III, who had refused him the imperial crown while Barbarossa was alive. Both disposition and environment, the example of his father and his personal experience of government in Italy and Germany, had prepared him precociously to bear the heavy burden of his father's policies.

On the death of William II, he should have gone down into Italy to claim his inheritance in Constance's name. But he had been prevented first by a new rebellion of the Guelph Henry the Lion with the backing of the kings of England and Denmark (in October, 1189), and then by the death of Barbarossa (June 10, 1190), which made the opportunity for coronation in Rome the most pressing of the many claims on his attention. After having quelled the rebellion more by means of shrewd diplomacy and concessions than by force of arms—the need for a settlement in Germany being pressing under the circumstances—Henry finally crossed the Alps during the winter of 1190-91 and made his way towards Rome and Sicily. He obtained the imperial crown at a price that Barbarossa might not have paid and which was echoed with reproof by the writers of the time: '*Imperium in hoc non mediocriter dishonestavit*'. He agreed to give up Tusculum which at the time was occupied by a German garrison as a condition of his coronation, which took place on April 15, 1191; as was to be expected, Tusculum was then subjected to the Roman hate and anger in full spate, and not a stone was left standing.

According to the information given to the imperial court by the chancellor, Diether, after his visit to southern Italy, the conquest of the Sicilian kingdom should have been an extremely easy matter: '*Omnia facilia captu*'; and considering the support offered to the imperial forces by the old partisans of Roger of Andria, this presumption was not an unfounded one. Being unable to count on his barons, Tancred fortified the cities of Apulia and Terra di Lavoro. The Germans advanced from Ceprano up to the gates of Naples almost without obstacles; but Naples resisted and had to be besieged. The Pisan fleet, which should have enforced a blockade to prevent supplies coming in by sea, was defeated by the Sicilian admiral, and the Genoese, who had only recently promised support to the emperor, arrived too late. Meanwhile, with the arrival of the summer, the army was badly reduced by disease and desertion; Henry VI himself fell ill, and Henry of Brunswick, the eldest son of Henry the Lion, who had come to Italy in the emperor's train as a hostage of peace, fled back to Germany where he cleverly spread a false rumour of the emperor's death. As a final stroke of misfortune, the empress herself was taken prisoner by the people of Salerno, who had taken her into their city when she was ill, and then rebelled during the siege of Naples. In these circumstances, Henry was left no alternative but to strike camp and return to Germany (in August, 1191).

The failure of the Sicilian expedition looked like the beginning of Henry's ruin. In a single movement, slow at first and then gradually faster and more and more widespread, all the forces hostile to the Swabian empire, in the great theatre of the old and new Europe, sought each other out and allied themselves against him. It was begun by the Church taking a firm stand on the question of the Sicilian kingdom: it put an interdict on the abbey of Monte Cassino, which was on the emperor's side, tried to intervene to effect a treaty between the contenders and, its services being rudely rejected, it replied by granting the investiture of Sicily to Tancred and giving the Guelphs a helping hand.

In Germany the two old centres of anti-Swabian feeling in the north-west and north-east, Saxony and Westphalia, the lands of the Guelphs, finally roused themselves. They were less interested in expansion in Italy and the Mediterranean, being drawn, under the influence of their great commercial cities of Cologne and Lubeck, rather to the North Sea and the Baltic, to England and Denmark.

Their alliance, which Barbarossa had managed to prevent, came about as the result of Henry's interference with the election for the bishopric of Liège. Both candidates had asked him for his support, but he set both of them aside and nominated Lothar of Hochstadt to the vacant seat on January 13, 1192. The man elected by the majority, Albert, brother of the Duke of Brabant, appealed to the Holy See and was consecrated; but not long after he was assassinated by a group of German knights, on November 24, 1192. The suspicion that the emperor had had his part in the crime was widespread, and the princes of the lower Rhine allied themselves with the Guelphs against their common enemy.

The final spark that set rebellion blazing throughout Germany, with plans for Henry's deposition and a new imperial election, was the enormous scandal of Richard Coeur de Lion's arrest by Duke Leopold of Austria on his way back from the crusade, and his delivery to Henry VI. A vast net, stretching from the extreme north of Europe down to Sicily, now threatened to suffocate not only Henry's Mediterranean ambitions, but the monarchy of the Hohenstaufen itself.

There was, however, one small lever in Henry's able hands, with which he could bring down the entire anti-imperial structure—the fact that he held the King of England prisoner. The old consciousness might rebel against the capture of the crusader; the new recognized no religious barriers to deeds of political necessity. After his heavy losses at Naples and Palermo, the emperor was thoroughly determined to settle his accounts with his challengers. When in the summer of 1192 Celestinus III had sent the abbot of Casamari to arrange a treaty with Tancred with him, he had replied in his usual haughty style: 'With regard to the treaty, it does not please us in the least, indeed we will not allow it to be mentioned to our Majesty again for any reason whatsoever.' Peace was possible only on one condition: that Henry should possess in peace the land wrongfully and treacherously occupied by Tancred. He remained immovable from this position, and his every care was in preparing the final blow against the Sicilian kingdom. Hence his policy of maintaining the balance of power in the states of Lombardy, and hence his moderation towards the Guelphs.

When it looked as if he had lost, the capture of Richard Coeur de Lion provided him with the money necessary for the expedition, the means to pacify the Germans, to rob Tancred of his allies and turn them to his own ends. A perusal of the documents of the negotiations for the king's delivery to the emperor and for his final delivery shows us clearly that the solution to the problem lay, in realistic twentieth century fashion, in a crude financial agreement; and that it was this that was to permit Henry to seize the Sicilian kingdom. 'I, Leopold, Duke of Austria, will give and present to my lord Henry, Emperor of the Romans, the King of England on these conditions: that the said king shall, as has been agreed, give the emperor 100,000 marks of silver, of which I shall receive half as dowry, etc.'; and, 'The lord emperor will send his messengers to London with the messengers of the lord king, to receive there 100,000 marks of pure silver by the measure of Cologne'. And so on from beginning to end.

One cannot follow the long series of negotiations to their conclusion without experiencing a strong sense of wonder and a certain pleasure at the beauty of the game, the complexity of the problem and the logical chain of its development, the skill of the player and the elegance of the solution. The king's capture was not just a small casual occurrence which produced unexpected and highly serious results. All sorts of different circumstances may have led Richard to fall into Henry's nets; but whatever they were, he was without a doubt the principle enemy, the man whose friendship and family connection was most sought after by the Guelph opposition and their kin on the one side, and the Sicilians of the Anglo-Norman alliance on the other. For various reasons, he was the common target of the Swabio-Capetian alliance; he was regarded by all of Europe as the most spectacular lord of war who had ever campaigned in west or east, as the prince and the crusader who was capable of obscuring the renown of the emperor with the fame of his deeds of war and his adventures.

Now Henry VI had him in his hands. The negotiations went on for a whole year, from February 14, 1193, to February 4, 1194—the whole fraught with dramatic alternatives, in which the two rivals gave proof the one of regal firmness and the other of the most impressive prudence and cunning. The destiny of a man was at stake, and with it the fate of the empire.

Henry drew all the advantage he could from his threat to hand over his prisoner to Philip Augustus or to his rebellious brother John Lackland, or to prolong the period of imprisonment at their request. By this means he first forced the princes of the Lower Rhine, under Richard's auspices, to put an end to their insurrection and return to obedience; then a second time he forced Richard himself into his vassalage—a true masterpiece of imperial politics. His liberty was in fact obtained for a ransom of 100,000 marks of silver, the feudal homage paid to the emperor for the crown of England, and the guarantee of an annual payment of 5,000 pounds sterling, and finally the promise of his help with the conquest of Sicily.

However, since the king flatly refused to betray his old ally Tancred or to take part in the Sicilian expedition in person, they found a solution in an alternative plan which at the same time made way for Henry VI's reconciliation with the Guelphs. Richard undertook to pay another 50,000 marks of silver to be released from the humiliating condition, or else to arrange for his brother-in-law Henry the Lion to take on the task in his place. To smooth over the reconciliation, Henry VI finally agreed to the marriage of his cousin, Agnes, only daughter of Conrad, the Count-Palatine of the Rhine, and the eldest son of Henry the Lion, Henry of Brunswick. This brought the Guelphs closer to the emperor in family relationship, and secured for them the rich inheritance of the Palatinate. Thus peace was achieved on this side too, and sealed at Tìlleda in March, 1194; and Henry of Brunswick promised as a pledge of his loyalty to accompany the emperor in the Sicilian campaign.

Thus the chain of alliances was broken, the German insurrection checked, the opponents brought to heel and made to support Swabian policy, the empire was provided with vast financial resources and aggrandized by the addition of a great kingdom to its vassals, and the Kingdom of Sicily was now destined to fall.

During the negotiations, there was also talk—which finally came to nothing—of investing Richard Coeur de Lion with the Kingdom of Arles, either because Henry thought this was the only way he could ensure the vassalage of the king and hence his feudal obligation to follow him with his own army on the Sicilian expedition, or else as a move directed against the King of France. It is hardly possible to exclude the latter intention from the emperor's plans. For, although the duel being fought at this moment was apparently between Henry VI and Richard Coeur de Lion, the true protagonists were Henry VI and Philip Augustus. The affair of Richard Coeur de Lion stands, as it were, on the border between the old and the new history of Europe. And between the emperor and the King of France a grim struggle for European domination was beginning, and this contest had for its immediate object the subjugation of England and its king. For the new Europe of the Capetian monarchy, the fettering of Richard and his kingdom meant a large step towards its goals: the exclusion of the Anglo-Norman powers from the continent, the eventual inheritance of their Mediterranean policies, and the possibility of threatening Germany from the flank through the princes of the Lower Rhine and the Guelphs. For the medieval empire it meant the pacification of Germany itself, the surrounding of France, and a good start for universal dominion, which to Henry meant that Philip Augustus also must be reduced to feudal subservience.

What motive could the emperor have had to give up so precious a pledge to his old ally or to prolong his imprisonment, and what interest in allowing Philip to reduce England to his will? And what motive could Richard have had to prefer his own ruin in the hands of the King of France, to submitting to the overlordship of the emperor? It is by these considerations that we can best explain Henry's lack of interest in the French proposals, except in so far as they could be used to put pressure on Richard and his allies. They also serve to explain how a crisis provoked by the common yet diverse interest of the Swabio-Capetian alliance to reduce the Anglo-Norman power to servitude, should have broken, at least temporarily, the bonds tied between them in 1187 by Frederick Barbarossa and Philip II, and given rise to an estrangement between France and the empire. One sign among many of this new hostility was the second marriage of the French king with the daughter of the King of Denmark, and hence the divorce of Denmark itself from the Guelphs and England and the birth of the Franco-Danish alliance against the empire.

Having won the diplomatic battle, and secured the loyalty of the states of Lombardy by the Peace of Vercelli (January 12, 1194), Henry VI set as high a price as he could on Richard's ransom and then struck the decisive blow at Sicily. The expedition was prepared with every care, the lessons of experience being carefully heeded. The departure took place in late spring, so as to avoid the dangerous heat of the South Italian summer, and the Genoese and Pisan fleets were both placed under the command of an imperial officer, Marcwald of Annweiler.

This expedition was as blessed by fortune as the first one was disastrous. Since Henry had left the peninsula, the war against Tancred in the south had been continued with no decisive results by the Abbot of Monte Cassino and the German captains, Berthold of Künsberg, Conrad of Lutzelinhard, and Diepold of Vohburg. Tancred had taken precautions against the isolation that was liable to leave him defenceless in the west by maintaining good relations with the

Holy See and by converting the old and natural enmity with Byzantium into an alliance which he sealed in 1193 by the marriage of his firstborn Roger, to Irene, daughter of the emperor Isaac Angelus. But as it turned out, both father and son died one after the other on February 20, 1194, just when the danger was reaching its height. The regency fell into the hands of a weak woman, the widowed Queen Sibylla, who was left with the support of her young son, William III, three daughters and their nurse.

Even before Henry crossed the Splügen Pass in May, 1194, all governmental organization had broken down and all provision for war came to nothing. Naples opened its gates before the advance of the imperial army, Salerno, being an object of revenge, had the courage to resist, and its sack served as an example to other towns. On November 20, 1194, the emperor entered Palermo, and on Christmas Day he had himself crowned in Sibylla's presence. She had obtained Tancred's county of Lecce and the principality of Tarantum for William III when she capitulated; but four days after the coronation even this faraway threat of a Norman restoration was removed: Henry accused the royal family of plotting against him, whether truly or falsely we do not know, and on these grounds they and some of their followers were exiled to Germany, while others were killed by the most atrocious tortures.

The aim so doggedly pursued had finally been accomplished. The palace of Palermo, with its immense treasure of silks, gold plate and silver tables, precious stones and gems, lay open to the avid gaze of the conquerer. And the most grandiose schemes presented themselves to ambitious mind.

Cesar erat omnia, fata tunc favebant.
Duces, reges, comites, proceres timebant.
Montes, colles, alpes, maria tremebant.

At that time there was no hope too proud to appear certain of fulfilment. As a pledge for the future, even the old Ghibelline trunk sprouted almost prodigiously. On the day after the coronation in Palermo, in a pavilion erected on the Piazza di Iesi and amid a throng of cardinals and bishops who had rushed to the scene, the forty-year-old empress, after nine years of unfertile marriage, gave birth to a son. The child was prophetically christened Constantine, Frederick and Roger; he was the future Frederick II. And already the poet saw him as the heir to the Roman name, born to a better destiny, which would lead him to bring peace and felicity to a world restored to its ancient grandeur by the arms of his father:

Felix namque pater, sed erit felicior infans:
hic puer ex omni parte beatus erit.
Nam pater ad totum victrici cuspide partes
ducet et imperium stare quod ante dabit.

O votive puer, renovandi temporis etas,
exhinc Rogerius, hinc Fridericus eris,
maior habendus avis, fato meliore creatus,
qui bene vix natus cum patre vincis avos!

II

The conquest of Sicily marked a decisive turning-point for the empire. What to some might have looked like an end, was in reality merely a beginning. The real aim, dictated by an undeniable inner force and served by a lofty spirit and inflexible will, was nothing more nor less than *ad totum ducere partes*, to reduce the parts to a whole, to embrace the new world before it fled, and to restore to the empire, or give it for the first time its universal domination. Personal ambition remains no more than a word, with no persuasive force, unless we feel it animated and relentlessly pushed forward by the twofold Swabian and Norman tradition, compounded of pride, interest, and the will to conquer. It remains meaningless unless we remember that Henry VI could only justify his enterprise in the eyes of Sicilians and Germans alike by claiming the whole of this inheritance, and that the empire was now placed in a position where it could either lay low all its enemies and become all-powerful or abdicate its pretence to universality *de iure* and *de facto;* and that a whole new Germany of soldiers, knights and *ministeriales*—something analogous though different to the crusading France of the previous century—had moved to the Swabian call; it had served, and it now had to be given land, booty and pay.

Having entrusted the regency of Sicily to Constance, Henry put almost all of central and southern Italy into the hands of German officers: Conrad of Urslingen was made Vicegerent of the kingdom, Diepold of Vohburg, justiciar of Terra di Lavoro; Conray Lützelinhard, Count of Molise; Marcwald of Annweiler, Duke of Ravenna, with the March of Ancona and the Romagna; Philip of Hohenstaufen, the emperor's brother, Duke of Tuscany.

While in the west England had been set onto France's flank, incited and provided with money to continue the war, the empire, being provided with almost inexhaustible financial resources and naval forces, was now for the first time conducting a great Mediterranean campaign, which was a combination of the joint and separate plans of Frederick Barbarossa and Roger II. In virtue of the former Norman conquest, the Arab potentates of North Africa and the Balearics, who were harrying Spain, were reduced to paying tribute. Aragon was an old object of Henry VI's ambition; he would have liked to make it feudally subordinate to the Kingdom of Arles, in order to make use of it for his Sicilian expedition or in the struggle with the Arabs, or as a part of his continent-wide strategy against England and France. Now its maritime activity was rousing his suspicions as well, so he tried to move Genoa, a rival power that he disliked equally, against it.

When in 1194 he had needed the Genoese, he had spoken to them after this fashion:

'If with the help of God I conquer Sicily by the use of your fleet, the honour will be mine and the advantage yours. I cannot stay there with my Germans, but you and your descendants can. The kingdom will belong to you, not me.'

And he had backed up his words with formal privileges. But then, when after the final conquest they asked that he maintain his promises and took out their documents, he replied to this effect:

'I have a copy too, and know well what it contains. Do you want to quarrel with me? I should like to give you satisfaction. You must know, however, that I shall give you no part of the Sicilian kingdom and that you cannot be my companions in its rule. Dismiss from your minds all possibility of possessing lands in common with me. If you would like to undertake an expedition, I am willing to help you to conquer another kingdom, which will belong to you alone. Sail against the King of Aragon and I will support you.'

The Genoese, however, would not bite, and nothing came of it. Nevertheless his intention was clear: to use the two rivals in the western Mediterranean basin for his own ends by setting them against each other. Such cunning was not unworthy of the man.

But the real showdown was to take place in the east. The time had come to settle all the old accounts: to reconquer the lands won by William II in the Balkan peninsula from Thessalonica to Epidaurus (in 1183); to avenge Byzantium's obstinate hostility to Barbarossa both in its Italian policies and in the crusade; to fulfil the aspiration of the Norman kings by resolving the age-old conflict between the two empires once and for all in the favour of the Swabians and the west. This was the intention behind the marriage Henry arranged between his brother Philip and the daughter of Isaac Angelus, Irene, the widow of Prince Roger, who had been found in the palace at Palermo and should have secured the succession to the Byzantine throne for her husband. Isaac Angelus was too hard-pressed by internal troubles, and too much in need of help, to put up any resistance. Then when he was deposed, blinded and substituted by his brother Alexis III on April 5, 1195, Henry, by posing as the champion of violated rights and threatening to make war on the usurper, succeeded in extorting great sums of money from him, which he earmarked immediately for his final campaign against the east. He conducted his diplomatic manoeuvres in the east with such energy, and created so convincing an impression that the monarchy of the Comneni was about to fall before the triumphant west, that Leo, King of Little Armenia, and Amalric of Lusignano, King of Cyprus, refused to recognize the overlordship of Byzantium and asked for and obtained their crowns from Henry VI, in 1194 and 1195 respectively.

The conclusive and culminating point of the imperial strategy was the decision to embark on the crusade, which, after being taken in secret by the emperor on March 31, 1195, was made public two days later at the solemn Diet of Bari. The letter in which Henry announced his intention to the German clergy was conceived in the traditional terms: 'The Kingdom of Sicily having been subdued and set in order by the Grace of God,' he had decided, 'in honour of Him who stretches his arms on the cross, sacrificed for us, and being mindful of the misery and hardship that the Promised Land was undergoing on account of men's sins, being intolerably oppressed by the cruelty of the pagans', to send at his own expense to conquer the Holy Land, for one year from the following March, 1,500 knights and as many foot soldiers.

This was a truly formidable undertaking, which, all religious considerations aside, embraced all the great themes of imperial policy. Henry VI was following on his father's path, but not because the liberation of the Holy Sepulchre was a sacred task of the empire, nor to end a life heroically lived according to the imperial faith in the pious service of the Church. This crusade was an expedition of German knights financed by conquered nations, a vindication of Barbarossa's ill-fated heroism against the first conquest of the Franks and the boldness of Richard Coeur de Lion; it was the affirmation of the empire and the foundation of a new Mediterranean universality, that would be above all and against all, and would triumphantly reconcile within itself the keen but disappointed hopes of the Norman kings and the German Caesars.

It was also an act which could wipe away the memory of the crusading king's capture, of the deceptions, the cunning and the cruelty with which he had built up his power. And above all it was an offer of peace to the Church.

For the structure of the empire, imposing though it seemed, was balanced on extremely shaky foundations. An irresistible force continued to push Henry VI from one enemy to another, from one great conquest to an even greater one, and he was always more and more behind the times. The very rhythm of his ascent seems to betray a consciousness of inner weakness, the anxiety of an enterprise that must be continued without respite to its final goal, so as to avoid falling into the void or being irremediably compromised.

The two great enemies of Henry's creation were the Church and the medieval empire. Having arrived close to his goal he thought he could negotiate, and boldly tried to remould both these institutions to suit his own political ends. In the eyes of the Church, Henry was a usurper, who had unjustly occupied the Kingdom of Sicily, which was a fief of the Church, and the lands of the Donations, which included the Matildine possessions in central Italy; he also ordered at his pleasure and misgoverned bishoprics and abbeys and property and servants of the Church both in Italy and Germany, in defiance of all the Concordats. The Church might watch and wait in silence, as it had done up till now, but its silence was a condemnation. The oppressive regime of the foreign power was not enough to pacify and reconcile the people. When the time was ripe, Rome could once more make its influence felt on both sides of the Alps, in its invaded lands, in the communes of Lombardy, among the German princes and in the western monarchies.

As far as the empire was concerned, the problem had been made more complex by the addition of the feudal crown of Sicily to the imperial crown, which already comprised those of Germany, Italy, and Burgundy, and also by the birth of an heir to Henry VI. In comparison with the hereditary monarchies of France and England and the other states of Europe, the empire was a different kind of organism, and one that was severely behind the times. Under the Franconian dynasty it had looked as if even in Germany the principle of hereditary succession might finally prevail, and the election of the King of the Romans by the German princes be transformed into a mere formality or fall peacefully into disuse. But instead of this, the two emperors who succeeded to the throne after the Struggle of the Investitures and the Concordat of Worms, both signed an unequivocal declaration of the elective principle—a triumph for the great lay and ecclesiastic nobility in conjunction with the Church. Frederick Barbarossa had aimed to widen the territorial basis of his monarchy, to rein in the anarchic and centrifugal tendencies of his princes, and to reclaim from the old national church *de facto* what the empire had lost *de iure* with the Concordat of Worms. And he had succeeded at least in getting his second son Henry elected King of the Romans at the age of four. Henry in his turn had followed his father's example with unprincipled energy and ability in his relations with the Church, and had made the *ministeriales* his instrument of government and conquest against the princes.

The empire had been the hegemonic power, and the religious and political conscience of the west. This conscience somehow justified the election and the devotion of the man to his sacred task, and some kind of universal recognition. Now, in the new Europe, such a title had lost its significance. The more the hereditary monarchies asserted themselves, the more the empire seemed to dwindle in comparison, as the bare bones of its constitutional weakness showed through the shrinking flesh. It could only maintain its pretensions to universality on one condition: that it did not deny itself, which meant dominating the world effectively by virtue of its might, by the right of conquest, with good legal sanctions to back it up. But how could even Henry VI's enormous accomplishment give him confidence for the future, as long as the fate of the empire was left to the whim of the princes, and the imperial coronation—whatever its value might now be—depended on the good will of the pope? And what human satisfaction could he expect from his heroic labours, if there was no guarantee that his son would wear the imperial crown, and if his posterity was destined to fall from the dizzy heights of world dominion to the more modest fortune of a kingdom?

The very possession of the Sicilian kingdom, even if it were sanctioned by the Church—a condition which remained highly questionable—still put the emperor in an absurd and humiliating position. While as emperor he was the universal overlord, he would have to become the vassal of the pope as the King of Sicily. In this capacity he would be uniting in his own person two powers of different and even contradictory natures: the one merely lifelong but sovereign, restricted in time but with unlimited authority, the other hereditary but subject to feudal duties, having greater security of tenure and less autonomy. Yet at the same time kingdom and empire were closely united in their policy and interests, not only because they were ruled by one and the same man, but on account of the layer of German knights and administrators, who had conquered the kingdom and were now governing it, and finally, because Sicily had become the principle instrument of imperial expansion.

Henry looked to solve all these difficulties by starting negotiations with the princes and the Church, this at the same time as he was preparing for the crusade with immense energy. The plan he proposed to the princes was practical and radical. Reading the words of this chronicler, we can feel the astonishment of his contemporaries through the simple language: 'In the year of Our Lord 1196 the emperor held a diet around the middle of Lent, and many men took the Cross there. At the same diet the emperor wanted to establish a new and unprecedented decree for the Roman kingdom with the princes: that in the Roman kingdom the kings should succeed to the throne by hereditary right, as in the Kingdom of France and the others.'

The scandal was more than legitimate. The proposal was no less than an attempted subversion of the constitution, a total modernization of the empire which would deprive the princes of the right to elect and be elected. Henry offered his German vassals more than the gift of Sicily in return for this sacrifice, which might be more or less according to each individual case. For his lay vassals in all the fiefs of the crown he would recognize the unqualified right of hereditary succession in both the male and the female line, and in direct and collateral descent—a concession that some nobles had already obtained as a privilege which could now become general; for the ecclesiastic vassals he renounced his assumed *ius spolii* over vacant benefices and the *regalia*, both of which had been so fiercely contested by the Church.

If put into practice, this plan would have given stability, peace and security to the monarchy. After various negotiations the emperor managed to obtain the consent of fifty-two princes at the Diet of Würtsburg in April, 1196. But in the face of the opposition of the Archbishop of Cologne, on whom the coronation of the King of the Romans depended, and the support for his stand in the old anti-Swabian centres of the Lower Rhine, Saxony and Thuringia, he felt it more prudent not to press the matter further and to adopt a more devious strategy. In the summer of 1196 he went down to Italy a third time, almost unarmed and with only a small train, to take the offensive in negotiations for peace with the Church.

A chronicler relates that ten years before this, when Henry VI was ruling in Italy in the absence of his father, he had one day had a bishop brought before him and had asked: 'Tell me, cleric: from whom did you receive your episcopal investiture?', to which the bishop replied: 'From my lord, the pope.' After repeating his question three times, always with the same result, he had scornfully told his servants to give him a good dose of blows and to 'tread him in the mud of the piazza'.

Now times were changed, and circumstances dictated a certain prudence and moderation. And yet even now, in the thick of the diplomatic formalities, the man did not bely the disproportionate pride, the violence, the contempt for his eternal enemy, and the blind faith in force, that lay in the depths of his soul. He declared that, 'Nothing is more useful or more salutary than a solid and unbroken peace between Church and empire', that he, . . . intended to use all his power to establish a concord that would be able to withstand any occurrence'. But of course, it had to be *his* peace, *his* concord; woe to those who asserted their rights, or complained to him of outrages they had suffered. When Celestine III reproached him for the violence of his brother Philip of Tuscany, the imprisonment of the Archbishop of Salerno, his refusal to endorse the nomination of the Archbishop of Siponto, the deposition of other bishops from their sees in the Sicilian kingdom, and the mutilation and robbing of the Byzantine ambassadors on their way to the papal court, he replied with apparent courtesy but in fact in an arrogant and even threatening fashion, refusing all responsibility, while confirming the accusations, and solemnly stating that more respect was due to him in Sicily than to his predecessors '*ex eo . . . quod illis sublimiores iudicamur at potentiores*'.

Such exchanges were no more than skirmishes which scarcely brushed the surface of the deep-seated differences of their irreconcilable conflict. Indeed while the emperor needed to win acceptance for his hereditary plan as fast as possible and to free the lands he occupied in Italy of all papal interference, the Church was totally unable to approve the plan and thereby renounce its own rights in Italy, without betraying itself and its whole history by abdicating its own independence, a large part of its domains, and renouncing all political activity on both sides of the Alps.

Being unable to break down the princes' resistance to his scheme, Henry VI proposed to the pope that he should annoint his son king, a move which would have avoided the obstacle of the German election and coronation, and also perhaps that of the union of Sicily with the empire; but he met with a refusal. When the pope asked him to pay homage for the Sicilian throne he in his turn refused, considering that this would be an offence to the dignity of the empire. In the end, in November, 1196, in order to remove all obstacles to the attainment of his two goals, he put forward a plan which, while harking back to the days of Barbarossa, was the equal of the hereditary plan in its revolutionary boldness and the unconstrained modernity of its conception; it also formed an interesting parallel with it in so far as its object this time was the other great universal body of the Middle Ages, the Church.

For some time the financial position of the Holy See had been extremely precarious, as a result of the occupation of the Italian territories. The plan was to buy with money the conditions that were indispensable to the stability of the empire and could not be otherwise obtained. Had not Frederick I attempted a solution of this nature at the Congress of Verona in 1184? And had not Gregory VIII himself recognized a few years before, 'that it was wrong for the pope and the cardinals to take up arms and go into battle', and that it was rather their duty to devote themselves entirely to works of charity and 'to raise hymns of praise to the Lord in the churches day and night'? Now Henry proposed that in return for his territorial and political sacrifices in Italy, the pope should be granted in perpetuity the greater benefice for each of the metropolitan churches and the larger episcopal churches throughout the empire; and the cardinals, according to their rank (excluding the chaplains and clerics attached to the papal chapel) should be allotted the annual income and prebends of the smaller episcopal churches. By means of universal Councils convened for the purpose, and by means of the propaganda of influential men—(there is a certain presentiment of a new era in this reference)—it would be possible to obtain the approval of both the empire and all the kingdoms of the Catholic world. The pope did not reject the proposal out of hand; his only reply was that this was not a step towards peace and that he would reflect on the matter until the coming Epiphany—this was on November 17, 1196. The Church was evidently in no hurry, because, among other things, the ancient enemies of the empire were perhaps working with her and for her.

Thus Henry was defeated on both his fields of battle. In Germany he had to abandon his great plans and content himself with having his son elected King of the Romans. In his relations with the pope he concealed the gravity of the blow he had been dealt, declaring that the refusal had caused him neither joy nor distress, and that he was willing to await the pope's decision. He then tried once more to obtain an agreement, but with no better result.

Henry still had two important weapons in his hands: the crusade and his oriental policy. He pushed both forward with alacrity, confident that they would open up new possibilities and new avenues to the resolution of the conflict. But in the midst of his preparations, around February, 1197, he was surprised by a vast conspiracy. It cannot be called a national movement in the modern sense of the word; and yet this was something new in the history of Italy and Europe, because over and above the traditional alliance of the Church with the communes against the imperial pretensions, there were Sicilians, Lombards and Romans joined together in the plot to shake off the greedy, cruel and despotic foreign domination. A further goad to the common exasperation had been the death of the Count of Acerra, brother of the unhappy queen, Sibylla, in December, 1196. He had been caught while fleeing, imprisoned and then handed over to Henry, who had him dragged from a horse's tail round the streets of Capua, hung from the gallows by his feet, and finally, when he was still alive after two days, strangled with a stone round his neck by the court jester, '*ystrio teutonicus nomine Follis, ut ipsi imperatori placeret*'.

The aim of the conspiracy was to depose the emperor, appoint a new king, and surprise and annihilate the German garrisons. It was said that Celestine III and the Empress Constance herself took their part in the plot, and difficult though it is to establish how far such participation went, the suspicion was very probably well-founded. The emperor was warned in time and withdrew to Messina, which was defended by Marcwald of Annweiler and Henry of Kalden, and with their help he quashed the rebellion. The mad barbarity of his revenge surpassed anything that had been seen up to that time in the revolts of the barons in Sicily. The Sicilians who had been held prisoner in Germany since 1194, with the exception of the ecclesiastics and members of the royal family, were all blinded on his orders. The pretender to the throne had a red-hot crown fixed on his head, and the empress was forced to assist at the spectacle. The types of execution were varied with the most exquisite and horrible fantasy. Some men expired on the gallows, others under the axe, drowned in the sea or burned, impaled or sawn in half.

After such proceedings, the emperor could once more call his life and kingdom his own.

> *Cesar erat omnia, cuncta disponebat,*
> *celum, terra, mare, pluto iam timebat.*

But just as he was sure of his coming victory, his luck betrayed him:

> *Fortuna volubilis gradum suum vertebat.*
> *Cloto colum baiulat, incipit filare,*
> *Lachesis est presens, vitam cepit dare,*
> *Atropos occurrit et facit detruncare.*

He had scarcely recovered from the serious illness which had struck him down immediately after his repression of the conspiracy, when the fever caught up with him again at the beginning of August, as a result of his over-exertion out hunting in the woods of Linari, near Messina. He was still able to salute the forty-four ships of his fleet that was sailing to the Holy Land at the end of August, but then six days after his crusaders had disembarked in the east, on September 28, 1197, he died on the road to Palermo, only just over thirty years old.

His last wishes, which he added to his will shortly before his death, closed this great period of imperial history with an act of political wisdom and an acknowledgment of defeat. Henry VI realized that with his death all hopes of bridling the Church were at an end, so with the sole purpose of keeping the two crowns for his son, he made the concession which he had inflexibly refused in the negotiations: the feudal dependence of Sicily and the restitution of the Matildine property and the lands of the Donations.

The body of the emperor, clad in the most splendid royal vestments, was placed in a porphyry sarcophagus in Palermo cathedral beside the founder of the monarchy, where it still lies to this day.

The age of Henry VI marks a critical point of history, in which the medieval empire made its last supreme effort to secure its own salvation and triumph. Beside the new Europe of the communes and the monarchies which was gradually evolving, the universal empire, being feudal and elective, and no longer supported by its faith, had become an anachronism.

Imperial policy was inextricably intertwined with the new European policy, and the new Europe penetrated the very system of the empire by means of Guelphism. Which of the two irreconcilable forces was to win? With a master stroke—the conquest of Sicily and a large part of Italy—Henry VI succeeded in establishing himself right in the heart of the Mediterranean, putting the Church and Byzantium on the defensive, and gaining control of the centre of the French and Anglo-Norman intrigues and ambitions. His possession of Sicily rendered the solution of the two fundamental problems inevitable, distinct and yet linked as they were, the one age-old, of the empire's relationship with Rome, the other more recent and decisive, of the constitution of the empire.

He attempted a powerful synthesis between the two worlds which was at once behind the times and daringly novel, reactionary and revolutionary. The Church was to be stripped of all its political functions and reduced to a religious institution of vast financial resources. The empire, enriched by the acquisition of Sicily and evenly matched with the hereditary monarchies in weight, was to be superior to them in power, and to realize the universality of its nature in a physical actuality which, *de iure* and *de facto* would be vaster and more powerful than it had ever been.

But the effort came to nothing. The forces he had repressed rose up in rebellion, and the Kingdom of Sicily, which should have been the catalyst in the great transformation, the point of departure of an effectively and humanly universal policy, was in the event the tomb of the empire.

Forty years after Barbarossa's assumption of the imperial throne there was much that was changed, both in the emperor and the world around him. Perhaps the most general and obvious feature of this change was the fading of the religious spirit which until then had animated the Middle Ages. The Germany of Henry VI was no longer the Germany of the great abbots and archbishops, the high court officials, the diplomats, and generals surrounding the emperor. Henry was in a way more alone, with his domestic enemies before him, with his *ministeriales* and his knights sworn for life and death to his fortune and theirs. He too, like the sovereigns of the other western kingdoms, began to loosen the bonds of the feudal classes on the monarchy, to lay the foundations of his state on people of the towns, on a new class of men of humbler origins and more devout obedience.

The human and divine drama of Church and empire, with its great scenes in the time of Otto I, Otto III, the three Henrys and Barbarossa, is now drawing to its close; the knot has been untied. The impenitent and perennial usurper of the Church's rights can now violate the Donations and the Concordats without being struck down by excommunication or obliged to find an antipope. The very crusade is intended to be a political master move, rather than an act of devotion to the outraged Christian faith and towards the empire. The problems that arise and the diplomatic and military moves, betray the existence of a new world of crude realism and reasons of State. The empire can become a question of inheritance, the object of the emperor's last wishes, just as the Church can be bought and sold for money in consideration of her poverty.

The solemn doctrinal polemics of court and Curia now give way to new voices of exhortation and investive: the voices of the troubadours, of Bertran de Born who celebrates Conrad of Monferrato's defence in the east and lets fly at Philip Augustus and Richard Coeur de Lion, of Pierre de la Caravana and Pierre Vidal who attack the horrors of the German regime in Sicily and encourage the Lombards to fight:

Lombart, beus gardaz
que ja non siaz
pejer que compraz,
si ferm non estaz!

De Pullaus sovegna
dels valens baros,
qu'il non an que pregna,
for de lor maisos;
gardaz non devegna
autretal de vos.[1]

[1] 'Lombards, take care that you do not become worse than slaves if you do not stand firm. Remember the valiant barons of Apulia, who no longer have anything that can be taken from them except their houses; take care that the same does not happen to you.'

Ben volgra que estes Lombardi' en defes
de croiz ribautz e de mals escarans.
Lombart, membreus cum Poilla fu conquisa,
de las dompnas e dels valens baros
cum los mes hom en poder de garsos![2]

And yet over and above the immediate political polemic there is a new expectation of a great tomorrow, a sense of living at a momentous time in the consciousness of the people. The spirit of prophecy reawakens after a century of silence; the biblical hermeneutics of Gioachino de Fiore are joined to the courtierly praise of Goffredo da Viterbo and Pietro Ansolino da Eboli. For the latter poets the sixth age of the world, which begins with the sixth Henry, will bring the world unity and peace. His successor, 'Constant in name and spirit', will be King of the Romans and of the Greeks and 'will have before his eyes the text that reads: "The King of the Romans vindicates all the kingdom of the Christians to himself".' Or else Henry himself will bring the Saturnian age back to the earth:

Imperium Cesar solus et unus habet.
Iam redit aurati Saturnii temporis aetas,
iam redeunt magni regna quieta Iovis.
Nam meus Augustus solus et unus erit,
unus amor, commune bonum, rex omnibus unus,
unus sol, unus pastor et una fides.

For the prophetic abbot, the sixth age of the world, which 'is already lightening the eyes of men with its dawn', opens the doors to the 'third state of the world', the age of the Spirit, which follows those of the Father and the Son, and is marked by a new spiritual Nativity and Resurrection, mission of the Apostles and foundation of churches. But first the Kingdom of Judas, the carnal Church, must be struck down and annihilated by Nebuchadnezzar—Henry VI—and the Kingdom of Babylon, the empire, minister of the divine retribution, must in its turn be undone. The hour is near, and yet men will not see.

'Alas, alas, how is it that that great city, that strong city which once with its multitude of people and the strength of its armies subdued the world, has now been submerged and reduced to nothing, so that there remains not a trace of memory of her greatness?'

'And these things are in truth about to happen, even if the sons

[2] 'How I wish that Lombardy would stand in defence of low rascals and adventurers. Lombards, remember how Apulia was conquered, how noblewomen and valiant barons were put into the power of knaves.'

of this world do not want it, and even if they defend their part with many authorities, jeering at those who announce these things and confuting them.

'And we on the day that God strikes down our rival shall sing Alleluia, not because she is ruined and perished, but because with her ruin we shall be left in liberty, and because the temple burned by the Chaldeans will be built again in living stone.'

The prophecy was a false one. And the celebration of the universal empire was not the prelude to new triumphs; instead these verses passed on to further generations, to Dante and others beyond him, the unrealizable dream of the harmonious Christian Republic under the imperial aegis, and re-echoed the Christian ideal of the family of man reconciled and set at peace in the faith. The first year of the thirteenth century, which according to Gioacchino da Fiore was the beginning of the new age, did not open the doors to the third state of the Spirit, although it did contain the clearest indications of the progressive decadence of the empire. But the prophet himself, whatever his doctrine, expressed, in his desire for spiritual liberty and his condemnation of the Church and its history, an exigency that was destined to provoke the most profound disturbances in the Catholic world.

The portrait of Henry VI that is probably the most penetrating that has come down to us is one he owes to the pen of an enemy, the Byzantine historian, Nicetas, lost in his own thoughts, a stranger to all pleasure, forgetful of food and sleep, the emperor turns over the greatness of the Caesars and ancient Rome in his mind. Throughout his life he is spurred on by a narrow, heroic and implacable will to power, which moves towards its goal with any kind of weapon: force and cunning, perjury and cruelty. This stain has remained on his name down the centuries, ever since the troubadours first taunted him with their invectives, and Bertran de Born, exalted the generosity of Barbarossa to shame him.

Papiols, ia N'Frederis
no feira aital barganha
com fetz son filhs N'Aenris
quan pres romieus ab bordos,
don pert Polha e Romanha.[1]

It is true: his father would probably not have captured and traded

[1] Papiol, Frederick would not have made such a bargain as did his son Henry when he captured pilgrims with their staffs, through which he has lost Apulia and Romagna.

Richard Coeur de Lion, or sold the Tusculanians, cheated the Genoese or blinded the Sicilian prisoners in Germany. But the nature of the man, the roughness of the times, and the occasional exacting demands of politics, which have been invoked a thousand times, are not enough to justify or explain his actions. If we want to go further than the various judgments, now moralistic, now episodic, now generally pessimistic, that have been passed on the age of Henry VI, and which leave us basically unsatisfied, we must above all take into account the battle of life and death which the empire had undertaken, and the break in the civil consciousness which left men's energies unbridled to the confused rule of their impulses or of immediate political convenience. We must remember too, the complexity and the breadth of scope in this game, which required shrewdness, prudence and boldness, and which confronted the Swabian with a man of equal calibre and greater fortune, Philip Augustus of France. For the victory of the morrow is to go not to the Swabian Empire, but to the new Europe of the Capetian monarchy.

'Henry the Emperor,'—I quote the funeral elegy of a contemporary chronicler, Otto of St Blaise—'after subduing the enemies of the empire on every side, and making himself powerful on land and sea, was surprised by an untimely death. His fate will be wept eternally by the race of the Teutons and all the peoples of Germany, because he made them famous with the riches of other lands; by virtue of war he struck terror into the surrounding nations, and showed how superior they were to the other races; he was destined to so much that, had he not been stayed by death, the honour of the empire would have been restored by his valour and actions to its ancient state of dignity.'

This lament has come down to us on the pages of historians, and even today we are liable to read that the undoing of Henry VI's work was due to his untimely death, that it was 'blind irrationality of the laws of nature', 'the blind force of nature that strikes at the course of events in the world'. Such statements mean effectively that if Henry VI had lived, the structure he had built would have been filled out and consolidated, with imponderably great consequences for the Mediterranean world in general and for Germany in particular. For such a figment of the imagination as is this hypothesis, we may as well substitute another, which though equally imaginary, is at least substantiated by what actually did happen. It is this: even if the emperor had lived, his work would soon have been undone equally. His life was not enough to break down the obstacles to his imperial dream; his death would not have sufficed to annihilate a solid construction. Whatever the necessity that impelled him and could not be denied without a betrayal of himself and his crown, it remains true that all his great achievements were attempts to move backwards in time, they repressed new forces, and trod underfoot a moral, civil and religious conscience which could be violated but could not be destroyed. This was the seed of death which destroyed his whole creation. The universal empire of the Middle Ages was no longer in the hearts of men, and Henry's heroic might and pitiless resolve were not enough to build it up on new foundations.

His tomb in Palermo beside Roger and Frederick II seems to symbolize the fate of Henry VI and of the empire—the conquerer of Sicily conquered on the land he had won.

CHAPTER 14

THE LAST BID FOR POWER OF THE MEDIEVAL PAPACY

BONIFACE VIII

I

When we see the triumphant papacy of Innocent III follow on the death of Henry VI and the collapse of the empire, we are liable to contrast the one with the other. We are astonished at the miracle of this giant and solitary pope who dominates the Catholic world in serene sovereignty for eighteen years, from 1198 to 1216, like a great peak rising from the lowlands of Clement II's and Celestine III's papacies, until the Holy See is forced once more to clash swords with the Swabians, and finally to yield to French domination.

This contraposition is in fact a totally superficial one. With a little reflection it becomes obvious that the two facts are correlated and that the one can be very largely explained by the other. This consideration is not intended to detract from the ability, energy and the high principles of Innocent III, or indeed from the results of his policy. It merely sets the man and his times in historical perspective, puts the right valuation on them, and shows that in this case medieval history is much more logical than it seems at first sight.

At the close of the twelfth century and the beginning of the thirteenth the advantage reaped by the Church was proportionate with the steep and sudden downfall of the empire. The imperial encircling of Rome, which looked as if it would suffocate it, had been broken as if by magic. Rome was once more mistress of her lands and held the overlordship of Sicily. The field of action, which until this point had been mortally narrow, was widened: no longer was the papacy faced with a Barbarossa or a Henry VI, but with two rivals of lesser stature, the Ghibelline Philip of Brunswick, Henry's brother, and the Guelph, Otto of Bavaria, the son of Henry the Lion, and then subsequently with the young Frederick II. The latter, when Philip was dead and Otto, though crowned, had failed in his duties to the Holy See, was thrown into the field against him with the promise of the imperial crown, on the condition that he would not unite the empire with the Sicilian kingdom and that he would go on a crusade. Thus the regime of repression and reaction that the Swabian Henry had founded on cunning, force and violence, gave way naturally to the moderating power of the Church, which, though absolute in its principles, was more temperate in its politics, being content with a relatively remote seigniory instead of direct and oppressive dominion, as the nature and necessities of its struggle with the empire led it to welcome and support the new forces of Europe rather than suffocate them.

Leaving this difference aside, the triumph of Innocent III was, from the point of view of the two universal potentates themselves, an exact parallel to that won ten or twenty years earlier by Henry VI. Both in their turn were engaged in a task of reconstruction, or better, of the greatest construction ever attempted in the Middle Ages in the name of the Church or of Caesar. But when we come down to details, the achievements of both Church and empire were equally transient: the absolutist empire had striven in vain to destroy the most vital part of the west for its own ends, and the universalist papacy took it back under its protection only to see the forces it had roused against the empire turned against itself.

There was in fact no great action of Pope Innocent III's that did not bear within itself a sign of weakness, foreshadowing or demonstrating the process of the medieval Church's dissolution. The Franciscan friars, who had arisen from the people and worked among them, were an expression of a religiosity that was lively and widespread, but at the same time rather turbulent and unsure, like the society they were born from. The ideal of St Francis, and his more rigid followers' antagonism to Friar Elias and his disciples, implied a condemnation of the temporal policy of the Church, a condemnation that was destined to make heretics of the friars who considered themselves his most faithful disciples, and to give the secular powers an effective instrument against the papacy in the Friars Minor. The Inquisition betrayed an anxiety to quench a hidden but uncontrollable fire which was growing more and more dangerous. The Church's solidarity with the state in the persecution of heretics finally developed into a mere service rendered to absolutist monarchy.

The great religious enterprises undertaken under the aegis of the Church sometimes changed their nature in mid-course, and in general were adapted to the interests and turned to the advantage of the men who controlled them. The Teutonic Knights of Germany and the Swordbearers in the Baltic provinces worked for themselves in this way. Aragon emerged from its minority by defeating the Arabs at Las Navas in 1212, and set to preparations to challenge the papacy by the conquest of Sicily and the western Mediterranean. Venice, rather than devoting itself to the liberation of the Holy Sepulchre, derouted its crusading ships to Constantinople and with the foundation of the Latin Empire in 1204 realized the dreams of Robert Guiscard, Roger II and Henry VI, and secured the Oriental trade for its own merchants.

The victories won by Pope Innocent III—over the weak John of England, over Otto IV through Frederick II, who was to betray the trust placed in him at the earliest opportunity, over Philip Augustus in the question of Ingeburga of Denmark, whom the king repudiated and pursued for twenty years in spite of the pope's thunderings, and then reinstated almost voluntarily in 1213—all lose much of their glory as soon as we consider them more closely in the light of the current circumstances and the events that followed them.

The very feudal seigniory that Rome could boast over more than one crown in Europe was for the most part no more than an illusion of power, based on a failing faith, imposed on the bargainer or the weak; and it was definitely outdated in comparison with the sturdy though more restricted development of the communes and the monarchies.

The greatest historical interest of the age of Innocent III consists perhaps not so much in the triumph of the theocracy as in the new characteristics developed within the papacy, characteristics which are to be thrown into ever clearer relief in the course of the thirteenth century up to the decisive period of Boniface VIII. The Church, which in the high Middle Ages was the great initiator and the moving force, now by reason of its own constitution and the constitution of the world in which it is obliged to work, can no longer pronounce such revolutionary and fertile words as 'reform of ecclesiastical life', 'liberty', and 'crusade'.

The theocracy becomes an instrument of order and conservation in the Europe that it has created and which is becoming every day more intolerant of its tutelage. Later than in the empire, in a different way and to a lesser extent, but analogously nevertheless, one can detect a decline of the religious spirit in the papacy, or rather a predominance of politics and administration over religion. To express it all in a word we have only to quote from the treatise 'On the corruption of the Church', written in the mid-twelfth century by Gehroh of Reichersburg:

'Nor is the fact that what used to be called the Roman Church is now called the Roman Curia a matter to which no blame should be attached. In fact, in the ancient writings of the Roman popes there is never any mention of this word Curia meaning the Most Holy Roman Church, which is more rightly called Church than Curia, because the word Curia is derived from *cruore*, or blood, or from *cure*, cares, as the poet says:

> *Curia, curarum genitrix, nutrixque malorum,*
> *iniustos iustis, inhonestos aequat honestis.*'

Leaving the poet to take the responsibility for his etymology and his condemnations, we must still accept the significance of the profound change in the Church which he noticed at that time and pinpointed in the change of titles. The Roman Church was gradually being transformed from a society of the faithful into an organization of vast temporal interests. And indeed, from the time of Gregory VIII on, Rome offers Europe the first great example of monarchical centralization. The Holy See becomes an immense bureaucratic organization which deals with the entire Catholic world in an infinity of public and private negotiations with both laymen and clergy: appeals, confirmation of bishops, the collation of benefices, dispensations, the relations with princes and sovereigns, truces and peaces, wars against rebels and infidels.

From this height of universal government, Rome becomes once more an authority on law. The *Decree* of Gratian, the *Gregorian Decretals*, the *Sext*, and later the *Clementines*, lay down the norm of judicial teaching and practice for Paris and Bologna. But this new supremacy is not gained without sacrifices; charity has to a certain extent to give way to law, the Gospels to the Decretals, and the vigour applied with such fervour to juridical problems and subtleties was lost to religion.

Until the beginning of the thirteenth century the finances of the papal Curia were nourished by the revenue of its dominion, by the income of the monasteries under the protection of the Holy See, the Peter's Pence levied in England, Scandinavia and Hungary, the feudal rights over the vassal states, and donations made by visitors *ad limina*. Now in the course of the thirteenth century the Church takes the lead in this field too, or in this field above all, leaving the lay potentates far behind by dint of its excessive fiscalism and the progressive centralization of its services. It is transformed into an enormous financial concern, infiltrating further every day into the network of economic interests, with its collectors scattered in every corner of the Catholic world, its deposits loading the houses of the Templars or the coffers of Tuscan bankers, with its remittances and bestowals of funds.

The ways in which this transformation took place were essentially two: the tithes imposed on ecclesiastical property and sometimes on the laity too by means of the crusades; and the *annatae* and *servitia*, which were the dues received by the Holy See in return for the bestowal and confirmation of benefices. After the example of Gregory VII and Urban II, the crusade became in effect the immutable task of all popes, the supreme manifestation of the sway they held over men's consciences. But the weapon that had been tempered for use against the infidels, was now turned against the Albigenses, Frederick II, or the Aragonese invaders of Sicily, and the money collected in the name of the Cross was put to uses which were too close to the immediate temporal interests of the Holy See, and too alien to those of the vast majority of Europe.

The reservation of benefices for the pope and the cardinals had been proposed, as we have seen, by Henry VI, so that the Holy See might be compensated for the abdication of all its political pretensions by a growth of economic security and independence. His offer was refused not because it was absurd or arbitrary in itself, but because at that moment the Church had quite different hopes and aspirations. So much so that when, in the new position assumed by the papacy after Henry's death, the financial exigencies, far from diminishing, increased enormously, the economic side of the idea came to light again in the Fourth Lateran Council, and its application was attempted by Pope Honorius III. And although his legates had to give way to the strong protests of the French clergy and the dilatory tactics of the clergy and the King of England, the work of the penetration and conquest of the benefices was tenaciously pursued by his successors, and towards the middle of the thirteenth century the idea was finally put into practice in the system of the *servitia* and *annatae*.

In this way Rome provided the money necessary for the support of the pope, the cardinals and the papal Curia, and at the same time, by means of the bestowal of benefices, guaranteed itself a way of relieving suffering, rewarding services, acquiring supporters, and making its will and presence felt in the widest circle possible. Here too, however, this financial independence which it craved for, finally turned into an earthly impediment, which was to check its impetus towards liberty and universal dominion.

The heaviest burden that weighs on the papacy in the thirteenth century, depleting its resources and its energy, is its political activity. The State of the Church is a patchwork of autonomous cities, old fiefs, and new seigniories. It is in the position to offer the stipend of a rectorship or a mayorship, or the land that was a prerequisite for the establishment on a lordly scale of the families of popes and cardinals; but in times of trouble, when the pope has greater need of help and loyalty, it is torn apart by the quarrels of rival factions, and needs much more vigilance and energy than it is able to provide.

The long and costly war against the House of Swabia and the

empire ends in victory at Benevento and Tagliacozzo; but the investiture of Charles I with the Sicilian kingdom is tantamount to a papal acceptance of vassalage to France and the Angevins—a distant prelude to Avignon. And when, after twenty years of interregnum, a pope of great spirit, Gregory X, is obliged to resuscitate the empire his predecessors had killed against the Angevins, its reappearance is so shadowy and wan that it can neither cause any apprehension on the part of Anjou, nor even help with the defence or share in the triumph of Rome.

Finally Sicily, which has already sealed the fate of the Hohenstaufen, becomes a malediction to the papacy as well. After all the Church's trouble over its conquest, it is suddenly lost through a popular insurrection and the wiles of the Aragonese. Being incapable of accepting the inexorable truth, the papacy weaves a web of intricate diplomacy, starts wars, squanders its treasures uselessly, and concentrates its every effort on the vindication of its rights.

The rights of the Church as stated in the papal bulls, the conciliar decrees, and the concordats are becoming more and more problematic every day at this time, for reasons much more complex than mere human corruption. Throughout the twelfth and thirteenth centuries there is an immense flowering of satire and invective against the venality and favouritism of the Church, against the *avaritia Romana*. And indeed, we cannot for love of argument or novelty close our eyes to the omnipotence of money, to the relentless race for stipends and benefices, the personal favours, and the parasitism that flourishes in the anterooms and offices of the Curia. But if the trouble had lain only in this, it would not have been irremediable for popes of the ability, energy and uprightness of Innocent III, Honorius III, Gregory IX, and Innocent IV.

The problem was not so simple. The Church had taken on enormous responsibilities, both spiritual and temporal, which it could not deny without admitting its own decadence, and which it was fatally forced to amplify, imposing a stricter degree of centralization the while, in proportion to the growth of difficulties of government. The '*Romanae Sedis inopia*', of which a contemporary writer spoke, was, in contrast to these responsibilities, a simple fact, just as Honorius III's request was a thoroughly honest one, in which he asked the churches of France and England to give help to their Mother, '*quae occupationibus multis et magnis involvitur pro necessitatibus filiorum*'. Quite apart from the unavoidable compromises all worldly governments have to make, and the concentration of ambition and greed around the fountainhead of power, the papacy did in fact need a great deal of money for its work and for its prestige. And its offspring, who were now adolescent or adult, were annoyed by the impositions, complaints and pleas of the Mother Church.

Europe, child of the Church though it was, was looking to its future not to its past; it was not conscious of its debt of gratitude, but felt only a craving for freedom and conquest, and a more or less distinct rancour against Rome, which continued to work and impose sacrifices to the end of its own grandeur, to speak a language that was now offensive and out-dated, and to announce new enterprises which were either out of tune with the western conscience, or damaging to particular interests. The sovereignty of the state, the autonomy of political activity, and the whole political system of Europe, were, in theory as well as in practice, in a period of gestation. The continual Roman appropriation of benefices, the proceeds of which went into the pockets of Romans or Roman favourites, never of the local residents, seemed to both state and clergy to be an uncalled for interference with local churches, and an intolerable and unjustified economic burden as well. The Holy See was still able to rally the Catholic world against the Turks, the Tartars or Frederick II; but the call was without echo, because the united political conscience of the west had had its day. The empire had its own problems to solve after its recovery: against the pope in Tuscany, against France between the Rhine and the Rhone, and in Provence, against the Angevins. The French monarchy was preoccupied with England's encroachment on the Continent, and Aragon with France and Anjou in Sicily. And the constant interference of the papacy in exciting wars, imposing peaces, and arbitrating in quarrels, was beginning to be looked upon with suspicion and annoyance as an intruder meddling with other people's affairs unasked.

Perhaps the most obvious indication of the burden of worldly cares on the Holy See, of the contradiction between its temporal politics and its religious misson, and of the inner weakness that undermines the absolutism of the papacy, is that presented by the figures of the popes and the cardinals themselves. In the days of Gregory VII or Alexander III all personal circumstances of family and birth were made insignificant by the enormous prestige of their office and by the unique and tremendous battle in which their lives were consumed. Their adversaries fought under imperial colours and were labelled antipopes. But the popes of the thirteenth century, especially after the fall of the Swabians, are distinguished by other characteristics: for their piety or their political strength, for their French or noble Roman origin, for their ready subjection to the kings of France or the Angevins, or for their strenuous action in support of the papacy, either on their own account or through their family. The political struggle does not give rise to antipopes; it is fought in and out of the Sacred College through influence and bargaining.

In other words, there is a tendency for the more fervent religiosity to move from the centre to the periphery; the crisis of politico-religious universalism, which was set in motion by the Gregorian reform and the Struggle of the Investitures, and firmly established by the victory of the Church and Europe over the empire, ends by putting the very titles of papal absolutism in jeopardy. And while the papacy keeps its precious rule over men's consciences intact in this changed world, and hence retains a certain supreme control over earthly government, it is alone, widowed of the empire, incapable of supporting itself with its own strength or of pronouncing words to move the multitudes, and it therefore finds itself obliged to find a material foundation for its ideal power, to cling onto lay potentates and submit to their self-interested guardianship.

And so the help and interference from France, which is now the leader of Europe and destined, by reason of its long standing loyalty to the patronage of the Holy See, is parallelled by the appearance of another equally new phenomenon, that of nepotism, favouritism, and the shameless race for office and for benefices. An occasional indication of this evil can, it is true, be traced back to the time of Innocent III; but its historical importance is shown by the fact that it only becomes rampant at just that time when the struggle against the empire is over and the old form of universal government, both twofold and single, of Church and empire, gives way to the hybrid Angevino-Papal system, in which the Catholic Church, anchored as it is in Sicily, is obliged to serve the house of France in order to retain its command.

This is the period in which popes and cardinals become senators in Rome and mayors in the cities of the Papal States, in which members of the families from which popes and cardinals were drawn, the Savelli, Annibaldi, Orsini, Colonna and Gaetani, grown rich on the fruits of office, dispossess the old feudal holdings, take possession of cities and castles with cunning, violence and money, and found family estates in Tuscia, the Sabina, the Campagna, and the Roman Maremma. There is a totally unprecedented flowering of avidity and ambition. And yet we have to recognize the fact that this unleashing of worldly passions in the very heart of the Catholic world had its obscure origin in profound, rather than base motives; it had its root in the Church's need, in order to defend her independence and her political prestige, to make sure of the kind of loyalty that only relatives and especially favoured clients can give, and of the strength that was constantly ambushed on every side, and perhaps more by friends than by enemies. These circumstances gave rise to one of the most salient characteristics of the time, which was the close relationship between the politics of the Church and the activity and personal or family fortunes of the popes and cardinals.

The age of papal absolutism, and, we may also say, of the medieval papacy, closes with Celestine V and Boniface VIII, men of strongly contrasting character, and significant even in this opposition.

Whatever judgment is passed on Peter Morrone, he was the personification of one of the great impulses in the heart of Catholicism. He represented freedom in poverty, the longing for individual salvation, disinterest and implied condemnation of temporal politics; all of which led, in his sudden fall, to the unleashing of the most unruly passions all around him, and to the removal of the papal seat from Rome to Naples by Charles II of Anjou.

At the other extreme stood Benedict Gaetani, who represented the most overbearing absolutism of the papacy, a Church which proclaimed itself the arbiter of princes, and was nailed firmly to the earth, to the world which it pretended to dominate from on high. He was a pope who carried the carnal weight of his magnanimous and robust humanity to the very top of the hierarchy.

As was written not long after his death: *'Nam Bonifacius incriminabatur quod fuerat multum carnalis contra consanguineos et carnaliter vel amicabiliter sibi coniunctos, et quod quasi in ditando istos ecclesias exspoliabat et nimis pecuniam et alia temporalia diligebat'*. In this the papal notary and the cardinal had foreshadowed the pope. The most remarkable occurrences in the life of Benedict Gaetani before his assumption of the tiara were the accumulation of appointments and benefices, Italian, French and English, in his hands, his investment of large sums of money in land and castles, and his participation in the large-scale diplomatic negotiations made by the Church. But this, as we have already mentioned, is an ambition and avidity for wealth that we cannot simply lay at his door as a culpable weakness towards himself and his kinsmen.

The most important point for a clear understanding of this period is indeed that this greed and ambition are not narrowly individual and sterile attributes. Their roots are sunk deep in the small native district of the Gaetani, and from there they spread in a vast and intricate network of personal relations to the north and south of Latium, and constitute the motive force of a complex family campaign for the consolidation of Benedict's position as cardinal and the challenging of other papal families who have achieved wealth and power before the Gaetani; finally they cleverly and in a way inevitably weave their way into the political dealings of the Church, exercise their influence and leave their seal upon them.

The links that bind together the interests of the man and his family with his office in the Curia are so close, and the reciprocal action so profound and so constant, that it is practically impossible to separate the one from the other with any degree of accuracy; and moreover, the most serious and the most tragic upheavals in the papacy are to have their root in Benedict's personal and family antagonisms.

From Anagni where he was born and Todi where he was educated by the Bishop Peter his uncle, Benedict Gaetani spread out his nets in the Campagna and the Roman Maremma, in Tuscia and the Neapolitan territory, the three great directions in which his conquering zest was to move in turn, and the lands where his house was to flourish for centuries. Beside him stood his brother Loffred II, and as time marched on a succession of nephews and grand-nephews, who were docile instruments for the purchase of castles, the receipt of investitures, the contract of lucrative marriages and the occupation of city magistratures. Himself he made acquisitions in Campagna and the Maremma, bought the Sicilian city of Calvi from Raymond of Balzo, the Count of Avellino, assumed the mayorship of Veroli, intervened as peacemaker at Viterbo and Nepi, Alatri and Perugia, occupied the castellanies of Fumone and Castro, and had himself appointed attorney for the government and defence of the county of Sovana, a fief of the Holy See, on account of its Tuscan interests and the promise of the eventual widowhood of Margherita Aldobrandesca, the mistress of the county.

His thorough judicial experience and his diplomatic ability gave rise to the quantity of his commissions, the flow of money into his private coffers from every quarter, the friendships that he made with the great, and the protection he was able to offer the needy whenever he found opportunities for aggrandisement and gain. The power of attorney he obtained over the Aldobrandeschi territory became a family affair, and gave rise to the marriage of Loffred III to the widow of Guido di Monforte. The subjection of the rebel Viterbo was concluded with a complicated financial operation by which the two peacemakers, Benedict Gaetani and Giacomo Colonna, lent the commune the several thousand florins they had condemned it to pay, and took the castles of Celleno and Sipicciano as security for the loan. The acquisition of the city of Calvi and various other favours of Charles of Anjou fit neatly into the negotiations for peace that Benedict conducted as cardinal between Charles himself and Alfonso of Aragon.

If one looked only at the results, one might judge this to be a splendid career favoured by good fortune and good friends; but if one patiently searches out the thousand ways, some more and some less open and direct, that Gaetani took to his success, we realize that it was a miracle of vigilance and cunning, courage and tenacity. He arrived last at the great banquet and had to push himself forward with whatever means were dictated either by circumstances or by his lively consciousness of his own worth and by his strong will.

Under such conditions he was bound to make enemies, and yet there was only one, the most important, the Colonna family, which came into the open at this time, and especially during the papacy of Nicholas IV, who was thoroughly devoted to this old Roman family. Most of the time there was no open or obvious conflict; it was rather a hidden game, a reciprocal surveillance and solidarity which tended to maintain the equilibrium between the two rivals. If Giovanni Colonna occupied the senate one year, Loffred Gaetani would follow him the next; where one family advanced, be it in the Campagna or the Maremma, Tuscia or the Naples district, they would without fail be overtaken, outflanked or confronted by the other. There was no transaction big or small, no opportunity for gain, in which each did not make a bid for its share. The family and personal interests are also questions of political direction—Angevin for Benedict Gaetani, Aragonese for the Colonna cardinals—and also questions of prestige and power, all of which are brought to the fore in the papal elections and the highly serious, but insoluble War of the Vespers.

Even after his assumption of the tiara, Benedict's conduct in this field remained much the same. An Aragonese ambassador to the Curia was to write one day to his king: 'The pope cares only for three things, which occupy his whole attention: long life, money, and thirdly, the enrichment, aggrandizement and exaltation of his own family. And he gives no thought to anything of the spirit.' In effect, wealth was the *sine qua non* of the worldly pomp and magnificence by which Boniface VIII delighted to exalt both himself and the Church, a kind of omnipotence with which he hoped to win himself favours and conquer all opposition. And he had no scruples, for 'the aggrandizement of the Church and his relations', in intriguing for offices in the communes, and stooping to compromises, threats, and all sorts of mercantile cunning.

During his papacy he remained the master mind of the economic policy of his family, and was no blind instrument of nepotism. Each one of his nephews could in the end boast of his own fine domain, and all of them would from time to time support him and take advantage of their control of cities and provincial governments. But in all these complicated manoeuvres, with their violence and trickery, whereby now one, now another of the family would take possession of the Aldobrandeschi territory, or of the county of Fondi, or of the cities and castles of the Campagna or the Maremma, the pope scarcely ever intervened directly; and in a kind of legalitarian spirit which reflected his culture, he never involved his own prestige or that of the Church, except in so far as his papal authority was necessary to ensure the juridical validity of the acts performed under his distant direction.

Although Boniface succeeded in founding the seigniory of the Gaetani for centuries by these precautions, he did not escape the hate of his victims, nor the blotting of his memory by posthumous condemnation. Just as, inversely, the fact that he was 'magnanimous and generous to people that he might please them', was of no avail in redeeming his reputation or in acquiring the certainty of loyalty from the men he had favoured in time of need. The Holy See had become an inexhaustible source of benefices for an infinity of postulants. The papacy had gathered an immense clientele around itself, and one which extended beyond Boniface's kinsmen, to the people of Anagni, the provincials and the Romans, and to all those who had been paid for the losses they had suffered or had found themselves suddenly raised to high office by the unexpected favour of the sovereign. But at the time of trial, the rancour was larger and more powerful than the gratitude.

The despotic and impetuous nature of the man, his harsh manner, and the frank and lively outspokenness of his language, which constantly reveals his Campanian origin overlaid with the new Roman consciousness, all contribute to the multiplication of his enemies. It is these that cause the hate that he finds building up against him, and the sense of terror and oppression that fills the atmosphere around the pope; and it is these which contribute even to his sudden fall, which although it essentially goes back to far deeper reasons, still in the most decisive moments shows the influence of the personal passions of the contenders.

The occasion on which the full rigour of Benedict's greatness first makes itself felt is one which merits a close examination, on account of the valuable picture it gives of a strength of will that is to stand firm amid even the harshest trials. A papal bull of Martin IV had given the Mendicants the right to preach and hear confession in parish churches even without the consent of the priest in question, and this had given rise to violent opposition between the French bishops and the masters of the University of Paris. So in 1290 Benedict, who was then a cardinal, was sent with Cardinal Gerard of Sabina to sort the matter out, while attending to various important political questions. On their arrival in France the word went round that they had been sent simply to revoke the decree. So they listened without comment to the public protestations of the Bishop of Amiens, who had borrowed all the arguments of the Parisian doctors, and resisted all attempts to discover their intentions with sealed lips.

In the end Cardinal Gaetani rose to his feet before the assembled council and spoke thus:

'Brothers and fellow bishops, I most diligently commend the Bishop of Amiens, your procurator and advocate, to your kindness. Indeed he worked against the aforesaid privilege in the Roman Curia with all his might, but achieved nothing; so he has tried to avenge his loss of pride here. And, as you see, the effort and expense have worn him out. But I declare before you all, that our mission is not to revoke the said privilege, nor to molest the friars whom you decry, but rather to confirm the privilege itself; because this is the only healthy limb we have found. On this account they will not be hindered but rather favoured. And therefore we wish that the privilege remain as it was originally decreed.'

He then added:

'It is a pity that the masters of Paris are not present to see their stupidity shown up in the light of day. With impious and rash temerity they presumed to interpret the aforesaid privilege as if the Curia had conceded it without the necessary deliberation. They must know that the Roman Curia has feet not of feathers but of lead. Indeed these masters think that we consider them wise; on the contrary, they are more foolish than all fools, because they have filled not only their own heads but the whole world with their pestilential doctrine. Nevertheless, in virtue of the authority that has been delegated to us to this end, we revoke and annul whatever any one has attempted against the aforesaid privilege. Otherwise, every privilege granted by the Holy See could be similarly nullified by the machinations of the masters.'

Henry of Gand, the most famous professor of the University of Paris, who had given the matter lengthy study, tried to persuade his colleagues to resist with the specious argument: *'Cum liceat nobis de Evangelio disputare, cur non de privilegio?'*; but he was suspended from his post. And when the masters appeared before the cardinals to intercede in his favour Benedict Gaetani harangued them thus:

'You, masters of Paris, have made nonsense of your teaching of knowledge and continue to do so, disturbing the whole world, which you would not do if you knew the state of the Universal Church. You sit on your professional chairs imagining that Christ is dependent on the results of your discussions; because so many consciences are taken in by your empty reasoning. It is bad, my brothers, bad. But as the world has been entrusted to us, we have to seek out not the course that suits you clerics as you see it, but that which is right for the whole universe. You think that you have a great reputation with us; but on the contrary, we consider you mere vanity and foolishness. You should discuss useful questions, but instead you busy yourselves with frivolous and imaginary trifles. Foolish indeed is this proposition of yours, which a fool puts forward foolishly and a master foolishly accepts and decides on. I have seen your arguments, and they are valid, but they can be resolved. And let this be the solution: We ordain by virtue of obedience, under pain of forfeiture of office and benefice, that from this time forward no master shall preach on, discuss or define the aforesaid privilege either openly or clandestinely. The privilege of the friars is to remain in full. And any one who is in doubt or who in the future starts to doubt about this privilege is to ask the pope for the interpretation. I say to you in truth, that the Roman Church would send the School of Paris to its ruin before it would deprive the friars of this privilege. Indeed we were not called here that we should acquire knowledge or make a fine show of ourselves, but that we should save our souls. And since the life and teaching of these friars procures salvation for many, their privilege shall always remain intact.'

These two speeches can not perhaps be quoted as examples of eloquence, but they certainly lack nothing in the way of clarity and force. When Gaetani refers to 'the state of the Universal Church' and says '*quia nobis commissus est mundus*', we hesitate for a moment, and wonder whether he means to speak of the Curia of which he is a member or whether he is not already feeling the weight of the government of the Church on his shoulders, whether it is a cardinal or a pope that is speaking through his mouth. The only thing that matters is the salvation of the soul, the only instrument of salvation, the Roman Catholic Church. And from the height of this certainty he dismantles the whole carefully constructed edifice of the French clergy and the Parisian professors with a word, he makes mock of the useless efforts of the Bishop of Amiens, hits out with his authoritarian and provocative tone at the theorizers and their scholastic arguments, which, while still cherishing them, he has learned to understand and to despise.

This is the way the new pope will treat sovereigns and cardinals. When Jean Le Moine of Picardy remonstrates with him for not asking the Sacred College its opinion, he replies: 'Picardian, Picardian, you have a Picardian head, but by God I shall pick and pitch at you and do as I please in everything, and I shall give up nothing for you or for all these others who are here like a lot of asses.' And when Charles the Lame refuses to sell him Gaeta, which he wants to endow as an ecclesiastical fief in favour of a nephew, he covers him with insults telling him that, 'He is no man, but a most base rascal; that he has held him up, otherwise the earth would have engulfed him', and asking him threateningly 'if he is aware that the kingdom could be taken from him by force'. Every one is bullied into abject submission; no one dares to speak for fear of his despotic and vengeful will, his 'tongue murderous in the ill it speaks', that spares neither kings nor emperors; and the suppressed hate grows out of all proportion.

Boniface, for his part, in spite of the passing years and troubles, 'is healthy and robust, and says that he will live until all his enemies die of suffocation'. He has himself exalted in the admiration and gratitude of Arnaldo of Villanova, the author of *De Regimine sanitatis*, the inventor of those gold seals and the *bracale* which preserve him 'from the ill of the stone and many other pains', the man 'who makes him live', in his own words: *'Iste homo maior clericus mundi est, et hoc fatemur et adhuc per vos cognoscitur.'* But the cardinals to whom he is speaking, secretly curse the arrival of Arnaldo for putting off the day of liberation, and sarcastic verses against the evil-doing Boniface and the evil-speaking Benedict are passed from mouth to mouth in the Curia.

II

We have been anticipating events: but this was indispensable if we were to give some indication of the nature of the man who, on December 26, 1293, ascended the papal throne. Boniface was mature in both years and experience at his accession. His many years in the Curia, and the important diplomatic missions this involved, had given him the mind of a lawyer and made him fully conscious of large-scale European politics and the conditions of the Church. His election was a reaction against the weakness and abuses of Celestine V's papacy, and the beginning of a regime of force; this in itself made it a cause for anxiety for the whole Catholic world from the very beginning. Indeed the abdication and flight of the old hermit in his search for solitude, his capture by Charles II and subsequent delivery to Boniface, his transfer under heavy guard to the isolation of Fumone and his immediate death, were all liable to give rise to unwarranted suspicion and accusations of violence and illegality. Hence the danger of a schism, the new pope's alarm and the severity of the measures he took against the Colonna, and his feeling that the prestige, unity and peace of the whole were threatened in his person.

But as we have already noted, we can see on closer inspection that the evil was deeper and more widespread than appeared from the complete contrast of the natures of these two popes or from the limited period of the abdication and its immediate consequences. Celestine V's renunciation was an indication of the gulf that lay between his spiritual and anarchic tendencies, his essential denial of the entire Catholic tradition, and the iron will of Boniface, who was conscious of the history of the Church as a whole and felt responsible for it to God and to mankind. It was a symptom of the crisis of the medieval papacy, faced as it was with the dilemma of either letting itself be peaceably dispossessed by the new Europe or pulling in the reins and re-establishing its absolute rule. Almost independent of Celestine V's abdication, the problem of Boniface's legitimacy and the danger of schism (which were to grow from mere forebodings at the beginning of his papacy to being the questions on which the final dramatic crisis of the Middle Ages was based), were signs of Europe's effective intolerance towards the papacy and of her insidious challenge to the papal theocracy.

The Church of Boniface VIII no longer has to deal, as friend or foe, with the one power that is its like, in its universality and historic and religious significance, the Holy Roman Empire. Her opponent is now one that she may rightfully consider to be her own creature, even though they are closely related by a thousand spiritual and temporal ties—the Europe of the new states with France at its head. The nature of the relationship is changed on one of the two sides, but just as the papacy and the empire used to be the two focal points of western politics, so the papacy and France are now. And yet the clash that marks the end of the medieval Church is to come about through France, and to come about because of the maturity her monarchy has developed and the central position that she has taken in European politics.

All the partial groupings that already existed in Europe, France against England, German Guelphs and Ghibellines supporting first one and then the other, Aragon against France and against the Angevin domination in Sicily in her bid for control in the western Mediterranean, were now firmly centred on the French monarchy. There was no question of importance in Europe that did not come back to France, or in which she had no part. The vassal kingdom of England continued to be her great enemy—Philip the Fair followed the example of his forbears in enticing her forces onto the continent and then having the Scots attack from the rear. This he did for the sake of territorial unity, and, in fine, for the triumph of the modern, monarchic and territorial state over the old order of feudal Europe. The empire was now confined within the limits of this conflict, in which, having fallen from her position of political universality, she sided now with England under Adolf of Nassau, now with France under Albert of Austria. Finally, the Sicilian question was especially a French concern, for France and Naples had joined forces to snatch the island from the hands of Aragon, and what was more, the crown of Aragon itself was placed by Martin IV on the unlucky head of Charles of Valois, the second son of Philip the Bold.

And before France stood the Church. Just as the conquest of Sicily had been in a way the cross and the tomb of the medieval empire, so the reconquest, or the restoration of the Church's high seigniory over the kingdom, mutilated as it was by Peter III's energy and ability, was the irresistably challenging task which drew the Holy See into direct participation in European politics and thus chained it to France. But there was basically no question of importance in Europe that did not touch the Church—Germany and the empire, the Anglo-French conflict, and even more, the party struggles in Italy—for all of them in one way or another had bearing on the War of the Vespers, and on the fate of the Papal States and the peninsula, they also had repercussions on the whole of the papal system of finance and taxation and came within the bounds of the supreme authority which the papacy still claimed over the Catholic world and the imperial crown, powerless though it had become.

Between the Church and the French monarchy there was finally the bank of Italy, which was primarily a Tuscan and Florentine affair. This was a new power, of a different nature; it was not tied exclusively to any state or territory, but spread its vast and intricate network over the greater part of Europe. Based primarily on Rome and Paris, it was at the service of the two very different monarchies, who had first set up large-scale financial systems, each on the model of the other. It was a power whose political efficacy in the broad field of Europe it is hard to evaluate, but in examining the passage of events at this time, we can conclude that it was there more to serve than to command, and was better able to give support to those in command than to impose its own financial policies.

The election of Benedict Gaetani brought the age of weakness and compromise to its end. This authoritarian and provocative prelate, jealous of the power that the Colonna and their supporters threatened to take from him, and almost physically conscious of the limitless scope it gave him, set himself resolutely to dominate the discord of the young Europe and to reduce it to order. His ultimate and unattainable aim was both simple and lofty: peace among men, divine and human justice, and liberty under the law of Christ. And it was in a spirit of heroism that he undertook this mission ordered by God and modelled on the examples of Gregory VII and Innocent III.

But unfortunately, as we have seen, states and princes were developing minds of their own, they began to go their own way, and to settle their quarrels with their own arms. The pope and the Church, while they proclaimed and vindicated such solemnly high principles as these, were in their turn trapped into becoming intimately involved themselves in the world they had intended to govern from above. Their immediate ends and the means that served them were all the more base because of their contradiction of the high-sounding words, and their identity with the practices of the secular potentates of Europe. Their actions were the less efficacious because they were not performed in the service of an ideal, they were no longer interpreting the profound exigencies of the Catholic world, but were debasing religion to the point where it became an instrument in the pursuit of worldly wealth and dominion, instead of making it, as before, a symbol of civilization, liberty and conquest to the masses.

The ultimate salvation, regularly put forward in the pope's letters as an argument for peace and an objective for a peaceful Europe, was held to be another Crusade. But there were too many intricate problems to be solved first, and grave though the Turkish threat was, the idea of liberating the Holy Sepulchre and bringing relief to the Christians in the east was one which had now lost its appeal in Europe. The pope might tread every highway, be everywhere at once with his imperious manner, warning, judging, and pacifying, he might use cunning or force, play his alliances cleverly and excite the animosity of whole towns against others, pour out money and dispense crowns to the favoured, coax or threaten—the result was almost always the same: his weapons turned to wax in his hands and he had to start all over again. Seldom has a man of such gigantic force suffered such enormous disappointments and obtained such insignificant results.

The recovery of Sicily was a real labour of Sisyphus. As a cardinal, Benedict had managed to isolate James of Sicily by setting his brother Alfonso of Aragon against him, and making up a quarrel between the latter and Charles of Anjou. As pope he succeeded in persuading James, now King of Aragon, to renounce the island altogether, by making him high admiral of the Church, helping him out of his financial difficulties, and investing him with Corsica and Sardinia, over which incidently the Church had no rights whatsoever. But the banner of rebellion was merely passed on to sturdier hands, those of the Sicilians, whose wishes had been ignored, and of Frederick, James' brother, whose ambition Boniface had briefly hoped to break. In one way and another even his allies betrayed him: Philip of

Taranto, who, after being beaten on the plain of Falconaria, allowed himself to be taken prisoner as had his father Charles of Anjou, and Charles of Valois, the brother of Philip IV.

The secret plots, the negotiations with Albert of Austria, the errands of peace entrusted to Cardinal Acquasparta and Charles Valois to take possession of Florence and Tuscany, lowered the prestige of the Holy See, set the city into mourning and financial ruin, and had no further result apart from laying bare the irremediable antagonism between the much advertised *plenitudo potestatis* of the Holy See, and the rights of the commune, which would now brook no interference in the jurisdiction in the city. The difficult negotiations with Adolf of Nassau and Albert of Austria to get freedom of action in Lombardy and Tuscany and recognition of the papacy's supremacy over the empire reached an artificial last-minute conclusion when Albert and Boniface were of necessity thrown into each others arms by the threats of Philip the Fair.

The papal claim to act as peace-maker between France and England was firmly resisted by the French king as an unwarranted interference in the affairs of state; and in the end he grudgingly allowed Benedict Gaetani as a private individual to act as arbiter, but denied him this privilege as pope. And even further afield, in the younger lands on the periphery of Europe, Denmark, Poland, and Hungary, we find the same situation: a faith and will that are unshakable, that are met with first resistance then failure. The reactions of the European states to Boniface's almost pathologically recurring need to clarify and test papal doctrine against hard facts were varied in intensity but never in kind.

The structure of the theocracy was everywhere in a state of imminent collapse. If we are in the habit of comprehending the whole of this crisis of the medieval Church in the jurisdictional conflict between Philip the Fair and Boniface VIII, this is not so much because of the heroism and vitality of the drama that ends with the insult of Anagni; it is rather because of France's political maturity and her position of leadership in Europe, the length, breadth and the desperate tenacity of the struggle, the fact that it brings into consciousness the tremendous problem of the death of a world and accelerates its decay, and because in this situation the germ of more than a century of Europe's immediate future was contained.

The conflict developed in three stages. On March 3, 1297, Stefano Colonna attacked and robbed a train of eighty mules two miles out of Rome on the Via Appia. They were carrying a load of papal treasure worth two hundred thousand gold florins. This was in a way the reply of the Colonna family to the early acquisitions of

Peter II, the pope's nephew, in the Maremma, on the lands of the declining Annibaldi estates. It was the mark, as has been said, of an old personal and family feud, both patrimonial and political, at once a vendetta and a provocation against the proud pope and his enterprising young nephews, performed on the part of the two Colonna cardinals and their family, who were linked by secret agreements with the Aragonese in Sicily and were supporters of the Spiritual Franciscans, who denied the legitimacy of Boniface's election.

The day after the assault the pope summoned the Colonna brothers to appear before him 'to hear what he shall please to say and to ordain', '*quod vult scire si papa est*' (because he wishes to know if he is pope), and then several days later he found a pretext to ask that their lands and their castles be handed over to him. The only effect produced by the summons and the request was that it induced the two cardinals to retire to the capital of their own seigniory.

But on May 10th, at the meeting held at Lunghezza sull'Aniene, they replied to the question that Boniface had imprudently challenged them with in a solemn manifesto containing the following words:

'Even if the renunciation (of Celestine) had been a valid one—which we neither state or believe in any way—there were many subsequent events which rendered the successive election null and void, so you, who are the person most closely affected by this, have good reason to doubt, saying that you wish to know if you are pope'; and, 'Now we, who speak in perfect faith, and with enlightened conscience truly believe that you are not the pope, cannot in conscience remain silent, so that the truth of so serious a question which touches the universal Church so profoundly is not clarified. Therefore we instantly and humbly request that a general council shall meet, so that the truth may be declared and all error removed concerning all these questions.'

The pope thus stood accused by two members of the Holy College; and the invocation of the council to judge the pope emerged from the abstract of juridical casuistry into the field of real live action; the bandits' attack on the road from Anagni had been transformed with dizzy rapidity into a fundamental problem, a threat against the unity of the Church that was all the more dangerous because the Colonna brothers found a supporter for their personal hatred in the France of Philip the Fair, which was prepared to make its own their call to rebellion against the absolutism of the papacy.

On finding themselves hard pressed by the financial demands of their mutual struggle, neither the French nor the English king hesitated to violate the clergy's immunity from taxation. By taxing them they were in fact doing the same thing on their own authority and in the interests of their own monarchies that the Church had so often authorized them to do on her behalf. Boniface replied to the protests of the French and English clergy with the *Clericis laicos* (on February 25, 1296), in which he made a violent attack on the hostility and usurpations of the lay world on the clergy, and went on to forbid all ecclesiastics to pay or promise to pay any tribute whatsoever and the secular powers to exact or receive any without the express authorization of the Holy See, both on pain of the severest of penalties.

Now while Edward I of England declared, after some hesitation, that he would no longer levy taxes without the consent of the clergy (in 1297), Philip the Fair published a decree to the effect that no kind of money or merchandise should be exported from the country, with the evident intention of not only providing for the country's needs for the duration of the war, but also hurting the interests of the Curia. This time, however, the knife did not quite strike home. For Boniface, being faced with the attitude of the French king and his counsellors and caught in the midst of his troubles with the War of the Vespers and his crusade against the Colonna family, also not improbably being put under pressure from the Florentine bankers, was forced to give way little by little, to the point of compromising on the actual execution of his orders.

But the bitterness remained on both sides, and the stage was set for the final encounter. Even in his withdrawal, Boniface VIII had taken the opportunity of the king's decree to set himself up as a severely paternal judge of all his political conduct, external and internal, and to enunciate, admittedly in a slightly less rigorous manner than formerly, the principles to which he firmly adhered, especially that of the theocratic tradition, the prerogative granted by Christ to the Church, and through her to the pope, 'of governing (*praeesse*) the faithful peoples with free dominion, just as a mother with power over each of her children, who all honour her as their universal mother and lady with filial reverence'.

The third stage of the conflict began with the arrest and condemnation for high treason by Philip the Fair of one of Boniface's favourites, his legate Bernard Saisset, Bishop of Pamiers. The years that preceded this event had apparently been peaceful ones. But the pope had been repeatedly releasing statements on the papal supremacy in the spiritual and temporal order, and the king had in his turn had no scruples in forming an alliance with Albert of Habsburg, maintaining his relations with the Colonnas, tampering with the ecclesiastical privileges and grinding down the clergy with his fiscal impositions.

At this point Boniface raised his hand and struck. He revoked the tributary privileges conceded to Philip the Fair four years before and summoned the French clergy to a synod to be held in Rome on November 1, 1302, and which the king himself was to attend, in order to 'do and to ordain that which would seem fitting for the honour of God and the Apostolic See, the increment of the Catholic faith, the conservation of ecclesiastical liberty, the reform of both king and kingdom, the correction of past excesses and the good government of the kingdom itself'. The representatives of the whole of France, clergy, nobles and city, replied to him from Paris on April 10, 1302, saying that they were willing to give their blood and their possessions for the defence of the crown. On April 13, 1303, Boniface notified the king that he was excommunicated for having prevented the clergy from attending the synod. And two months later, on June 13th and 14th, a new solemn assembly of nobles, clergy and lawyers convened in Paris by the king, accused the pope of the most infamous crimes, and, considering the Church to be deprived of its legitimate leader, decided that there should be an appeal to a Council, before which he should be forced to appear. Messengers from Philip the Fair ran from the Alps to Sicily announcing the decision of the Parisian assembly, while the vice-chancellor, Guillaume de Nogaret, the public prosecutor of the assembly, busied himself with its execution, making up to the aristocracy of Anagni and the Campagna, who had been dispossessed by the pope's nepotistic practices.

The pope's reply, his last one, was contained in the bull which began:

'Seated on the elevated throne of Peter, we, by divine dispensation, take the place of Him to whom the Father said: "Thou art my beloved Son, this day have I begotten Thee . . . Only ask it, and I will give thee even the uttermost parts of the earth for thine inheritance, and Thou shalt have power over them. Thou shalt govern them with a rod of iron, and like pots of clay Thou shalt break them." Let this be a warning to the kings and a lesson to the judges of this earth.'

The excommunication was confirmed and the king's subjects released from their oath of loyalty. The bull was to be nailed to the door of the cathedral at Anagni, where the pope was in residence, on September 8th.

But at dawn of the day before this, the gates of the city were treacherously opened to admit Guillaume de Nogaret and Sciarra Colonna with their troops.

The words uttered by the Cardinal Matthew of Acquasparta in the thick of the crisis in 1302: 'The discord which has sprung from a modest, even tenuous and trivial cause', might well make us wonder whether with a little good will on both sides, especially Philip the Fair's, the final and decisive encounter might not have been avoided and peace re-established.

Certainly, we are free to imagine all the alternative developments we please; but the hard facts of history remain the same. The clash of interests represented in the persons of the pope and the King of France had reached the point of no return. On one side there stood the greatness of divine and human doctrine, the wisdom born of centuries of experience of diplomacy all over the world, and with them tradition and law; on the other a new kind of statesmanship, which, though it too was supported by its own doctrinal justifications, was inspired with the energy of revolution, jealous, provocative and unprincipled. Boniface VIII might make compromises in practice, moderate his words out of consideration for the king of the most catholic France and the grandson of St Louis, and forbear for a long time before making his final condemnation. But his faith always remained that which he had implacably stated for the last time in the bull *Unam sanctam* of November 18, 1302, according to which the Church had two types of power, the spiritual and the temporal, the first to be exercised by the Church through her priests, the second by the laity but *pro Ecclesia, ad nutum et patientiam sacerdotis*'; and the secular power was distinct from the ecclesiastic, but subordinate to it. And this was precisely what the France of Philip the Fair was no longer prepared to tolerate.

To prepare public opinion for the assembly of Paris in 1302, wide circulation had been given to an extremely brief bull of Boniface which began: 'Fear God and observe his commandments. We wish you to know that you are our subject in both spiritual and temporal matters'; and to an equally brief reply from the king: 'Your sovereign stupidity must know that in temporal matters we are subject to no one'.

Both the one and the other were unashamed falsifications; but they came to the root of the matter, laid bare what diplomatic courtesy was liable to disguise, and made all further compromise impossible. The Council convened by the pope was now set against the General States of the kingdom, and the revolutionary Council before which the pope himself was to be brought for judgment. The solemn theocratic propositions were challenged by the frank statements of the royalist polemic, which no longer understood any law but that of the state, and reproached the clergy for their absurd claim that they should enjoy the benefits of living in the kingdom without contributing to the expenses of its defence.

Being strong in his own faith, Boniface could not reconcile himself to the idea of a Council not convened by the pope, and of an accusation of heresy, which, quite apart from being false, could, with this precedent, become a routine weapon of all princes against papal justice. And equally legitimately, the author of the *Disputatio inter clericum et militem,* who had lost this faith, could scorn Boniface VIII for his claim to exercise a right simply on the grounds that he had attributed it to himself verbally.

The gulf was indeed irreconcilable. With Boniface VIII and the France of Philip the Fair face to face, the battle-hungry faith of a medieval pope against the revolutionary audacity and zeal of the monarchy, the course of history could not be turned back. The time had come to break out of the circle of equivocations and to put things to the final test, to shoulder the full burden of their respective responsibilities. And the two adversaries did not hesitate to throw into the balance, with their own fortunes, the civil patrimony, old and new, of Europe. This was their heroic achievement, their magnanimous contribution to the great history of the west, the free necessity of their creation.

Leaving aside the falsifications, the legal sophistries and the petty personal attacks, it was through their efforts that the process of the disintegration of the Holy Christian Republic, which had begun with the Struggle of the Investitures and been ratified by the decline of the medieval empire, drew to its close with the birth of the modern state and its definition in theory and in practice.

And indeed, amid the confusion and intrigue of the struggle, we see France created almost before our very eyes, a France with a religious belief in herself, in her dynasty, and in the sovereign power of her king. It was many centuries since an organization so vast and compact, held together by its triumphs, its benefices and its common sacrifices, had challenged the condemnation of a pope. At one time, Boniface had reproached the clergy that 'fearing where they had no need to fear, seeking transitory peace, and being more afraid to offend the temporal majesty than the eternal', they let the laity abuse them and usurp their office without protest. But now even the clergy of France had sided with the monarchy against him and his theocratic papacy. This was the dawn of the new Europe.

In the course of the conflict, the pope, too, grows in stature and is transformed before our eyes. His greed for money, his passion for his nephews, his vendettas against his enemies, his violent threats and insults, all are far away. As shown in his solemn words of warning and his condemnations, he is the true personification of the majesty of the medieval papacy, making its last immortal testimony.

'Quod vult scire si papa est,' he had said, in his summons to the cardinals Colonna; *'Quod vult scire si papa est'* becomes, in a much broader sense, the purpose of the whole of his life.

In his profession of faith at the beginning of his papacy, Boniface had promised: *'Quamdiu in hac misera vita constitutus fuero, ipsam (Ecclesiam) non deseram, non abdicabo aliquatenus, neque ex quacumque causa cuiusque metus vel periculi occasione dimittam, vel me segregabo ab ea; sed vere fidei rectitudinem, totis conatibus meis, usque ad animum et sanguinem custodiam.'* And he made the same statement on the occasion of his first clash with Philip the Fair: 'We and our brothers, if God on high concede, are ready to suffer not only persecution, damage to our property and exile, but to undergo bodily death itself for the liberty of the church.' And this was the almost prophetic pronouncement that he made on the eve of the irrevocable day:

'And we boldly affirm, that if all the kings and princes on earth were today in league against us and the Church, provided that we were in possession of the truth and stood for the truth, we would not give a straw for them. And without a doubt, if we were not in possession of truth and justice, we should do well to be afraid; but otherwise we should confound them all, and the truth would confound them.'

The surprise of Anagni was the day he was brought to the test, for which he had long planned his course of action. It was also a day of vendetta. Around Guillaume de Nogaret and the standard of the King of France, there flocked the Colonna family and their followers, who had seen the destruction of Palestrina, and its ruins furrowed by the plough 'after the example of ancient Carthage in Africa'; and with them the Supinos, the Rubeos, the Ceccanos, the multitude of the petty lords of the Maremma and the Campagna, who had been expropriated by force, cunning or money. A single motivation, the personal and familiar one of petty hates and ambitions, linked the last act of the drama to the first. But the pope was by now outside the world of the shabby competitiveness of his fellow creatures, alone in the gigantic solitude of his conscience and his desperate resolution, the living symbol of the Roman pontificate that had for centuries been the lord and master of Europe. Guillaume de Nogaret had replied to the question he had asked the Colonna brothers that the absolutism of the papacy was dead. Boniface could have died quietly in Naples in the shadow of Charles of Anjou, through the piety of Celestine V; instead he chose to fall heroically in Anagni. He appeared before the invaders of his palace, arrayed in his papal robes, holding the cross to his breast and kissing it, and to

Nogaret's request that he renounce the tiara he replied: 'Here is my head, here is my neck. For the faith of my Lord Jesus Christ I wish to die.'

And in view of this end, we may, in a different spirit, adopt the words pronounced six centuries ago by Augustine Triumphus, in which he exalted Boniface VIII as, 'The confessor and martyr of Christ, taken by the tyrants of the Church, blasted with insult and injury, and at last dying for the defence of justice and the conservation of the liberty of the Church'.

CHAPTER 15

THE CRISIS OF THE MEDIEVAL WORLD

THE COUNCIL OF CONSTANCE

I

Amid the fervour of all the publicist polemics aroused by the conflict between Philip the Fair and Boniface VIII, one of the most interesting supporters of the French king was an imaginative and prolific lawyer from Coutances called Jean Dubois, who was the author of a treatise entitled *De recuperatione Terrae Sanctae*. The policy he put forward was, as the title indicates, the recovery of the Holy Land, but since this could only be accomplished by a Europe in which the Church was pure and the Christian republic at peace, Dubois also unfolded a large-scale plan for universal, if not immediate, reform, which was to pave the way for the conclusive effort.

To establish peace the European states were to reunite in a kind of society of nations, in which the restored Latin Empire of Constantinople was also to have its place. The president of the society would no longer be an elective emperor but a hereditary one, the King of France; and the crown of Byzantium would fall to the king's brother, Charles of Valois. To ensure the purity of the Church, it would be necessary to free her from the burden of temporal cares; so the Papal States were to be entrusted to the administration of the king, and through him to one of his sons or brothers, to be entitled 'Senator Romanus'. Ecclesiastical property would be liquidated by the state, and the proceeds devoted partly to the liberation of Palestine and partly to the support of the clergy. The elections of the cardinals would be organized in such a fashion as to ensure that the French would permanently remain in possession of the Holy See. With these reservations, the pope was still to remain the '*caput universalis Ecclesiae*', the successor of Peter and the vicar of Christ. A council convened by him was to proceed with the work of the great political and religious reform, after the completion of which he would be the highest court of appeal for the Papal States and the supreme organ of control over sentences pronounced by the tribunal for the conservation of peace.

Dubois was obviously a dreamer, who suffered from the illusion that he could lay down the most minutely detailed prescriptions for the regeneration of the world; but his dream interests us all the more for the very reason that, being free from the responsibilities and pressures of officialdom, he was able to give a truer picture of the passions and demands of his time. So at the centre of all the construction, there is a consciousness of a crisis in the Christian republic in its unitary constitution and in the principles of its government. With all due respect to the vicar of Christ, Dubois's main object of study, and of condemnation, is the temporal Church; according to him, the salvation of the Christian Republic lies in the house of France; and a kind of constituent assembly convened by the pope should sanction all arrangements and judgments in the interests of peace in the New Europe. In the *De recuperatione* the old political and religious faith is fused with an understanding of the present and a vague presentiment of the future.

Apart from his prophetic fantasies, Dubois's ideas about the relationship that should obtain between the French monarchy and the Holy See does in fact correspond to a certain extent with reality. The papal theocracy, after being crushed with Boniface VIII, had been obliged to take shelter in Avignon, under the protection of what was, for all its lack of the imperial title, the supreme power in Europe. For seventy years the Holy See was virtually in the hands of French popes, although some of them were officially English; a hundred and thirteen of the hundred and thirty-four cardinals elected in the same period were French, and French, too, were many of the officials appointed to the government of the Papal States. What Dubois did not foresee, on the other hand, and this was in any case all too far removed from the developments he and many of his contemporaries hoped for, was that the papacy was to receive no stimulus to renewal from the French influence, that the old ways would be followed to the bitter end, and the evils that were so universally lamented were to grow out of all proportion.

Only in the abstract was it possible to consider the restoration of a purely spiritual Church, which would be the arbiter of peace in Europe, and totally abdicate its own secular rights and its own principles. Instead, the papal supremacy was constantly and tenaciously reasserted against the empire, and wealth and energy were dissipated in the desperate effort to make a stand against Henry VII, Ludwig of Bavaria, and the Ghibellines in Italy, to snatch the Papal States away from the confusion and the usurpations rampant among the nobility and in the communes, and to save the vassal kingdom of Naples from disintegration in the toils of a dynastic crisis which was in effect the crisis of the entire Middle Ages.

To the grave dissatisfaction of the bishops and the ordinary collators, dispensations grew apace and the number of benefices reserved for the Holy See increased at a giddy rate. Over and above the dues paid by bishops and abbots on their appointment or confirmation in office by the pope, and the rise in the dues of chancery payable by the recipients of bulls, extraordinary tithes were levied on the income from ecclesiastical property, the yield from benefices that were being kept vacant were collected on behalf of the Curia, and, after their collation, the fruits of the first year. The *procurationes,* which originally consisted of the provision of entertainment for bishops on their pastoral visits, were converted into a tax payable to the Apostolic Chamber; with ever increasing avidity and ever wider pretensions, the Church laid its hands on the inheritances of its beneficiaries at their death; charitable donations, which were nonetheless obligatory, were collected on various pretexts: now the Holy Land, now the needs of the Church, now the struggle against heretics and rebels. An awe-inspiring system of collector's offices, its branches spread through all the provinces of the Catholic world, implacably collected the money of the faithful in every quarter and poured it in to the centre of administration in Avignon.

The fiscal avidity of the Church at this time must have suggested the image of a giant octopus stretching out its greedy tenacles to suck the blood of Christianity. The clergy suffered, being taxed exorbitantly and unremittingly, and hindered and degraded in their spiritual ministry itself. Peoples and princes suffered, seeing the wealth of their countries removed over the frontier for the use of others. And the religious life of the whole continent was affected, wearied and worn down as it was by the burden of wars and taxation, by the absences of the incumbents of benefices and their long holidays, by the dubious elections on the part of the Curia and the ever-diminishing surveillance exercised by the bishops on the clergy of their diocese. Although it was not infrequently that extraordinary tithes and annates were conceded for certain periods and territories to lay potentates, especially the King of France, the Holy See was the object of hatred and condemnation from every side.

By a fatal impetus the Church of Avignon, in its material and moral impoverishment, and its confrontation with the new Europe, was constrained to seek its salvation where its ruin lay. The more it enlarged and tightened the net of its temporal interests, the closer it clung to the earth to suck at its life-blood, the more it squandered its religious substance and lowered its prestige. Wealth was the indispensable condition that could ensure the Church's independence from France, by which the papacy could keep control of the Papal

States, conduct a vigorous policy against the empire and the Ghibellines in Italy, intervene with authority in the great European issues, wage war on the infidels, grant and accept favours, and gain the respect of the people. But wealth could only be acquired by contaminating the holiness of the papacy and by arousing widespread hostility.

We can, it is true, make distinctions between one pope and another, hold Clement V responsible for the most abject obedience to the French crown and the impoverishment of the treasury on account of his prodigal testamentary donations; we can attribute to John XXII the major impulse to the development of the fiscality of the papacy. But the line of development can be traced much further back than the former, and goes much further on than the latter, and the good natures and worthy intentions of a Benedict XII or an Urban V are not enough to arrest the evil, which rather grows daily greater. It was obviously not in the power of any one pope, however heroic the strength of purpose that moved him, to fight and win against an entire political and religious system, which had been evolving over the course of generations, and which respond to the undeniable exigencies of the society of the time.

Thus began the universal indictment brought against the Roman Curia by kings and their countries, members of the clergy and the university. Simultaneously and implicitly, it was also the rebellion against the authoritarian and unitary principles on which the medieval world was based, and the debate on the foundations and the limits of authority in the religious and civil fields.

This was not, of course, the first time that the greed and corruption of the Holy See had been bewailed. The literature of the twelfth and thirteenth centuries offers enough material on the subject for the most generous of anthologies, in which the severe condemnations of St Bernard of Clairvaux find a place beside the gay satire of the *Carmina Burana*. Evidently there is continuity here, but in the fourteenth century the general or episodic reproaches, sporadically or personally expressed, become something quite different. The unique importance of this period in history derives from the fact that the assault on the papacy now came from all quarters, from the representatives of the great political, religious and cultural forces of the time, and it went beyond the individual abuses to strike with revolutionary criticisms at the entire system of the *plenitudo potestatis*, the fiscal policy of the Curia, and finally the very institution of the Church and the papacy.

It would have been hard for a declared enemy to hurl bitterer reproaches or fiercer insults at the '*avara Babilonia*', than did Dante and Petrarch, St Bridget and St Catherine, all of them great souls who, though betrayed, were unshakable in their faith. The seeds of the revolt sprouted almost imperceptibly in full view of the Curia, in the midst of both regular and secular clergy, and especially among the bishops, who were subjected to the twofold oppression of papal centralization and royal sovereignty. In all their zeal for the independence and prerogatives of the Holy See, the papal theologians—such as Alvarus Pelagius, and Augustine Triumphus—did not hesitate to denounce the flood of corruption and to invoke a concerted effort on the part of the cardinals to bring the pope back to Rome and snatch him from his enslavement to France. When Clement V put ecclesiastic reform on the agenda of the Ecumenical Council of Vienne (1311-1312) and asked the bishops to express their views freely, he doubtless expected to put an end to a few abuses practised by the high and low clergy, but without this action in any way impairing the authority of the papacy or the constitution of the Church.

But there were bishops who took his invitation literally, and had no scruples in telling the whole truth. The Bishop of Angers, Guillaume Lemaire, did not limit himself in his statement to deploring the decadence of religious life in general as a result of the corruption of the clergy and the interference of the state. He indicated what he felt to be the primary cause of so much evil: the system of papal centralization with its exemptions, reservations, expectatives and its plurality of benefices, through which the ordinary collators were defrauded of their rights, the local clergy, however deserving, disappointed in their legitimate hopes, and thus alienated from the divine service and turned against the Church; benefices were distributed unjustly, the Divine Offices neglected by the better priests, who were living at the Curia or in the courts, or entrusted to incompetent strangers who had bought the expectatives from them.

Guillaume Durand, the Bishop of Mende, set out his proposals in a veritable treatise, the *De modo generalis Concilii celebrandi*, and with all his faith in the Roman primacy and the *plenitudo potestatis*, went much further than his colleague of Angers. The reform had to be completed immediately, both at the head of Christianity and in its limbs, but especially at the head, for otherwise 'both faithful and infidels would say that the prelates and ecclesiastical persons had lost their faith', matters would go from bad to worse and the blame would be thrown on the pope, the cardinals and the Council. For Durand, too, the greater part of the disorders are derived from the papal centralization and fiscal rapacity, which, in the case of the *servitia*, he refers to clearly and simply as simony: '*Proverbium vulgare est: qui totum vult, totum perdit. Ecclesia sibi vindicat universa, unde timendum est quod universam perdat.*' He laments the nepotism of the Curia, its unworthy acquiescence towards the secular potentates in the granting of tithes, the facility of gaining dispensations, the interminable suits for elections which leave the churches widowed, and the universal market of all things holy.

Rich and lively though it is in style, the treatise would still have little new to show us, were it not for the vigorous conscience of the bishop, his resentment at the humiliation and offence to which his own order had been subjected and his reaction against the omnipotence of the papacy. Primacy, yes; but it was important to define the scope of its authority in spiritual and temporal matters, and not to exercise it without due care, more particularly, without consulting the cardinals. The pope should not be given the title *Universalis Ecclesiae Pontifex*, and the bishops, who were the successors of the Apostles, should be once more given the honour due them and restored to their ancient position of privilege. The exercise of power should be governed by the *ratio* and the indefeasible norm of the canons; the canon law was simultaneously a commandment for whoever was in power, and a defence against his abuses for his *subditi*, who were warned, in Durand's lively and almost revolutionary expression, '*ne plus quam expediat sint subjecti*', not to be more subjected than was expedient. In virtue of the biblical adage: '*Ibi salus ubi consilia multa*', or rather, in virtue of the new significance being given to the wisdom of *Proverbs*, Durand saw the absolutism of the papacy being tempered by the counsel of the Holy College, by the provincial councils, and finally by the Ecumenical Council, which should be convened every ten years and to which all innovations in legal matters and all general provisions should be submitted for approval, '*cum illud quod omnes tangit ab omnibus approbari debeat*'.

These suggestions are, as we see, still far from the explicit affirmation of the supremacy of the council. Nevertheless, the pope had been put on the defensive, his *plenitudo potestatis*, though admitted in principle, is in fact hampered by a thousand reservations and restrictions, and, with a reference to the ideal of the primitive Church, the whole process of reversal is set in motion, whereby the ecclesiastical authority and power, instead of radiating from the centre or summit of the papacy, was to accrue to it from the communities of the faithful.

The precise formulation of a revolutionary doctrine, which was a reflection of the new consciousness of the time, was developed in the heat of the struggle between John XXII and Ludwig of Bavaria, by Marsilio of Padua, John of Jandun and William Ockham.

They had been preceded in this pursuit some ten years before by a Dominican, Jean Quidort, who, having become involved in the controversy between Boniface VIII and Philip the Fair, had written a treatise entitled *De potestate regia et papali*, in which he had, with rare independence of judgment, dissociated the spiritual from the temporal, declaring that the Council was the final authority on all questions of faith, and indeed superior to the pope himself; he had further traced the power of both kings and bishops directly back to God, through the elections of the people, had made a thorough examination of the problem of the deposition of popes and emperors, and finally recommended a form of Church government in which '*omnes haberent partem suam*', or in greater detail, '*sub uno papa eligerentur plures ab omni provincia et de omni provincia*'.

Now Marsilio, his mind unencumbered by the old doctrinal impedimenta, capable of a vision of the whole that was without prejudice and therefore subversive, vindicated in his *Defensor pacis* the sovereignty of the people and the universality of the state, and went on to exterminate, by reference to the Gospels, the ecclesiastical hierarchy and the primacy, canon law, and the temporal pretensions of the Church.

The same practical conclusions were reached in these same years by the Franciscan Ockham, although he had started from theoretical premises that were substantially different. Faithful though he was to the doctrine of the primacy, he was nonetheless convinced that the power granted to Peter by Christ was of an exclusively spiritual nature, that the clergy should content themselves with what was necessary to support life and for the exercise of their ministry, and that the question of whether there should be one pope or more was one to be settled according to which course would most benefit the community of the faithful.

The arguments published by the theologians and politicians in their treatises were diffused among the more receptive populace by those errant sons of St Francis, the Minor Friars. Heretical sects sprouted all over the Catholic world. And the English parliament in spite of the reluctance of the king, who had his share of the ecclesiastical booty, promulgated legislation that was directly opposed to the fiscal and jurisdictional pretensions of Avignon with the *Stature of Provisors* in 1351, and the *Statute of Praemunire* in 1353.

In 1378 the Great Western Schism broke out, and for the next forty years and more it was to occupy the entire political and religious forces of Europe. From that time to this, the circumstances have been thoroughly weighed and investigated to establish where right and wrong lay, in Rome or Avignon; and there has been no lack of enthusiasts, even in quite recent years, to reopen the debate to lend energetic support to Clement VII against Urban VI, and to exalt or condemn the doctrine and practice of the Council.

These factual circumstances are certainly of interest to us, too, even though, or rather, all the more because, we have no desire to take sides with either one of the contenders. Leaving motives of a spiritual nature aside, we find that the first attempt of Urban V, and the second of Gregory XI to move the Holy See back to Rome both coincided with a decline in the French hegemony and were accompanied by a correlative, more resolute effort at restoration in the States of the Church. They were signs, then, of either a need or a desire to regain the dignity and the liberty of action afforded by residence in Rome, but without the conditions necessary for the exercise of that liberty being assured either externally or internally. The College of Cardinals was divided, and this division was shown up in all its asperity when, at a papal election, it became necessary to opt for France or Italy, for Rome or Avignon. Of Gregory XI's twenty-three cardinals, six had stayed in Avignon, one was away in Tuscany acting as legate, and of the remaining sixteen who went into conclave at his death, one was Spanish, four Italian, and eleven French. The French, then, would have been in a position to impose their will, had it not been for the fact that the six cardinals from Limousin found their compatriots more disposed to make common cause with the Italians than to allow the election of yet another Limousinian after Clement VI and his nephew Gregory XI. Without a doubt, various kinds of pressure and intimidation had been brought to bear, and the authoritarian and brutal conduct of the newly-elected pope, Bartholemew Prignani, Archbishop of Bari, certainly helped to provoke the secession of the ultramontane cardinals, who, having retired first to Anagni and then to Fondi, raised the cardinal Robert of Geneva to the papal throne as Clement VII.

Nevertheless, the representations of the Banderesi, the cries of the crowd: 'We want a Roman pope, a Roman, or at least Italian', and the imprudence of a single pope, can scarcely be considered sufficient cause for the abyss which continued to divide the Catholic world for more than forty years, and in whose depths, we might even say, the whole of the medieval world was lost. The idea often occurs to students of this period that if only everyone in that ill-starred year had proceeded with a little more prudence and moderation, Europe would have been spared a long period of confusion, and the Church need not have undergone the humiliation to papal dignity or even, perhaps the lasting damage of the protestant reformation. But if we only turn our minds first to the Church, which was being attacked on every side, by laymen and clergy, heretics and theorists, peoples and princes, or else supported by the latter on the condition that their demands be granted, and if we look secondly at the extreme difficulty of healing the wound, we shall easily be convinced that the Schism was not an evil which could have been avoided with a little good will on all sides, but that it was in itself the climax of a tremendous crisis that was by this time unavoidable. The papacy was torn apart and divided physically because this had already happened in reality, and because the Church did not have sufficient prestige, or the people of the time the consciousness, to take prompt action to reconstitute the religious unity that was lost.

While the question of papal legitimacy was providing endless material for discussion in the universities of Oxford and Paris, Prague and Bologna, and St Catherine and St Vincent Ferreri were kneeling with equal purity and devotion to Urban VI and Clement VII respectively, the states of Europe were grouping themselves according to political conveniences and rivalries around either the pope or the antipope. Those who declared for Avignon were first, of course, France, then Scotland, her ally against England, and the French lineage of the Kingdom of Naples. For Rome were England and Flanders, her ally against France, and then Hungary, on account of its age-old designs on the crown of Naples, the Emperor Charles IV and his son, Wenceslas on the basis of Urban VI's recognition of the latter as King of the Romans. The Spanish remained neutral for some time and finally sided with Clement VII.

The enormous problems of the empire, Naples, the Anglo-French hostility, and the dynastic crisis which struck all the major powers, indicating a deep-seated malaise in European society, gave the Schism a solid foundation from the beginning, and such rich nourishment, that it was impossible to turn back. The war between France and England came to a standstill from mutual exhaustion, and because the monarchy in both countries was in a state of collapse. First the minority, and then the madness of Charles VI of Valois, gave rise to rivalry between his relations, his uncles Philip, Duke of Burgundy, Louis of Anjou, and Louis Bourbon, and his brother Louis Duke of Orleans, all of them wanting to gain control of the regency and thus satisfy their own personal ambitions. Both within the kingdom and in foreign affairs—in relation to the Holy See, England, the Spanish kingdoms, Italy and the Empire—each one of them followed his own policy and the country went to rack and ruin. With Clement VII in their favour, the Angevin ambitions turned naturally to Naples, and those of Orleans, with Louis's marriage to Valentina Visconti and his acquisition of Asti, to Genoa and Northern Italy. But the costly efforts of Louis I and Louis II of Anjou were without fruit; and Louis of Orleans died without realizing his hopes at the hands of the assassins sent by his cousin, Jean Sans Peur, Duke of Burgundy, the son of Philip the Bold. With this provocation, the furious civil war between Armagnac and Burgundy broke out, which was to soak the country in blood, and annihilate the power of the royal house.

The English monarchy was in similar straits, with Richard II's succession to the throne at the age of twelve, the rivalry of his uncles, and his enforced abdication and subsequent assassination on the orders of Henry Bolingbroke, who was then occupied for years, as king, in dealing with opposition and revolts all over the country. The Anglo-French antagonism was still alive; it lasted on in spite of the more or less peaceful alternatives, and was expressed both directly in exchanges between the two countries, and indirectly in their reciprocal meddling in the dynastic affairs of Spain and the empire. But the clash had lost much of its clarity, vigour and effectiveness, on account of disintegration of the unifying power of the monarchies, and the substitution, on both sides of the frontiers, of personal and family interests, for the great political directives of former times.

The Kingdom of Naples was, on account of its feudal subordination to the Holy See, the great field of papal politics, and on account of its geographical position and dynastic history, the meeting-point of the Franco-Angevin ambitions on the one hand and the Hungarian on the other. The absence of direct heirs, in spite of the four marriages of Queen Joanna, gave rise to competition for the succession, which was eventually secured for the Durazzo branch of the Angevins, under the aegis of Lewis the Great of Hungary, in Charles III and his heirs, Ladislas and Joanna II. Central and Northern Europe were no less disturbed, but more productive of new and lively developments than the other regions. The event of greatest prominence and the most general in character was the checking of the German expansion and its gradual retreat before the younger powers, who had now become conscious of their own identity and were reacting against the interference and competition from beyond their frontiers. The Hanseatic League was now challenged by the union of Baltic states formed at Kalmar; and the Teutonic Order's penetration of the Slavs by the official conversion of Lithuania and by the Duke of Lithuania's assumption of the Polish crown after his marriage to Edwige, the daughter of Lewis the Great, who had united Poland and Hungary under his rule.

The German character of the old empire was being gradually obscured, its constitution no longer responded to the needs of the day, and its strength ebbed away. With Charles IV of Luxemburg, it had been centred in Bohemia, and had reached a high peak of national splendour under his rule. At his death the imperial crown was overtaken by the common fate of almost every crown in Europe at that time: Charles' son and successor, Wenceslas, King of Bohemia, was overcome, in his vacillation and indolence, by the anti-Catholic and anti-German movement of the Hussites; he also betrayed the interests of the empire in Italy, by first selling his title of duke to Gian Galeazzo Visconti, and then indulging the ambitions of his son-in-law, Louis of Orleans. He was deposed by the princes and substituted, equally infelicitously, by Robert of the Palatinate; upon whose death in 1410, the crown was contended after a double election by no less than three princes, Wenceslas, Jost, Duke of Moravia, and Sigismund, another son of Charles IV, who had become King of Hungary by his marriage to Maria, the second daughter of Louis the Great. Sigismund was shortly to succeed in putting an end to the imperial schism, and was also, as we shall see, to take a leading part in the Council of Constance.

But his strength was derived not so much from the empire in itself, as from the crown of Hungary, which lead him in the wake of his father-in-law to fight against Venice and Ladislas of Naples. This was by no means the last sign of the powerful reaction, or even counter-attack, of the north-eastern peoples on the old Europe, which is one of the fundamental characteristics of this period.

Under the conditions that we have briefly sketched above, the religious schism grew more bitter and deeper every day. The relations between Rome and Avignon on the one side, and between the governments of Europe on the other, which had originally been relatively easy to grasp, acquired a giddy volubility as time went by. There seemed to be no fixed point left in the public life of Europe. There was no prince who could not find a pope willing to approve his intentions, and no pope who could not count on the support of one or more potentates to uphold his legitimacy. The arms of excommunication, interdicts, and crusades, brandished by the rival popes, were used by each half of the Catholic world against the other. The problem of the collation of benefices, which was already so serious in the past, was complicated to infinity now that the Church was making a dual assault on the pockets of Europe, and one that was all the more persistent because of the need of securing authority and financial resources by the occupation of bishoprics and abbeys. In contended territory and in border districts double provisions became practically an accepted norm, and the alternation of obediences in these districts naturally brought with it a change in the persons of the ecclesiastical government.

It is not difficult to imagine the consequences of such a state of affairs. The whole of Catholicism was disturbed by the doubt as to who was the legitimate successor to Peter and whether the sacraments administered in his name were valid. The authority of the papacy were subverted by its own indifference to the over-riding interests of the Church, and its unavoidable resort to violence, cunning, and all the compromises of petty personal and temporal politics. The uncertainty and inconstancy of both public and private relations had repercussions on the society, the economy and the states of Europe. In both practical and spiritual life, Europe fell prey to a unique and immense crisis, of which schism was only an element, but an element of such a nature that it engendered a universal malaise, inspired a sense of hopelessness and disaster in the people, and excited a revolutionary thirst for salvation and liberation in the more alert and enterprising spirits of the day.

The road to salvation, which meant both the end of the schism and the purification of the Church, was sought from many and various points of departure, by reformers, princes, cardinals, and universities.

The movement that started in Oxford and Prague, and which we commonly refer to by the names of John Wycliff and John Huss, in reality went much further than mere reform, and in its immediate application implied the complete destruction of the Roman Church.

The early actions of Wycliff were a part of the national and anti-Roman opposition of the *Statute of Provisors* and the *Statute of Praemunire,* in as much as he made himself the champion of the crown against the papal collectors and their exaction of the annual tribute, which had been promised to the Holy See by King John, suspended for thirty-three years, and finally demanded by Urban V. But the outbreak of the schism and the piteous spectacle afforded by the popes put his words and his actions in a thoroughly radical and subversive context. He took refuge from the corrupt Church that surrounded him in visions of a Church of the predestined—known to God alone—who were triumphant in Heaven, dormant in purgatory and militant on earth. Against the ecclesiastic hierarchy he set the universal priesthood of the faithful; against the roman discipline and teaching, the Holy Scriptures; against the primacy of the pope, whom he deemed the antichrist, the Redeemer, sole head of the Church; and he called to the people to share his faith in the Gospels, and his assault on the time-honoured structure that was Rome.

In Prague the campaign undertaken by Charles IV against the corruption of the clergy gave rise to the affirmation of national sentiment against the predominant German element in the country. Hate of the clergy and hate of the Germans united to build and to cement the Bohemian consciousness. Huss took up the inheritance of Conrad of Waldhausen, Milicz of Kremsier, Matthew of Janow, and Thomas Stitny, all preachers of reform and evangelic purity. He stretched out his hand to Wycliff, and preached to his people, in their own language, in spite of the papal bans and excommunications, that 'we must obey God rather than men in matters which affect our salvation'. Then when Wenceslas was persuaded by political convenience to banish him from Prague, he set himself with indefatigable enthusiasm to the diffusion of his message by the written word; and he too opposed the Church of the Elect to the Church of Rome, the Holy Scriptures to Catholic tradition, and taught that 'true Christians must resist presumed power which tries to remove them from the imitation of Christ by force or by deceit', and that the faithful had been granted the grace, 'even when there is temporarily no Roman pope in existence, of being able to reach their home in Heaven under the guidance of Christ the Lord'.

Wycliff and Huss had thought to cut the Gordian knot by wiping out ten centuries of history, at least as far as the Church was concerned. But Europe was not prepared to follow them along this road.

There is probably no modern historian, who has not, when confronted by the very length of the Great Schism, given way to recriminations against the princes, cardinals, popes and scholars, and in his mind's eye substituted for the actual damage done in those forty years of chaos the advantages that would have accrued to European society if everyone had been able to sacrifice their own interests and resentments to the common good of the restoration of Catholic unity. There is no doubt that, as usually happens, and especially with the most serious issues, there were many thoroughly dishonourable interests at work, and that the parliamentarianism, of the universities in particular, found in the schism such a magnificently inexhaustible subject for dialectical exercises, that they were slow in making any statement of a definite principle, or putting forward one or more resolute and capable men who could put an end to the scandal.

However, we need not look with too much severity on this contest of words, which is partly the self-assertion of the new individual and national energies against authority and tradition, the confused and clamorous beginning of modern Europe. And the long hesitations and persistent resistance deserve to be considered not as objects of condemnation but as signs of the times, as indications of the Europe that has lost its unitary faith of the Middle Ages, and can no longer find in it the strength necessary to recompose itself as a Christian republic. Instead, torn within itself, firmly rooted in the past and yet pulling away towards the future, it tries painfully, desperately, to heal the wound under a single pope and with a programme of reform, giving vent to the most ferocious invectives against the Church, and at the same time trying to restore the papal authority.

The schism was nothing really new in the Catholic world. What constituted its novelty, and threatened to draw it out indefinitely, was the disordered vitality of the lay potentates and of the general culture in contrast to the moral impoverishment and the profound prostration of the Holy See. Since the reciprocal excommunications of the two popes, even when backed up by political pressure, were to no purpose, the task of restoring unity slipped from the hands of the opposing parties and became the concern of the universities, the princes and their subjects; and since, in spite of all efforts, the problem of papal legitimacy remained unsolved, it finally became necessary to leave it on one side and to have recourse to more practical and effective measures. All possible expedients were from time to time proposed or attempted. A personal agreement between the popes was considered, recourse to arbitration, the resignation of the two rivals and a new election, the reunion of the two obediences at the death of the first pope, who would have no successor. But the obstacles were too great: on the one hand the good faith of the pope who considered that renunciation would be an unworthy defection, and on the other the ill will of the pope who by surrendering his rights would be betraying his own interests and those of his supporters. The trouble was that a weak body and an enfeebled and enslaved mind were being asked to supply heroic energy and sanity of judgment; and could make no response to all the appeals.

As the proceedings became more and more revolutionary, and hostility mounted towards the popes and the Holy College, who were held personally responsible for the situation, newly elected popes were asked to promise to abdicate if this could contribute to a religious settlement, there was a withdrawal of obedience from each of the popes and a proclamation of neutrality, and there was even recourse to force. But the results were always the same. Nobody could in conscience force a pope, who considered himself legitimate, to abdicate, especially as, even if the abdication were secured, it would be no more a guarantee of peace than of a disturbance of the existing equilibrium which would provoke even more universal chaos. The withdrawal of obedience, which consisted in the establishment of a French Church in 1398, apart from the disturbance it caused to the inevitably Catholic consciences of its members, showed itself in practice to be much more oppressive than even the extortionate rule of the papacy. It was revoked in 1403. The French were equally unsuccessful in their attempt to use force against the inflexibly obstinate Benedict XIII, who, for his part, could recall the very different treatment the monarchy had given Clement VII, whose legitimate successor he was, in the first years of the schism.

The only way out of the impasse was to appeal to the Church, which meant convoking an Ecumenical Council, which could then make provisions for the unification and pacification of Europe. This proposal had been advanced from the beginning by Conrad of Gelnhausen and Henry of Langenstein, and it was supported increasingly by the masters of Paris University, especially by Pierre d'Ailly and his pupil Jean Gerson, as the hopes of a settlement receded.

The trouble was that it was considerably easier to propose the remedy than to put it into practice. The practical difficulties were, in fact, enormous. According to tradition, the General Council could only be convoked by the pope, and might otherwise be declared null and void; and the pope himself could only be subjected to the judgment of the Church if he were guilty of heresy. Now the two popes could obviously not be relied upon to convoke the Council; then, even if this irregularity were overcome, there was no foundation on which to base an accusation of heresy; and lastly it was by no means an undisputed fact that the conviction of heresy could be grounds for deposition. So the Council could only be used against the papacy on two conditions: that it was established as being superior to the papacy, and that it could make the continuance of the schism on the part of the two rivals count as heresy—a rather dubious supposition. This is the point at which we are struck by the profoundly and inevitably revolutionary character of this period, and by the turmoil of the Catholic conscience, which is forced to deny tradition in order to restore it, and uses all its ingenuity to demonstrate the orthodoxy of the new doctrines, for fear that, if taken to their logical conclusions, they might turn into full-scale heresies.

In the desperate situation of the time, the summons to the Council was felt to be a necessity by the most enlightened representatives of Catholic thought. In 1415 Jean Gerson was to propose that the superiority of the Council be made an article of faith, to be carved on the stones of each and every church; a few years later, Nicholas of Cusa was to speak of the '*eminentissima potestas*' of the General Councils, as being a doctrine that had been long forgotten '*non sine maximo publicae utilitatis et fidei orthodoxae dispendio*', and then almost suddenly, by some divine influence, born and defined '*ex conquassatione ingeniorum*', after the disagreement between the pope and the Council. But there is no doubt that the doctrine concerning the Council referred back to the two turbulent rebellions against Boniface VIII and John XXII as their immediate precedents, and that it had affinities with the principles of the sovereignty of the people, contractualism, and political convenience, put forward by Marsilio of Padua and William Ockham, who went further than simply referring to the Gospels and the customs of the primitive Church to justify a Council not presided over by the pope, in that he threatened to undermine the Church itself, by removing one of its primary foundations—tradition.

There was another less remote misfortune liable to result from this solution to the problem, namely that the schism could in fact continue in spite of the formal deposition of the two pretenders and the election of a new pope. And this is what occurred in fact. At one point it had appeared that Benedict XIII of Avignon and Gregory XII of Rome were disposed to work seriously for peace, and to this end a personal meeting was arranged for them at Savona. But their mutual diffidence had brought the whole plan to nothing; the one had managed to reach Portovenere, the other Lucca, both of them plagued by a thousand doubts and unable to steel themselves to take the final step.

Amid the general scandal caused by the behaviour of the two popes, the two Colleges of Cardinals denied their respective obediences and convoked the Council of Pisa. It was inaugurated on March 28, 1409, and on June 9th of the following year it proclaimed the deposition of Gregory and Benedict on grounds of heresy and unworthiness of the tiara. On June 26th the cardinals went into conclave and elected the seventy-year-old Peter Philarges, a native of Candia, and Cardinal and Archbishop of Milan, to occupy the throne that they had declared vacant.

But, contrary to the hopes entertained by so many people, the results were disastrous. While France, England, Portugal, and part of Germany and Italy, all recognized the newly-elected Alexander V, Aragon, Castille, Scotland, and the counts of Armagnac and Foix remained faithful to Benedict, and Gregory was still supported by Poland, part of Germany, Naples, and the Papal States in the power of Ladislas of Durazzo. The first attempt at religious restoration had only succeeded in aggravating the schism by adding a third obedience to the two in existence and causing an even more profound disturbance in men's minds.

II

The failure of the Council of Pisa was perhaps less surprising than it seems to us when we consider only the universal confusion and the need for unity and peace. There was too much room for queries regarding the legitimacy of a Council convoked not by a pope but by cardinals who were deserters from their respective obediences and therefore of uncertain legitimacy themselves. Its pretensions to universality were on extremely shaky ground, as it had not been attended by or received representatives from the whole of the Catholic world, and, at the period of the greatest fervour, it had attracted no more than five hundred persons. Lastly, the lack of faith and indeed the hostility towards a project so tainted by the influence of France and the ill-famed Colleges of Cardinals was presumably fairly widespread, and this opposition was neither overcome nor organized into a general agreement either before or during the Council's proceedings.

And yet the experience of Pisa was not without its uses. The most serious danger had been that the schism would become indefinitely prolonged, that the evil would, as it were, acquire all the attributes of normality. But this point was now passed. The addition of the third obedience to the existing two gave wider scope for the juggling of political combinations, and the very aggravation of the scandal brought the end in sight. At the death of Alexander V on May 3, 1410, the Neapolitan cardinal Baldassare Cossa was elected to succeed him, under the name of John XXIII. He was the man least likely, from the moral point-of-view, to gain the respect of the faithful for himself and the papacy. One of his contemporaries wrote that 'he was more interested in shields and helmets than in palls and mitres', 'that he was brilliant in temporal matters, but absolutely inept in the spiritual', that it was common knowledge in Bologna that 'in the first year of his pontificate he had seduced two hundred married women there, widows, virgins, and also a large number of nuns'. Then when things finally swung against him it became known that he had committed every crime in the book: homicide, incest, simony, heresy, and practically anything else you care to name.

Certainly, he was a man more suited to the management of arms than to ministry in the Church; his term as pope was spent in a continual battle of wits, his sole concern, when finally brought to bay, being to save his life and possessions; and his fall from power was ignominious. A character of great dignity would no doubt have enhanced his reputation and been in the interests of Catholicism. But, however valid the accusations against him, his crimes were not alone responsible for his punishment, any more than the universal chaos can be explained by his immorality. He was, indeed, a living symbol of the Europe of the day, in moral corruption and ambition of government, in the lapse from the Roman tradition and servitude to the turbulent demands of the times. Drawn into the centre of a gigantic struggle for which he had no responsibility, and which completely dwarfed him and every action he might take, to a position which he could not refuse without making a heroic sacrifice, he was to use the common weapons of deceit and violence, until, faced by betrayal on all sides, he was subjected to the enormous indignity of the Council of Constance, and fell victim not so much to the fruits of his own transgressions as to the disruption of the medieval world.

The two men who are his opponents, Benedict XIII and Gregory XII, are of quite a different moral fibre, though their fate is not dissimilar. Benedict is a warrior spirit, inflexible to the end in his certainty of his rights, and holding out against both financial pressure, and the trials and depositions of the Councils. Gregory too, stands firm in his faith in his own legitimacy and hesitates to renounce the tiara, but he is animated by a lively and sincere desire to reunite the Catholic world, and supported in his work by Carlo Malatesta, Lord of Rimini, who was perhaps the noblest figure of the whole period of the Great Schism.

As though by fate, the skirmishing now started up around John XXIII, the most recently elected pope, and also the possessor of the largest obedience and the greatest political and military enterprise. The immediate object of contention was the Kingdom of Naples, which at that point, and others in the Middle Ages up to the invasion of Charles VIII, constituted the centre of the European disturbances, a sort of cyclonic area to which all surrounding forces were attracted. After the amputation of Sicily at the close of the thirteenth century, the kingdom had been steadily losing, with the decline of the empire in the course of the fourteenth century, its universal office of protecting the Church and the Guelphs; but it had not succeeded in compensating for this loss by becoming its true self, as it were, by breaking away from the Middle Ages, breaking the bonds of its vassallage to the Holy See, and founding a stable monarchy, which would turn its feudal constitution into a modern one. The protagonists in the struggle for Naples were, apart from John XXIII and Ladislas of Durazzo, the pretender Louis II of Anjou, and most important of all, Sigismund, King of the Romans, who by his actions in this field dealt the death-blow to the schism.

It is not without some astonishment that we see at the close of the Middle Ages the empire once more take upon itself, quite suddenly, the religious and civil responsibilities for the whole of Europe; as if, after a Rudolf of Hapsburg and an Adolf of Nassau, a Henry VII of Luxemburg and a Charles IV, it were still possible to have a Charlemagne or an Otto, who had in their own times, though under rather different conditions, castigated the bad popes, purified the Church, and set the Catholic world in order. Only the imperial tradition, alive and active as it was in this troubled time in European history, was no more than a part, and perhaps not the most important part, of Sigismund's activities. He was, as we mentioned above, the son of Charles IV and the half-brother of King Wenceslas of Bohemia, he was the son-in-law of Lewis the Great and his successor on the throne of Hungary. His election as King of the Romans put an end to the imperial schism to the disadvantage of Wenceslas. By his personal qualities, his inheritance, his relations with Bohemia and Poland on one side and Germany and Italy on the other, Sigismund reconciled and embodied all the vigour of the new Europe of the east and all the strength that remained in the old idea of the empire.

His way to power had been a tough one; now conquered, now conquering, he was unafraid of personal sacrifice and unhesitating before violence and crime. A champion of Catholicism, he had undertaken the first great action against the threat of the Turks, and been defeated at Nicopolis. Although the anti-Germanic and anti-Catholic movement of the Hussites did not constitute an immediate threat to him, it did impinge closely on his political interests, especially in Bohemia and Germany. He was drawn to Italy, the hot-bed of the schism, by four things: his need for an established pope who would restore peace to his domains and give him the crown of Rome; the conflict he had inherited with Venice for the possession of Dalmatia, Friuli, and the Adriatic; his plan to vindicate the rights of the empire in Lombardy, which Wenceslas had alienated in favour of Gian Galeazzo Visconti; and finally, the military triumph of Ladislas of Durazzo, who a few years before had had himself crowned King of Hungary, and against whom he could inversely, stake a good claim to the inheritance of Naples.

In the various stages of the struggle between the king and the pope, Ladislas had forsaken the obedience of the Roman pope for that of John XXIII, and he was about to embrace the cause of Benedict XIII when he was surprised by death in 1414. Pope John, in his turn, had been awaiting the intervention of Louis II of Anjou whose claim to the throne of Naples he supported; but when these plans ended in failure he was obliged to make peace with Ladislas; and then, when the latter robbed him of Rome and the Papal States, he was forced to throw himself into the arms of Sigismund.

The strongest of the European potentates thus came into contact with the most authoritative, but at the same time the weakest, of the popes. The empire vindicated its Catholic mission by extorting the convocation of the Council of Constance from the pope who needed his help so much.

There is a tale told of Gabrino Fondulo of Cremona, that not long after he had acquired control of the city by the extinction of the entire Cavalcabò family, he was tempted to earn immortal glory by flinging his illustrious guests, Sigismund and John XXIII, down from the campanile of the cathedral, where he had taken them to admire the beautiful view of the Po valley. He is said to have grieved for the rest of his life at having missed so splendid an opportunity. It is not easy to say what the consequences of so sprightly a venture as this might have been for the Council, and for the future of the west in general. Certainly the pope would have been spared the infamy of his fall; but this would hardly have quieted the profound turmoil of European society.

After so many years of division and disorder, Europe needed to rediscover her own identity, and recompose her religious and civil life. None of the preceding Councils could compete in nature or in procedure with the modern and revolutionary Council of Constance, and indeed of Europe; for it united, by the convocation of a pope and a king of the Romans, all the great powers of the Catholic world—patriarchs, cardinals, archbishops, bishops, abbots, lay potentates great and small, the representatives of sovereigns, delegates of the universities—and it constituted the first and perhaps the greatest parliamentary experiment that the whole western world had ever attempted. Although the occasion for the Council was provided by the division of the Church and the need for reform, there was no political question of importance that was not discussed before the assembly or that did not provoke some reaction from it—the internal troubles in France and the Anglo-French conflict, the disturbances in Bobemia and the threat of Turkey, the rights of Joanna II of Naples in Hungary and Poland's antagonism for the Teutonic Knights. The very taking of sides on problems that were essentially religious, such as unity, heresy and reform, revealed not so much an interest in religion, as opposing political and cultural tendencies. Speaking in even more general terms, it can indeed be said that the Council, which was summoned to restore the Church, expressed as a whole a sense of rebellion that was diffused throughout states, universities, the national clergy, the primacy, and the papacy and the Sacred College in Rome.

The new constitution of Europe was in a way reflected in the organization of the Council on a national basis, on a principle which we might consider to be derived from the practice of the universities; it was in point of fact not based on political or religious differences, but, while the whole was in the final analysis ordered under the principal sovereigns, the great formations and historic affinities of Europe were delineated, and the representatives of clergy and laity classified under them. There was the Italian nation, the French, which included, as well as the kingdom, Savoy, Provence, Dauphiné, and Lorraine, the English, including Ireland, and the German, which comprehended not only the German territory of the empire, but also Hungary, Dalmatia, Croatia, Dacia, Bohemia, Poland, Sweden and Norway. Later the Spanish realm, composed of the states of the Iberic peninsula, was to be included. The questions to be brought before the plenary session of the Council were first discussed in specially elected commissions and in smaller gatherings of the separate nations.

The first blow to the pope, the cardinals, and also to the Italian nation, was the Council's recognition of the right of not only bishops and abbots to vote in the deliberations, as John XXIII and his supporters would have wished, but also doctors of theology and law, kings, princes and their ambassadors. Had this been all, there would still have been some hope for the pope, on account of the conspicuous following of loyal prelates with which he had crowded the assembly.

However, even this weapon was taken from him, by the Council's adoption of the vote by nations, which, it was all too easy to foresee, would assure him at most the votes of the Italians against the English, French and Germans. In this field, the Sacred College, which was the object of accusations and misgivings from all sides, was subjected to the gravest humiliation. Their request for a separate collegial vote having been rejected, the cardinals were forced to vote with their own nations. What was more, it was even proposed later on that they should be excluded from the deliberations of the Council, and the pope with them, on account of their being interested parties in the question of Church reform; and finally it was suggested that they should not participate either in the new papal election.

Certainly the system of voting adopted cannot be said to have assured the harmonious progress of the work. Apart from the revolutionary element in the procedure, it sanctioned an inequality, which, in critical moments or under the stress of political rivalries, was to give rise to the most violent discussions, and put the very existence of the Council in peril. The nations who suffered most were the Italian and the French, on account of the great numbers and authority of their delegates, their populations and the number of their ecclesiastical provinces. The English had the best of the bargain, as they counted as a quarter, and later as a fifth of the Catholic world, in spite of the small number and inferior status of their representatives. This was the cause of the clashes in questions of precedence. France's attempt to deprive the English of the vote when she found them allied with Sigismund against her, and the lengthy negotiations for the concession of voting power to the Spanish. Remembering the thousand reasons for discord, the monstrous task before them, the predominance of the university spirit and parliamentary enthusiasm, it is easy to imagine the excesses, the alternatives and the bewilderment of this assembly that was called to give peace to Europe. Let us leave on one side the personal acts of violence in mid-Council, the whistles, the '*pedum strepitus et clamor*', which often blotted out the voices of the orators. For three years there was an orgy of eloquence and doctrine, a triumph of theological and legal subtlety over the Catholic faith, proclamation of the boldest theories, an insidious sport and at once a spectacular effort to restore tradition through revolution, and at the same time, to hamstring revolution in order to save orthodoxy.

No sooner had the work started, than the easy prediction made by John XXIII as he approached Constance came true: the Council that he had convoked started to treat him as a culprit. For the pope of Pisa and his supporters, it had seemed obvious that the conclusions of the Council of Pisa would be ratified at Constance, and that the Council would then proceed, under his presidency, to the reunion of the three obediences, and also, eventually, to Church reform. But instead Guillaume Fillastre, Cardinal of San Marco, made a proposal, and one that met with widespread approval, that the abdication of the three rival popes was an absolute necessity for the re-establishment of peace. And to overcome the pope's understandable resistance to this proposal, an anonymous denunciation was presented to the nations, and an enquiry begun into the many serious crimes of which he was accused.

When John XXIII complained to one of his cardinals, Pierre d'Ailly, that he had supported the Council's right to depose the sovereign pope, he replied that the thesis of conciliar superiority went back to the decisions made in Pisa, on which his very legitimacy depended; what had been done in Pisa could be done again in Constance—the pope could be deposed. Whichever way he turned, John was met either with a legalistic quibble which made papal legitimacy the laughing stock of the whole assembly, or with a new principle of faith which made the Council the foundation of the Church. His dilemma was an indication of the extreme difficulty of arresting the constitutional crisis provoked by the dissolution of the medieval world, and of Europe's weary struggle to bend the principles of tradition and reason to deal with the exigencies of the time.

The pope could only resign himself to fate; but when he saw that the Council wanted an unconditional renunciation made through procurators, and began to feel that he was the prisoner of Sigismund, who was kept informed of his every action and had placed a close watch on the gates of the city, he made an agreement with Frederick, Duke of Austria, and on the evening of March 20, 1415, left Constance disguised as a groom with a cross-bow on his saddle, and made for Schaffhausen.

The news of his escape provoked an enormous panic. What would happen to the Council, abandoned and doubtless soon to be disavowed by the pope? Once again, the universal bewilderment, the profound contradiction within the conscience of the age, which was at once faithful and antagonistic towards the past, the absurdity of the compromise between old and new, and the instability of the balance between Papacy and Council, all reappeared in the clear light of day. But Sigismund's energetic activity stopped the assembly dispersing. And the very action the pope had taken, the Council's desperate desire to end the uncertainty, to find a solid base for reconstruction, had the result of eliciting a much quicker and more uncompromising affirmation of the superiority of the Council, which only a few months before, when Wycliff's books were condemned, had been denied.

A decree of a definitely revolutionary character, sanctioned on April 6, 1415, established, in fact, that 'the Council of Constance, legitimately met in the Holy Spirit, forming an Ecumenical Council and representing the Church Militant, derived its power immediately from God, and all, including the pope, were obliged to obey it in matters regarding the faith and the extinction of the schism'; it further threatened temporal and spiritual punishment to anyone, not excluding the pope himself, who should obstinately refuse to conform to the decrees, statutes and ordinances of the holy Council and of every other General Council canonically convened.

Having thus legitimized its own omnipotence, the Council proceeded to clear the field of the three competitors. While John XXIII fled from Schaffhausen to Laufenburg, to Freiburg-im-Breisgau, to Breisach, and finally to Radolfzell, he was being declared an absconder, suspended, then prosecuted for the most vile crimes, deposed, and imprisoned, all without the slightest movement of protest or resistance on his part. Shattered in mind and body, he submitted to the decisions of the Council, asking only that his honour and his person be respected. By the beginning of July, the abdication of Gregory XII and the unification of the two benefices was also an accomplished fact. Benedict XIII would not bend, and was tried and deposed on July 26, 1417, after the countries in his obedience, Aragon, Castille and Navarre, had sent their delegates to Constance as a result of the Treaty of Narbonne, stipulated by the mediation of Sigismund. The unification had formally been achieved; it remained only to proceed to a new papal election and to reform.

During the delays in the negotiations and the proceedings against the popes, another serious problem had been tackled, a problem that was apparently of quite another kind, but in essence very close to the first one, because it too had its roots in the crisis of the principle of authority; it was the heresy of Wycliff and Huss. The struggle against the Hussite heresy is the most significant testimony of the almost superhuman effort of the Council to take revolutionary action without allowing itself to be subverted by revolution.

Before leaving for Constance, Huss had taken leave of his friends, asking them to pray to God for him that he should have the strength of spirit necessary, 'so that, if death were inevitable, he could support it with fortitude, and if it were granted him to return, he should be able to do so with his honour intact and without betraying the truth'. Perhaps it was a presentiment of his end, and certainly a recognition of the hard battle he had to fight before the Council. There is no need now to tell the tale of his trial before the Fathers and the Emperor Sigismund, who condemned him to death at the stake. He was submitted to the horrors of imprisonment and the clamour of the assembly in full cry against him, but at least he had his wish in being given a public hearing more than once, and before he was condemned, all possible ways to persuade him to recant were tried with persistence. If, in spite of the Council's efforts and Huss' almost ingenuous and ever-recurring illusion that he had only to proclaim his faith to convince his adversaries, the two parties remained inflexibly in their respective positions. This was not due to any misunderstanding or any human malevolence; it was the result of a profound and substantial conflict. And the martyr gained human and historic greatness by his refusal to deny what he believed to be the truth, which had awakened the conscience of his people and was destined, in the space of a hundred years, to split the unity of the Catholic world in two.

Even when he had cleared the field of the false accusations of his enemies, his doctrine of predestination, and his insults to princes and priests alike, whom he considered morally unworthy of their office, both shook the foundations of the hierarchical and sacramental structure of the Church, and with it the constitution of the state. He made his appeal to the Holy Scriptures and to the Fathers; he had come to seek enlightenment; as though astonished, he declared himself willing to recognize his own errors provided that they were explained to him by the use of reasoning and scriptural witnesses superior to his own. But his voice was drowned by shouting. Sigismund confessed to the elector-palatine that in the whole of Christendom there was no greater heretic than Huss, and Pierre d'Ailly inveighed against him, that, not content with having abased the dignity of the Church, he had attacked even the princes. In a word, Huss wanted to discuss, to convince or be convinced by the force of reason and the Scriptures, he was deluded enough to think that history could be wiped out and everything begun again with the purity of the primitive Church. This would have meant, in reality, taking to their logical conclusion the revolutionary principles regarding nations, states and religion that had matured in the course of the Great Schism. The Council, on the other hand, would brook no discussion, it wanted a 'Yes' or a 'No', a pure and simple recantation of the propositions declared heretical by the Council.

In order to recompose the Catholic unity of Europe, the Council of Constance had been forced to violate its first principle. It is hardly surprising, then, that it should have attacked the preacher of reform, the heretic, the schismatic, and that the greater it felt the danger of civil and religious subversion to be, the more rigidly it clung to orthodoxy. Small wonder, either, that Sigismund, trembling for the fate of his states and his empire, rose at the end of a session, when Huss had been led away, to advise the 'most reverend Fathers' charitably to condemn him to be burned and deal with him as the law prescribed, but, whatever happened, even if he recanted, not to believe him, not to let him go back to Bohemia, and to enlist the support of bishops and prelates, princes and sovereigns, to break down and eradicate the heresy.

Sigismund's name was permanently blackened by this, but the remedy he suggested did more to promote than to suffocate the spirit of independence and reform. Here again, the logic of history was more powerful and tremendous than the will of a single man; the clash was inevitable, and the martyrdom fertile. The interpreter of new exigencies, standard-bearer of a twofold yet single revolution, Huss had created with his followers a Church of his own, which believed in him. The Catholic Church, guardian of a more than age-old tradition, could only condemn him; no compromise was possible without one side or the other denying its own nature.

While waiting for his final sentence, between the end of June and the first days of July in 1415, Huss asked Stephen of Paleč, a compatriot of his and the staunchest of his opponents, to hear his confession. After entering the confessional, they wept together for a long time, then Huss asked the other's pardon for having so often insulted him, and especially for having called him a liar, but also reproached him for his injustice, without managing to convince him, however. In this dissent, and these shared tears, there is almost a symbol of the fatality of history, which caused a tragedy no human charity could prevent.

On July 6, 1415, the sentence was given its public reading by the Bishop of Concordia:

'The holy Council, in view of the fact that John Huss is obstinate and incorrigible, and refuses to return to the bosom of the Church and abjure his errors, decrees that the guilty party be deposed and defrocked in the presence of the assembly, and since the Church can have no further dealings with him, abandons him to the secular arm.'

After his unfrocking, when they put the tall paper mitre on his head, inscribed with the words '*Hic est haeresiarcha*' and said to him: 'We abandon your soul to Satan', he replied, joining his hands and raising his eyes to Heaven: 'And I abandon it to my merciful

Lord Jesus Christ'. Then he started on his way to the place of torture, from time to time raising the invocation: *'Jesu Christe, Fili Dei vivi, miserere mei: Jesu Christe, Fili Dei vivi qui passus est pro nobis, miserere mei'.*

On May 30, 1416, Jerome of Prague suffered the same fate; after having recanted, he had defied the Council, by reconfirming his faith and praising the goodness, justice and sanctity of his master, who had been unjustly killed. In Bohemia, the fire of anger blazed, and the statues of John Huss and Jerome of Prague were adored as saints in the churches.

The Council had been unanimous in its fight against heresy, and with a few ups and downs it had also succeeded in putting an end to the schism. But when Christian unity lacked nothing but the seal of a papal election, and the restoration of the Church was complete but for reform, the assembly became divided and the ambiguity of its position, the conflict between medieval Catholicism and the young Europe of the future reappeared in all its clarity. On the actual existence of the evil everyone was agreed, cardinals and bishops, princes and professors. Amid all the parliamentary eloquence of the Council, the Fathers had listened without protest to the occasional sermons against the Roman Curia and the clergy, the simony and debauchery of churchmen, which were often on a par with the violent lamentations of the *Squalores Ecclesiae Romanae* and the *Speculum aureum*, and used the same rebellious accents as Wycliff and Huss.

When it came to the remedies, however, opinions differed. In the Council the reform of the Church had been revealed in its true colours, as revolt and reform *against* the Church, against a vacant papacy and a Holy College that had lost all its authority. But the Europe of this time could not resolve the problem in the radical and subversive manner chosen by the heretics, even though they had many premises in common. It wanted to achieve several quite contradictory aims, to take its revenge on the Holy See, deprive it of strength, riches, and prestige, make it serve the interests of various persons, groups, states, and national groups, and, at the same time, it wanted to re-establish the unity of the Catholic Church around the papacy. Under these circumstances it is understandable that the committee appointed to study the problem encountered grave difficulties. Every proposal of a general character concerning the Curia, the centralization of the Church, or the fiscal policy excited a thousand animosities. Some people wanted the old constitution of the hierarchy to be kept intact, others claimed that the papal monarchy, flanked by the aristocracy of the cardinals, should be substituted by a democratic parliament of the bishops to which the pope would be subject, some approved the system of papal collations and reservations, as did the members of Paris University, who took advantage of it, and others again wanted the rights of the bishops to be restored. Every single subject was material for disagreement, not only between one nation and another, or one group and another, but between the delegates of a single nation, between princes, cardinals, bishops and delegates of the universities.

On top of all this, there was the need for the new election which further embittered men's hearts and increased the task of the Council. If the election had been made by the cardinals and had preceded the reform, there was the danger that, as with Pisa, the reform itself might become a dead letter. If on the other hand the pope was not elected until the Church had been reformed, there was no knowing how long the Church might remain without a shepherd. And the election and the reform were to a certain extent dependent on each other, in the sense that only an established pope in the fullness of his power could be an effective guarantor and promoter of reform, and only a reform of the Church could produce a pope who could effectively unite the whole of the Catholic world in his obedience.

This was perhaps the most dangerous moment for the Council, which seemed to be on the point of adjourning. On the question of precedence, those in favour of an immediate election were the cardinals and the Latin nations, Italians, French and Spanish, who were more closely tied by tradition to the Holy See, and were represented respectively by fifteen delegates, seven, and a member of the Sacred College. But Sigismund, who was by now accustomed to lording it over the Council, was immovable in his wish to see first the reform and then a pope of his own choosing, and he resorted to all means, fair and foul, to get his own way. When on September 9, 1417, the Archbishop of Bourges made an official protest in the name of the cardinals and the three Latin nations against the obstacles the emperor was raising, and asked that the procedure for the election should be settled, Sigismund interrupted him, shouting: 'These Italians and these Frenchmen think they can give us a pope. But, by God, they won't succeed!' What was more, a few months before this he had had no hesitation in declaring to the Castilian ambassadors that 'this time the election was his affair, and no one else's'. And when the Bishop of Cuença replied: 'How, my lord, can it be your affair? The right belongs to the cardinals and to no one else', he had said 'that there were no cardinals, and that these were not cardinals, because the Church was unoccupied, and that under the circumstances it was the emperor and the King of the Romans who should elect on this occasion'. Such was the exasperation of the delegates that there was open mention of Huss, and public talk of schism and heresy on the conscience of anyone who delayed the election, in other words of Sigismund and his supporters.

Finally a compromise was reached. On October 9, 1417, the decrees of reform on which agreement had been reached by all the nations were promulgated. Above all, the regular convocation of General Councils was established and measures taken against the occurrence of another schism with the most minute casuistry, which revealed by its very existence the lack of a solid Catholic conscience, the one indispensable and irreplaceable prerequisite of unity. The oath to be taken by popes before their proclamation was prescribed, and the rights of procuration and spoliation usurped by the Holy See were revoked.

The interminable question of the papal election, which Sigismund wanted reserved for himself and others wanted deferred to the Council with the absolute exclusion of the cardinals, was finally resolved by a compromise. The electoral body was to consist not only of the twenty-three cardinals, but also of thirty prelates, six from each nation. Secondly, the cardinal elected to the papal throne had to get two-thirds of the votes in every single national group as well as in the College of Cardinals.

Simultaneously, on October 30, 1417, another decree was promulgated which laid down that the future pope should, before the adjournment of the Council and with either its assistance or that of delegates from the nations, attend to the reformation of the Church 'in its head and in the Roman Curia', with special reference to the quality and nationality of the cardinals, the papal fiscal policy and centralization, and the thousand questions that had been giving rise to protest all over Europe, without any plan of action being agreed upon.

On November 11, 1417, Cardinal Oddone Colonna, called by a contemporary 'the poorest and most simple of the cardinals', was elected by the conclave and took the name of Martin V.

Was the schism then finally vanquished, and was Europe to return in peace to one shepherd and one fold? It was only an appearance. As though nothing had happened, the day after his election Martin V confirmed, *sic et simpliciter* (and he perhaps could not have done otherwise without provoking another revolution), the rules of John XXIII's chancery, including all the abuses that had caused such rivers of ink and eloquence to flow.

When, on the basis of the decree of October 30th, Sigismund and the nations asked the pope to help with the reform, he consented to the nomination of a new committee of six cardinals and six delegates from each nation. But in practice it was impossible to take a single step forward, because there was always someone with different ideas from the rest. When this state of affairs was explained to him, the pope replied that for his part he was willing to accept all the points on which the nations reached agreement: a reply which was a reflection of the sad truth, and which, were we not assured of the candour of the man, might appear to be a cloak for the most diabolic cunning. When the emperor was begged to use his authority, he replied: 'When I insisted that the reform should be attended to before the election of the pope, you would not consent. Now we have a pope; go to him; the matter is no longer any concern of mine.'

In effect, his greatest worry, which was that a French pope might be elected, was now a thing of the past. Martin V lost no time in formally recognizing him as King of the Romans (on January 23, 1418) and, in recompense for the expenses he had sustained for the Council, made him a concession of a tithe on almost all the benefices in Germany.

For a true reform of the Church to be possible, single individuals, groups and nations would have had to be spiritually fused in a new religious unity. Since this was not the case, exactly the opposite happened, in the sense that the reform had to demean itself and dissipate its energy by adapting to the complex demands of European society, and was reduced to a mediocre systematization of European interests to the detriment of the Holy See, instead of being a response to a noble determination to effect a renewal.

After many labours, agreement was reached on a few points of relatively small importance, which were promulgated in seven decrees on March 21, 1418: the revocation of exemptions and incorpations granted from the death of Gregory XI onwards; the renunciation, on the part of the pope, of the income of vacant benefices; the condemnation of simony; new provisions on dispensations; the imposition of tithes, and the propriety of clerical behaviour; in short, all the reforms which could, without subverting the system, give some material and moral satisfaction to the malcontents. Further than this it was not possible to go.

Questions for which various partial arrangements could be made were no longer the subject of the general deliberations, but were dealt with in concordats between the Holy See and the 'nations', and varied considerably both in content and in length. The English agreement was extremely short and made in perpetuity; it did not touch the burning questions of the annates, reservations and papal collations, which had already been settled internally by the *Statute of Provisors* and the *Statute of Praemunire*. The others were even shorter and were quinquennial. A single concordat seems to have been agreed by all the Latin 'nations', which were united in the

Council's most decisive period, and were destined in time to band together to defend the Church against the Protestant Reformation.

The only matter of substance to come out of these agreements was the guarantee given to both English and German nations that they should be granted equal participation in the Sacred College and the staff of the Curia, and, after all the dissension, the recognition that under the obtaining circumstances the Holy See could not afford to renounce the collection of the annates.

The Great Schism and the Councils formed the resolutive crisis of the Middle Ages, a crisis which was, like all the great moments in history, concerned with the principle of authority. The adult Europe of the states and nations rebelled against her mother, Rome; it vindicated its rights against a papal centralization and fiscal policy which seemed totally without reason; and it prepared a case which looked for its target beyond John XXIII, Gregory XII or Benedict XIII to the papacy itself and the whole of the Catholic government of the Middle Ages. The conciliar superiority, considered as a historical problem rather than a question of doctrine, was the victory of the European system over the Holy Roman Republic.

The Council of Constance stands on the watershed between two ages. Like a two-faced Janus, it looks backwards to the past and forwards to the future; and by its contradictions it makes manifest the suffering of a separation which is not yet complete, and the restlessness of a creation that can be felt in the air, but which has not yet broken the surface of consciousness. The guiding light shines from behind, and in spite of the illusion of footsteps retraced and the lost way found again, the new road, in the opposite direction, is grievously, laboriously being built. The greatest endeavours of the Council had been spent in the extermination of heresy and the re-establishment of the Catholic unity of the Middle Ages; but it was already clear that this unity was dying in men's hearts and that no superficial skill in drafting amendments would suffice to revive it. When a cardinal, like Pierre d'Ailly, and a man of the moral stature of Jean Gerson, proclaimed that the pope was fallible and could be judged, that in matters of faith he could have no more knowledge than had the Fathers in council, and that the Council was superior to the vicar of Christ, they gave clear proof that the faith of former days was shaken.

The real purpose of the Council of Constance was to bring civil peace to Europe and to strike a blow at the papacy; political interests and doctrinal discussions prevailed over religion. John XXIII had good reason to condemn the division into nations at the General Councils and to say that all members should have voted together. But never before had national consciousness expressed itself with such rank exuberance as now in the monarchies of France and

England, nor with such self-awareness as in the actions of John Huss and Jerome of Prague, or in the words of John of Jenšlejn when he said:

'God has pleased to give each people their kingdom, which belongs to no one but that people; in Bohemia there were once only Bohemians; so the Bohemians should be free to enjoy their laws and their rights as they did in former times, and without being molested by the Germans. Make way, therefore, teachers who have looked only for your own advantage, make way for the sons of the house, the sole possessors, and may they retain their power in perpetuity.'

The new countries of the west are the reality that the Holy See now has to face, the reality that is concealed under the religious, unitary mantle of the General Council. Dissentient among themselves, and in various states of disagreement with the Curia, they discuss, deliberate, and pass decrees on the deposition of the popes, the superiority of the Council, the heresy of Wycliff and Huss, political questions, and reform. They want to have their part, or even to have a free hand, in the new election; and their indestructible individuality appears once more in the concordats, no sooner than unity seems to be re-established with the election of Martin V.

The road taken by the Fathers was a fearful knife-edge, with tradition on one side and full-scale revolution on the other. To escape from the confusion of the schism, they had recourse to a revolutionary principle, and one which Martin V was quick to deny in the early days of his reign, as soon as the Poles tried to appeal to the Council against him. The way was so strewn with traps that the most solemn champions of conciliar doctrine and practice, Sigismund, d'Ailly and Gerson, more than once ran the risk of facing an accusation of heresy, and much labour was needed to quench the flames already licking the thrones of princes, when the sinful among them were deprived of their authority by Huss's words, and when tyrannicide was justified and exalted by the pens of Jean Petit and the Dominican, John of Falkenberg.

The results of the great European parliament obviously show signs of its contradictions and ambiguities. Developments are still in a state of fluidity, so there is nothing conclusive, the war closes with a series of compromises and the occasional defeat. A general Catholic consciousness does exist, but the soul of the new Europe now resides in the states, the nations; and the political and religious Hussitism, or rebellion against the Church, is livelier than ever. The match between pope and Council is not over: ideally they coexist and are each the negation of the other. The reform has been left stranded, because no one has had the courage for renunciation and revolution. The only certainty is that the Holy Roman Republic no longer exists, and that it is impossible to turn back.

There are probably readers who will grieve that salvation had to be sought in human reason instead of being awaited as a gift from divine Providence, that the Church never completed its reforms and had later to suffer such serious consequences, or that popes and cardinals, instead of supporting the effort to reform, opposed it for selfish reasons. But we feel, once again, that such an attitude substitutes an empty phantom for reality, and degrades one of the most tragic and fertile periods in European history to the level of personal morality. Once again, men were answering for themselves and for those who had gone before them, they were chained to their post of responsibility and combat, condemned to neither retreat nor stay, impelled to tear themselves from the past and to build for future generations.

The Church had created Europe; and Europe denied her, precisely because she had been the common mother and mistress of all the nations, which now, aware of their own strength, were preparing with all the drive of youth to compete for the hegemony of the west.

CHAPTER SIXTEEN

CONCLUSION

The purpose with which we started this work was to take note of the substance and the value of the Middle Ages, to show that the dark ages have, contrarily, an extremely clear significance, which is the foundation of Europe on a Christian and Roman base, the process of its articulation and dissociation, and finally the basic structure of the modern world.

A quick glance at the road we have travelled will perhaps help to decide whether we have attained this goal.

The empire and Christianity, with their triumph and their reciprocal relations, are the presupposition of the entire Middle Ages, in as much as they are to be the common faith of all men for the whole millenium, and the very substance of the age. The unitary and universal government, the principles of civil order and Christian purity may be denied a thousand times by actual events; but men continue to believe, to hope and to work in the light of the Church and the empire; and politics and religion constitute only two aspects of a single reality.

The first great period of our history is that of the progressive fusion of the conquerors and the conquered. This was a complex problem, whose difficulties lay in the moral forces of civilization and the faith even more than in the questions of arms and economic pressures. From the violent clash of Alaric and Ataulf's dream of a Gothic empire, we come to the Germanic and Roman monarchy of Theodoric, the static compromise between force and law, orthodoxy and heterodoxy, and thence to the family constellation of Romano-Germanic kingdoms which revolved around the palace at Verona. But the spirit of Rome, with its civil and religious consciousness, was an almost insurmountable obstacle to the union. The cultured thousands of the Catholic hierarchy, rooted to the earth and full of vital energy, was a far more powerful army, for both resistance and conquest, than the Goths, Burgundians, Franks, and Alemanni, stationed in enemy territory. The first victory of note was gained over the Franks, who, after Clovis' example, were converted to Catholicism and became in time the pillar of the papacy, the most effective instrument of Roman and Catholic expansion among the invaders and the peoples beyond the frontiers, and for the defence and unitary development of the west.

A development along these lines was almost a foregone conclusion on account of the different nature, culture and history of the two parts of the Roman Empire, the effective division of the empire itself, the fate that had preserved the east from the invasions which the west had to suffer, and finally on account of the incompatibility of the two powers which claimed to govern the world, albeit in different spheres, from Rome and Byzantium. In theory the unity of the empire could continue, provoking military and diplomatic conflicts and the vindication of rights on either side down the centuries; but in fact, the west becomes more and more estranged from the east, withdrawing into itself with a strong and forceful consciousness of its own interests and its own worth. St Benedict gives the model for its culture; St Gregory, under pressure from the Lombards, accentuates the separation from Byzantium by taking on the military defence of Italy, and by the conversion of the Lombards and the Anglo-Saxons, the subjection of the Irish Church and his relations with the Frankish potentates, he sketches the outline of a new papal policy which is concerned primarily with the west. In the end, a little more than a century after the pope's death, the clash between the inflexible force of the Roman primacy and the Byzantine Caesaropapism renders the divorce between east and west irreparable.

Two different forces, separate from each other and yet conspiring, now move towards the foundation of Europe: the Church with its prestige and its civil wisdom, its Apostolate and its spirit of independence; and the sons of Pippin, the flower of the palace aristocracy, heirs to the Merovingian monarchy, who halt the Arab invasion, spread the rule of Christianity with their arms in competition with the English missionaries consecrated by Rome, and reform their national clergy on the directive of Rome. When, under the pressure of the Lombard threat, the axis of papal policy moves decisively from Byzantium to the court of the Franks, the divorce is complete and European history begins.

The coronation of Charlemagne, however the act be judged in its immediate context, is the sign that in the contemporary consciousness the separation from Byzantium and the unification of the conquerors and the conquered are complete; his consecration by the pope, that the empire is invested with a religious mission. The disseminators of the Gospel are the missionaries of Rome and the soldiers of Charles; the literary splendour of his court is in great part an offshoot of the insular monastic culture; bishoprics and monasteries become the most conspicuous centres of political, cultural and economic activity.

But the unity of which we speak is neither the Roman Empire nor a modern state. There is something superficial and almost accidental about it; it is more a shared religious consciousness, an aspiration to a cultured society, and a practice of government, than a profound reality of Carolingian Europe. For if we study its social, political and economic constitution, it appears to be a rather haphazard ordering of conquerors and conquered, an aggregate of peoples with their own laws under a personal regime, an elementary society of feudal armies, ecclesiastical culture and servile labour.

The eclipse of Charlemagne does not, in spite of appearances, point the way to a halt and a regression, the absurd dissolution of a world of civilization and its return to even darker barbarism. The consciousness of empire and priesthood, as the Christian and Roman unity of the west, is now so strong that even through the most fearful crises it remains the fundamental principle for the rest of the Middle Ages. The protagonists of the new age spring from the very heart of the creation of Charles and his predecessors. They are the military aristocracy promoted by the wars of the sons of Pippin, who break down the summary order of the empire from the inside, and sink their roots deep into the earth.

In this profound travail, the two heads of the Catholic world go into a decline; clergy and laity, lost without their respective leaders, become inextricably entwined. The universal particularism, which with Alberic and Octavian takes over even the papacy, seems to throw the entire economic and political life of Europe into confusion and anarchy. But what in fact is happening is that a more stable edifice is being built by the construction of firmer foundations. Between the ninth and tenth century, a twofold development is taking place in European society: the feudal hierarchy orders itself increasingly under the monarchies of France and Germany, and the ecclesiastic hierarchy looks more and more decidedly to Rome.

These two movements, which are animated by the Christian ideal and respond to the common need to overcome the civil disorder and moral corruption of feudalism, meet together in the Saxon monarchy, which is destined to take the lead in feudal Europe. Otto III, like his father and grandfather before him, but more resolutely than they, directs his attention to Italy and Rome. He makes himself the champion of the ideal of the Roman Empire, and makes it tower above the local factions; he makes the final bid to incorporate the papacy in the empire, to absorb the mission of the Church and the religious impulse of the west into the imperial structure.

Charlemagne was his model, but Europe had changed since his day. The old frontiers had gone, and with them the threat of the Arab, Hungarian, Slav and Norman invasions. The Arabs and Byzantines were beginning to withdraw from Spain and Italy, and

European recovery and conquest were settling into a steady stride. England, Bohemia, Poland and Hungary were now a part of the European orbit. There were no longer capitularies, but laws; no longer counts, bishops, abbots and *missi dominici*, the personal servants of their lord, but a hereditary lay feudality, and a church of bishop-counts, who formed the body and foundation of the state. If the empire still signified the Christian government of the world, or at least of the west, its political foundations lay in the crowns of Italy, Germany and Burgundy. Outside this Italo-Germanic nucleus, stable political organisms had been developing, the foremost of which was the Kingdom of France. New classes, sprung from the hierarchic formation of the feudal state, came onto the stage of history in a turmoil of hate, ambition and exuberant vitality: the French knights, the German *ministeriales*, and the Italian vavasours, citizenries bred in the shade of episcopal immunity, peasants freed from their former serfdom. If we take a look at the culture of the time, we feel the pulse of new life bursting out and breaking the old sheath: the first babbling of the vulgar tongues; a few shining classical reminiscences of heroic civil life: the lowly, lively humanity of the bishop Liudprand; the serene classicism and scientific curiosity of Gerbert.

The soundest stimulus to these emergent energies was given by the Church. The Ottonian policy contained an irremediable contradiction and therefore necessitated a further development. It was impossible to elevate the Church materially and morally while at the same time incorporating and imprisoning it within the feudal empire. The demand for the reform and the liberation of the Church from territorial and private interests, which had been made first by the theorists of the Carolingian age, and then by Ratheri of Liège, Atto of Vercelli, Odo of Cluny, the hermits like St Romuald and St Nilus, and by the great lay potentates themselves in the interest of the state, which had found a certain satisfaction in the mutual restoration of the papacy and the empire, was now reaffirmed, against the empire, by the papacy itself, which had now regained consciousness of its universal mission.

And so we come to the Struggle of the Investitures, which is the crisis of the Middle Ages, of the Christian, unitary government of the west. On the one side stand ecclesiastical freedom and hierarchy, on the other, feudalism and the territorial church. The empire, which represents the medieval state in general, stands firm on its historical rights and its unity, strong in the tradition of centuries; the Church, which has spread Christianity and Romanism through the whole of Europe, penetrated its entire society and been to a certain extent absorbed by it, now raises its tremendously revolutionary demands for reform against the secular powers. The crisis was general throughout the west, but it developed with a more tragic finality in Italy and Germany, on account of the universal aspirations of the empire, its fatal attraction to the papacy, and the German crown's substantial interest in retaining its control over the national church.

The Holy See waged the war on the political and religious fronts simultaneously. On the one hand, it renewed the ecclesiastical cadres, papal legates were sent to England, France and Spain to make known the will of Rome, the hierarchy developed into a tight-meshed network of clerks and prelates, all of them responsible to the pope, their supreme judge and master. At the same time, it appealed to all the young forces of the continent, which were in a ferment of revolt and conquest—the townsfolk, the great feudal lords who were enemies of the empire, Poland, Bohemia and Hungary in their thirst for independence, the Normans of the north and south—and around the original nucleus of the kingdoms of France, Germany, Burgundy and Italy, a new peripheral Europe was established, over which the Church claimed a remote seigniory of a feudal type, the details of which varied according to the circumstances. The empire emerged from the struggle mortally wounded. Bereft of its claim to dominate the papacy, shaken in its political and economic structure, which rested on the principle of the private national church, it was placed in a position of lasting inferiority, whether it accepted its enforced attenuation or, neglecting all prohibitions, flew in the face of the condemnation of Rome and the Catholic world.

The Holy See celebrated the most clamorous of triumphs. As the interpreter of the religious spirit and the turbulent energies of the young Europe, it had raised high the banner of liberty and conquest against the old, feudal and imperial Europe. And under the command of Rome, conquest and religion were united in the proclamation of the crusade, which was to open the door to the colonization of the Levantine Basin by the French knighthood, and to hold the interest of a large part of Europe for two centuries. Thus the papacy provided the stimulus and the discipline for the spiritual elevation, the liberation and the expansion of Europe.

After the Struggle of the Investitures the unity of the Christian republic of the west is broken, its politico-religious consciousness divided. The two universal powers go their separate ways; clergy and laity, now disentangled from their mutual embrace, begin to constitute two different worlds, each with its own ends and interests.

The empire, deprived, as it were, of its religious substance, rediscovers Roman law as its claim to universal dominion, and takes refuge in an absolute sovereignty which is not derived from God, not bound to the Church, but founded on juridical titles and born of this world and of man. But the world of the twelfth century no longer responds to the historical conditions from which the absolutism of Rome had arisen, and this new principle of absolute sovereignty, far from legitimizing the empire, clashes directly with the political exigencies of the territorial potentates who are challenging the two supreme powers.

From now on, the empire has two irreconcilable adversaries: the Church and the new Europe of the communes and the monarchies. Henry VI makes a last, most heroic bid to dominate them both, or rather to absorb them in a new universality. With the conquest of Sicily and the Patrimony of St Peter he can indulge in the illusion that he has the hostile pope and rebellious Europe in his power. He negotiates for the union of the crowns of Sicily and Germany, the hereditary constitution of the empire on the model of the French and English monarchies, and the subjection of Rome in exchange for a few external signs of honour and some liberal financial benefits. He dreams of uniting the Norman and German traditions, of renewing the *élan* of the Crusades at his command, and of restoring the unity of east and west. But his early death only sanctions a failure that is already implied by the very vitality of the Church, the peoples of Europe and their kings and princes, and by the oppressive and reactionary character of his policies.

After this time, the universalism of the empire continues to survive for a long time in the European consciousness as a nostalgic dream. But in fact, not only is the unitary order of the Christian government of Europe obsolete by the end of the thirteenth century, but, even within the narrowed boundaries of the empire, new political organisms, the communes, are gaining their autonomy and growing towards independence and even sovereignty. Beyond its frontiers the individual states stake definite claims to a life of their own, they defend their own interests, make alliances, and display preferences and antagonisms which foreshadow the political system of the future Europe. If the empire is still the protagonist of the dying Europe, the leader of the new Europe is France, which has consolidated its monarchy, gained the upper hand over England, allied itself with Rome, and in the service of Rome brought light to the west with the schools of Chartres and the University of Paris.

The war being fought on both sides of the English Channel, the political and economic growth of the commune in Italy, the levelling monarchies, which are the founders of royal justice, call the third estate to form a part of their constitution, and create their own ministers, bureaucracy, army, and finances—all these are so many aspects and illustrations of the medieval structure giving place to the modern state.

And here the Church, in its reaffirmation of its supremacy, comes into conflict with this new adult Europe. Now that it has lavished all its strength in fostering and guiding the Catholic world, now that the empire is beaten and the communes and seigniories and monarchies have acquired a measure of self-confidence, the Church appears, sometimes even to its champions, not so much the great salvation-bearing institution, as a formidable juridical, fiscal and political organism; and this is partly because the temporal is in effect in the ascendant over the spiritual, and partly because it is inevitable that children revolt against their parents when they want to go out into the world.

The countries which are most violently opposed to the political and fiscal interference of the Church, are of course France and England, where on account of the dynastic tradition, the centralization of the monarchy, and the continual wars and sacrifices, a strong national consciousness is developing. Whatever its foundations according to doctrinal speculation and publicist polemic, the temporal monarchy is no longer a sacred ministry, a bond of faith between men, but dominion and jurisdiction on the one side, and subjecthood and servitude on the other; the state is not born from on high, from the religious need to put the law of God into practice among men, but from men themselves, voluntarily, because they need to assure for each man his own and to guarantee that they can live together in peace. So the sovereign state grows up in the face of Church and empire, recognizing no power superior to itself in temporal matters. Amid political entanglements and continual financial necessity, the states work energetically for the abolition of the ecclesiastical privileges, and for the establishment of a national church subordinate to, or preferably incorporated in, the state. The people of the cities, the middle classes, take their place beside the nobility and the clergy in the fight for a national monarchy and for the protection of their own economic interests against the monarchy itself. The parliaments with their three orders are at once the expression of the sovereignty of the people and the formation of national unity around the crown. These are the forces which Philip the Fair has behind him. With his gigantic spirit, Bonifice VIII moves against the advancing tide, and solemnly repeats his profession of faith, which is that of Gregory VII. But the Christian Republic no longer responds to the call of the Church, and for the first time the modern state asserts its own exigencies with resolution. The theocratic government, having lost its vital substance and fallen to being an instrument of nepotism, fiscal imposition and worldly government, is now a structure without foundations, for it represents the temporal expression of a universal and transcendent ideal, which has itself lost all hold on the imagination of Europe.

Avignon, for the humiliated and now powerless Church, was the only hope of salvation; for France, it was the prize of victory, the token of her effective hegemony, and a debt of help and devotion paid to religion. The Great Schism was the French recovery after disillusion and the conflict between Catholicism and the national churches.

And it was also the crisis that brought the Middle Ages to an end, in which the Holy See, ravaged by the lay potentates and weighed down by the burden of its centralization and its fiscal complications, was called to defend itself before the assembly of the nations. With its mind fixed on the past, Europe tried to reconstitute the unity of the Christian republic which it was in fact denying by the very act of holding its revolutionary assembly. The result was the restoration of the monarchic papacy, which was limited, however, by the declaration of conciliar superiority, the obligation to reform the Church and collaborate with the Council to that end, and the compromises made in the national Concordats. In reality the Holy See emerged deeply wounded from the long crisis of the fourteenth and fifteenth centuries, not only because the *reformatio* that was so insistently demanded was now an unavoidable necessity and at the same time a task which presented tremendous difficulties, but also because an attack had been made from several quarters, on various principles, against the hierarchic and sacramental institution of the Roman Church itself.

Thus the Middle Ages came to an end. After softening the impact of the invasions, pushing back the frontiers of the west, controlling the feudal particularism and setting it on the way to civil organization, the threefold and single universality of Europe, at once religious, cultural and political, was lost in the world it had created; and from the common ground of Roman and Christian Europe which it had established, there emerged, with increasingly sharp differentiation, nations with their own characteristics of faith, constitution and culture.

The *renovatio*, which in the perennial youth of history, had been invoked and saluted continually throughout the Middle Ages, was accomplished once more, not within the universality of the Church but against it. It was a new political conception, which found the fountainhead of its power and its ambition in the state; a new religious conception, which opposed the Holy Scriptures interpreted by free examination to the Catholic tradition; it was the rediscovery of classicism as the model of life and beauty, the revaluation of man and nature, the irresistible impulse to discover and conquer the world.

FINIS

BIBLIOGRAPHY

CHAPTER 1

The bibliographies placed at the end of the book make no claim to be complete, they are merely intended to give a summary indication of the principal sources and the specialist and general works which may serve to furnish deeper or more detailed acquaintance with the subjects discussed to those who desire it. I should like to thank my friends and colleagues, Gina Fasoli, Arsenio Frugoni and Pier Fausto Palumbo, for their assistance in bringing these notes up to to date for the second edition in 1954. My thanks are also due in particular to Professor P. Classen and to my friend Raoul Manselli, professor of Medieval history at Turin University, whose excellent suggestions I have made use of for the notes of the fourth edition.

Chapters 1 and 16 contain the introduction and conclusion of this work, which in the main are drawn from: G. FALCO, *La polemica sul Medioevo*, I, in *Biblioteca della Società Storica Subalpina*, CXLIII, Turin, 1933; IDEM, *Albori d'Europa, Pagine di storia medioevale*, Rome, 1947. For a study of the thought of the Renaissance, in which the historical period of the Middle Ages originates, W. K. FERGUSON, *La Renaissance dans la pensée historique*, Paris, 1950.

On the political and religious consciousness of the Middle Ages: H. EICKEN, *Geschichte und System der mittelalterlichen Weltanschauung*, Stuttgart u. Berlin, 1923; A. DEMPF, *Die Hauptform der mittelalterlichen Weltanschauung*, Munich, 1925; IDEM, *Die Ethik des Mittelalters*, Munich, 1927; IDEM, *Sacrum Imperium. Geschichts-und Staatsphilosophie des Mittelalters und der politischen Renaissance*, Munich, 1929 (trans. by C. ANTONI, Messina and Milan [1933]).

To avoid tedius and unnecessary repetition in subsequent bibliographies, it is convenient to note here a few general works which can be referred to for fuller information and more detailed bibliographic guidance.

For medieval history in general:

The Cambridge Medieval History, edited by J. R. TANNER, C. W. PREVITÉ-ORTON, Z. N. BROOKE, Cambridge, 1911 sqq.;

C. W. PREVITÉ-ORTON, *The Shorter Cambridge Medieval History*, Cambridge, 1952;

Peuples et Civilisations, edited by L. HALPHEN and PH. SAGNAC, Paris, 1626 sqq.

Histoire Générale, II, edited by G. GLOTZ, Paris, 1928 sqq.

Historia Mundi, F. KERN, vols. 4-7. Bern, 1956 sqq.

For the history of the Church and the Papacy:

A. FLICHE and V. MARTIN, *Histoire de l'Eglise depuis les origines Jusqu'à nos jours*, Paris, 1934 sqq.: volumes II-XIV;

E. BUONAIUTI, *Storia del Cristianesimo*, II, Evo Medio, Milan, 1947;

E. CASPAR, *Geschichte des Papsttums*, Tübingen, 1930 sqq., unfortunately only up to the eighth century;

J. HALLER, *Das Papsttum. Idee und Wirklichkeit*, 2nd ed. 5 vols., Stuttgart, 1950-53 sqq.

Die Kirche in ihrer Geschichte, ed., K. D. SCHMIDT and E. WOLF, Gottingen, 1962 (further edns. in preparation).

The following learned works on the whole of the Middle Ages should be born in mind: G. VOLPE, *Il medio evo*, Florence, 1933; S. HELLMANN, *Storia del medio evo dalle invasioni barbariche alla fine delle Crociate*, Florence,

1930; K. KASER, *Il basso medio evo*, Florence, 1923; C. BEMONT, G. MONOD, R. DOUCET, *Histoire d'Europe au moyen âge*, Paris, 1921-1931; H. PIRENNE, *Histoire de l'Europe des invasions au XVIe siècle*, Paris and Brussels, 1936; C. BARBAGALLO, *Il Medioevo* (476-1454), in *Storia Universale, Turin*, 1935; F. SCHNEIDER, Das Mittelalter bis zur Mitte des 13. Jahrhunderts, and B. SCHMEIDLER, 'Das spätere Mittelalter', in the *Handbbuch fur den Geschicts-lehrer*, ed. O. KENDE, Wien u. Leipzig, vol. 3, 1039, vol. 4, part 1, 1938; L. GENICOT, *Les Lignes de faîte du moyen âge*, Tournai, 1952; P. L. GANSHOF, *Le moyen âge*, in *Histoire des relations internationales* edited by P. RENOUVIN, I, Paris, 1953.

Other works on medieval historiography to be born in mind are: WATTEN-BACH-LEVISON, *Deutschlands, Geschichtsquellen im Mittelalter, Vorzeit u. Karolinger, Weimar*, 1952-57; WATTENBACH-HOLTZMANN, *Deutschlands Geschichtsquellen im Mittelalter, Deutsche Kaiserzeit*, Berlin, 1938-43.

The following books are extremely useful for obtaining a quick idea of the state of research, sources, and for bibliographies of single periods and problems of the Middle Ages: J. CALMETTE, *Le monde féodal*, Paris, 1951, in *Clio. Introduction aux études historiques*; and the *Questioni di storia medievale*, edited by E. ROTA, Milan.

CHAPTER 2

The principal narrative sources for the life and times of Constantine are: the *Vita Constantini* (ed. J. A. HEIKEL, *Eusebius Werke*, I, Leipzig, 1902, in *Die Griechischchristlichen Schriftsteller der ersten 3, Jahrhunderte*, VII) and the *Historia Ecclesiastica* by EUSEBIO DI CESAREA (ed. E. SCHWARTZ, *Eusebius Werke*, II, Leipzig, 1909, *Ibidem*, IX); *the De mortibus persecutorum* attributed to LATTANZIO (ed. S. BRANDT and G. LAUBMANN, Vindobona, 1897, p. 171 sqq., in *Corpus scriptorum ecclesiasticorum latinorum*, XXVII); the *Panegyrici latini*, IV-VII, XII (ed. G. BAEHRENS, Leipzig, 1911); ANONYMUS VALESII (ed. R. CESSI, *Fragmenta historica ab Henrico et Hadriano Valesio primum edita, Città di Castello*, 1913, in *Rerum Italicarum Scriptores*, new ed., XXIV); the Ἱστορία νέα of ZOSIMUS, representing the anti-Christian tendency (ed. L. MENDELSSOHN, Leipzig, 1887). A good collection of texts on the relations between Christianity and the Empire will be found in: E. PRESCHEN, *Analecta, kursere Texte zur Geschichte der alten Kirche und des Kanons*, 2nd ed., p. 1, *Tubingen*, 1909; K. KIRCH, *Enchiridion fontium historiae ecclesiae antiquae*, 4th ed., Freiburg i.B., 1923; P. BREZZI, *Christian-esimo e Impero Romano fino alla morte di Costantino*, Rome, 1942.

On Constantine in particular: L. SALVATORELLI, *Costantino il Grande*, Rome, 1928; A. PIGANIOL, *L'empereur Constantin*, Paris, 1932; IDEM, *L'Empire Chrétien* 325-395, Paris, 1947, in G. GLOTZ cit., *Histoire Romaine*, IV, 2; K. HÖNN, *Konstantin der Grosse*, Leipzig, 1940; I. VOGT, *Constantin der Grosse und seine Jahrhundert*, Munich, 1949.

The most important works of the extremely full bibliography on the relations between Constantine and the Church are: E. SCHWARTZ, *Kaiser Constantin und die Christliche Kirche*, Leipzig, 1913; N. BAYNES, *Constantine the Great and the Christian Church*, in *Proceedings of the British Academy*, 1929; M. VOGELSTEIN, *Kaiseridee-Romidee und das Verhältniss von Staat und Kirche seit Constantin*, Breslau, 1930, in *Historische Untersuchungen*, ed. by E. KORNEMANN, VII; H. DÖRRES, *Das Selbstzeugnis Kaiser Konstantins*, in the *Abhandlungen der Gottinger Akademie*, 1954; H. KRAFT, *Kaiser Konstantins religiose Entwicklung*, Tubingen, 1955.

For information on recent studies on Constantine see: A. PIGANIOL, *L'état actuel de la question constantinienne*, 1930-49, in *Historia*, I, p. 82 sqq.; J. VOGT and V. SESTON, *Die Constantinische Frage*, in *Relazioni del X Congresso Internazionale di Scienze Storiche*, Rome, 1955, p. 733 sqq.

For fuller information on the history of the later Roman Empire, of the works of eighteenth century historians, see: L. S. LE NAIN DE TILLEMONT, *Histoire des empereurs qui ont régné durant les six premiers siècles de Eglise*, Paris, 1693-1738, and E. GIBBON, *The History of the Decline and Fall of the Roman Empire*, ed. J. B. BURY, London, 1894 and later editions; and of more recent authors: O. SEECK, *Geschichte des Untergangs der antiken Welt*, Berlin, 1893 and later editions; E. STEIN, *Geschichte des spätrömichen Reichs*, I, Vienna, 1928; IDEM, *Histoire du Bas Empire*, II, Paris, Brussels, Amsterdam, 1949. See also the article and accompanying bibliography by A. MOMIGLIANO in the *Enciclopedia Italiana; Roma Età imperiale*, in which the process of the Christianization of the Empire is already shown in the perspective of its intrinsic development, rejecting the nineteenth century pattern of the relations between Church and State.

On the decline of paganism the work of G. BOISSIER, *La fin du paganisme*, Paris, 1913, will always be read with interest. On Christianity and the Church in the early centuries remember: L. DUCHESNE, *Histoire ancienne de l'Eglise*, Paris, 1906 and later editions; A. V. HARNACK, *Mission und Ausbreitung des Christentums in den ersten drei Jahrhunderten*, Leipzig, 1934 (trans. P. MARUCCHI, *Missione e propaganda del Cristianesimo nei primi tre secoli*, Turin, 1906); E. CASPAR cit.; A. FLICHE and V. MARTIN cit.; H. LIETZMANN, *Histoire de l'Eglise ancienne*, III, Paris, 1941.

As an illustration of the historical consciousness of the first centuries of the Christian era, the extremely rich though unfortunately nebulous, *Sacrum Imperium* of DEMPF, sopra cit. may prove useful.

F. LOT's, *La fin du monde antique et le début du moyen âge*, Paris, 1951, in *L'Evolution de l'Humanité*, ed. by H. BERR, whose title leads us to expect a treatment of the link between antiquity and the Middle Ages, and hence a work that concerns us closely, does not in fact touch on the subject of Christianity, which is reserved for another volume in the collection. It is nevertheless an extremely useful work on account of the full and reliable information and the rich bibliography it contains. For the transition from the ancient world to the Middle Ages see also: H. ST L. B. MOSS, *The Birth of the Middle Ages* (395-814), London, 1935; C. DAWSON, *Religion and the Rise of Western Culture*, London, 1950; and H. DANNENBAUER, *Grundlagen der mittelalterlichen Welt*, Stuttgart, 1958; IDEM, *Die Entstehung Europas*, Stuttgart, 1959-1962, 2 vols.

CHAPTER 3

The most important literary sources for the age of the Valentinians, Stilicho and Alaric are: the precious historical work of the contemporary AMMIANUS MARCELLINUS, of which a part is unfortunately lost (*Rerum gestarum libri qui supersunt*, ed. C. U. CLARK, Berlin, 1910 and later editions); the Ἱστορία νέα by ZOSIMUS sopra cit., which is hostile to Stilicho; the *Carmina* of the Alexandrian CLAUDIUS CLAUDIAN, the poet of his triumphs and his family joys (ed. TH. BIRT in *Monumenta Germaniae Historica*, Auctores Antiquissimi, X); the *Historiarum adversus paganos libri septem*, by PAULUS OROSIUS, inspired by the *De Civitate Dei* of St Augustine (ed. K. ZANGEMEISTER, in C.S.E.L. sopra cit. V). For the quotation of the rhetor LIBANIUS, who was so devoted to Julian the Apostate, see: Περὶ τῆς τιμωρίας Ἰουλιάνου (in LIBANII *Opera*, ed. R. FOERSTER, II, Leipzig, 1904, XXIV, p. 514 sqq.).

On Alaric see: A. THIERRY, *Alaric, L'agonie de l'empire*, Paris, 1880; on Stilicho: R. KELLER, *Stilicho oder die Geschichte des weströmischen Reichs von 395-408*, Berlin, 1884; S. MAZZARINO, *Stilicone. La crisi imperiale dopo Teodosio*, Rome, 1942, in *Studi pubblicati dal R. Istituto Italiano per la Storia Antica*, III. E. NISCHER-FALKENHOF, *Stilicho*, Wien, 1947; E. DEMOUGEOT, *De l'unité à la division de l'Empire Romain* (395-410), Paris, 1951

For fuller information on the whole period see in addition to the general works listed in previous bibliographies: J. B. BURY, *A History of the Later Roman Empire from the Death of Theodosius I to the Death of Justinian* (395-565), London, 1923; F. GREGOROVIUS, *Geschichte der Stadt Rom im Mittelalter*, Berlin, 1903 sqq. (trans. by R. MANZATO, *Storia della città di Roma nel medio evo*, Rome, 1900 sqq.); H. GRISAR, *Geschichte Roms und der Päpste im Mittelalter. I. Rom bei Ausgang der antiken Welt*, Freiburg im Br., 1901 (trans. by A. MERCATI new edition, revised by A. BARTOLI, *Roma alla fine del mondo antico secondo le fonti scritte e i monumenti*, Rome, 1930); G. ROMANO, A. SOLMI, *Le dominazioni barbariche in Italia* (395-888), Milan, 1940; TH. HODGKIN, *Italy and her Invaders*, London, 1892 sqq.; L. HALPHEN, *Les barbares, Paris*, 1940, in *Peuples et Civilisations* sopra cit., p. 311, V; L. SCHMIDT, *Geschichte der Deutschen Stämme bis zum Ausgang der Völkerwanderung. Die Ostgermanen*, Munich, 1941; F. LOT, *Les invasions germaniques. La pénétration mutuelle du monde barbare et du monde romain*, Paris, 1935; R. LATOUCHE, *Les grandes invasions et la crise de l'Occident au Ve siècle*, Paris, 1946; GONZAGUE DE REYNOLD, *Le monde barbare et sa fusion avec le monde antique. Les Germains*, Paris, 1953.

On the spiritual opposition between Rome and the Germans see in particular: P. COURCELLE, *Histoire littéraire des grandes invasions germaniques*, Paris, 1948; J. FISCHER, *Die Volkerwanderung im Urteil der zeitgenossischen Schriftsteller*, Heidelberg, 1948; H. HELBLING, *Goten und Wandalen, Wandlung der historischen Realitat*, Zurich, 1954.

CHAPTER 4

The fundamental source for the age of Theodoric is the twelve books of Cassiodorus' *Variae* (ed. T. MOMMSEN and L. TRAUBE in *M.G.H., A.A.*, XII). Twelve more books by Cassiodorus on Gothic history have been lost except for a meagre summary in JORDANES *Getica* (ed. T. MOMMSEN in *M.G.H., A.A.*, V). We are indebted to MAGNUS FELIX ENNODIUS, a native of Gaul and bishop of Pavia (d. 521) for a *Panegyric* of Theodoric (ed. F. VOGEL in *M.G.H., A.A.*, VII). For the ANONYMOUS VALESIAN, see above p. 312; for the *De consolatione philosophiae* of BOETHIUS see the edition of G. WEINBERGER in *C.S.E.L.*, XXXI.

The first important historian of the Franks and Clovis is GREGORY, bishop of Tours (538-594), the author of a *Historia Francorum* in ten books (ed. G. ARNDT, in *M.G.H., Scriptores rerum Merovingicarum*, I), in addition to many religious writings.

On Theodoric in particular: T. HODGKIN, *Theodoric the Goth, the Barbarian Champion of the Civilisation*, New York, 1891; G. PFEILSCHIFTER, *Theoderich der Grosse*, Mainz, 1910, in *Weltgeschichte in Charakterbildern* ed. by F. KAMPERS; W. ENSSLIN, *Theoderich der Grosse*, Munich, 1947; P. LAMMA, *Teodorico*, Brescia, 1950. On the Goths: *I Goti in Occidente*, Spoleto, 1956, in *Settimane di Studio del Centro Italiano di studi sull'Alto Medioevo*, III. On Clovis: G. KURTH, *Clovis*, Brussels, 1923; *IDEM*, *Sainte Clotilde*, Paris, 1905, in *Les Saints*.

For fuller information on the whole period see, in addition to the books mentioned in preceding bibliographies: L. DUCHESNE, *L'Eglise au VIe siècle*, Paris, 1925; H. V. SCHUBERT, *Geschichte der christlichen Kirche im Frühmittelalter*, Tübingen, 1917 and later editions; L. M. HARTMANN, *Geschichte Italiens im Mittelalter*, Gotha u, Leipzig, 1897 and later editions; C. BAYET, C. PFISTER, A. KLEINCLAUSZ, *Le Christianisme, les barbares, Mérovingiens et Carolingiens*, Paris, 1903, in *Histoire de France* ed. by E. *Lavisse*, II, part 1a; R. CESSI, *Le vicende politiche dell'Italia medievale*, Padua, 1938; O. BERTOLINI, *Roma di fronte a Bisanzio e ai Longobardi*, Bologna, 1941, in *Storia di Roma* ed. Institute of Roman Studies, IX; L. SALVATORELLI, L'Italia medievale, Mondadori, Milan, in *Storia d'Italia*, III; G. PEPE, *Il Medioevo barbarico d'Italia*, Turin, 1942; IDEM, *Il Medioevo barbarico d'Europa*, Milan-Verona, 1949.

On the political and moral value of the period: E. SESTAN, *Stato e nazione nell'alto medio evo*, Naples, 1952; H. LÖWE, *Von Theoderich zu Karl d. Gr.*, Darmstadt, 1956.

CHAPTER 5

The sources for the life of St Benedict are the *Regula Monasteriorum* (editions: C. BUTLER, Freiburg im Br., 1927; B. LINDERBAUER, Bonn, 1928; R. HANSLIK, in *C.E.S.L.*, 75, 1960; text with translation and commentary by A. LENTINI, Montecassino, 1947; text with translation by G. PENCO, in *Biblioteca di Studi Superiori*, XXXIX, Florence, 1958; and the second book of the *Dialogi* of GREGORIUS MAGNUS (ed. U. MORICCA, Rome, 1924, in *Fonti per la Storia d'Italia* edited by the Istituto Storio Italiano). Faithful and effective Italian translations of both texts are to be found in: P. LUGANO, *San Benedetto, Vita, Regola*, Rome, 1929, which we have used occasionally for quotations in this chapter.

On St Benedict: L. SALVATORELLI, *San Benedetto e l'Italia del suo tempo*, Bari, 1929; on Benedictine monasticism: PH. SCHMITZ, *Histoire de l'Ordre de Saint Benoît*, Maredsous, 1948-1949; U. BERLIERE, *L'ordre monastique des origines au XIIIe siècle*, Paris, 1921 (trans. by M. ZAPPALA, Bari, 1928); *Il monachesimo nell'Alto Medioevo e la formazione della civiltà occidentale*, in *Settimane di Studio* sopra cit., IV Spoleto, 1957; G. PENCO, *Storia del monachesimo in Italia dalle origini alla fine del Medio Evo*, 1961.

For a particular and important viewpoint on the *Regula*: G. AULINGER, *Das Humanum in der Regel Benedikts von Nursia*, St Ottilien, 1960.

For fuller information on the age of St Benedict see the general and ecclesiastical histories cited in preceding chapters.

The story of the Moslems on their return from the devastation of the monastery mentioned at the end of this chapter is to be found in the *Chronica Sancti Benedicti Casinensis* (in *M.G.H.*, *Scriptores rerum Langobardicarum et Italicarum*, p. 472 sqq.) and is repeated in the *Chronicon* of LEO and the *Dialogi* of the abbot DESIDERIUS. The 'sweet Cassinian poet, who will also be considered in future chapters, is Alfanus, the bishop of Salerno.

CHAPTER 6

The fullest and most direct evidence on St Gregory is furnished by his own writings. The most important of them are the 848 *Epistolae* in fourteen books, all that has come down to us of the papal *scrinium* which was split up (ed. P. EWALD and L. M. HARTMANN in *M.G.H.*, *Epistolae*, I-II, 1891 and 1899). For the *Dialogi*, an extremely important source for the knowledge of Italy at that time and for the life of St Benedict, and also for many problems connected with Gregorian and medieval culture in general, see the edition of U. MORICCA, sopra cit., on p. 315.

Treatises which deserve particular mention are the *Expositio in librum Job sive Moralium libri XXXV*, an enormous moral and doctrinal encyclopedia which Gregory began as apocrisiary in Constantinople and completed in Rome as pope; the *Homiliae quadraginta in Evangelia,* composed between 590 and 593, some of them pronounced in person and some read out by a *notarius;* the *Viginti duae homiliae in Ezechielem,* composed in Rome under the pressure of the Lombard army in 593 and prepared for publication eight years later; finally the *Liber regulae pastoralis* of 591, which is, in a way, a parallel to the *Regula Monasteriorum* of St Benedict. For this last work see the editions of H. HURTER, Oeniponte, 1872, and of A. M. MICHELETTI, Tournai, 1904; for the other treatise: MIGNE, *Patrologia Latina,* LXXV-LXXVI.

On the Roman plague, the death of Pelagius II and the beginning of Gregory's papacy, important information is furnished by the tenth book of the *Historia Francorum* of GREGORY OF TOURS, sopra cit., p. 314, on the conversion of the Angles, the first chapter of the second book of the *Historia Ecclesiastica Anglorum* of the VENERABLE BEDE (ed. K. PLUMMER, Oxford, 1896, or alternatively, MIGNE, *P.L.,* XCV). Other brief details, apparently the work of a contemporary author, are to be found in the *Liber Pontificalis* (ed. L. DUCHESNE, Paris, 1886-1892).

Works of little biographic importance are: the anonymous *Vita,* composed in the first decades of the eighth century in the cloister of Whitby, and discovered in a codex by P. EWALD and published by F. A. GASQUET, *A Life of Pope St Gregory the Great,* London, 1904, and two *Vitae* written respectively by PAULUS DIACONUS in the second half of the eighth century (ed. H. GRISAR in *Zeitschrift für katholische Theologie,* XI, 1887) and by JOHANNES DIACONUS at the request of Pope Gregory VIII (ed. MIGNE, *P.L.,* LXXV).

For the period preceding Gregory's papacy see W. STUHLFATH, *Gregor der Grosse, Sein Leben bis zu seiner Wahl zum Papste nebst einer Untersuchung der ältesten Viten,* Heildeberg, 1913, in *Heidelberger Abhandlungen,* XXXIX; on the life and work of St Gregory: F. HOLMES DUDDEN, *Gregory the Great, His Place in History and Thought,* London, 1905; H. GRISAR, *San Gregorio Magno,* trans. A. DE SANTI, Rome, 1904; F. TARDUCCI, *Storia di Gregorio Magno e del suo tempo,* Rome, 1909; E. CASPAR, *Gregor der Grosse,* in *Meister der Politik,* Stuttgart u. Berlin, 1923; F. ERMINI, *Gregorio Magno,* Rome, 1924; P. BATIFFOL, *Saint Gregoire le Grand,* Paris, 1928; for the relations between Gregory the Great and the monasteries, see: O. M. PORCEL, *La doctrina monastica de San Gregorio Magno y la 'Regula monachorum',* Washington, 1951, and especially K. HALLINGER, *Papst Gregor der Grosse und der hl. Benedikt,* in *Commentationes in Regulam S. Benedict,* Roma, 1957; on the mission to the Anglo-Saxons: S. BRECHTER, *Die Quellen zur Angelsachsenmission Gregors d. Gr.,* Münster, 1941, and W. LEVISON, *England and the Continent in the Eighth Century,* Oxford, 1946.

For fuller information on the whole period see the general works cited in preceding chapters.

CHAPTER 7

The principal sources for the train of events are: of western works the *Liber Pontificalis* sopra cit., p. 186; and of eastern, the Χρονογραφία of THEOPHANES (ed.) C. DE BOOR, Leipzig, 1883-1885 and the Ἱστορία σύντομος of NICEPHOROS (ed. C. DE BOOR, Leipzig, 1880).

For the crisis provoked by the *Typos* of CONSTANS II see the Acts of the Lateran Council of 649 (ed. in J. D. MANSI, *Sacrorum Conciliorum amplissima Collectio*, X, Florence, 1764, col. 863 sqq.), the *Commemoratio eorum quae saeviter et sine Dei respectu acta sunt a veritatis adversariis in sanctum et apostolicum, novum revera confessorem et martyrem, Martinum papam.* (*Ibidem*, col. 853 sqq.), and the letters of Martin I (in MIGNE, *P.L.*, LXXXVII, col. 135 sqq., and in *M.G.H., SS. rerum Merovingicarum*, V, p. 452 sqq.). Cf. also E. CASPAR, *Die Lateran-Synode des 649*, nella *Zeitschrift fur Kirchengeschichte*, 51 (1932), p. 95 sqq.

The contrast between the attitudes of the pope and the emperor in the struggle against monotheletism and of the papacy and empire in general towards religious questions is indicated by the Acts of the VI Ecumenical Council and the letter addressed by Pope Agatho and the Roman Synod to Constantine IV (in MANSI cit., XI, coll. 195 sqq., 286 sqq.).

For the work of Justinian II concerning the ecclesiastic discipline and the liturgy, see the acts of the *Trullana* or *Quinisexta* Synod (*Ibidem*, col. 921 sqq.).

The most significant documents of the first period of the struggle against iconoclasm are: the two letters sent by Gregory II to Leo III (ed. E. CASPAR in *Zeitschrift für Kirchengeschichte*, LII, 1933, p. 72 sqq.), probably partly authentic and partly interpolated; the letter from Gregory II to the Patriarch Germanus (in MANSI cit., XIII, col. 91 sqq.); the treatise on heresies and the letters of the Patriarch GERMANUS (in MIGNE, P.G., XCVIII, coll. 49 sqq., 155 sqq.); the three orations of JOHN OF DAMASCUS (*Ibidem*, XCIV, col. 1232 sqq.).

A few of the many works dedicated to the struggle against iconoclasm in particular are: K. SCHWARZLOSE, *Der Bilderstreit, Ein Kampf der griechischen Kirche um ihre Eigenart und Freiheit*, Gotha, 1890; E. J. MARTIN, *A History of the Iconoclastic Controversy*, London, [1930]; G. OSTROGORSKY, *Les débuts de la querelle des images*, in *Mélanges Charles Diehl*, I, Paris, 1930, p. 235 sqq.; IDEM, *Studien zur Geschichte des byzantinischen Bilderstreites*, Breslau, 1929, in *Historische Untersuchungen* ed. by E. KORNEMANN and S. KAEHLER, V; E. CASPAR, *Papst Gregor II und der Bilderstreit*, in *Zeitschrift für Kirchengeschichte*, 52 (1933), p. 27 sqq.

For fuller information see the general works listed in preceding chapters, in particular: BERTOLINI cit. p. 315; A. FLICHE and V. MARTIN cit. p. 312, V; J. B. BURY cit. p. 83; also G. OSTROGORSKY, *Geschichte des byzantinischen Staates*, in *Byzantinisches Handbuch in Rahmen des Handbuchs der Altertumswissenschaft* ed. by W. OTTO, Munich, 1940; A. A. VASILIEV, *History of the Byzantine Empire* 324-1453, 2nd English edition, Madison, 1952; L. BREHIER, *Le monde byzantin*, 3 vols., in *L'évolution de l'humanité*, Paris, 1947-1950. On the acts relevant to the iconoclastic struggle, see V. GRUMEL, *Les régestes des actes du Patriarchat de Constantinople*, Istanbul, 1932-36.

The problem of cultural relations between east and west is treated fully in C. DAWSON, *La formazione dell'unità europea dal secolo V all'XI*, Turin, 1939.

CHAPTER 8

The principal narrative source on the age of Charlemagne is provided by the so-called *Annales Regni Francorum* (ed. F. KURZE, Hanover, 1895, in *Scriptores rerum Germanicarum*), which were previously entitled by PERTZ, *Annales Laurissenses maiores* after the monastery of Lorsch where they were composed. They cover the period from 741-829 and are almost official in character. An indisputable source for Charlemagne's character, and one of absorbing interest is the *Vita Karoli* of EGINHARD who was for a long time a friend and companion of the king. His style is modelled on Suetonius, but the classical imitation does not detract from the effectiveness and truth of his narrative. Of the many editions we will mention that of L. HALPHEN, EGINHARD, *Vie de Charlemagne*, Paris, 1923, and that of O. HOLDER-EGGER, Hanover, 1911, in *SS. rerum Germanicarum*.

For the diplomatic sources see: E. MÜHLBACHER, *Die Regesten des Kaiserreichs unter den Karolingern* (751-918), Innsbruck, 1899-1908; *Diplomata Karolinorum* (ed. E. MÜHLBACHER, in *M.G.H., Diplomata*). The capitularies have been collected by A. BORETIUS and V. KRAUSE, in *M.G.H., Capitularia regum Francorum*.

Collections of letters which merit particular notice for their political, religious and cultural importance are: the *Codex Carolinus* (ed. W. GUNDLACH in *M.G.H., Epistolae Merovingici et Karolini aevi*, I), which contains the correspondence of the pope with Pippin, Carloman and Charlemagne which Charlemagne had collected in 791; the letters of ST BONIFACE (ed. M. TANGL, in *SS. rerum Germanicarum*) and of ALCUIN (ed. E. DÜMMLER, in *M.G.H., Capitularia Karolini aevi*, II).

The most important poetic testimonies of the Carolingian age have been collected by E. DÜMMLER, L. TRAUBE, B. VON WINTERFELD, K. STRECKLER, in *M.G.H., Poëtae Latini aevi Karolini*.

On Charlemagne: K. HAMPE, *Karl der Grosse*, in *Meister der Politik*, Stuttgart, 1923 (trans. A. BORTOLINI, Venice, 1928); A. KLEINCLAUSZ, *Charlemagne*, Paris, 1934; J. CALMETTE, *Charlemagne. Sa vie et son oeuvre*, Paris, 1945 (trans. G. LOMBARDINI, Turin, 1948); IDEM, *Le moyen âge*, Paris, 1948; G. PEPE, *Un problema storico: Carlomagno*, Firenze, 1952.

On the Carolingian Empire: S. ABEL and B. SIMSON, *Jahrbücher des Frankischen Reiches unter Karl dem Grossen*, Leipzig, I, 1888, II, 1883, in *Jahrbucher der deutschen Geschichte*; F. DAHN, *Die Könige der Germanen*, VIII, Leipzig, 1897 and later editions; E. MÜHLBACHER, *Deutsche Geschichte unter den Karolingern*, Stuttgart, 1896, in ZWIEDINECK-SÜDENHORST, *Bibliothek deutscher Geschichte*; L. HALPHEN, *Charlemagne et l'empire carolingien*, Paris, 1949, in *L'Evolution de l'Humanité* ed. by H. BERR, XXXIII; H. FICHTENAU, *Das karolingisches Imperium, Soziale und geistige Problematik eines Grossreiches*, Zurich, 1949; F. L. GANSHOF, *Recherches sur les Capitulaires*, Paris, 1958.

On the renewal of the Empire and the imperial ideology: R. MORGHEN, *L'impero medievale da Carlo Magno a Federico II*, in *Medioevo Cristiano*, Bari, 1951, p. 52 sqq.; R. FOLZ, *L'idée d'Empire en Occident du Ve au XIVe siècle*, Paris, 1953; P. E. SCHRAMM, *Die Anerkennung Karls d. Gr. als Kaiser, nella Historische Zeitschrift*, 172 (1951); H. FICHTENAU, *Karl d. Gr. und das kaisertum*, in the *Mitteilungen des Osterr. Instituts f. Geschichtsforschung*, 61 (1953), pp. 257-334; J. DEER, *Die Vorrechte des Kaisers in Rom*, in the *Schweizer Beitragen zur allgemeinen Geschichte*, 15 (1957), pp. 1-63.

On the foundation of Europe: G. DE REYNOLD, *La formation de l'Europe*, Fribourg, 1944; C. DELISLE BURNS, *The First Europe. A Study of the Establishment of Medieval Christendom*, A.D. 400-800, London, 1949 (trans. H. FURST, Milan, 1951); C. DAWSON, sopra cit., p. 317; TH. SCHIEFFER, *Winfrid-Bonifatius und die christliche Grundlegung Europas*, Freiburg i. Br., 1954; J. FISCHER, Oriens, Occidens, Europa, Wiesbaden, 1957.

On the culture of the Carolingian Age remember: M. ROGER, *L'enseignement classique d'Ausone à Alcuin. Introduction à l'histoire des écoles carolingiennes*, Paris, 1905; E. PATZELT, *Die karolingische Renaissance, Beiträge zur Geschichte der Kulter des früheren Mittelalters*, Vienna, 1924; E. SHIPLEY DUCKETT, *Alcuin, Friend of Charlemagne*, New York, 1951; J. FLECKENSTEIN,

Die Bildungsreform Karl d. Gr., Freiburg i. Br., 1953; *I problemi della civiltà carolingia*, in *Settimane di Studio*, sopra cit., Spoleto, 1954, I.

There has been considerable controversy over the theory of H. PIRENNE, *Mahomet et Charlemagne*, Paris, 1940, (trans. M. VINCIGUERRA, Bari, 1942), which makes the Middle Ages start with Charlemagne and the fragmentation of the economic unity of the Mediterranean by the Arabs. See also on this subject: P. E. HUBINGER, *Spätantike und frühes Mittelalter, Darmstadt*, 1958.

On Charlemagne's conflict with Byzantium see: F. DÖLGER, *Byzanz und die europäische Staatenwelt*, Ettal, 1953; W. OHNSORGE, *Abendland und Byzanz*, Weimar, 1957; on Islam: F. W. BUCKLER, *Harunu'l Rashid and Charles the Great*, Cambridge, Mass., 1931.

For fuller information on the whole period, see the general works mentioned in preceding chapters; for further bibliographical details see: P. F. PALUMBO, *Dall'impero di Roma al Sacro Romano Impero e Carlomagno*, in *Studi Medievali*, Naples, 1949.

CHAPTER 9

On the feudal system and its period, in addition to the general works listed in preceding chapters see: F. L. GANSHOF, *Qu'est ce que la féodalité*, Brussels, 1947; M. BLOCH, *La société féodale*, Paris, 1939, in *L'Evolution* cit., XXXIV-XXIV bis (trans. B. M. CREMONESI, Turin, 1949); H. MITTEIS, *Der Staat des hohen Mittelalters*, Weimer, 1953; C. G. MOR, *L'età feudale*, Milan, 1952, in *Storia politica d'Italia*, ed. Vallardi; G. FASOLI, *I re d'Italia*. Florence, 1949; IDEM, *Le incursioni ungare in Europa nel secolo* X, Florence, 1945.

Narrative sources on the history of medieval Rome are extremely scarce. The most important ones dealing with the time of Marozia and Alberic II are: the *Antapodosis*, written by LIUDPRAND when a fugitive in Germany, between 958 and 962, which contains Italian, German and Byzantine history from 888-949, an extremely lively work which passionately attacks the enemies of the author and his protector Otto I (ed. J. BECKER in *SS. rerum Germanicarum*); the extremely incorrect but equally precious *Chronicon*, written by BENEDICTUS, a monk of St Andrew's of Mt Soracte, between 972 1000 approximately, covers the period from Julian the Apostate to 972 (ed. G. ZUCCHETTI, Rome, 1920, in *Fonti* cit. p. 315); finally the *Liber Pontificalis* cit. p. 316. The poems of AUSILIUS and VULGARIUS have an important historical bearing on these works (ed. E. DÜMMLER, *Auxilius und Vulgarius. Quellen und Forschungen zur Geschichte des Papsttums im Anfange des* X. *Jahrhunderts*, Leipzig, 1866).

For documentary sources see: for the diplomata of the Italian kings, the the edition of L. SCHIAPARELLI, Rome, 1903-1924, in *Fonti* sopra cit.; for the papal bulls P. F. KEHR, *Italia Pontificia*, I-II, Berlin, 1906-1907. For the relations between the family of Theophylact with Sergius III and the future John X, *Il rotolo opistografico del conte Antonio Pio di Savoia*, edited by A. CERIANI and C. PORRO, Milan, 1884; and for the struggle against the Arabs, the treaty of 915 (ed. O. VEHSE, *Das Bündnis gegen Sarazenen vom Jahre* 915, in *Quellen und Forschungen aus Italienischen Archiven und Bibliotheken*, XIX, 1927, p. 181 sqq.).

Much work has been done on the history of Rome in the first half of the tenth century, especially after the fundamental *Ricerche per la storia di Roma e del papato nel secolo* X by P. FEDELE (in *Archivio della R. Società Romana di Storia Patria*, XXXIII-XXXIV, 1910-1911). On John X, the battle of the Garigliano, see in particular: P. FEDELE, *La battaglia del Garigliano dell'anno 915 ed i monumenti che la ricordano* in *Archivio* sopra cit., XXII

(1899), p. 181 sqq.; O. VEHSE sopra cit.; T. VENNI, *Giovanni X*, in *Archivio della R. Deputazione Romana di Storia Patria*, LIX (1936), p. 1 sqq. On Alberic II there is a limited study by W. SICKEL, *Alberich II und der Kirchenstatt*, in *Mittheilungen der Instituts für Oesterreichische Geschichtsforschung*, XXIII (1902), p. 50 sqq., and also an excellent article devoted to him by G. ARNALDI in the *Dizionario Biografico degli Italiani*, Roma, 1961, vol. I, p. 647 sqq. On local administration: T. HIRSCHFELD, *Das Gerichtswesen der Stadt Rom vom 8. bis 12. Jahrhundert wesenlich nach stadtrömischen Urkunden*, in *Archiv für Urkundenforschung*, IV (1913), p. 419 sqq.; L. HALPHEN, *Etudes sur l'administration de Rome au moyen âge* (751-1252), in *Bibliothèque de l'Ecole des hautes études*, CLXVI, Paris, 1907; W. KÖLMEL, *Beiträge zur Verfassungsgeschichte Roms im 10. Jahrhundert*, in *Historisches Jahrbuch*, LV (1935), p. 521 sqq. On the formation and political action of the local aristocracy: L. M. HARTMANN, *Grundherrschaft und Bürokratie im Kirchenstaate vom 8. bis 10. Jahrhundert*, in *Vierteljahrschrift für Sozial-und Wirtschaftsgeschichte*, VII (1909), p. 486 sqq.; O. GERSTENBERG, *Die politische Entwicklung des römischen Adels im 10. und 11. Jahrhundert*, Berlin, 1933. IDEM, *Studien zür Geschichte des römischen Adels im Ausgang des 10. Jahrhunderts*, in *Historische Vierteljahrschrift*, 31 (1937).

For a general picture of Roman history in the tenth century see, in addition to GREGOROVIUS, of course, F. PAPENCORDT, *Geschichte der Stadt Rom im Mittelalter*, Paderborn, 1857; L. DUCHESNE, *Les premiers temps de l'Etat pontifical*, Paris, 1911 (trans. A. M. SALVATORELLI CASALEGNO, Turin, 1947); W. KÖLMEN, *Rom und der Kirchenstaat im 10. und 11. Jahrhundert bis in die Anfänge der Reform*, in *Abhandlungen zur Mittleren und Neueren Geschichte* ed. by PH. FUNK, TH. MAYER, G. RITTER, Berlin Grünewald, 1931; P. BREZZI, *Roma e l'impero medievale* (774-1252), Rome, 1947, in *Storia di Roma*, Istituto di Studi Romani, X; C. G. MOR sopra cit.

The opinions of this period of Roman history referred to in the text of this chapter are those of F. SCHNEIDER, *Rom und Romgedanke im Mittelalter*, Munich, 1926, p. 179, and of L. SALVATORELLI, *Italia Medievale* sopra cit., p. 530 sqq.

For fuller information on the entire period, remember the general histories listed in preceding chapters. See also: R. HOLTZMANN, *Geschichte des sächsischen Kaiserzeit* (900-1024). 3rd edition, Munchen, 1956; *I problemi dell'Europa postcarolingia*, Spoleto, 1955, in *Settimane di Studio*, sopra cit., II.

CHAPTER 10

The principal narrative source for Otto III is the chronicle of the bishop THIETMAR of Merseburg, written between 1009 and 1018 (ed. F. KURSE in *SS. rerum Germanicarum*); subsidiary sources which are important for one reason or another, and from which many of the quotations in this chapter have been drawn are: the acts of the Council of Rheims in 991 (ed. in *M.G.H.*, PERTZ, III); the *Vitae* of St Adalbert, Bishop of Prague (ed. G. WAITZ and M. PERLBACH in *M.G.H.*, PERTZ, *SS.* IV and XV, 2), of St Nilus (in MIGNE, *P.G.*, CXX), of St Romuald (in MIGNE, *P.L.*, CXLIV), and Bernard, bishop of Hildesheim (in *M.G.H.*, PERTZ, *SS.*, IV); *the letters of Gerbert* (ed. J. HAVET, *Lettres de Gerbert* (983-997), Paris, 1889, in *Collection de documents pour servir à l'étude et à l'enseignement de l'histoire*).

The final reference to the dead Emperor's exit from Rome on horseback is taken from the *Chronica Regia Coloniensis* (ed. G. WAITZ in *SS. rerum Germanicarum*, p. 32).

The diplomata of Otto III have been published by TH. VON SICKEL in the

M.G.H., *Diplomata regum et imperatorum*, II; the imperial legislation by L. WEILAND in the *M.G.H., Constitutiones et acta publica imperatorum et regum*, I. All the documentary material on Otto III, listed in the *Regesta Imperii* of Bohmer, has recently been re-elaborated by M. UHLIRZ, Graz u. Köln, 1956.

The broadest and most comprehensive study of Otto III to date is still R. WILMAN'S, *Jahrbücher des deutschen Reichs unter Otto III*, Berlin, 1840, in *Jahrbücher der deutschen Geschichte*, which has recently been thoroughly revised and replaced by a work of the same title by M. URLIRZ. Particularly important for the evaluation of the emperor's political and religious activity: M. TER BRAAK, *Kaiser Otto III. Ideal und Praxis im frühen Mittelalter*, Amsterdam, 1928; P. E. SCHRAMM, *Kaiser, Rom und Renovatio*, Leipzig, 1929, in *Studien der Bibliothek Warburg*.

On Gerbert: F. PICAVET, *Gerbert, un pape philosophe d'après l'histoire et d'après la légende*, Paris, 1897, in *Bibliotheque de l'Ecole des hautes études. Sciences religieuses*, IX; J. LEFLON, *Gerbert humanisme et Chrétienté au 10e siècle*, Paris, 1946; M. UHLIRZ, *Untersuchungem über Inhalt und Datierung der Briefe Gerberts von Aurillac*, Gottingen, 1957.

On the influence of Charlemagne on the imperial tradition: A. FOLTZ, *L'idée d'empire* sopra cit. p. 318; IDEM, *Le souvenir et la légende de Charlemagne dans l'Empire germanique médiéval*, Paris, 1950, in *Publications de l'Université de Dijon*, VII; on the new Europe which is born from the disintegration of the Carolingian Empire: J. CALMETTE, *L'effondrement d'un empire et la naissance d'une Europe (IX-X siècles)*, Paris, 1941, in *Les grandes crisis de l'histoire* ed. by J. CALMETTE; on Germany and the Empire: W. GIESEBRECHT, *Geschichte der deutschen Kaiserzeit*, Leipzig, 1855-1895; K. HAMPE, *Das Hochmittelalter, Geschichte des Abendlandes von 900 bis 1250*, Münster, 1953; A. CARTELLIERI, *Die Weltstellung des deutschen Reiches (911-1047)*, Munich u. Berlin, 1932; G. TELLENBACH, *Die Entstehung des deutschen Reiches*, Munich, 1940; R. HOLTZMANN, *Geschichte der Sächsischen Kaiserzeit*, Munich, 1941; J. CALMETTE, *Le Reich allemand au moyen âge*, Paris, 1951; C. G. MOR sopra cit. p. 319; H. KÄMPF, *Das Reich im Mittelalter*, Stuttgart, 1950.

On the history of the Church and Italy, see the works listed in preceding chapters.

CHAPTER 11

The fullest testimony of the figure and the work of Gregory VII is furnished by his *Registrum* (ed. E. CASPAR in *M.G.H., Epistolae selectae*). For the diplomata and imperial statutes: K. F. STUMPF, *Die Reichskanzler vornehmlich des X., XI. und XII. Jahrhunderts*, Innsbruck, 1865-1883; *Constitutiones et acta publica imperatorum et regum*, I, ed. by L. WEILAND, in *M.G.H.*; *Die Urkunden Heinrichs IV*, edited by D. V. GLADISS, in *M.G.H., Diplomata*.

On Henry IV we have an anonymous *Vita* written by a familiar after 1106 (ed. W. EBERHARD in *SS. rerum Germanicarum*); on Gregory there is a *Vita* written by the monk PAUL OF BERNRIED around 1128 (ed. J. M. WATTERICH, *Pontificum Romanorum vitae*, Leipzig, 1862), both these lives are apologetic in character.

Some chroniclers on the papal side are: the *Annales* of LAMBERT of HERSFELD, a Thuringian monk, composed between 1077 and 1080, which only go up to 1077 (ed. O. HOLDER-EGGER in *SS. rerum Germanicarum*); the *Annales* attributed to BERTHOLD OF REICHENAU (ed. G. WAITZ in *M.G.H.*, PERTZ, *SS.*, XIII), which go up to 1080; the *Chronicon* of the monk BERNOLD of CONSTANCE, begun between 1072 and 1073 and continued up to 1100 (ed. G. H. PERTZ in *M.G.H., SS.*, V).

Some chronicles on the imperial side are: the *Chronicon Universale*, composed around 1100 by the monk EKKEHARD of St Michael and Bamberg (ed. in *M.G.H.*, PERTZ, SS., VI) and the *Chronicon* of the monk SIGBERT OF GEMBLOUX from the beginning of the twelfth century (ed. L. C. BETHMANN in M.G.H., PERTZ, SS., VI).

The extremely full publicist literature on the Struggle of the Investitures is collected in the M.G.H., *Libelli de lite imperatorum et pontificum saec*, XI, *et* XII. *conscripti*, Hanover, 1891-1897. Of the greatest importance for the development of the struggle between the papacy and empire are vols. IV, 2 and V, 1, of the *Histoire des Conciles* of HEFELE, trans. H. LECLERC, Paris, 1913-1914; G. MEYER v. KNONAU, *Jahrbücher des deutschen Reiches unter Heinrich IV u. Heinrich V*, Leipzig, 1890-1909; and A. HAUCK, *Kirchengeschichte Deutschlands*, Leipzig, 1902-1920.

On Gregory VII, the period of reform and the investitures, the relations between Church and empire: A. FLICHE, *Saint Grégoire VII*, 1927, in *Les Saints*; R. MORGHEN, *Gregorio VII*, Turin, 1942; *Studi Gregoriani* collected by G. B. BORINO, 4 vols., Rome, 1947 and later editions; A. CARTELLIERE, *Der Aufstieg des Papsttums in Rahmen der Weltgeschichte*, Munich, 1936; P. BREZZI, sopra cit. p. 320; A. FLICHE, *Les Prégrégoriens*, Paris, 1916; G. B. BORINO, *L'elezione e la deposizione di Gregorio VI*, in *Archivio della* R. *Società Romana di Storia Patria*, XXXIX (1916); G. LADNER, *Theologie und politik vor dem Investiturstreite. Abendmahlstreit, Kirchenreform, Cluni und Heinrich III, Brünn*, Leipzig, Prague, 1936, in *Veröffentlichungen des Oesterreichischen Instituts für Geschichtsforschung*, ed. by H. HIRSCH, II: A. FLICHE, *La réforme grégorienne*, Louvain, 1924-1925, in *Spicilegium Sarcum Lovaniense*, VI, IX; IDEM, *La réforme grégorienne et la reconquête chrétienne*, Paris, 1946, in *Histoire de l'Eglise* sopra cit. p. 311; VIII; IDEM, *La querelle des investitures* Paris, 1946, in *Les grandes crises de l'histoire* sopra cit. p. 321; A. SOLMI, *Stato e Chiesa secondo gli scritti politici da Carlomagno fino al Concordato di Worms*, Modena, 1901; E. VOOSSEN, *Papauté et pouvoir civil à l'époque de Grégoire. Contribution à l'histoire du droit public*, Gembloux, 1927; H. X. ARQUILLIERE, *Saint Grégoire VII. Essai sur la conception du pouvoir pontifical*, Paris, 1934, in *L'Eglise et l'Etat au moyen âge*, IV; G. TELLENBACH, *Libertas, Kirche und Weltordnung im Zeitalter des Investiturstreites*, Stuttgart, 1933; R. MORGHEN, *Libertas Ecclesiae e primato romano nel pensiero di Gregorio VIII*, in *Medioevo Cristiano* cit., p. 120 sqq.; C. VIOLANTE, *La Pataria milanese e la riforma ecclesiastica*, in *Studi Storici*, ed. Istituto Storico Italiano per il medioevo, fasc. 11-13, Roma, 1955.

On monastic reform: K. HALLINGER, *Gorze-Kluny*, in *Studia Anselmiana*, 21025, 2 vols., Roma, 1951-52; on the Eastern Schism: A. MICHEL, *Humbert und Kerullarios*, in *Quellen und Forschungen* of the *Görresgesellschaft*, 2 vols., 1924-30; M. JUGIE, *La schisme byzantin*, Paris, 1941; S. RUNCIMAN, *The Eastern Schism*, Oxford, 1955; 1054-1954, *L'Eglise et les Eglises neuf siècles, de douloureuse séparation entre l'Orient et l'Occident*, 2 vols. Chevetogne, 1955.

For fuller information on the papacy and the empire, Italy and Germany, see the books and collections quoted in previous chapters.

CHAPTER 12

The most important Greek and Latin narrative sources for the first crusade are: the *Gesta Francorum et aliorum Hierosolymitanorum* (ed. in *Recueil des historiens des Croisades* published by the Académie des Inscriptions et des Belles-Lettres, *Historiens Occidentaux*, III, 1866; H. HAGENMAYER, Heidelberg, 1890; L. BREHIER, *Histoire anonyme de la première Croisade*, Paris, 1924, in

Classiques de l'histoire de France au moyen âge, IV), *an* anonymous work by a follower of Bohemund; the *Historia Francorum qui ceperunt Jerusalem* by RAYMOND DE AGILES, the chaplain of Raymond of Toulouse (ed. in Recueil cit., III); the *Gesta Francorum Jerusalem peregrinantium* by FULCHER OF CHARTRES, who also went on the expedition (ed. H. HAGENMAYER, Heidelberg, 1913; MIGNE, *P.L.*, CLV; *Recueil* cit., III); the *Gesta Dei per Francos sive Historia Hierosolymitana* by GUIBERT OF NOGENT (1053-1121), who includes direct information from Crusaders in this work as well as from the anonymous *Gesta* and the work of Fulcher (ed. *Recueil* cit., IV; MIGNE, *P.L.*, CLVI); finally the *Alexias* of ANNA COMNENA, the daughter of the Emperor Alexius, which reflects Byzantine opinion (ed. A. REIFFERSCHEID, Leipzig, 1884; trans. E. DAWES, London, 1928). An interesting collection of letters and documents on the first crusade is contained in the volume of H. HAGENMAYER, *Epistulae et chartae ad historiam primi belli sacri spectantes* (1088-1100). *Eine Quellensammlung zur Geschichte des ersten Kreuzzuges*, Innsbruck, 1901.

For the European recovery see the bibliography of chapter XIII.

On the origins and the character of the crusades: C. ERDMANN, *Die Aufrufe Gerberts und Sergius IV für das heilige Land*, in *Quellen und Forschungen aus Italienischen Archiven und Bibliotheken*, XXIII (1931-1932); IDEM, *Die Entstehung des Kreuzzugsgedankens*, Stuttgart, 1935, in *Forschungen zur Kirchen-und Geistesgeschichte*, ed. by E. CASPAR and W. WEBER; M. VILLEY, *La Croisade*, Paris, 1942; P. ROUSSET, *Les origines et les caractères de la première Croisade*, Geneva, 1945.

On the first crusade: R. RÖHRICHT, *Geschichte des ersten Kreuzzuges*, Innsbruck, 1901; F. CHALANDON, *Histoire de la première Croisade*, Paris, 1929; S. RUNCIMAN, *A history of the Crusades. I. The First Crusade*, Cambridge, 1951; on the crusades: L. BREHIER, *L'Eglise et l'Orient au moyen âge. Les Croisades*, Paris, 1928, in *Bibliothèque pour l'enseignement de l'histoire ecclésiastique*; F. COGNASSO, *La genesi delle Crociate*, Turin, 1934; R. GROUSSET, *Histoire des Croisades et du Royaume Franc de Jerusalem*, Paris, 1934, and later editions; A. SARTELLIERI, *Der Vorrang des Papsttums zur Zeit der ersten Kreuzzüge*, Munich, 1941; A. WAAS, *Geschichte der Kreuzzüge*, Freiburg i. B., 1956.

For a general perspective on the crusades and the related bibliographies see P. F. PALUMBO, *Studi Medievali* sopra cit. p. 319.

See the preceding chapters for works and anthologies of a general character.

CHAPTER 13

Some of the principal narrative sources from north of the Alps are: the *Chronica* of OTTO OF ST BLAISE, a continuation of the *Historia de duabus civitatibus* by OTTO OF FREISING, up to 1209 (ed. A. HOFMEISTER in *SS. rerum Germanicarum*); the anonymous *Annales Marbacenses*, which cover the period from 1184 to 1200 (ed. H. BLOCH in *SS.* cit.); the *Chronicon* of BURCHARD OF URSPERG, which goes up to 1229 (ed. O. HOLDER-EGGER and B. VON SIMSON in *SS.* cit.); the *Chronica Regia Coloniensis*, listed on p. 356, which was begun in 1175 and goes up to 1242 with its various additions; the *Speculum regum* and the *Pantheon* of GODFREY OF VITERBO, probably of German origin, are important for the imperial consciousness of the period, also the anonymous *Gesta Heinrici VI* (ed. G. WAITZ in *M.G.H.*, PERTZ, *SS.*, XXII).

For the relations with Southern Italy, see in particular: the *Historia de rebus gestis in Siciliae regno* (1154-1169), *sive de calamitatibus Siciliae sub Wilhelmo I et II regibus* by HUGO FALCANDUS (ed. G. B. SIRAGUSA in *Fonti* of the Istituto Storico Italiano); the *Liber ad honorem Augusti,* or *De rebus Siculis carmen* by PETER ANSOLINUS of EBOLI (edition G. B. SIRAGUSA in *Fonti* cit.; E. ROTA in *RR. It. SS.*, new edition XXXI); the *Chronica* (1189-1243) of RICHARD OF SAN GERMANO (ed. G. H. PERTZ in *SS. rerum Germanicarum*).

An important Greek source is the *Storia Bizantina* of NICETAS ACOMINATUS, which covers the period from 1118 to 1206 (edd. J. BEKKER in *Corpus Scriptorum Historiae Byzantinae*; MIGNE, *P.G.*, CXXXIX-CXL).

For the English chroniclers, that is the *Gesta* of Henry II and Richard I by WILLIAM OF NEWBURGH and ROGER OF HOVEDEN, etc., see the extracts edited and compiled by F. LIEBERMANN and R. PAULI in M.G.H., PERTZ, SS, XXVII-XXVIII; for complete editions of their works see: *Rerum Britannicarum medii aevi scriptores*, London, 1858 and later editions.

For imperial legislation and diplomata: K. F. STUMPF sopra cit. p. 321; R. RIES, *Regesten der Kaiserin Constanze, Königin von Sizilien, Gemahlin Heinrichs VI*, in *Quellen und Forschungen aus Italienischen Archiven und Bibliotheken*, XVIII (1926); D. CLEMENTI, *Calendar of diplomas of the Hohenstaufen emperor Henry VI concerning the Kingdom of Sicily, Ibidem*, XXXV (1955), p. 86 sqq.; M.G.H., *Constitutiones et acta publica imperatorum et regum*, I, ed. L. WEILAND.

On Norman Italy: F. CHALANDON, *Histoire de la domination normande en Italie et en Sicile*, Paris, 1907; on Henry VI: T. TOECHE, *Kaiser Heinrich VI*, Leipzig, 1867, in *Jahrbücher der deutschen Geschichte*.

All the most important events of Henry VI's life, his marriage, his relations with Constance, with Richard Coeur-de-Lion, with the Communes of Lombardy, his hereditary plan, his negotiations with the Church, the crusade, his will, have been the subject of lengthy controversies. Works of special note from the very full bibliography are: H. BLOCH, *Forschungen zur Politik Kaiser Heinrichs VI in den Jahren* 1191-1194, Berlin, 1892; J. HALLER, *Heinrich VI und die römische Kirche*, in *Mittheilungen* sopra cit. p. 320, XXXV (1914); V. PFAFF, *Kaiser Heinrichs höchstes Angebot an die römische Karie* (1196), Heidelberg, 1927, in *Heidelberger Abhandlungen*, LV; E. PERELS, *Der Erbreichsplan Heinrichs VI*, Berlin, 1927; C. E. PERRIN, *Les negotiations de* 1196, in *Mélanges L. Halphen*, Paris, 1951. On the relations between papacy and empire: F. KEMPF, *Papsttum und Kaisertum bei Innocenz III*, Rome, 1954, in *Miscellanea Historiae Pontificiae*, 19; *Sacerdozio e Regno da Gregorio VII a Bonifiacio VIII*, Rome, 1954, in the same collection, 18; P. ZERBI, *Papato, Impero e 'Respublica Christiana' dal* 1187 *al* 1198, Milan (1955).

On the other European states: C. PETIT-DUTAILLIS, *La monarchie féodale en France et en Angleterre*, Paris, 1950, in *L'Evolution de l'Humanité*; R. MENENDEZ PIDAL, *La España del Cid*, Madrid, 1947, in *Obras Completas*, VI-VII. On the origins of the European political system: W. KIENAST, *Die Anfänge des europäischen Staatensystems im späteren Mittelalter*, in *Historische Zeitschrift*, CLIII (1936); IDEM, *Deutschland und Frankreich*, Göttingen, 1957; F. HEER, *Aufgang Europas*, Zurich, 1949, and IDEM, *Die Tragödie des Heiligen Reiches*, Stuttgart, 1952 (these two books have in fact been received with many reservations); R. W. SOUTHERN, *The Making of the Middle Ages*, London, 1953.

On Gioachino da Fiore: E. BUONAIUTI, *G. da F.*, Rome, 1931, in *Collezione di Studi Meridionali*, XIV; also by BUONAIUTI, the edition of the *Tractatus super quatuor Evangelia* and the *De articulis fidei*, in *Fonti* of the Istituto Storico Italiano; J. BIGNAMI ODIEZ, *Notes sur deux manuscrits de la Bibliothèque du Vatican contenants des traités inédits de Johachim de Flore*, in *Mélanges d'Archéologie et d'Histoire*, LIV (1937); J. C. HUCK, *Johachim von Floris und die johachimitische Literatur*, Freiburg im Br., 1938; L. TONDELLI, *Il Libro delle Figure*, Turin, 1939; H. GRUNDMANN, *Neue Forschungen über*

Johachim von Flore, Marburg, 1950, in *Münstersche Forschungen* ed. by J. TRIER and H. GRUNDMANN, I; E. BENZ, *Ecclesia Spiritualis*, Stuttgart, 1934; F. RUSSO, *Bibliographia gioachimita*, Firenze, 1954.

For the Provencal poets quoted in the text of this chapter, see the edition and translation compiled by V. DE BARTHOLOMAEIS, *Poesie provenzali storiche*, in *Fonti* sopra cit.; the date of March-April, 1194, attributed to Peire de la Caravana in this work is very probably erroneous.

For fuller information on the history of both Germany and the empire, and indeed of the whole period, see the works and collections listed in preceding chapters.

CHAPTER 14

The principal source for the papacy of Boniface VIII is the collection of bulls published by G. DIGARD, M. FAUCON, A. THOMAS, *Les registres de Boniface VIII*, Paris, 1886 and later editions in *Bibliothèque des Ecoles françaises d'Athènes et de Rome*. In addition see: the extensive material collected by P. DUPUY, *Histoire du différand entre le pape Boniface VIII et Philippe le Bel*, Paris, 1955; the documents edited by H. FINKE, *Aus den Tagen Bonifaz VIII*, Münster, 1902; by FINKE again in the *Acta Aragonensia*, Berlin, 1908; by G. CAETANI, *Regesta chartarum, I, Perugia*, 1925, in *Documenti dell'Archivio Caetani*; the *Codex diplomaticus dominii temporalis Sanctae Sedis* (ed. A. THEINER, Rome, 1861); the *Regestum Clementis papae V* edited and compiled by the Benedictines, Rome, 1884 and later editions.

We will limit ourselves to listing the following biographical sources and chronicles; the *Opus Metricum* of the Cardinal JACOPO CAETANI STEFANESCHI, which contains the *Vita* of Celestine V (ed. in *RR. It. SS.*, III); the *Historia Ecclesiastica* of TOLOMEO DI LUCCA (ed. *Ibidem*, XI); the *Vitae* of the Roman Popes by BERNARD GUIDONIS (ed. *Ibidem*, III), the continuations of MARTIN OF TROPPAU'S *Chronicon* (ed. L. WEILAND, in *M.G.H.*, PERTZ, *SS.*, XXIV); the *Relatio de Bonefacio VIII papa capto et liberato* (ed. F. LIEBERMANN, *Ibidem*, XXVIII, p. 622 sqq.); DINO COMPAGNI, *Cronica* (ed. I. DEL LUNGO in *RR. It. SS.*, new edition, IX); GIOVANNI VILLANI, *Historie Fiorentine* (ed. in *RR. It. SS.*, XIII); the *Historia rerum in Italia gestarum* of FERRETO DEI FERRETI (ed. C. CIPOLLA in *Fonti* of the Istituto Storico Italiano); the *Chronicon* of WILLIAM OF NANCIS and its continuation (ed. in *Recueil des historiens des Gaules et de France*, XX, Paris, 1840).

On Benedict Gaetani, cardinal and pope: W. DRUMANN, *Geschichte Bonifacius des Achten*, Koenigsberg, 1852; L. TOSTI, *Storia di Bonifacio VIII*, Rome, 1886; T. S. R. BOASE, *Boniface VIII*, London, 1933; G. CAETANI, *Caietanorum Genealogia*, Perugia, 1925; IDEM, *Domus Caietana*, I, San Casciano Val di Pesa, 1927; H. FINKE sopra cit.; G. FALCO, *Bonifacio VIII* in *Enciclopedia Italiana*, s.v.; IDEM, *La Signoria dei Caetani* (1283-1303), in *Albori d'Europa*, Rome, 1947, p. 293 sqq.; A. FRUGONI, *Il giubileo di Bonifacio VIII*, in *Bullettino dell'Istituto Storico Italiano per il Medio Evo*, no. 62 (1950); G. LEBRAS, *Boniface VIII symphoniste et modérateur*, in *Mélanges d'histoire du moyen âge L. Halphen*, Paris, 1951, p. 383 sqq.

On his relations with the Colonna see: L. MOHLER, *Die Kardinäle Jacob und Peter Colonna. Ein Beitrag zur Geschichte des Zeitalters Bonifaz VIII*, Paderborn, 1914, in *Quellen und Forschungen aus dem Gebiete der Geschichte*, XVII; on his relations with Florence: R. DAVIDSOHN, *Geschichte von Florenz*, Berlin, 1912, III, p. 1 sqq.; on Rome in the time of Boniface: R. DUPRÉ THESEIDER, *Roma dal comune di popolo alla signoria pontificia* (1252-1357), Bologna, 1952, in *Storia di Roma*, ed. Istituto di Studi Romani, vol. II;

on Boniface VIII's conflict with Philip the Fair: A. SCHOLZ, *Die Publizistik zur Zeit Philipps des Schönen und Bonifaz VIII*, Stuttgart, 1903, in *Kirchenrechtliche Abhandlungen* ed. by U. STUTZ, VI-VIII; J. RIVIERE, *Le problème de l'Eglise et de l'Etat au temps de Philippe le Bel*, Louvain and Paris, 1926, in *Spicilegium Sacrum Lovaniense*, VIII; H. KAMPF, *Pierre Dubois and die geistigen Grundlagen des französischen Nationalbewusstseins um 1300*, Leipzig u. Berlin 1935, in *Beiträge zur Kulturgeschichte des Mittelalters und der Renaissance*, ed. by W. GOETZ; G. DIGARD, *Philippe le Bel et le Saint Siège de 1285 à 1304*, Paris, 1936, and the review of this work by G. MARTINI, *Per la storia dei pontificati di Niccolò IV e Bonifacio VIII*, in *Rivista Storica Italiana*, LVIII, 1941; P. FEDELE, *Per la storia dell'attentato di Anagni*, in *Bullettino dell'Istituto Storico Italiano*, LXI (1921); M. MELVILLE, *Guillaume de Nogaret et Philippe le Bel*, in *Revue d'histoire de l'èglise de France*, 36 (1950).

A few works of interest on some of the subjects mentioned in this chapter are as follows: on Celestine V: F. BAETHGEN, *Der Engelpapst*, Leipzig, 1943; A. FRUGONI, *Celestiniana*, Rome, 1954, in *Studi Storici* ed. by the Istituto Storico Italiano per il Medio Evo, nos. 6-7; on Frederick III of Sicily: A. DE STEFANO, *Federico III d'Aragona re di Sicilia* (1256-1317), Palermo, 1937; on the question of the universal powers and the sovereignty of the state: E. E. STENGEL, *Kaisertitel und Souveränitätsidee*, in *Deutsches Archiv für Geschichte des Mittelalters*, III, 1939; H. WIERUSZOWSKY, *Vom Imperium zum nationalen Königtum*, Munchen-Berlin, 1933; F. BOCK, *Reichsidee und Nationalstaaten*, Leipzig, 1943; W. ULLMANN, *The development of the mediaeval idea of Sovereignty*, in *English Historical Review*, LXIV, 1949; IDEM, *Mediaeval Papalism*, London, 1949; F. CALASSO, *I glossatori e la teoria della sovranità*, Milan, 1951; IDEM, Rileggendo il Liber Augustalis, in *Atti del Convegno Internazionale di Studi Federiciani*, Palermo, 1952, p. 461 sqq.; S. MOCHI ONORY, *Fonti canonistiche per l'idea moderna dello Stato*, Milan, 1951; IDEM, *La crisi federiciana del Sacro Romano Impero*, in *Atti del Convegno* sopra cit.

For fuller information of a general character, see the works and collections listed in preceding chapters.

CHAPTER 15

The principal sources on the Council of Constance are collected in E. H. VON DER HARDT, *Magnum Oecumenicum Constantiense Concilium*, Frankfurt and Leipzig, 1696-1700; J. D. MANSI, op. cit. p. 187, XXVII-XXVIII; H. FINKE, *Acta Concilii Constantiensis*, Münster, 1896-1928; IDEM, *Froshungen und Quellen zur Geschichte der Konstanzer Konzils*, Paderborn, 1889; ULRICH VON RICHENTHAL, *Chronik der Konstanzer Konzils* (ed. M. R. BUCK, Tübingen, 1882, in *Bibliothek der literarischen Vereins in Stuttgart*, CLVIII).

On the Council of Constance and the conciliar period: N. VALOIS, *La France et le Grand Schisme d'Occident*, Paris, 1896-1902; C. J. HEFELE, *Histoire* cit., p. 289, VII, Paris, 1916; E. F. JACOB, *Essays in the Conciliar Epoch*, Manchester, 1943.

On the Emperor Sigismund, see for the diplomatic sources: in *Deutsche Reichstagsakten*, vols. 7-12, *Kaiser Sigmund*, Gotha, 1878-1901; in the *Regesta Imperii*, vol. II, *Die Urkunden Kaiser Sigmunds*, ed. M. ALTMANN, 2 vols., Innsbruck, 1896-1900; for bibliography: the old but always useful work of F. ASCHBACH, *Geschichte Kaiser Sigmunds*, Hamburg, 1838 sqq.; on papal centralization and fiscal policy: C. SAMARAN and G. MOLLAT, *La fiscalité pontificale en France au XIVme siècle. Période d'Avignon et du Grand Schisme d'Occident*, Paris, 1905; in *Bibliothèque des Ecoles françaises d'Athènes et de Rome*, XCVI; *Die Inventare der päpstlichen Schatzes in Avignon*, ed. H. HOBERG, Citta del Vaticano, 1944, in *Studi e Testi*, vol. III; on the struggle for reform: J. HALLER, *Papsttum und Kirchenreform. Vier Kapitel zur Geschichte der ausgehenden Mittelalters*, Berlin, 1903; on Marsilio of Padua and William Ockham: G. D. LAGARDE, *La naissance et l'esprit laïque au déclin du moyen âge*, II, St Paul-Trois-Chateaux, 1934; *Marsilio da Padova. Studi raccolti nel VI centenario della morte*, Padua, 1942; A. G. GEWIRTH, *Marsilius of Padoa*, New York, 1951; A. HAMMAN, *La doctrine de l'Eglise et de l'Etat chez Occam*, Paris, 1942; R. SCHOLTZ, *Wilhelm von Ockham als politischer Denker and sein* Breviloquium de principatu tyrannico, Stuttgart, 1944, in *Schriften der Reichsinstituts für ältere deutsche Geschichtskunde* (M.G.H.); L. BAUDRY, *Guillaume d'Occam*, I, Paris, 1950; on contemporary European politics: M. DE BOÜARD, *La France et L'Italie au temps du Grand Schisme d'Occident*, Paris, 1936, in *Bibliotheque* sopra cit., CXXXIX; G. PEYRONNET, *Les relations politiques entre la France et l'Italie principalement au XIVme et dans la première moitié du XVme siècles*, in *Moyen âge*, LV-LVI (1949-1950); W. T. WAUGH, *A History of Europe from 1378 to 1494*, 3rd edn., New York, 1951; P. BAETHGEN, *Europa in Spätmittelalter*, Berlin, 1951. On Wycliff and Huss: H. B. WORKMAN, *John Wyklif*, Oxford, 1926; J. LOSERTH, *Hus und Wiclif*, Munchen u. Berlin, 1925; M. VISCHER, *Jan Hus, Aufruhr wider Papst und Reich*, Frankfurt, 1955

For general information: G. HERGENRÖTHER, *Storia universale della Chiesa*, recast by G. P. KIRSCH, trans. E. ROSA, V, Florence, 1906; A. PRUTZ, *Storia degli Stati Medievali nell'Occidente de Carlomagno fino a Massimiliano*, Milan, 1898, in *Storia Universale illustrata* ed. G. ONCKEN; L. VON PASTOR, *Storia dei Papi dalla fine del medioevo*, trans. A. MERCATI, I, Rome, 1910; G. MOLLAT, *Les papes d'Avignon*, Paris, 1950, in *Bibliothèque pour l'enseignement de l'histoire ecclésiastique*; E. DUPRÉ THESEIDER, *I papi d'Avignone e la Questione Romana*, Florence, 1939; L. SALEMBIER, *Le Grand Schisme d'Occident*, Paris, 1921, in *Bibliothèque* sopra cit.; M. CREIGHTON, *A History of the Papacy from the Great Schism to the Sack of Rome*, London, 1897, I and II; A. C. FLICK, *The Decline of the Medieval Church*, London, 1930.

INDEX